THY I

IS

VODUN

CONVERSATIONS
WITH
MAMIWATA PRIESTESS

Published by BEHUMBEZA FOUNDATION

The material in this book is intended for educational purposes only. No expressed or implied guarantee as to the effects of the use of the recommendations can be given nor liability taken.

Library of Congress Control Number: 2015932946

ISBN: 978-0-692-90161-8

First printed 2015, Second Edition Published 2017
Printed in the United States of America

10 9 8 7 6 5 4 3 2 1

COVER PHOTOS

1. Temple BEHUMBEZA background
2. Ouidah, Ceremonies in temple of the Supreme Chief of Vodun, circa July 1998
3. 2001 January 10th Vodun Fete, Republic of Benin
4. Mami Wata Priestess and mother-in-law, Behumbeza, at the 2000 January 10th Vodun Fete, (Grand Popo) Republic of Benin
5. The Venerable Maman Edoh, High Priestess of Guin-Vodun and Mami Dan Divinities, The First BEHUMBEZA
6. Hounnon BEHUMBEZA, Supreme Chief of Mami Wata Dan, in temple
7. Hounnon BEHUMBEZA, Supreme Chief of Mami Wata Dan, in offering to GU

SPINE

1. Spotted Panther of Agassou

BACK COVER

1. Mami Wata Priestess
2. Hounnon BEHUMBEZA and Vodunsi at night ceremony

DEDICATION

This book is dedicated to the following: Hounnon Behumbeza, my husband and spiritual father, my ancestors, the divine spirits that gave me life; and, in particular, my mother (1940-1974) and my paternal grandfather (1912-2012).

EPIGRAPH: I would rather serve my God in the Benin* way; I would rather worship him in the Benin manner; I will sing songs of praises to him in the Benin custom; unless it can be proven to me that he does not understand the Benin language. Oba Akenzuwa / Akenzua N'iso N'orro II (1933 - 1979 CE)

*speaking of Benin, Nigeria

Contents

FORWARD

It is with great honor that I write this forward. It is a privilege. I must say thank you to all that have come before that have patiently and with grace, put the hard work into making this book happen. I truly owe great gratitude to the hands of the unseen that have made sacrifices beyond imagining so that this voice may come to the people. It has been a long time coming, but now, the knowing that has been passed down for generations, of a change whose time has come, is here.

The challenges faced in learning about Traditional African Vodun, a religion and way of life whose foundation is most ancient, may seem to be insurmountable in the age of globalization. It is rare that an authentic voice of guidance that has undergone the rigors of initiation arises. It was when I first came across Mami's writings that I knew, this was a voice rooted in the deep and rich relationships of ancient Africa.

The challenge to learning about Vodun is that one must have a guide who is ancestrally chosen, as ancient mysteries systems all over the world respond to the power invested in ordination. Thus, an introduction to Vodun that is on par with the perennial ancient order, in depth and nuance. Such an ordination cannot be faked and there are witnesses and accountability checks in place to ensure that only those sent may give justice to a subject that forms the foundation of humanity's trust and devotion to the sacred.

In the modern world, where there are many who walk with titles, the correct one is difficult to discern. In the rush to find authentic spiritual information, many seeking to understand give up what the original archetypal guru, guide, and teacher should bring and how they should operate. Yet, in these essays, the caliber of spiritual, historical, and practical understanding is of the few that can be tested and accepted among the original standards of authentic spiritual guidance imprinted within each us.

The essays in this introductory volume are written in such a way as to speak to extraordinary depth and spiritual necessity. Learning from what they contain requires a well rooted desire to comprehend the vast amount of information presented. In authentic form of ancestral storytelling, these essays, when combined, tell a story whose breath spans centuries. Within that, a rich and fertile ground for academic research and personal transformation waits for those whose interests glean in that direction. For those that seek to know more from an authentic insider's perspective of the ancient priesthood of Mami Wata Vodun, they can hear the voices of the ancients speaking in this volume, authenticating the legitimacy of this work, the legitimacy of Mami's many initiations, and the legitimacy of the deep call from within them to learn of the Vodun, from the Vodun.

The techniques and anecdotes of discernment presented here are necessary in approaching a subject that is dense and sensitive. For those who trust the truth within them, these tools of discernment will help in understanding an arena of wisdom as majestic as the great oceans themselves. The information here is simply not available to the western researcher. It has taken a synthesis of approaches to articulate. the perspectives here in an accessible fashion.

Namely, Mami's scope of mastery in historical and psychoanalytic research grounds her voice in accuracy. Moreover, her initiations, training, and ancestry takes common research approaches to the realm of lived experience, access to the ancient chambers of wisdom, and understanding of the scope of ancestral tenets for expressing knowledge. It is not an easy task and not something that is available to everyone, for to do so, one must meet the rigorous demands and tests of the ancestral review process many times over. Mami has done this, with each fact presented in this volume being able to checked by anyone who seeks to inquire. So now she can tell the story. It is a story that takes volumes, yet in seeking to understand its tenets, the larger purpose and scope of this introduction to Vodun may be approached.

There are some manuscripts that have a certain quality, a rare and ancient touch that speaks of destiny, that I immediately sensed in Mami's work. Perhaps, there will be those whose spiritual and intellectual senses can engage to see the threads of destiny woven elegantly through each essay. I pray that those with ears to hear may receive what is destined for them to hear.

It is written. As it is written upon the walls of the heavens, so shall it be written upon the land, for the earth to clearly see and have say. Destiny requires a gust of the epic. To accomplish the mythological in this time, is the bring the words of the ancients alive into the open to dance. Each word, carefully designed, is part of a design most holy, befitting those who have not forgotten that majesty is real and that wholeness is encoded in all of creation. Thus, religion gives way to knowledge and mastery of knowledge systems gives way to the divine, and in that way the divine mysteries may speak unto the earth, as it has been ordained from the beginning of man.

Emenike La

CEO Water Oracle Publishing, LLC.

PREFACE

Since the winter of 2007 I have been writing about African vodun on the internet. While recuperating from a knee surgery I was surfing the internet in hopes of finding like-minded people who had no reservations about discussions on vodun. Thinking, immediately, of our Haitian cousins, and their well-known relationship with vodun, I found myself on a Haitian site for several years. Being a political junkie as well as someone who served the spirits I found many hearty discussions, on various subjects including vodun, during my sojourn there. However, the thing that struck me, the most, was many of its member's preference for popular 'bought in priestesses' of Haitian vodou. After a number of years, while surfing the internet yet again, I came across a vodun group on a site carrying various tribes. Because it appeared that these folks had genuine interest in vodun I hung out with them, for a while, hoping to be helpful. However instead of accepting vodun, as per saith the voduns, many of them preferred to make vodun what they chose it to be rather than what it really was. There appeared to be a built-in resentment towards anyone who promoted African spirituality, it's preeminence or dared to challenge their "New Age" beliefs of what they assumed African spirituality was to be. My insistence that one cleave to the tenets of traditional African vodun, above all else, appeared to be a personal affront or perceived notion that I was indulging in pure and overt racism towards them. These vodun enthusiasts were generally of non-African descent and felt that they were, somehow, on my spiritual level. They did not fully understand the rigorous initiation process, nor the training involved in someone who had become a servant of the spirits within the African priesthood. They did not accept me nor my spiritual authority. As a result, many, eventually, left the vodun thread to go and form their own thread so as not to be bothered with someone like me. When joining other diaspora spiritual threads such as the Orisa, on that same site, these were generally dominated by a Cuban element consisting of many who were either rude, disrespectful or suffering from extreme machismo. Some were choosing to perpetuate the myth, and downright fabrication, that vodun began in Cuba. As a result, much infighting occurred; and, a war torn, battered and bruised Mami Wata Priestess, after much encouragement from a very internet savvy spiritual child, joined facebook.

It has been within this setting that I, a woman who was once told that I had no writing abilities, began my written conversations on African vodun. Couched in my preferred genre of storytelling I began to share the journey of my life and reflections, to this point, in African vodun. Since my first writings on facebook, in September 2013, many on the internet have come to depend on these writings for understanding and guidance into the mysteries of African vodun. Many, of my facebook friends, have encouraged me to write a book. In fact, it was often pointed out that I already had a book that I simply needed to collect the writings and put the book together. So, due to the encouragement of many; and, after being approached by a very capable young man with his own publishing company which promotes true spirituality, this is what I have done. This book consists, primarily, of my earliest conversations with my facebook friends from September 2013 to December 2014. I hope you enjoy!

ACKNOWLEDGEMENTS

First, how can I not thank my most beloved ancestors and the divine spirits who gave me life. It was you oh majestic ones, led by a mighty Dattatreya and a Da Zodji (Sakpata), that found a way that I might come to this earth and embark upon a spiritual mission that you yourselves designed and I contracted to. It was you oh mighty ancestors, that accepted me and made me your own by implanting your specific DNA in me and allowing me to dwell among the living and represent you, thus, giving me a grounding in this physical world in order to pursue this spiritual work. It was you oh honored ancestors, that touched me with your invisible hands; and, after hundreds of years led me, a descendant of African slaves and traditional priests, across a deep blue sea back to our African homeland. It was you; and, it has always been you, even when I did not know you, that have stood by me in the good times and the bad. I thank you my beloved ones with everything in me I thank you, because, without you this book would have never been.

And, secondly, how can I not thank or forget to acknowledge one of the greatest gifts that the spirits have ever given me, Hounnon Behumbeza, my husband. A man who is an example of the African priesthood personified. Behumbeza, a priest so beloved that he has been designated as A National Treasure in the Republic of Benin. Thank you, my love. I thank you for all that you have done, to make this book possible, and for all that you continue to do, for me, on a daily basis. I couldn't ask the spirits for no greater gift of love than you!

Next, a young man that walked into our lives over seven

years ago carrying the head spirit of Rama, Mami Wata Priest, I thank you. You are more than just our spiritual child you are the son that I never had. You have walked with me, learned from me, put up with my temper tantrums, encouraged me and let me bark at you. You have persevered a temperamental middle-aged woman. You have been invaluable to Behumbeza and me. You have nurtured us, encouraged us; and, at times even fed us. You are developing into a mighty priest. I am so very proud of you. You are a true testament to the divine spirit that lives within you...the great Lord Rama. You have been encouraging me to write a book for a very long time. Thank you, my son, thank you!

And, last, I would like to thank a young man that has entered my life in a more recent time. A young man who has followed my writings, unbeknownst to me, all over the internet, Shaman Emenike La, of Water Oracle Publishing, who was the first editor and publisher of this work. Thank you for your faith in me and your being the avenue that has made this endeavor possible. I salute you and the mighty Dattatreya that lives within you.

INTRODUCTION

I arrived in that place, (Cotonou) the Republic of Benin, in the middle of the night not understanding the language nor knowing a single soul. I was frightened out of my wits! Visions of zombies were filling my head! I had only a Lonely Planet, two bottles of high grade gin and a name...Daagbo Hounnon Houna. And, for eight continuous years (1998-2006), I laid in initiation chambers from Benin to Togo to Ghana, sometimes near death, with malaria, begging that the spirits allow me to return home. It was an experience that changed my entire life! It became more than a pilgrimage to the motherland it became, and still is, a journey towards the divine!

Vodun! The word alone puts the fear of God in most people. For it has been a combination of westernization, Hollywood, media, and the tenets of Christian thought that has promoted and perpetuated this fear. Guided by the deep-seated prejudices and intolerances toward the 'other' vodun has consistently bore the brunt of one of the world's greatest misunderstandings towards the African continent. For even prior to the trans-Atlantic slave trade black Africa was considered a bastion of darkness, evil and a place where its inhabitants did not know God.

Christian missionaries, since their first visits there, have come with this incorrect assumption coupled with the notion that by converting Africa's populace they would give them a chance to be saved from damnation, thus, affording them the opportunity to have access to the divine. Yet, it has turned out to be a very sad state of affairs, because, in reality Africans have not only been proven to be one of God's first creations, from whence all mankind was derived; but, locked inside of Africa's various cultures and traditional spiritual systems are the keys that unlock the spiritual mysteries, of the world, and the answers to life itself. Christianity, in hindsight, has done more damage to the African traditional way of life than anything that has come before it!

The word vodun means 'spirit' in the language of the Fon people. In the Republic of Benin, when we speak of the Orisa, we refer to it as Nigeria's vodun. Togo and Ghana is also vodun. In fact, contrary to popular belief in the diaspora, the Akan tradition is vodun. But what we are referring to, when we speak of the African voduns, are spirits originating from a specific region peculiar to a specific group of people. The researchers do not understand this. Wherever traditional spiritual systems are practiced in Africa it is vodun. But because of vodun's emphasis, on the spirits themselves, I refer to vodun as 'that which is sacred'. And it is that sacredness, in the world of the spirits, which is the emphasis of this book. Vodun is not a series of spells and potions to which one throws a few dollars out to a priest or priestess to perform a specific work. African vodun, original traditional vodun, is a relationship between mankind and those ancestors and divinities, specific to each person, which has given them life. In essence, it is the relationship between God and his creations; and, Thy Name is Vodun.

What I am discussing, in this reading, is why the African ancestor is so important, not only for those of African descent but, for all humankind. And, in particular for those of African descent, why our reconnection to the African ancestor and our ancient traditional spiritual systems will bring about a better understanding of the self and thus promote psychological as well as spiritual healing for a people who have been stripped of so much as a result of the trans-Atlantic slave trade. But this can only happen if we cleave to the original tenants of African vodun. Due to the transatlantic slave trade much of the original tenants of these African traditional spiritual systems, brought over by the African slave, has either been lost or fell out of favor because of the rigorous demands of chattel slavery. Now that the overt and physical bondages of slavery are over it is the desire of the African ancestors and the divinities that vodun be restored, in the diaspora, to its former glory and power thus helping us to overcome the blight that slavery has left on both our psyches and our souls. In addition, it is our duty to reach back and help those loved ones who have come before us and died in these foreign lands to eat with their ancestors and rest in eternal peace. Vodun has the power to make all of this possible. Yet, contrary to popular belief, vodun in the diaspora is not a new and separate branch of African spirituality.

Vodun, in the diaspora, is African vodun as originally brought over by Africans who were enslaved, but damaged by the trauma of the slave experience, itself, yet folded over into it local spirits and experiences. One cannot separate a tree's branches from its root or it will surely die. And the roots of African spirituality lay in Africa! The myth that vodun, in the diaspora, is separate from Africa is largely perpetuated by those who have 'bought into' these African-based spiritual systems and is used, by them, to cloak their desires to stamp on vodun their own unique brand, deny accountability for their unordained methodologies and justify their refusal to allow the authority of African vodun's leadership to regulate them. These are the people who see vodun as a means of profit. And the ones who are legitimate in the faith who initiate these people are equally to blame. These counterfeit priests and priestesses are an internal cancer to the work of diaspora vodun and will see recompense from the spirits whenever their portion is due.

It has become apparent to many that know me that after my sojourns, in Africa, I am no longer the same as when I left. Since my return to the United States, in 2006, I have become the wife of a prominent African priest, Hounnon Behumbeza, and am part of a vibrant African Mami Dan temple...Temple Behumbeza. As I continue to travel back and forth, to the continent, The Republic of Benin is now home. In fact, it has always been my home. I simply didn't know it before, that, my paternal ancestor hailed from this place...the great Agassou. Coming to know my ancestors and learning to serve the voduns is directly responsible for all of this. Yet, it is my contention that no one, in the diaspora, has seen authentic vodun...original traditional vodun... and its beauty, until you visit the continent of Africa! But, I am aware that with today's economy, and life's demands, many cannot simply pack up their belongings and travel. So, I invite you to take my hand, walk with me and let's converse. Let me help you to understand what vodun really is...its tenants, its beauty, its majesty and its hope. I firmly believe that as the African continent is the birthplace of all of humankind my journey is your journey and my hope your hope.

CHAPTER 1

AFRICA AND THE AFRICAN ANCESTOR

Mami in Agassou Temple, her paternal Ancestral Temple

John Adams: ...the test ahead of us is an exceptionally difficult one.
Cinque: We won't be going in there alone...
Adams: Indeed not, no, we will have right on our side, we will have righteousness at our side...
Cinque: I meant my ancestors. I will call into the past, far into the beginning of time, and beg them to help me at the judgment. I will reach back and draw them into me. And they must come...for at this moment I am the whole reason they have existed at all.
AMISTAD (1997)

REFLECTIONS

I do not believe that the divine spirits do anything by chance! Opportunities often befall us that give us the opportunity to learn and grow. In my isolation, I often forget what is around me. My mind is forever on the spirits, I spend much time on the phone, to Africa, speaking to my husband about the events there. The temple is large, ceremonies almost daily, and traveling, for the spirits immense. Most temples are like this whether in Africa or the diaspora, if one is out helping folk. But the thing I and the ancestors are adamant about is to understand that vodun came from Africa. And it is based and rooted in African culture, African ancestors and African traditions. This is not about racism but about giving a people their due. This is about respecting the African ancestor whose children suffered the trans-Atlantic slave trade. So, I do not care if folks brand me racist if I speak on these things. I could care less that many, due to their own inadequacies, try to turn our history on its head and say that somehow, we enslaved ourselves and whites have nothing to do with it. In reality history cannot be changed for convenience purposes. One has to accept the good, the bad and the ugly of life! When Africans had domestic slaves, we came back and now SERVE those very slaves...The Tchamba Voduns. So, this is not what it is about! Having racial pride IS NOT RACISM! Understanding one's history and knowing WHO did what and WHO is responsible IS NOT RACISM! Only those suffering WHITE GUILT think this way. As an American I have got sense enough to understand that in that Black folks are only 13% of the population some very well meaning white folks stood shoulder to shoulder to help us fight for the freedoms we now have. But does that change the history of what happened to us? The fact that we were literally enslaved, castrated and/or hung on trees, denigrated, our names, our cultures taken away? No! YOU CANNOT ERASE THAT! But, you can say, my sister, my brother, it happened, I'm sorry, and let's go on.... Some would say give a little RESTITUTION; but, this is still under debate!

As a vessel, for the spirits, I believe EVERYONE, no matter what race, gender, or sexuality has a right to know the spirits; and, if the spirits find fault let each man or woman take it up with their God. That is the way of the spirits.

For history buffs, out there Ana Lucia Araujo's book, Public Memory of Slavery: Victims and Perpetrators in the South Atlantic, explains a lot as to why Benin, West Africa began a campaign on the Public memory of slavery. That, to me, is part of a healing process. And healing, both spiritually and psychologically, is what we need.

VODUN AND ONE'S CAPACITY TO FORGIVE

For about a week, or so, there had been a post, that came across my news feed, that made me 'hot under the collar'. The post, obviously, was a good one because it was shared on several forums; and, at least on two occasions, I responded. The poster is a friend; and, has every right to give his opinion. But this thing simply will not leave me; so, I decided to write about it.

The subject was about Africans, who themselves, captured and sold slaves during the transatlantic slave era and the poster's complaint that diasporans had to, now, go and pay for what was theirs in the first place...initiations/ceremonies and spiritual work in general. The historical facts are there. One cannot dispute them. My ancestors, the Dahomeans, for instance, were notorious in the slave trade. They made war on their neighbors, took captives, the women they would marry or keep and the men would be sold to the slaver for cannons, guns and anything else they sought of value. Normally these captives would have been killed annually; but, they were convinced, by those dealing in the slave trade, that selling them was much more economically advantageous.

My response to this post was that it was impossible for the Africans to have known what would happen to the slaves once they were sold. Domestic slavery, for the black Africans, was very different from that which happened in the diaspora. In many instances slaves were treated as family members. Those who were sold, in most instances, were war captives; and, whether the Africans understood what would happen, to them, or not these were the spoils of war in an era that we, today, cannot begin to understand. Many others, as was my ancestor, was captured while hunting or roaming in the forest or going about their everyday lives.

My first reaction, to this post, was visceral. Even though valid the post made me feel a sense of betrayal. I knew that if I was annoyed the ancestors were livid! As African Americans, we must develop the capacity for forgiveness. I am not saying that our history and our experiences with slavery, or racism in America for that matter, is to be forgotten. By no means should we forget or neglect to teach our children the good, the bad and the ugly of our history. But, if we do not develop a capacity to forgive we will never be able to go forward as a people. Stewing in the pain of past hurts, injustices and wrongs immobilizes us from the promises of a better future. We do not know the mind of the Creator when this forced migration was put in place. Because of it, those of African descent encase the entire globe; yet, we do not know, exactly, why these things happened the way that they did. Yes, it has been man's inhumanity to man that underpins this great tragedy; but, what has been the underlying spiritual reasons if any? We simply do not know.

Those Africans, who lived during those very tumultuous times, have been long since dead. And, if they were wrong have been admonished, according to each man's deeds, by the divine. So, who, now, are we to not see it (our history), acknowledge it, make peace with it and move on? These very Africans are our present-day ancestors; and, they have been interceding for us with the divinities for eons. Can we not, therefore, have the capacity to forgive their former transgressions? These ancestors who are our first line of defense when something goes wrong in our lives, who raise up mightily against our enemies, who beg the divinities on our behalf and do so much more.

We want to point fingers? No, my friends this is not good. Dig into that history if you must, go read books on the African's perspective if you must; but, do not sit around pointing fingers and making comments against the very ones who are trying, daily, to help you have a more prosperous and fulfilling life. They were human beings, they lived and they made mistakes as we do today. Have the capacity to forgive and move on.

Having to pay for services, rendered, for ceremonies and spiritual work in general. Really folks...really? For ceremonies, in Africa, those involved, the vodunsi, drummers, cooks, those who prep the animals for sacrifice, Priests, in attendance, and others take off from their jobs to serve the spirits and participate in these ceremonies. The sacrificial animals, alone, are expensive. A medium sized white bull was over $1,000 or more as of this writing. African vodun...original vodun...doesn't deal in just chickens. Bulls, goats, large rams, forest animals, and fowls of all kinds are used. The sacrifice is particular to the vodun that the ceremony is for. These animals must be prepped, slaughtered and prepared for the voduns, as well as, the people in attendance. Drummers must be paid and the vodunsi must be tipped something for their services. Any invited Priests/Priestesses and their vodunsi fed as well as those already in attendance. Suffice it to say that these ceremonies are labor intensive, with drumming, dancing, spirits riding the vodunsi so as to communicate with the people and/or leave messages for the person sponsoring the ceremony. So, all of this is to be done for free because you happen to be of African descent? In what universe?

My prayer is that we understand that without the capacity for forgiveness we can become stagnant in our dislike or 'hate' for the 'other'. The incapacity to forgive fosters disrespect, in some cases, racism and all manner of bad things. As a young girl the very first Bible verse I ever memorized was Galatians 5:22-23 (NIV), " 22 But the fruit of the Spirit is love, joy, peace, forbearance, kindness, goodness, faithfulness, 23 gentleness and self-control. Against such things there is no law. Let's get over it folks! Let's get over the pains of the past and reach for the future.

THE AFRICAN ANCESTORS: WHY THEY ARE FIRST

People have asked me many things about our ancestors. Many African Americans, and others, are beginning to understand that our ancestors are an integral part of serving the spirits. Our spiritual journeys, in this life, begin with them...for it is an ancestor, that wants to be remembered, that molds the clay and makes the child then bargains with a divinity to give the child life; and, it is to them, the ancestor, that we return. But a particular question, from a young man, is what inspired this post. He wanted to know that if he served his African ancestors, then, what would become of his European ancestors, his interracial ancestors, his Native American ancestors and/or those ancestors who died upon diasporan soil? It was an excellent question!

My favorite movie, of all times, has to be La Amistad (1997). Steeped in actual historical events it is a movie depicting a mutiny, in 1839, by newly captured Mende slaves who took control of the ship La Amistad off the coast of Cuba, and the international legal battle that followed their capture by a U.S. revenue cutter. It became a United States Supreme Court case in 1841. Its main character is Cinque who was determined to see his people go free. John Quincy Adams, former President of the United States and Congressman, took the case to the Supreme Court and won! While discussing the difficulties, of the case in Adams' greenhouse, this verbal exchange ensued between the two men:

John Adams: The test ahead of us is an exceptionally difficult one.

Cinque: We won't be going in there alone...

Adams: Indeed not, no, we will have right on our side, we will have righteousness at our side...

Cinque: I meant my ancestors. I will call into the past, far into the beginning of time, and beg them to help me at the judgment. I will reach back and draw them into me. And they must come...for at this moment I am the whole reason they have existed at all.

Every time I have heard Cinque say those words, about his ancestors, tears, they don't just roll, they wash down my face! He said that he would CALL INTO THE PAST, FAR INTO THE BEGINNING OF TIME AND BEG HIS ANCESTORS TO HELP HIM! REACH BACK, DRAW THEM INTO HIMSELF, FOR THEY ARE COMING PEOPLE!. THEY ARE THE WHOLE REASON WE HAVE EVER EXISTED AT ALL!

The African ancestors are the oldest of mankind's ancestors. For Africa is the cradle of civilization no matter who you are. And when the African Priest stands, in the crossroads, and call the ancestors from the North, South, East and West they ALL come...from the oldest to the newest. EVERY ancestor knows his children and when that sacrifice is given, in that crossroads, they all come and partake because they see that their child has given it! In African vodun, therefore, we start with the oldest of your ancestors...the ones that started your clan and we pull FORWARD that ALL of them are included. That is the power of Ifa, he is hooked into the African ancestry and can find them for you!

When the African Priest begins his prayers, he shouts in Fon, "Ago! Ago! Ago!" Let me pass, let me pass, let me pass to the beginning of time itself! For he is asking to communicate with the very CREATORS of the universe! He is asking for an audience that the divinities might hear his prayers, on behalf, of his spiritual children. These divinities that were here long before the world ever existed! African vodun is that old! And our African ancestors were their first CREATIONS! So, as we approach another Black History Month, Feb. 2015, remember the ancestors, and remember that it is because of them that you are here!

THE VICTORY!

The route de l'esclave (the route of the slave) was a long and arduous route in Benin. Deep in the interior of the country, leaving northward, the slaves would walk days and weeks on end, heading south towards the sea, after being captured. Chained one to another they would travel by night, sometimes in circles, to disorientate them so they could not find their way home. Tired, underfed, whipped and manhandled, snatched from a life, and loved ones, that lay deep in their hearts. Loved ones that they would never see again in life. The weak and less strong died on the road, bodies discarded like animal carcasses...no ceremony nor dignity. And those that would make it to that last village...that village in Ouidah...would be housed in a dwelling with no windows and no light, made to circle the tree of forgetfulness numerous times before being put on a boat. An act, that the enslaver thought, would erase the memories, of a people, attached to a land they called home.

Such scenes were happening all over Africa! Its west coast was depleting in population and its shores bleeding from the blood of our ancestors. But there is much that the enslaver did not understand! He did not understand the POWER of our ANCESTORS. He did not realize that those to whom he chose to enslave had a special relationship with the DIVINITIES, themselves, and would take those traditions with him/her! He did not know that, one day, when the ancestors decided...they would WAKE UP their children. That the BLOOD, running through their veins, had a MEMORY all of its own! He did not know that one day the children, of the ones he stole, would COME BACK...come back to the shores of their ancestors and forefathers claiming the powers that had been left there. It is a SPIRITUAL VICTORY! And, each time a descendant, of a slave, reclaims his heritage or crosses that great ocean, retracing the root of an ancestor, and re-connects to that ancestry claims that victory. For each one, of us, who walks into that African ancestral village for the first time...We Claim Victory! Victory, for our ancestors, Victory for every slave that died on that route, Victory for every slave that was hung on a tree, Victory, for every Black Man or Woman who was raped, castrated, humiliated, or whipped by a massa. When it comes to material things most of us ain't got much! But for those of us who understand our plight and KNOW who we are as a people.... WE GOT THIS! And we can claim it...VICTORY! Claim it for yourselves, for your children and for your children's children!

WHAT IT ACTUALLY MEANS TO KNOW THE ANCESTORS

I know my peeps* especially that Afrocentric bunch! Every brotha is a king, every sistah is a queen, we gone pour libations to the ancestors, grow our hair in dreadlocks and afros, 'cause we be 'natural'; and, we gone vacation in the motherland wearing our kente cloth. My queen is gone birth me some exceptionally beautiful babies, who of course, are royal 'cause we are with no birth defects or issues, we gone live off the land with my king sitting on his throne with two great lions at his feet, being faithful until death, and everything gone be kum by yah! All hail to my naturally perfect Afrocentric life! Sounds familiar?

Look folks, even before we left the African continent things were not perfect. So, what makes you think our reconnection, to Africa, is going to be so? It is necessary, I feel for our wellbeing as a people, to reconnect and know self. But, just like anything else, one must see and accept the good, the bad and the ugly of who we are. My quest, in this writing, is to discuss what it really means to actually know the ancestor. African Americans, and anyone else for that matter, must be able to distinguish between that which is fantasy and that which is reality.

I have plenty of folks coming to me saying, "I was born with gifts; so, I am in constant contact with my ancestors. They tell me what to do and guide my life!" Well that's wonderful my dear! But while they were speaking did they happen to explain, to you, that they were

**People*

showing up because they wanted to be fed? Did they tell you where their village was and/or still is today? Did they happen to mention the name of the particular family they came from or tribe? Did they tell you what your head spirit was or about any of the other spirits that gave you life? How about what spiritual thrones or spirits you may have inherited from them? Did they talk about the day your ancestor was captured or how he or she may have ended up in the diaspora? Oh no, none of these? Well my dear, so sorry to inform you; but, if you cannot answer these questions, then, you still do not know the ancestor. For it is only Ifa/Fa/Afa that can tell you these things.

Many of us were born with spiritual gifts; and, we are visited by ancestors and spirits of all kinds. This denotes a very spiritual people which we, most definitely, are! However, when spirits show up, they are doing so to deliver a message, "Go to Bokono (or Babalawo) and find out what I want and need. Feed me that I might help you to have a more productive and prosperous life!" This visiting from an ancestor, or spirit, is to attempt deep communication; and, I don't care what you think you were born with, only an able and experienced diviner will be able to tell you what it is. These gifts are wonderful; but, they can only be truly activated by the ancestors and the divinities themselves. This happens during the initiation process. And, if you don't take heed to these visitations and request to communicate, one day you will wake up and find that these gifts have disappeared!

Pouring libations on the ground and using the term 'ancestor' while calling out in prayer is not knowing or feeding the ancestor. Knowing his name, his tribe, his people, his village, his history and giving blood sacrifice is. I know plenty of folks who claim that they have done DNA analysis and are Fon or Ashanti or Yoruba or some other tribe. But just knowing the tribe, or group, is not enough. There are countless families within these tribes...which one are you from? What was their vocation? And I can go on... One needs to find the ancestor; and, only Ifa can help you. And once you find him or her that is truly the beginning of your spiritual journey. For all things began with the ancestor and ends with the ancestor. He or she wants to be remembered, so, reaches down and molds the clay and ask a divinity to breathe life into you. And, when your journey in this life is done, it is to him or her that you return. But know your journey back will not always be perfect. For as humans we are imperfect. Do not idolize Africa. It can be a harsh place! Be able to accept the good, the bad and the ugly; and, in doing so you will be able to negotiate a more balanced perspective.

RETURNING TO OUR ANCESTRAL HOMES

One of my spiritual children sent me a trailer about a young man returning to his ancestral home in the Republic of Benin. It depicts one young man's journey back to his ancestral village in Dahomey. I, as many before him have made that same journey! This is the WILL of the ancestors and the divinities. Once Ifa tells you where you came from, and you travel there, they will verify these findings through their own divination system. We have done this for several people if they, themselves, were not able to come to Africa. If all can be verified, then, you are heartily welcomed. All that belonged to the ancestor, who left, will now belong to you. The elders will give you the story of his/her capture into slavery or however they entered the diaspora. If it was a man/woman, of the spirits, you will receive all of the spiritual inheritance, from this ancestor, as dictated by Ifa. It is in this process that one's spiritual thrones, opele and TRUE, African kingships are revealed. Names based on what is given from the tribal elders, steeped in one's familial traditions, not from a book on African names is what is bestowed upon you! To do Vodun one MUST start with the ancestors!

THE ASCENSION

Of the many experiences and stories, I have, in vodun, the one I am about to share is perhaps my favorite! It happened during a Tchamba ceremony in Benin, West Africa. I have attended several in Benin and Ghana; but, I always look back on this one with a smile coupled with awe. The Tchamba voduns are ancestral spirits from those of us descended from African tribes who owned domestic slaves. I, a descendant of the Ashanti, serve these spirits. As these domestic slaves served our families, we in turn serve them. In Africa, the Ashanti, is considered the first house of the Tchamba voduns. These spirits, as they must be fed at Zogbe, have their ceremonies outside of the temple. Zogbe is the place were those that have died unnatural deaths (disease, murder, accidents, animal maulings, fires, etc.) must be buried and fed. Every one of us, therefore, have someone at Zogbe. And, it is important that we perform the ceremonies for these loved ones because, without them, they are forever cut off from their ancestors. But back to my story...

On this particular night (ceremonies generally began around midnight) * all appeared to be proceeding well. The folks conducting the ceremonies were extremely busy preparing. Spirits started showing up; and, I one of the folks they were working to initiate was busy trying to hold my eyes open. So much was going on that I couldn't make heads or tails of it, but, was struggling to do what I was told! Sacrifices were being done right and left and to be honest I was about terrified! The spirits showing up were painting themselves in distinct tribal markings. Then a gentleman approached me and sat down. He motioned for a gentleman, who spoke English, to come that he may converse with me and he told me his story.

* *Ceremonies, in vodun, generally began around this time because from midnight to 6:00 a.m. is when the spirits are most active. They become extremely active around 3:00 a.m.*

During the times of human sacrifice this man lived. In fact, he was the one, of his tribe, that would go and procure the human sacrifice! When it was his time to join his ancestors, in death, instructions were given, from the spirits, as to how he was to be buried. So, upon his death sacrifices were, again, taken; but, the blood of these sacrifices was to be painted upon his body. In other words, he was covered in the blood of these human sacrifices, certain ceremonies were performed and he became a vodun! The story left me speechless and awake! Here was a spirit telling me his story. I was in awe to be chosen to hear it! About 15 minutes later this same man came again, but, running from somewhere behind me. He was annoyed at his fellow vodunsi for allowing him to fall asleep during the ceremonies. He had no idea that, for most of the night, a wonderful spirit had possessed him. In Africa, we never tell them.

ANCESTORS/OUR NEWEST ONES

Mankind's oldest ancestors hail from the African continent. Africa is the birthplace of man. Ifa helps us find them whoever they may be. And, when called to feast, they will come from the oldest to the newest and the darkest to the lightest. That is a fact. Every ancestor knows his children no matter where they are. However, this essay highlights our most recent ancestors; and, that is those who were born and have died on foreign soil. It may be a person of African descent, born in the diaspora, or one of European, Asian, or another descent immigrated to the Americas or, somehow, taken from their native soil. It may even be someone born of mixed race where cross-acculturalization has occurred. Or, it may be one of our closest loved ones who have died and crossed over. In any event, it is those to whom, many of us, perceive to be our closest relatives.... our most recent ancestry.

Not everyone chooses to immediately reach back to Africa. In fact, some may even choose to resist it...to their detriment I might add. Many in the Caribbean, for instance, are so loyal to their perspective islands that they tend to put aside the fact that their origins are African. And, there are others that may feel that, because they are of mixed heritage, to honor the African would somehow dishonor, or pay less respect and homage to, their ancestry that looks less black. This isn't true! All of us originate from somewhere on the African continent regardless of race, creed, color gender. Some are just more removed from that ancestry than others. In African traditional spiritual systems; however, all of one's ancestry matters. So, do not be deceived. If you want to serve the spirits you must reach back; and, it will become clear as to why by the conclusion of the essay.

In our 21st century world life expectancy is considered high...in the U.S. 76 years for men and 81 years for women. It is even higher in other countries. Yet, while the numbers say we should be living longer many do not due to disease and man induced tragedies such as murder, accidents and all manner of things. Our super enriched diets, inactivity, chemicals in foods, excessive alcohol, drugs and other such things are taking our loved ones far too early. As a result, many are going before their time and becoming lost in the spiritual realm.

In the world of the spirits we start out with our ancestors (we come from them) and it is to them that we wish to return after death. Dying from unnatural causes separates us from our ancestors and the process of that return. While each ancestral group has its specific ceremonies and rituals, that aid this return, those dying of unnatural causes have an even more perilous journey returning back. In Vodun we call this place...the place where the spirits of those who die of unnatural causes (disease, murder, accident etc.) go "zogbe". This is the place that separates our loved ones from eating with their ancestors. Ceremonies must be performed in order to allow these persons now living outside of the temple, in the spiritual realm, to be able to eat and join one's ancestors. African-Americans who have suffered slavery, lynchings, drive-byes, drugs, disease and every manner of mishap, imagined, desperately need to perform these ceremonies.

That is why it is so important for us to reconnect to our oldest ancestors. They know the ceremonies, these ancient ceremonies, to perform to redeem our loved ones and put them at peace. Too many beautiful souls wander aimlessly, disoriented and afraid because we have lost our abilities to perform such ceremonies. And, if not done, they will continue to wander and become privy to those who wish to feed them in return for bad acts done against others in our physical world. Those who use the dark arts can elicit these wandering souls/ spirits for their own purposes.

The diaspora has begun to put more emphasis towards our ancestors and putting up shrines for our aunt Sadies and uncle Joes. This is making me extremely happy! However, if aunt Sadie and uncle Joe died of disease, or some other unnatural occurrence, I can assure you that neither is at peace. These remembrances and shrines, with photos and mementos, are lovely; but, what our loved ones really need are the proper ceremonies to put them at peace and to allow them to eat with their ancestors. When we read of an African, of great age, saying that they have lived their life to the fullest and now are ready to join their ancestors this is a beautiful thing! But contained within that statement is the knowledge that their loved ones will perform the proper ceremonies to put them at peace and allow their reconnection to their ancestors in the spirit world.

My beloved grandfather passed over on November 7, 2012, the day Barack Obama won his second bid for the Presidency, at 100 years old. I adored him. A disease took him before his time. Who knows how much longer he would have lived. That day my husband, a Priest, was in the forest, in Africa, working for the spirits. As he was about to leave the spirits commanded that he wait. When he did the spirit of my grandfather came forth as I was trying to contact, my husband, by phone. We later performed all of the ceremonies, at zogbe, that were commanded of us; but, the most beautiful thing occurred as my husband was preparing. A great spirit showed up, one waiting for my birth for many years. He had died before my birth....it was my grandfather's father. He too had died, at zogbe, and had waited all of these years. So, for the two we performed the ceremonies. My sisters and brothers these things are important. These ceremonies are important for all of our ancestors...the old, as well as, the new.

Mami returning through the Door of No Return, February 1998

CHAPTER 2

DREAMS: VODUN'S ARCHETYPAL COMMUNICATION SYSTEM

"The dream is the small hidden door in the deepest and most intimate sanctum of the soul, which opens to that primeval cosmic night that was soul long before there was conscious ego and will be soul far beyond what a conscious ego could ever reach."

- Carl Jung

The Meaning of Psychology for Modern Man (1934)

DREAMS

The great Psychoanalyst, Carl Gustav Jung (1875-1960) had it right when he said that the unconscious [subconscious] was not animalistic, instinctual, or sexual; as his mentor Sigmund Freud (1856-1939), the father of Psychoanalysis, had assumed, but rather more spiritual. While Freud believed that dreams are wish fulfillment... attempts, by the subconscious, to resolve old and new conflicts Jung realized that inside of the subconscious a bit of the divine lived. They are both correct!

While in training as a Psychoanalyst, in NYC, in the 1990s I got where Freud was coming from; but, as a priestess, I live what Jung has said We all do! For many who began a spiritual journey the subconscious becomes the backdrop or domain/place where the ancestors guide us and the spirits direct us. It is through our dreams that these divine beings send us messages, signs, signals, picture-graphs or small movie plots to show us the spiritual path and guide us to it. Sometimes there is an urgency, sometimes not. But in any case, it is their way of guiding us to a place where we can find out why we have com, our purpose on this earth and help us to fulfill a divine mission which we have all come to do. The ancestors protect us by interceding, for us, with the divinities and the divinities, themselves, impart the power and the wisdom to succeed. Dreams are powerful! For those of you who have such dreams but do not always understand what they say, start writing them down in a journal. Recall your week with events etc., to see if they relate to a personal issue. If not then see if a pattern, of some type, is emerging. There might be some spiritual quest that you might be journeying on or a yearning, deep inside of yourself, to do, try or know a certain thing. And, if so, this may be some ancestor, or personal divinity, pushing you toward something. Pay attention, then, go to Ifa, the answers lay there.

And know this! When a person comes to serve the spirits...it is not about that person...but it is about ALL of those who have come before him/her and after. ALL of these souls, through your actions, can be fed and tended to. For it is because of them that we live! We take on these missions not to glorify ourselves or wallow in our spiritual titles but to humbly the spirits and mankind.

DREAMS 2

As said in my first writings on dreams...Dreams are powerful One of the most notorious dreams, that we all know, is Martin Luther King's 'I Had a Dream Speech' orated August 28, 1963. We can all attest to this dream's effect on the world. This great man fulfilled his spiritual mission; and, when it was over was taken from us. This is the hand of the ancestors and the divinities. They use us, as vessels to right wrongs and/or change the courses of history. Others on such divine missions stand with Martin Luther King, like Mahatma Gandhi, Harriet Tubman, Mother Teresa and others. These greats were born to be used by the hand of the divine. And even further back look at the Old Testament prophets. They were not perfect human beings; but, there was something in them that made them usable by the spirits.

What I find interesting about King's speech is that it was almost not told. The story I hear is that King was not happy with the speech written, for him, and he was at odds as to what to say. Then Maya Angelou said. "Tell them about the dream Martin!" And, history was made! Make no mistake! It is not us humans who run and command this world...it is the spirits! We are but players in THEIR universe. It is THEY who have designed it all!

Again, dreams are powerful! Christendom is STILL, today, trying to decipher the Book of Revelations a dream/vision handed down to John of Patmos. I have learned much through my dreams. It is where the spirits have shown themselves and revealed WHO and WHAT I am in the spiritual world, as well as, my mission here. And in a continuation of this theme I will share a couple of my own personal dreams and the lessons learned so as to impart knowledge to those who would wish to learn.

DREAMS 3: THE BAGGED SERPENT

I learned early on, in vodun, that if the spirits have you on a spiritual journey and they want you they will succeed. Africans and Islanders seem to know this best! Africans, whom the spirits have chosen, are usually harassed until they give in. The spirits have a way of taking things away, from your life, in order to get your attention. Where one has fortune, he/she may lose it. Where a home has been peaceful, dissension begins to occur. Where one may have a loved one, the love may dwindle. Where one is healthy, illness may befall him/her. One's life literally begins to fall apart. It forces you to seek help. One goes to Ifa; and, Ifa will diagnose the problem...you are a child of the spirits, you were born to serve, go and initiate. If one heeds the call then steps are made to began the process; but, if not, a person's life continues to spiral. Some may go and take a spiritual bath with the appropriate sacrifices. However, this is simply a temporary measure telling the spirits, I hear you and I promise to do it later. If later takes too long the plummet downward begins again! The Voduns go no place! And, they have LONG memories! This lesson came to me in the following dream: 'THE BAGGED SERPENT'. Why I named it such will become self-evident.

I had just returned to Benin, West Africa in December 1998. Two trips had preceded it. The first in Feb. 1998 and again July 1998. I did not realize it then; but, once I put my foot down on African soil (originally in South Africa in 1997) I was captured by the ancestors. I simply could not stay away from the place. After the death of both my paternal and maternal grandmothers in span of two weeks, in 1997, something unexplainable began to happen to my life. It was as if I was obsessed. On a deep dark night, traveling alone, not understanding French or the local language I entered Benin, West Africa carrying a tour book, two bottles of gin and asking to be taken to Daagbo Hounnon Houna, the Supreme Chief of Vodun. Telling myself I was there for research I really was not sure WHY I was there. After seeing him I found myself sitting in a hotel, with no flush toilet, terrified! With fears of zombies coming through the small grated window I simply could not sleep! But fast forward to my 3rd visit and here is the dream.... As a child, I was always afraid of snakes! As an adult...it's gotten worse! But in this dream, there was this huge python! I was scared to death of it! In an earlier dream two huge pythons had come as I was attempting to go to the outhouse. They were so huge that I could hear them approaching me with the great noise they were making. I ran for my life! But on this night, I had managed to bag one huge python that was sunning itself on my bed. I took him to the airport and left him there. When I returned he was on the bed again! The next time I took the bagged serpent to a train station; and, again upon my return, he was laying there! No matter where I took the bagged serpent, upon my return, he would STILL be there! I woke up in a cold sweat! For weeks I would wake up, from dreams of me sleeping in a serpent's den with snakes slithering all around me! The next day I would go screaming to Daagbo Hounon. Ifa later revealed...It is YOU who is the serpent! YOU are Mami Wata; and, no matter what you do...THIS spirit isn't going anywhere! I now understand that I am not just Mami, but, Mami Dan. These spirits manifest themselves, in animal form, as serpents. And, inside this pantheon of Vodun is Mawu Lissa...the CREATOR. Many are known as the Hindu Gods; but, they are universal to all mankind.

But the lesson here was that I had to contend with who I was and make decisions in my life accordingly. Daagbo Hounnon Houna informed me, while standing on the Ouidah beach, "Your visit here was planned." I have not looked back.

DREAMS 4: TAKE ME TO THE KING!

I never know just what to say about this last dream I would like to share with you. It has only been named within the last year as 'Take Me to the King'. I have been in awe of it for so many years because it has made such a profound impact on my life. For one, it has taught me that if one chooses to take on this spiritual mission, that one was born to, it is a serious matter. Oh yes, it is a choice! See, many folks can take a spiritual journey; but, it is always up to you...a choice...to accept the mission or not. I can't tell you how many folks I have worked with and brought right up to the brink but then decided not to follow through. In many cases, as mentioned earlier, the spirits can harass you or seek a way to get your attention; but, still you must choose. The consequences of you NOT choosing, to accept the mission, is something you, personally, will have to deal with; but, choice is there just the same.

In late 1999, after 3 and a half months in a Mami Wata temple, in Benin, I came out for a breather. I had finished a portion of an initiation and had to go back in later for more. I headed to my little home in Ouidah. Disoriented and worn it had been an ordeal. When I got back I was told that the elderly lady living behind my little place was very ill. I went to see her. As I walked to her house the son of Daagbo Hounon Houna said, "The Fa said she is dying Mami, do not bother." I went anyway. She was a bag of bones. She had no strength to hold her body up. It was obvious she had been suffering greatly. I headed to the pharmacy and bought vitamin B12. I thought this would give her appetite; so, I began to nurse her. For a small while she did well. She was able to sit up, the family took photos of her and she had a bit of an appetite; but, she still died. I was saddened. They took her away and buried her.

Two weeks later I found myself dreaming of her. In my dream, I was walking with her in my arms, a bag of bones, disheveled hair and a shadow of her former self. As I walked I kept looking down at her, cradled in my arms saying, "They won't accept her, she is not worthy, she is too broken, too unfit!" I continued my journey along this long dark road, sad and worried carrying her in my arms. After much walking, and mutterings to myself, I came upon this great light. And as I lifted my arms up to offer this broken woman, to the light, two arms reached out to grab and accept her and a voice said, "It is NOT because of HER that we take her, it is because of YOU!"

People, serving the spirits, in whatever capacity, is a noble calling. Do not take it likely!

VODUN, ITS COLORS AND DREAM INTERPRETATION

I was perusing another forum, checking for email, when I came across a young lady who had posted a long dream for interpretation. According, to her, it had been bothering her, for some time, and she wanted to understand what it meant. She had been washing down her ancestral alter, with Florida water, and made a point to mention that she was wearing a red scarf, with a red shirt and blue jeans. Later she went to bed, wearing the same red scarf. In her dream, a woman appeared telling her about serving her as she kneel before an alter with rosaries and blue and red cloth. She assumed that the woman, who was mulatto, was Yemoja/Mami Wata. Upon reading it my response was three simple words "Go to Ifa."

Another poster appeared, after me, and told her that the dream was very simple to explain, "You could start building a relationship with her [Yemoja], by getting her image and decorating a small space in red and blue for her, with roses etc., that should be a good start. Is she your met tet, only time will tell or you will find out once you get initiated? Good luck!"

Again, I answered and repeated, "Go to Ifa! The color red has nothing to do with Mami. In fact, it is opposed to Mami or anything INSIDE the temple walls. Red is associated with spirits that have died unnatural deaths. Red is about the dead not Mami Wata/Yemoja etc. Divination will tell you what the dream is about. There are also many spirits in the pantheon of Mami Wata. The spirit that may have come could be associated with what you were doing with your ancestral shrine. These spirits need sacrifice in order to eat with their ancestors. Unnatural deaths separate us from re-joining our ancestors after death. These people are caught at zogbe, the place outside of the temple that they are at after an unnatural death. Diasporans must understand that questions, about the spirit world, must be taken to the spirit world, and through authentic divination, answered by the spirit world. Human guessing does not always arrive at the correct answers."

In vodun, each spirit is associated with their own colors, songs, foods/food restrictions, sacrificial animals, dances, ways the vodunsi are mounted, pearls/beading, sacred days of the week, and many other things peculiar to that particular vodun. An initiated person recognizes these colors, from their own pantheon, of spirits and maybe a few others. These colors, habits, of the voduns, etc. gives us clues as to what spirit one might see in a dream; however, my issue today, is with the layperson putting their spiritual dreams online and trusting the average 'Joe Schmoe' to interpret them.

A person's spiritual life is one of the most important and sacred things there is. Trusting total strangers, online, to interpret something that could affect one's life in such a profound way is not something one should do. Matters of the spirits should be taken to the spirits. It is they and they alone, through authentic African divination or another such ordained method, who can interpret such dreams. It is only they who know what they truly want. While the Internet has opened up the information highway, to the world, vodun simply cannot be learned by this medium. One can learn generalities; but, the spirits, and their nature, are only learned in a temple and by dealing with them on a daily basis. It is the same with one's spiritual dreams. One should go to the spirits, themselves, through divination to find out what the spirits want from our lives and ascertain why they approached them in the first place.

While I had an idea of what the poster's dream was about, as an initiated person, it is still necessary for, even me, to consult Ifa. In understanding the colors, of the voduns, in the African Mami, I knew what the dream DID NOT MEAN. The young man who claimed, that the interpretation was simple, had no clue that, based on the colors, he was giving out incorrect advice. The color red is Ade (accent over the e). This is the hunter in the Tchamba voduns. This is an ancestral vodun dealing with Zogbe, the place where those who have died of unnatural deaths reside/eat. This dream was not about the Mami spirits inside the temple; but, it was possibly about an ancestor asking to be fed outside of the temple at zogbe.

I implore all of you. If you want to know about a dream that is obviously of a spiritual nature...go to Ifa! We, as diasporans, descendants of the African chattel slave, have many ancestors that died unnatural deaths. Many due to slavery, and many more to lynchings, murder, executions, drive-by, disease and more. When these spirits, appear in our dreams, go to Ifa and ask what they want and what they need from us. Putting up an alter, with photos, is one thing...A form of acknowledgement to a few of them; but, tending to the needs of all of our ancestors, from the oldest to the newest, with the appropriate sacrifices and ceremonies is what is most essential. Only Ifa, or a spirit, can reveal this to us that our ancestors may eat together, draw strength from 'the blood' and, thus, finally.... Rest in peace.

CHAPTER 3

IFA: THE WEST AFRICAN DIVINATION SYSTEM

"FA NA GU NU, YOU ARE A WONDER TO BEHOLD!"

- Mamiwata Priestess

THE GREAT IFA: THE WEST AFRICAN DIVINATION SYSTEM

Over and over again folks ask me about Ifa. They seem to think it is some type of college course that you can take; and, in so doing become efficient in it! That simply isn't how it works! Those who take it up as a course can NEVER be as efficient, in it, as those born to it! This Eurocentric approach to that which is sacred simply doesn't work. Why? Because one coming from the outside can never understand it, or perform its duties, as someone born into it.

The priesthood, of Ifa, is a specialized priesthood, in Vodun, and entails a lifetime of training. Every priest or priestess is given the spirit Ifa during the initiation process. However, not EVERY priest or priestess is an Ifa priest carrying the opele. That is because with whatever divination tool (and there are several) one ends up with, as a priest(ess), one must communicate with the spirits. Ifa/Fa Afa is that spirit that travels through to the spirit world and returns with answers to our questions. He is thus separate from the 'tool', of divination, known as opele. This is a highly specialized person and a specialized diviner which many in the diaspora do not understand.

Let me give an example. When I was initiated into the priesthood of Mam Watai, in 1999, the three diviners present (there must be 3) determined that I was an Ifa priestess...A rarity for some women. But my spirits are male. For 16 days, while in initiation, I was taught the beginning rudiments of Ifa to be trained more extensively later. Opele was made for me. Several years later the voduns sent my husband on a trip without telling him why. He ended up in Ghana amongst the Ashanti tribe. They took him to an old diviner that was, at this time, 120 years old. He was blind and my husband was led to him by his son. He asked, "Who is that fat woman behind you?" It was my own spirit; but, Behumbeza was afraid to answer. The old papa sent for his wife and said, "The stranger has come!" According to the old diviner when he was 85 years old, the spirits commanded him to make an opele for a stranger. He did, the stranger was me; and, he had been waiting all these years. He was now ready to go to his ancestors. When Behumbeza returned to perform the ceremonies, for this opele, the old diviner died in his arms; and, his spirit, as well as a Tassinon (a woman of prayer) and all of his other spirits came to dwell in my opele. This was the first time my husband every said to me, "Mami I was afraid!" And it was at the old papa's death that it was revealed that I was his relative and heir to the large opele of the Ashanti tribe. Upon hearing this, I fell to my knees praising the ancestors and the spirits!

This is what I am saying folks, one, INHERITS one's opele as with many of one's other spirits! The Ifa priesthood is not one that you can enter haphazardly and think you can do with it what those born to it can do! I don't care how many courses you take or how big your pocketbook might be! The key is finding one's ancestry in vodun. These spirits, opele and spiritual kingships are passed down from generation to generation. Africa is STILL there! The seats are STILL there! The families are STILL there! And, Ifa can point you to them! One becomes one with one's opele. The diviner is born with gifts that no one else is. One sees without seeing, understands and knows without someone telling you anything, for, it is in the blood! The blood of the people who came from the motherland. These persons of African and non-African descent running around claiming they are Ifa priests without connecting, in anyway with African ancestry, that which we all have, in my opinion, are simply wasting their time. Because, that which is African will ALWAYS remain African!

THE SACREDNESS OF IFA/FA/AFA

Ifa/Fa/Afa is the west African divination system or oracle if some choose to call it that. It is referred to as Ifa in Nigeria, Fa in Benin and Togo, and Afa in Ghana. Because of a conversation I had, yesterday, I would like to reiterate a few basics, and a few elements, about the sacredness of Ifa/Fa/Afa. As I live in Benin, in some instances, I will simply use the term Fa.

Everyone that the spirits reveal is of the Priesthood, of vodun/orisha, or a child of the spirits (vodunsi or some other capacity) and they begin the initiation process is given the spirit (vodun) Fa.

1. It does not mean, however, that one is of the Fa Priesthood. This is a specialized Priesthood.
2. There is Fa the spirit and there is Fa the divination system. Many, in the diaspora, confuse or conflate the two.
3. Fa, the spirit, is prepared for the person that they are able to communicate with their spirits because it is the vodun Fa that goes into the spirit world and returns with the answers to our spiritual questions. So, all headed to the priesthood must receive this spirit, regardless, of what your head spirit is.
4. One is only a part of the Fa Priesthood if revealed by Ifa/Fa/Afa.
5. One is given either one hand of Fa or two hands. Ifa/Fa/Afa reveals how many hands we are to receive.
6. One hand is generally given to women and two hands are generally given to men; however, if one's head spirit is distinctly male; and, they were born to a large and/or significant spiritual throne they may have been born to receive two hands of Fa as I have.
7. If it is revealed that one was born of the Priesthood of Ifa/Fa/Afa, then, one will receive some initial training while in the initiation chamber (16 days), initiating into their head spirit, to later continue with more specialized training and or initiations into Ifa. Each pantheon of spirits treat this process differently.
8. If born of the Ifa/Fa/Afa Priesthood one's opele is generally passed down from generation to generation or specially prepared, for them, by an elder family diviner. The ability to divine is also passed down. It comes through one's ancestry.

9. Inside one's opele (or divination tool) if prepared correctly, generally lives the spirits of other family diviners and/ or Tassinons (women of prayer). That is why one must find the ancestor. These divination tools are endued with family spirits and divine power. They are not simple instruments... They, themselves, are vodun and are sacred. They must be fed (animal sacrifice) and cared for like any other vodun.

10. The Odu/Du are the sacred stories of Ifa. One generally is taught these stories through oral history as one is trained in the art of Ifa if of the Priesthood. They are sacred. They are not to be privy to any and every 'Joe Shmoe' that exists.

11. The Odu/Du being sacred are also secret to those 'outside' of the Priesthood. The tendency, in the diaspora, is to make these stories public and debate them or attempt to explain them. This is not the desire of the spirits. These are sacred and secret stories; and, it is the one who trains you, in Ifa, that explains them to you. They do not not exist for public scrutiny and debate. If one wants to learn them go to Ifa. Discover if you were born to be a diviner; and, if so go, initiate and train. There are too many 'bought in' and 'boot leg' diviners in the diaspora. I would not trust my spiritual life to such people.

12. The training of an Ifa/Fa/Afa priest develops over a lifetime. One's divination tool and the priest become one.

13. I would like to add, also, that in African vodun or in African traditional spiritual systems, in general, if one wants to know about someone of the Priesthood...one simply goes to Ifa. As a priest or priestess, of the spirits, we are born to our calling. And, when we heed the call of initiation, and one's initiation is conducted at the direction of the ancestors and the divine spirits, themselves, then you are known by them. Therefore, Ifa, the bringer of spiritual answers, will tell you about any priests or priestesses that has so been ordained. So if anyone

wants to know who I am or of my legitimacy or anything else.... go to Ifa.

THE HANDS OF IFA/FA/AFA

Over the years I have heard, while on the internet, folks speaking of the hands of Fa...whether one gets one or two hands of Fa. This is directly related to one's voduns. In Africa, generally, women receive one hand of Fa and men two. However, there are some women whose head spirit is distinctly male as mine is. These women are given BOTH hands of Fa. Why? Because all voduns (spirits) come in the male/female duality. If one has Ayidowedo, for instance, there is a male and a female of this spirit. The person, therefore, receives the male and female counterpart of each vodun he/she has. Most females would receive the female version of this spirit when one's voduns are set down/made. Ifa determines, or tells us, how many hands of Fa we receive when our Fa (the spirit itself) is being set down/made. In Benin, he is called Fa Na Gu Nu! Fa Na Gu Nu, you are wondrous to behold!

AUTHENTIC AFRICAN DIVINATION (IFA): THE PRACTICALITIES... WHY USE IT?

I wanted to speak, today, on the practicalities of using authentic African divination in the diaspora. I have spoken on this west African divination system, through essay, on numerous occasions; but, I want to discuss the practicalities of using it. In other words what makes it different from what we have always done in the diaspora? Why is it necessary and what makes it different from that of a diaspora 'reading'?

As a quick overview Ifa/Fa/Afa, called by either of these names, is the west African divination system or oracle as one may term it. This system, of divination, was given to us by the divine ones, themselves, and came as a part of the traditional spiritual systems, of Africa, as a means of communication between us and the spirit world. Therefore, it is intrinsically linked to African traditional spirituality and, thus, African based spiritual systems, in the diaspora, since these systems were brought over by the African slave during the transatlantic slave trade. And, if anyone is practicing, any of these traditional African-based spiritual systems, in the diaspora, without the benefit of Ifa, then, they are not practicing these systems in their entirety. But why?

Look at it this way. When one has an illness one generally goes to a physician. Most physicians, today, will do a series of tests. He is attempting to discover the underlying medical or chemical issues, within the body, that might point him to a clear diagnosis. In other words, he wants to know what, specifically, is causing this patient's illness so as to proper diagnose, treat and, thus, heal.

In the spiritual world, this is the function of Ifa. Ifa is not just a simple messenger. Ifa is a system that helps diagnose the spiritual problems of a client. In other words, Ifa, goes into the spirit world, seeks the answers to our spiritual ills, after consulting with the spirits or making various other inquires, returns with the spiritual causes that form the root of our manifesting woes (pointing to a diagnosis), and shows us how we may go about treating them (the various sacrifices, ceremonies, etc.) that we may return to spiritual wholeness, thus, a more productive life.... a healing. The breathe of the work of this great spirit and ordained divination system goes far beyond these so-called diaspora 'readings' and psychic friend networks or clairvoyants. While some of these persons, or systems, may have some talents, I can assure you that they are not even, remotely, in the league of the great Ifa. So, it is not about whether one is better over the other but a matter of restoring these African-based spiritual systems to their full potential, of healing, by restoring the use of Ifa that which came with these systems in the first place. It is the 'bought in' folk that has helped pollute these systems with these alternative replacements to our own original divination system because they have not understood or been trained to do Ifa. At least not by the normal or traditional ordained routes anyway.

Ifa helps us better diagnose and treat our spiritually ill clients. Ifa goes in and comes out with the names of our head spirits and accompanying spirits and finds our original ancestors. With him we can know the pantheon of spirits to which we were born. He helps us with our inquiries that we may live more productive lives. He is a mighty bridge from us to the spiritual realm. But above all he is the mighty re-connector to our motherland, our ancestors and the great divinities themselves. This is why his Priesthood is so specialized and so honored. For a diviner sees that which others cannot see, he/she senses that which others cannot sense; and, with the divine opele, in his/her hands, brings the spiritual and the physical worlds in perfect alignment.

AFRICAN SPIRITUALITY: IN AUTHENTIC AFRICAN DIVINATION (IFA/FA/AFA) TO WHOM ARE WE SPEAKING?

The answer, of course, is the spirits. But which spirits? Many think that when we speak of African divination, or Ifa, we are simply calling down a bunch of random spirits to ask questions about one's particular situation. This is not the case. Authentic African divination calls upon the spirits that gave YOU, in particular, life. It is YOUR personal spirits, your ancestors and the spirits that breathed life into YOUR body that we are calling upon. That is why divination is so important in consulting on our spiritual and personal issues. And, it is this divination system that is SPECIFIC to African or African-based spiritual systems and was handed down, by the divinities themselves, as an avenue to communicate with them.

By far the greatest handicap to diaspora vodun, in my opinion, is the non-use of Ifa. During the transatlantic slave era, the use of Ifa was either lost, or fell into disfavor, because the culture of slavery did not allow these skills to flourish or be handed down. The skills of an Ifa priest or priestess takes generations to cultivate, learn and train. It is a priesthood of the highest spiritual order. As a result, many in the diaspora vodun community, are using anything from simple playing cards, to Tarot, to nothing at all to divine. Clients are putting their faith in such priests/hougans or priestesses/mambos simply to know and to intuit what they need. And, because of it, very few diasporans, have the opportunity to truly know who their head spirits actually are. Other mechanisms, during the slave era, fell into use where one, if gifted, would either attempt to intuit the spirits, through dreams, possessions or other methods. This works fairly well with ancestral spirits and those loved ones who may have passed over and know you well; but, even then one may not understand the message clearly or diagnose the reason, for the spiritual appearance, correctly. And, to hit the mark any at all, it must come from a person that has generations of family seers and the gift has been passed down. But it is not definitive. For instance, why else would a European, who was born and bred in Europe, with no ties to Haiti think that they are carrying spirits particular to Haiti? It is because someone told them so without the benefit of authentic African divination. What many do not understand is that a great many of the spirits, that we possess, are culturally specific and/or inherited from one's ancestors. But, one's head spirit, could hail from anywhere across the globe. Such divinities, that existed before the world was even formed, cannot be called by just anyone. These held over "slavery days" divination methodologies cannot and will not summon them. Divine beings do not respond to random calls from people who do not know them. One has to be aware that, first, they exist, possess the knowledge needed to summon them and then be ordained, by them, to call upon them. And it is only through authentic African divination that one can determine one's oldest ancestor and their origins. After all the human race, itself, evolved from that one place...Africa. DNA analysis, which has recently hit the scientific community and us, can only take you but so far.... 1,000 years...and it doesn't differentiate between who is who. Ifa tells you who that first ancestor was, where he came from and anything else you choose to know about your ancestral history. With authentic African divination, your own ancestors show up to speak, on your behalf during the consultation, as well as the divinities. And these personal spirits, who see the past, the present and the future, all at once, are best able to guide you through your times of difficulty.

And this is WHY we seek their counsel.

But, now, let me take a moment and address you folks running up and down the internet searching for priests or priestesses to do love spells. First of all, for me personally, I do not like the ethical issues surrounding someone attempting to bind another to you unbeknownst to the person to be bound. I am referring to girlfriend/boyfriend relationships. If somebody doesn't want you, anymore, why not pick yourself up and go on. One needs to develop a bit of self-respect. If the person finds out, later, that separating from you was a mistake, then, they will eventually attempt to come back. But many of you, hormone laden, young people done lost your ever lovin' minds! When you fall in love you fall down! But getting back to the subject at hand...look! Too many of you are running up and down the internet from, priest to priest, handing out your money on a promise, from them, that your love object will come back and they don't. But, let me explain how this thing works in the spiritual world. If the spirits that live within you...your ancestors and divinities...see that this person is unsuitable for you, in any way, these spirits will put a wrench in that relationship. Our spirits come down, with us at birth, to not only guide us but to protect us. So, stop handing your money out to folks offering bogus promises without seeking authentic African divination, first, in order to find out if your ancestors and/or your divinities even approve of or want you with this person. And if they do agree, then, only authentic African divination is going to tell you what you need to do to get them back!

When one is ill we seek a qualified specialist in the medical field for consultation. This person has been trained in the illness, or problem, that concerns us and is duly seasoned. He or she has also been certified by an appropriate governing body in his/her field or specialty. In the spiritual world, this is what authentic African divination does; however, it goes one better. One is able to access the spirit world through a duly qualified, seasoned and ordained diviner and consult, specifically, with one's own ancestors and the spirits that gave us life spirits that see the past, the present and the future all at once. How cool is that?

IFA: THE WEST AFRICAN DIVINATION SYSTEM (ORACLE) AND OUR RELATIONSHIP TO IT

Several months ago, I posted an essay on Ifa. I felt it was important because of the proliferation of people attempting to "buy-into" a system that one must be born into...as with all African Priesthoods. Now I am seeing solicitations, from individuals, attempting to make 'how to' videos; and, I am simply shaking my head. Look my diasporan brothas and sistahs. Truth be told, very few to ANY of us, born in the diaspora, have the skills to teach Ifa; and, that includes me. While my opele came, to me, through inheritance, as it is supposed to, I couldn't even begin to count myself as some type of expert on Ifa. In this Priesthood, I am an infant; and, I have more time, in Africa, than most. Ifa involves a lifetime of training. And not only that; but, is something that one is born to do. And in that opele lives a multitude of ancestral diviners and spirits. The Ifa Priest and his tool are as one unit. He sees that which is unseen; and, his skills accumulate over a lifetime. Promoting a 'how to' video, on Ifa, only highlights the misunderstanding, in the diaspora, of what Ifa is, how one comes into it (through birth) and the extreme high regard in which this particular priesthood is sanctioned by the divinities.

DIVINATION

In the diaspora, many people come to ask me questions. While my experiences with spirit matters allow me to answer many, still, I refer people to Fa. Ifa/Fa/Afa is the West African divination system. One of the things least used in a diasporan's attempt to serve the spirits is the use of Fa. And it is because of it that there are so many problems with serving spirits here. As it is initiations have been grossly shortened in the diaspora as a result of the slave era. The slave, if caught practicing African spiritual systems, could be whipped or worse. We did what we could; but, Africans would find only two weeks spent in an initiation chamber, and someone calling themselves initiated, laughable. What can one learn in two weeks? Most say a Haitian kanzo is only nine days. This can be debated later; but, Fa must be consulted in spiritual matters. This great spirit goes into the spirit world and brings back answers to our questions. One must understand that in spirit matters one must consult the spirits, themselves, for the answer. Africans have no problems finding reputable diviners; but, diasporans do. I will discuss this issue later. However, coupled with it is just what to expect in a divination. An initial divination, for someone, should uncover certain things...ancestry, head spirit and accompanying spirits, the nature of one's problem and what sacrifices one must give to correct these problems. I'll cover each as I continue this topic this week.

DIVINATION 2

As mentioned earlier, most Africans know their ancestry. However, sometimes, Africans, who have been in the diaspora a while might have disconnected from their village and/or are Christians who may no longer serve them. Like us, those born in the diaspora, they too must start from the beginning. In an initial divination (if you've never experienced one before) learning ancestry is a must. Why? Because no one can serve the spirits without them. In African spiritual systems, they are an integral part. THEY are why we are here. In addition, they intercede, on our behalf, with the divinities asking for help for their children. Many of the spirits that we have are passed down from them to us; and, when they leave this life they can pass on spiritual kingships/thrones, strong spirits and their protection. I want to tell you a story that even today STILL touches my heart.... A young lady came to us for a divination. She had been experiencing dreams in the night of being under water. She thought she was losing her mind. She would see seaweed and would wake up gasping for air terrified from these dreams under the sea. When my husband began her divination, he could not see the ancestor. He was instructed to travel to the Togolese/Ghana border and head towards the sea. Her ancestor would meet him there. When my husband made the journey, her ancestor appeared and told this story:

He was AGASSOU (the same as my husband and I) and had been caught by the slavers. After months of traveling, in chains, and many dying around him he got to Goree Island, in Ghana, where he met a woman. Both slaves were put on the boat. He had impregnated the woman; but, he was thrown overboard and drowned on the shores of Goree Island. This child who has come to us, centuries later, is of his seed and a descendant from the impregnated woman who made it, shackled in chains, to the Americas. This great ancestor had reached out his hand from a water grave. When I heard this, I fell to my knees. This child has now become my child...this ancestor I will honor and feed until the day I die!

DIVINATION 3

As mentioned in the previous divination posts, in an authentic African divination one's ancestors generally show up. A deceased person will often speak on behalf of the person from his/her family giving the name of the clan/tribe or discussing something of importance for that person. Next a person's head spirit will come; but, not always. Divinities are very particular. If the spirit sees that the person calling is not qualified to do one's initiation that spirit will not show itself. Ruining a person's initiation could damage a person's life or kill them. An example is what happened to me. Upon my initiation, even though there were three bokono (diviners) in attendance. My true head spirit did not show himself until I came into contact with someone he (my head spirit is male) * considered pure of heart and the type of person that would follow that vodun down to the letter on my initiation. It is my second spirit, Ayidowedo, who stood up on his great tail to hide the three heads of the great Dattatreya (Den'su in Africa).

* *Physically I am female, spiritually I am male.*

That is why I was initially initiated as Hounon Ayidowedo. It took the great African priest Behumbeza to find my true spirit. I must complete further ceremonies for him in order to know his personal name. In divination, the experience and character of the diviner is paramount! If the head spirit comes others will follow also. The ancestors and the spirits will discuss any problems that are going on in the person's life, as well as, those sacrifices needed to correct these problems. It is then up to the person to proceed with the various ceremonies if he/her so chooses. These divinations can be most involving. There are times the spirits may ask for special sacrifices before giving information or even tell the diviner to come back at another time.

THE IFA PRIESTHOOD

I had a question about Vodun tidbit #8 today: Everyone initiated, in Africa, gets Fa; but, not everyone is an Ifa priest. The Ifa priesthood is a separate priesthood. For better clarification it means that, in Africa, one of the first ceremonies done, toward initiation, is the installation of the vodun Fa. Fa is an actual spirit! It is needed in that whatever medium you use to divine can be used. If you use the shells, for instance, you need to install the vodun (spirit) Fa.

It is this spirit that goes through the spirit world to bring us back the answers to our spiritual concerns. If you do not take/install this spirit you will not be able to communicate with the spirit world. It is by this spirit that we are able to communicate with the spirit world regardless of what method of divination that you are using. However, the Ifa priesthood is a separate priesthood. These priests specifically use the opele; and the opele is passed down from generation to generation! Tarot cards are not hooked into the African ancestry nor can it give us answers to our problems. The divine ones gave the African a direct contact with them; and it is called Ifa/Fa/Afa.

WHEN SPEAKING OF IFA

On a vodun thread, several months ago, a young lady said and asked the following question in a post. I have simply copied and pasted it verbatim here: The young lady said, "Generally speaking the Diaspora recognizes sovereignty for each ATR among those that practice it. Meaning that if some Spirits in the Nago Nation of Haitian Vodou are viewed as Orisha, I would still bow to the authority of a Houngan or Mambo before working with Them even as a Lukumi...... Or even though Candomble and Lukumi both venerate Orisha, I recognize and respect that we each may do things differently. We all recognize roots in Africa but are all siblings of each other now in other parts of the world, influenced by the environments we have found there. You, Wedosi seem representative of a practitioner of the Mother Religion we may have roots to. Do you feel as much of a connection to Spirits in the Diaspora that have originated from the Voduns you work with as you do with your own Spirits and, maybe more importantly, do you feel a sort of authority over them all. I was thinking about the comment of Ifa Priests in the Diaspora perhaps not being properly trained and my first thought was....in WHAT. I mean, if we are acknowledging Lukumi Ifa and African Ifa and you are representative of one.... why should it necessarily have the same modes of training as the other. If you are saying that African Ifa as the origin should dictate for all Ifa in the Diaspora, then that is another thing that may be debatable. However, knowing how you view African Ifa within the family of ATRs the world over may better help me understand some of your responses."

HERE IS MY ANSWER:

"...I am trying to figure out the best way to answer you. I'll do my best; but, it is YOU that will have to tell me if it makes any sense. I see two things here. One is about training and one is about serving the spirits themselves. In the AA community, we have always had the debate of us being Africans, living in the Diaspora, or Americans who are simply of African descent. One theorizes that we are STILL an integral part of Africa while the other assumes us cut off from our ancestors, through slavery, therefore a new breed of folk developing new norms (and everything else associated) while we are. I, and the voduns, subscribe to the first. And in that instance, one starts with serving one's very first ancestors, born/inherited spirits, and pull forward. Haitians serve the local spirits but reach back to the Rada spirits (those in Africa) occasionally. Therefore, as Africans, we must go back and re-instate our spiritual practices as our ancestors did them. But it is not only for that reason that I say this; but, it is the training. A properly trained priest/priestess, of any kind, in Africa can call a spirit from anywhere. The African's relationships with the spirits, their understanding and training in spiritual matters simply surpasses all others. AFRICANS are the Priest/Priestesses of this world. The spirits say Africa is FIRST in spirit matters. So why not train and learn from the best! The things I have seen in Africa are true miracles to the human eye. For example do you know that some of these priests have the power to bring the dead back to life and actually ask them how they died? Of course, there are certain conditions that must be met for these circumstances; but, this is today people...in the 21st century. These secrets lay in Africa not anywhere else. And we, as the inheritors of this knowledge, can know it. What priest, anywhere in this diaspora, can do what the great BEHUMBEZA did almost two years. ago. This man walked on the bottom of the sea for 4 hrs. while camera crews/media and the whole of Benin, West Africa waited on the shores! No gimmick but truth! The African training is simply unparalleled. And, everyone who visits Africa and sticks around for any period of time will tell you so!

Our power is in the land that we left. By re-instating it we can only gain! But lastly, this message I bring is not from me. I did not theorize any of it! It is the mission that I was told of as I initiated into the priesthood. It comes from the spirits themselves. If one visits Benin, in particular, one will find that the things I am saying were prophesied long ago in traditional culture. And, if one honors priest/

priestesses, in Africa, as vessels of the spirits one should honor those properly initiated, from there, as well. I personally serve EVERY spirit and ancestor I have...those from Africa and in the diaspora. That is the way of African vodun. "

ANCESTRAL SEARCH SITES/DNA ANALYSIS/IFA

Many are interested in DNA analysis today! Even I have been using governmental records to compose my family tree. For it appears that the more modern we have become, the less tendency we have of our elder family members sitting around, a glowing fireplace, relating family history. And if yours is anything like my own family, folks don't want to talk for being horribly ashamed of those who had the TB, those prone to drink, those jailed or the ones who spent time in the insane asylum and the like. And whether it was true or not...those who died of the "bad disease" as my grandfather used to term it. But the desire is still there...the desire to know who we are and where we came from.

DNA analysis is a short cut and a most convenient method to discover ourselves for those of us with roots as a result of the transAtlantic slave trade. It gives us an idea of our general genealogical makeup and that's a good thing! But the one thing I must remind you all of, and, that is that ALL of mankind has been traced back to a single African man and woman. Africa, without a doubt, is the birthplace of mankind. All starts there and branches outward. And while DNA analysis shows us that make up of ancestry, for at least 1,000 years, only the great Ifa can reveal that beginning ancestor, his tribe and/or his origins. While DNA analysis goes from you to those within that 1,000-year span Ifa STARTS with the oldest and pulls forward catching the oldest to the newest, the darkest to the lightest. And only he and he alone, or a spirit directly, can tell you the story of how they came to be and what, spiritually, you may have inherited from them all. I am always thankful for new science. For I know that what we, as humans, discover has already been placed there for man to discover. This is the beauty of the divine. But when it comes to the spiritual only that which is spiritual can reveal what is. DNA analysis and those sites that aid in our search, for who we are, are helpful indeed; but, with the information revealed by the great Ifa it can change our very lives.

TO REINSTATE AUTHENTIC AFRICAN DIVINATION IN DIASPORA VODOU: WHAT THAT ACTUALLY MEANS AND HOW ONE GOES ABOUT IT

I have said continuously, in my writings, that one of the greatest handicaps to diaspora vodou has been the lack of using authentic African divination. Why? Because unless one actually goes to the spirits, themselves, and inquire many things about the spiritual life of a person may never be discovered. Many traditional practices were either lost or fell into disuse due to the vestiges of slavery after African slaves were brought into the diaspora. Many of these ancient arts were not able to be passed down through the generations. As a result, much has been lost. While not so much in the past, today, there has been a proliferation of people buying into these African based spiritual systems. Many have initiated these folk, and others, without either finding out whether they were born to the spirits or to identify their true head spirits or ancestry. This has weakened diaspora vodou and people's understanding of it. Instead of it being seen as a priesthood of the spirituality ordained it is far too often viewed as a series of good luck spells, potions, charms and a system where anybody and everybody can enter its priesthood who show up with a fist full of dollars. That is not what vodun is or has ever been. The African priesthood, from whence these systems came, is a divine priesthood. Set up by the divinities, themselves, it was set up to offer spiritual assistance to those to whom the divinities created...mankind. For underlying every problem, we encounter in our everyday lives a spiritual issue is usually at its root. Those born to the priesthood came with special spiritual missions and gifts to be able to complete these divine missions for the benefit of mankind.

Giving initiations to every Tom, Dick and Mary Jane who shows up with a fist full of money, not only pollutes the pool of ordained people calling themselves priests/houngans and priestesses/manbos but brings dishonor to this royal priesthood. These people are often not fit to serve and generally only do so for financial gain. Reinstating authentic African divination practices will not only serve to root out those who were not born to the priesthood but help to keep them out. In addition, it will allow one to hear what the spirits, themselves, desire for each individual client coming to us, identify their ancestry, spirits, underlying spiritual issues and how to correct them in order for them to lead a more fruitful and fulfilling life. So, how do we go about it?

We start out by taking ourselves to Ifa. We, first, want to know who and what we are in the spirit world. For those born in families where priests and priestesses may abound you still need to go. Not ALL in a family are born to the priesthood or if they were one still needs to know to what station, one's spirits, and one's particular spiritual mission. Being a priest or a priestess IS NOT the spiritual mission it is simply the vocation. In every vocation, one specializes. And, in vodun, we need to know to what our particular spiritual gifts and skills are best suited for. Ifa can reveal all of this to us. For instance, I am a born teacher, my husband an excellent practitioner, a particular spiritual child of mine excellent in dealing with women chasing folks who don't want them no mo'. He can listen to them for hours. I have absolutely no patience. As a result, my bedside manner needs great improvement according to most. As a warrior priestess unless we are talking 'bout gettin rid of some bad spiritual stuff, clinging to the tenets of African vodun and/or discovering one's ancestors I might appear to be abrasive and uninterested. So, discovering one's priesthood mission is most important.

If one has never been to Ifa before I suggest that one goes to the source...Africa. One's spiritual life is far too important an issue to trust in the hands of amateurs. I have been hearing about these so called "roots readings". Ridiculous! All authentic African divinations are "roots readings" by their very nature. This is simply a marketing gimmick! I don't mean no harm my brethren and sistren; but, the diaspora is amateurville when it comes to these things. Beware of these diaspora 'self styled' Ifa priests and those calling themselves elders when they may have visited Africa in the 1970s, for three weeks, and haven't been back since. Make inquiries and contacts with gifted priests, in the motherland, and hook up with your ancestors and began your journey there. Do not be deceived. You cannot serve the spirits effectively without the ancestors. Too much of who you are and what you are, spiritually, comes from them. If you are of the Ifa priesthood or any priesthood, for that matter, it came from them. It was all inherited. Your spiritual and/or earthly thrones come from them and are passed down through the generations. For those of us living in the diaspora it simply lies dormant until we go to Ifa and discover it all. The ancestors are your spiritual grounding. These "bought in" folk can holler Africa is not important all they want. But they straight up lying! They simply do not know what they are talking about!

Depending on what Ifa reveals depends on whether you are given one or two hands of Ifa. Having the spirit Ifa/Fa will allow you to use whatever methods of divination that you were destined to use. Ifa will reveal all of that too. And, if you happen to be of the Ifa priesthood it will be revealed also. Many in the diaspora do not understand that just because you have been given the vodun or spirit Fa does not mean necessarily that you are of that priesthood. What it means is that you are a priest or priestess and have been given the spirit Fa which underpins whatever divination method you will eventually use. It allows you to communicate with the spirit world. Folks claiming to be throwing cowries on your behalf without the benefit of having the spirit Fa is simply counting on gravity to divine. Absolutely nothing is happening there. But the Ifa priesthood is a very special priesthood within itself. Very few born to the priesthood are also Ifa priests. Many temples consist of the priests/priestesses and one specializing in Ifa. For instance, my husband's divination tool, the mirror, is different from my own...the opele. Both methods used were inherited through our ancestors. But we both have the spirit Fa.

So, depending, on what Ifa says about you, your ancestry, your station to the priesthood and other particulars taking the actions described above should begin your journey in re-instating authentic African divination in your practices. I know that many, in the diaspora, have depended on spirits possessing the adapts and speaking when they arrive; but, this is only one way to seek spiritual answers. Spirits don't show up all the time and we are not having ceremonies 24/7. Using Ifa, the divination system that came with these spiritual systems in the first place, allows us continual contact with the spirit world.

CHAPTER 4

AFRICAN VODUN AND IT'S MAJESTY

"REMEMBER THAT A PRIEST OR PRIESTESS IS ONLY AS POWERFUL AS THEIR RELATIONSHIP WITH THE SPIRITS IS STRONG."

-Mamiwata Priestess

THY NAME IS VODUN

I am older than time itself, for, it is I that created it! I was here before the world come, for, I created that too! The beasts of the fields, the fields themselves, the mountains, the valleys, the hills, the waters and all that the earth contains is my handy work. But, my greatest creation was one in my own image...mankind. And of this creation I made male and female...in this place known as Africa. And through this creation the earth populated itself into clans, tribes, groups with a common ancestry and common blood.

I gave my children systems to communicate with me directly. It is called Ifa for some, oracle for others, visions, dreams, tarot cards and divination tools of all kinds. With each group, of my children, I have made myself known. My emissaries are in charge of their care. They are divine beings, from me, that aid and assist, my children, in their hours of need. And, among them are born those sent, from me, with divine missions, spiritual missions, to facilitate in the care of those who need me. These ordained ones embark upon a journey, of discovery, of who they are spiritually and what their missions are; and, if they find them, are molded and refined to complete these divine missions. Some are called Shaman, some Gurus, some Priests, others Imams and still others by names by which their spiritual vocations are known.

As time passed many of the world's spiritual systems organized themselves. My children are always busy and have many needs; so, I have sent my prophets. Among my children they often fight. But in all, of these systems, I live inside. They all began with me, for, all things began with me. But those who hold the traditional ways often know me best.

Their arrogance, of knowing, has not taken them away from me. They have not set themselves up as Gods, for, they know that I am their God; and, so they hear and obey my tenants. Many have lost their ability to hear, see and obey my divine will. I have tested them all.

I am called many things depending on the language of my children. In the broadest terms, I am known as 'religion'. But to the ones that know me best they understand that I am much more than this. Traditional societies describe me in their own languages and pen upon me many names. For I am all that is pure, clean, holy and divine. Yet, I am the giver of all things; and, thus, all things lay within my hands. Even the bad spirits heed my commands. I am the creator of all things. I am the beginning and the end...the alpha and the omega. In the Fon language I am known as 'spirit' but my child refers to me as 'that which is sacred'. But to the world thy name is vodun.

THE PRE-EMINENCE OF VODUN

This spiritual system termed "vodun" which means "spirit", in the Fon/Mina language, per-dates all known spiritual systems that have ever existed on the earth. Vodun is this ancient because MawuLissa, and those whom he/she designated to control various domains of the earth, existed BEFORE the world was even formed. Once the world was formed our Creator, thus, communicated to its creations (us) directly, through nature and Ifa or traditional African divination systems. Thus, the indigenous peoples, of the world, know vodun/ the spirits through that nature and have given these spirits names from their own languages. These divine ones have shown themselves in every culture and every era of mankind's existence interceding, when necessary, and using, as it's vessels, those chosen before birth and sent with specific missions and contracts to accomplish a work on earth. In more traditional cultures they possess the chosen, send miraculous healers, gifted Shaman and divine seers. During Old Testament times they have sent prophets, visions, dreams and miracles in order to accomplish their agendas here. And, cloaked, in these Old Testament writings are the traditional Priests, of old, who walked on water (the domain and feats of Agwe/Mami Wata), brought the dead to life, as traditional African priests do today, traveled great distances, overnight, by foot...as some of these priests still do, spoke in tongues...those possessed by spirits, speaking in the languages of their origins, and much much more. It is ALL vodun! Some of these gifts disappeared when many of these great priests died; but, in Africa, I have seen such gifts returned when one is born and deemed worthy enough that the spirits chose to teach them these ancient feats. So, in every known spiritual system today, whether written or oral, we see the invisible hand of vodun...that which is sacred...that which is spirit.

AFRICAN SPIRITUALITY: THE BASICS

Since slavery, those of African descent have been spread throughout all four corners of the globe. We are everywhere. While many of us are the offspring of those who arrived, in chains, others have come by plane, boat and/or other modes of transportation looking for economic prosperity. Whatever may have been the plan, of the divinities, in master mining this forced migration, or even how we may feel about it, we are here now. One cannot put the toothpaste back in the tube. Regardless of our faith, Christianity, Islam, Judaism, Buddhism or any other, I argue that there are two basics that we need to know; and, only authentic African divination, or possession of a vodunsi who speaks to us directly, can tell us. It is our ANCESTRY and that SPIRIT and accompanying SPIRITS that gave us life. Much can be done with just this knowledge, alone, whether one chooses to serve the spirits or not.

What I admired about those Africans that I met, and those who I meet today, is the understanding that ancestry is important. Many, in Benin (Dahomey), for instance attend church. But once a year you will see them sending sacrifices and/or monies, to the villages, that these ancestral sacrifices can be done just like those who openly serve the voduns.

The ancestors know their children...each and every one of us! They intercede, for us, with the divine ones if we are in trouble. They are our first line of defense, when this trouble comes; and, they have their own spiritual powers in helping us prosper. Potential spouses, homes and things that we need, in our everyday lives, are their domain. They will also rise up, if properly fed and cared for, to smite our enemies with power and finality. Do not estimate their power and do not take them for granted. They are a force to be reckoned with! And regardless of where we choose to be on Sunday morning, or any other holy day, our ancestors need to be identified, acknowledged, fed and served. And because we were snatched from their bosom, due to the slave trade, only divination can find them.

More, today, are availing themselves to DNA analysis; but, Ifa goes back much further. Not only does it take us to our roots but it also brings up any spiritual problems that may be looming and gives solutions (prescribed ceremonies to be performed) on how to deal with these problems.

Knowing the spirits that gave us life is also a must. These divine beings work, diligently, daily to provide the things we require for our lives on this earth. Knowing them and honoring them, whether we choose to regularly serve them, can only be a benefit to us. If we need to we can readily seek their assistance. These, to me, are the basics of spirituality in general, not just for those of African descent. Ancestry is important in ALL cultures; but, it is most important to those, of us, whose ancestors had no choice into what country they were taken to. I am confident that our re-connection, to ancestry and spirit, will help lift us out of centuries of oppression, poverty and degradation regardless of faith.

REINCARNATION AND VODUN

This is one of those subjects that I ran into by accident if I may describe it as such. As a person, I have always felt that I had an old soul. I never had an interest in reincarnation because, after this hard life I done been through, I had/have no interest in returning in another life. So, when one of my spiritual children kept bringing up the subject, I not only told him I did not know, I made sure he understood that I wasn't even trying to know! "Go ask your spiritual father", I said (speaking of my husband Behumbeza), "Mami ain't interested in that!" After Ifa revealed that this Haitian born man was Lord Rama he 'bout worried me to death! In a good way, of course, 'cause I love the boy to pieces; but, inquisitive he is!

So after almost 5 years of preparing for this big initiation, of his, and the spirits sending my husband to Ghana, Togo and Nigeria, on his behalf, chasing his ancestry, bringing back royal seats, collecting his opele, visiting sacred waters, digging up his pearls from sacred places and doing sacrifices and ceremonies all over, the spirits said to my husband, "Go to India, for our son (speaking of our Lord Rama) left something there in his first life over thousands of years ago and then the preparations for his initiation will be complete". I like to fell down!

This young man instinctively knew something was there and pursued it until the spirits, themselves, revealed it! Behumbeza knew that he would, one day, have to travel, to India, on Rama's behalf as he did for himself but waited patiently on the spirits. Mami, with her totally impatient self, wasn't wanting to hear NOTHING about returning to this 'mug'. I was simply tired of being 'tired'! Lord Rama is on his 3rd visit to this place, we call earth, and Mami on her 5th. Of course, I listened about these 5 lifetimes reluctantly. Behumbeza knew I was not ready to hear these things and waited until I asked. For it was Behumbeza that my head spirit, Dattatreya, while standing on a mountaintop first revealed himself. My second spirit Ayidowedo stood on his great tail as Dattatreya hid his 3 heads because the person who did my initiation did not understand his ceremonies. Thus, I am called Hounnon Ayidowedo. So, be careful folks...if the ceremonies for your spirits are done incorrectly it could cause you your life. Most divinities, therefore, if see that the person you are employing, to do your ceremonies, could cause you harm simply will not reveal themselves! But getting back to the subject at hand.

Reincarnation is part and parcel of vodoun; however, it is only ordained and highly skilled priests that can access this information for you.

THRON: THE KOLA VODUN

In the diaspora, there is a tendency for folks to seek after a vodun (spirit), with the attributes they like, and then serve it. This is not correct. One should go to Ifa/Fa/Afa and find out what spirits one was born with and serve them. For it is THEY that has given life after the ancestor has reached down and molded the clay. However, there is a vodun that can approach any divinity on one's behalf. The diaspora does not know him. I met him in Africa; and, his name is THRON. I call this spirit the kola vodun. I am not entirely versed on this spirit; but, I know him, I respect him and honor him here. There are Thron priests on the Internet, out of Africa, that know him better than me. I know that this spirit can offer you protection, from your enemies, and approach any vodun, on your behalf, to ask favors. Many folk, for instance, that do not have Mami, or some other vodun in Africa, will seek out Thron. I know Africans who serve this great vodun. Once one visits a temple of Thron you will understand why I call him the kola vodun.

THE BLOOD

About three years ago I had a major surgery. I became extremely tired; and, it was discovered that I needed blood. When I received this transfusion, of two pints, I felt energetic and renewed. It reaffirmed my understanding, in vodun, of the concept of sacrifice and the blood. Many know that in vodun and other African traditional spiritual systems that sacrifice is done. But one shouldn't concentrate on the sacrifice itself but the concept of the blood. It is the blood that is the key. In Old Testament times when a sinning Israelite wanted to get right with God, it was the blood of the lamb (or goat) that had to be shed and sprinkled across the alter. In New Testament times, it is said that it is the blood of the lamb (Jesus) that offers continual cleansing from sin. Blood is seen as the purification agent, offering power over satan and giving eternal life. This concept of sacrifice with the shedding of blood per-dates all organized religions because it comes from the heavens, was relevant in ancient times and is still relevant today.

In vodun it is still through the shedding of blood, by sacrifice, that we purify ourselves and offer nourishment to the divine spirits that they may do the work needed for their children. This sacrificial blood regenerates the spirits as it does our physical bodies bringing the necessary nourishment. As Africans were displaced throughout the world in shackles a disconnection occurred. Cut off from our ancestral roots centuries of sacrifices were not done. Our people suffered and is still suffering throughout the diaspora. Without these sacrifices we, as a people, became weak. These sacrifices are still needed today. Diasporans must reconnect to that which was lost...our ancestry, our spiritual systems, our human dignity and the unique African way of life...and this can be done through the Blood.

VODUN AND THE MALE/FEMALE DUALITY

Yesterday I heard a lady repeat words that my grandmother, in her own words, used to say, "It is said that the man is the head of woman; but, I say to you that attached to every head is a neck. This neck is woman and it is the neck that turns the head any way it chooses." What she said was wonderful; and, it made me smile and think. So be the nature of man and woman. But vodun shows us something that the world does not readily see. That, in fact, the Godhead (MawuLissa)...the creator of this universe... is a male/female duality and not a patriarchal tyrant. Throughout ancient times man worshiped and served it's great goddesses; but, as organized religions took root modern man, in his great attempt for superiority, undertook the task of subjugating woman. And, while every religion speaks against it some men still have difficulty giving woman her due.

I once minored in Women's Studies while working on a Master's Degree in Psychoanalytic Studies. Feminist issues were the course of the day. Classes were composed of militant feminist, vocal lesbians and me...A Black woman just wanting to know. For me feminism would be something different from that of a white woman that I might be employed to clean for.

Feminist rights were not my problem but freedom from prejudice of all kinds was. Vodun somehow solved all these great problems for me. It showed me who I was (ancestry), what I was spiritually and what my purpose in this world is to be. It showed me that beneath the skin we are spirits that walk of different backgrounds and missions (destinies). It showed me that through woman all creation flows, therefore, she is to be (and should be) held to a higher standard. That there is male and female in all of us not to be fought against but to flow harmoniously. In all of the great temples, of Africa, we see this male/female duality. If there is a Daagbo there is a Naagbo...the male/female counterpart of the same spirit. The Bible says: "It is not good that man should be alone". But vodun says that it was never intended.

HOW OLD IS VODUN?

I have read that people date vodun at 10,000 years old. I smile. The term vodun means "spirit" or my preferred meaning, "that which is sacred" in the language of the Fon people. The meaning, within itself, should give a clue as to its age; but, anthropologist, and the like, by pass this clue and attempt to put a numeric age on it anyway. These are folk who do not communicate with the spirits on a day to day basis or even believe that such communication can happen. Their clues are the written words or oral records of those who can bare witness. My understanding of vodun's age is what they personally tell me. And, in lieu of this, their ages vary because there are many different types of spirits; but, the oldest spirits of all are the creators of the universe and all it contains.

Since man's creation, God (Mawu/Lissa, the spirits, the voduns, the orisha, etc.) have communicated with their children in one way or another either directly or through divination. Vodun, therefore, is at least as old as man's creation; yet, in reality it is much older than that. The spirits existed long BEFORE man's creation. Someone or something had to exist to create; and, that was vodun! So, does this mean, then, that all other African spiritual systems or other indigenous systems are less old? By no means! For the Fon people, the Orisha is Nigeria's vodun, the Akan tradition Ghana's vodun or the traditional spiritual systems in South Africa their vodun.

The term vodun is actually means 'spirit' in the Fon language. The term orisha would be the same, or an equivalent, in the Yoruba language. All over Africa one refers to particular spirits in that particular place or region that we are referring. Therefore, for us ALL of Africa is vodun. It is the anthropologist and researchers, in their attempt to list and quantify, that put up these divisions and subdivisions of this unified indigenous service to spirits that is pervasive all over Africa. It is only when a person is initiated into the spirit world, according to the tenants of the divine ones, that some of its mysteries unfold.

I have always felt that I had an old spirit. My Da Zodji had once teased me by mentioning that he was very old way before he ever came down with me. This comes up every year, during my birthday, when I have to give my voduns drinks and sweets to celebrate their time here on earth. But my Dattatreya, he took the cake! In the last dream in which I saw him, he said with a smile, "You date me, you were here before the world come!" I have been TIRED every since!

IN VODUN WHO ARE WE?

The question I am attempting address is what spirits are actually contained within us? In actuality, there are many; but, I would like to concentrate on two specific groups. The ancestors and the divinities themselves. I am covering this because there is a misnomer, among African Americans, that all of our spirits are from black Africa. That isn't true. Some come from other parts of the world. Review my post on 'Who is Mami Wata?' As for the ANCESTORS, those of us who are of African descent, know the deal. We are from Africa! Our ancestors and their descendants are STILL there. If Ifa tells us what tribe we originate from we can find them. And with the corroboration of Ifa (they may use their own diviners for verification) reclaim any spiritual thrones and spirits inherited, from your ancestor, spiritual titles, opele, any rights you may have in that tribe and land. Yes, folks land! If it is proven that your ancestor left that tribe, during the slave trade, you will get land. But Ifa must verify everything. Ain't nobody giving you nothing 'cause you cute! And, even for those most removed from African ancestry, one's oldest African ancestor can be found. Africa is the birthplace of man!

The DIVINITIES, however, may originate from any place! These spirits are the creators of heaven and earth itself. Folks do not often understand this because, in Haitian vodou, and many other diasporan African based spiritual systems the tendency is to deal with local spirits. A lot of these spirits lived, on earth at one time, died, and returned from the spirit world, to help their children. Some have even been elevated to voduns. But they are not the creators. The Africans, straight up, deal with the divine ones (not saying that others can't too); and, they can originate from anywhere. These priests and priestesses are STILL dealing with the mysteries as they came out of Egypt; and, that is WHY they are so powerful! These mysteries and secrets are buried deep, in African vodun, and is only privy to those destined to know. No researcher or tourist has access. That is also why folks rolling into Africa on a two-week vacation, returning, and claiming they are the grand poo pa, in vodun, is laughable to me and anyone that knows better. I laid in those temples, non-stop, for eight long years...still laying in them and folks telling me what?! You've got to be there, a while, to even get a hint at learning something. But, getting back to the subject at hand. In an earlier post, I explained how we come to be. An ancestor, who wants to be remembered, takes the clay and molds the child. But he cannot give life. He makes a argain with a divine spirit (one that he may have) to give the child fe promising that the child will serve that spirit all of the days of s life. These spirits that give life are those who created both the eavens and earth! And, if the child has come here for a specific nission his spirit may be like my own.... Arab, called Dattatreya, and riginating from the Red Sea. And, he could also be known in the Iindu pantheon of Gods; but, since he visits Africa and is often the pirit of kings, called Den'su there.

Those spirits that give us life can come from another part of the vorld. They are part of MawuLissa. Do not think that a brotha or istah cannot have a spirit that originates outside of black Africa. It s possible. As people, we often embody spirits originating from all ver the globe; but, the ancestry stays constant. Wanna know why ome brothas might have a propensity for white women? Could be nessed up priorities, but, could be spiritually based! I'm just saying.... vhaaaa! : lol: Sistahs gone get you for that one Mami....

/ODUN'S FLIP SIDE

I remember going on tribe's Vodun thread, many years ago, and eing a bit touched that these folks were interested in Vodun. I thought 'd help them out; but, it didn't take me long to realize that these folks vanted to make Vodun what THEY thought it should be as opposed o what it really is. Folks, immediately thought they were my equal ind wanted to argue the tenants of vodun; and, I wasn't having it! Why? Because you either know vodun or you don't...they didn't; and, ifter 8 years of laying in and out of African temples, I simply had no equal! This wasn't ego, it was simple fact! And Wedosi wasn't about to oite her tongue! So, these folks took their brand, of vodun, to another hread and closed me out! But one unusual thing about them, and, find in many folks interested, in vodun, is to think that the spirits ire these ALWAYS sweet loving, cuddly, fuzzy little things that loves everybody! Nothing, could be further from the truth!

I tell my spiritual children, if you want to see the voduns in action, read the Old Testament prophets! See how God dealt with the Israelites! These are the voduns that I know. They will test your obedience, they will mold you like a diamond in the rough. The road is rocky, many times difficult, long and arduous; but, if you can make it to the other side, if you can complete the mission you have come to do, you can sit down in the heavens on a throne of gold!

What folks do not understand is that the voduns are the CREATORS of heaven and earth itself! These are DIVINE beings! These aren't some folk who died and come back. These are the divinities that have given us life. They were here before the world come! They are the ones that our ancestors go to requesting that they intercede and help them in our difficult times! They are the God of the Israelites, the Allah of the Muslims, the God of the Hindu, and every other people on earth! So why do folks think that they, just any Ole' Joe Smo, can call them down? What is this "self-initiation" insanity? Since man's earliest times the divinities have given their tenants on how they can be approached. The purification rituals that must be adhered to. Yet the follies of mankind continue to exist that some would think that, now, even the highest divinities can be called down by men/women who are unwashed, impure and have attitude! The voduns are laughing at them! And, I'm falling out of my chair... But what is their TRUE nature? It is simple, they can create, they are the Creators of this universe; but, they can also destroy! And they do when they choose to.

VODUN'S FLIP SIDE 2

Why does God (the voduns) allow bad things to happen, we ask? Our idea of God, spawned by the New Testament, is that he/she is all knowing and all loving...cute, cuddly and non-malevolent! Our God wouldn't allow bad things to happen. The Old Testament teachings, and examples, are quickly forgotten! This is my greatest problem with this, canonized, New Testament that has left much out! It has cut out the true nature of the spirits and took the prophet Jesus and made him larger than life because they were promoting a new religion instead of the true nature of God (the spirits). This is also the attitude that I got from folk on various Internet sites and others that have interest in vodun. The thought that our ancestors had of God punishing somebody, or us, for bad acts is a barbaric thought! But, in essence, in some cases this is true! These natural disasters are sometimes spiritually induced. Human sacrifices are still being made today; and, it generally happens by these natural disasters. I know this is difficult to hear; but, hear it you must because one must take the good, the bad and the ugly in all that one seeks to pursue.

The voduns can and will chastise man if necessary. When one puts themselves in the hands of the voduns, through initiation, they began to mold and knead you that you are able to do their will. And, that means THEIR will not your own! If you are a hard head like me... they will literally knock you to your knees if they have to. They must mold and refine you in order that you become a vessel for their use. These divine missions are not often easy. We humans think we are in charge of this universe. I've got news for you. We aren't! THEY are! We are the actors in THEIR play! And, if you are the recipient of one of these little 'cookie cutter' initiations and do not know sacrifice, have not seen suffering and only sit on a throne, built on sand, basking in the glow of folks bowing before you all the time...you haven't a clue as what vodun really is! You are spiritually powerless because the voduns do not know you. For we are only as powerful as our relationships, with the voduns (spirits), are strong! And, a TRUE server of the spirits could knock you down where you stand!

I have told you about Mami-Dan. Dattatreya is not the only spirit that exist in this pantheon. If you do not understand that Vodun is not all cuddly and sweet, may I introduce you to a couple of more spirits, in that pantheon, and ones that I was born with: Shiva and Kali. Feel free to Google any one of these; and, then tell me if either one is cuddly.

DIVINE MISSIONS

Nelson Mandela (1918-2013); Martin Luther King (1929-1968); Mahatma Gandhi (1869-1948); Harriet Tubman (1820-1913); Mother Teresa (1910-1977) ...these are just a few of the many souls that have come to this earth to do great things. For it has been through the vessels of such human beings that the spirits have brought about changes in this world. These are DIVINE missions.

And, yet, we have ALL come here with divine missions no matter how large or small. We have ALL been born of spirits to help us find out, through Ifa, if we do not know these missions, what they are and complete them. None of us came here to fret away our lives. We were not born just to lean up against street signs, on a corner, or sell drugs to the vulnerable. We did not come here to rob, steal and cause petulance. Neither did we come here to spend our time chasing the opposite sex. We were born with purposes far greater than these.

Men such as Nelson Mandela will be very much missed. He made a profound and indelible effect on our world and his society at large. But so, can each and every one of us! And if you don't know what is that you have come here to do; and, if by chance you do not stumble onto it by whatever reasons out there...Ifa can point you to it!

ENVY, GRATITUDE AND VODUN

In the 1990's, I was training as a Psychoanalyst in NYC. While studying psychoanalytic theory I was intrigued by Melanie Klein (1882-1960). Klein was the mother of "object relations" theory...the belief that environmental factors, not internal conflicts, cause our psychological problems which can began with our first relationship, or object... our mothers or 'the nourishing breast'. I can't tell you just how much I've seen that validated over the years; but, her most intriguing observations were the ones on envy, jealousy, gratitude and greed. When in Africa I got to see some of these up close. Please do not misunderstand, it was NOT because Africans manifest these traits any more than any other; but, in environments where class distinctions are more pronounced one can study environmental affects a lot easier. As an observer of people, I often see much others don't. But how does this relate to vodun? I will show you; but, first, let me define my terms.

Jealousy exist when someone has something I do not have and want. It could be a new car, a guy you've always admired etc. They have the thing that I wanted; therefore, jealousy exist.

Envy exist when the person has something I want but NEVER can have. A college degree that is beyond my reach because of financial circumstances, or plenty of money because I married well or have 7 sons and all of them are rich or I'm living in the United States because I won the visa lotto in my home country. This person wants the thing that I have; but, for whatever reason, WILL NEVER be fortunate enough to have the thing. It is these people who can, then, run to the nearest bokono, babalawo, bokor, juju doctor, or whomever, to do you dirty! These are the people that will begin to hire out bad spirits to make your life unlivable. And, if this envy is coupled with greed they become dangerous because they want it all! They can literally try to snuff out your life to obtain the thing you've got! These folks may not necessarily serve vodun or the spirits; but, they will pay to use it against you! And, many folks have died in the vodun community because of it!

I have seen many Africans refusing to visit their villages because of fear of juju being thrown while there. I have seen Haitians afraid of NOT sending money home due to family members who may visit the bokor in retaliation. All of these, aforementioned, vices are bad... jealousy, envy and greed; however, envy is the most dangerous and when coupled with greed can kill. As for gratitude?

Klein states that gratitude felt towards the good objects, in a child's life, shapes it's capacity for love in subsequent love relationships throughout [one's] life. If the envy aimed at the nourishing breast [or mother] is intense, full gratification is obstructed because envy destroys and desecrates that which is good. While priests are taught that we are to not serve the voduns with BOTH hands there will always be some priests that will do so. Human nature often prevails. Envy, jealousy and greed will always live among us. It is prudent, therefore, to be aware and be protected.

VODUN'S SWEET SIMPLICITY

A young woman approached me recently. Her inquiry was most innocent. She asked to what books could she read to learn more about vodun and to what books had I been reading lately. My answer to the latter was none and to the first I no longer clearly remembered. For as a beginning researcher, several years ago, I read what was available; and, they gave me a cursory understanding of what vodun was supposed to be. However, when I became the very thing that I went, to Africa, to study I no longer needed books. As I have developed an intimate relationship with the spirits, now, THEY themselves are my resource. A practitioner has no need of books to know vodun. He or she goes directly to the source or should be able to if they are truly hooked into the spiritual realm. But in so many instances, on the Internet, I am observing these "neo-scholars/bought in/boot-legged" priests of Ifa and the like, in diaspora vodou/orisa, that spend all their time quoting bookish rhetoric instead of talking about what the voduns (spirits) are saying or discussing their nature or how they have affected their lives. To me it is a sure indicator of someone who knows nothing about the spirits. But to challenge them, at this point, is simply a waste of my time. But imagine my shock when I read, on a forum, about a "bought in" Ifa priest relating about how he was writing Odu/Du. I almost feel out of my chair! These ancient stories coming from ancient Africans, from a per-colonial/primordial African oral tradition and experiences; yet, he is over here, in the Americas, telling folks he is to write Odu/Du and they are too! What African or ancestor, anywhere, is going to acknowledge any of this!

What's even crazier is that there are folks who believe him! But, the voduns have a way of dealing with folks like this; so, I will simply wait on them to do their thing. But, might the spirits hear me when I beg that some of our brethren/sistren, instead of buying overly expensive gifts for their boyfriends and girlfriends, save up for a few tickets to Africa or at least the divination fee. Such would be life changing! But getting back to the subject matter at hand...

While vodun is indeed filled with untold mysteries many of these are to remain as such. For some things are only privy to the divinities, themselves, or to those whom they choose to know. Man/woman is not God but the children of Gods. However, to the average person vodun is one of sweet simplicity. All one needs to know is that we are ALL born of spirits. That these are ancestral as well as divine, and, that they love us regardless of race, creed, color or gender. We are all born in their likeness. And, further, that we come to this earth with a specific destiny or spiritual mission. That through the birthing process this knowledge is lost. That the great Ifa was sent to help us to regain this information. And, that if we discover this lost information and choose to proceed and follow the instructions of the spirits, using them as the light unto our paths, we can accomplish whatever it is that we came here to do and will live a better and more prosperous life. AMEN

THAT WHICH IS WITHIN US

In Africa, we say that when an ancestor wants to be remembered he takes the clay and molds the child. But he, himself, cannot give life. So, he makes a bargain with a divinity to breathe life into the child; and, in return, the child will serve this spirit all of the rest of its days. For it is the ancestor that starts us in this life and it is to the ancestor that we hope to return! These two, the ancestors and the spirits, are eternally connected. That is why we can not do vodun without one or the other!

It is further said that through the process of childbirth we do not remember our spiritual mission or why we have come. That is why, in traditional Africa, when a child is born and after 3 months of life ceremonies are performed and Ifa divinations are done to determine "who has come back" to us. In other words, what ancestor is wishing to be remembered and what work have they returned to do. Therefore, sistahs and brothers, of African descent, we seek that which is within us not that which is without.

In that we are in the diaspora, and not Africa, we come to these spiritual revelations late in life. But, if we go to Ifa, he will tell us WHO our ancestors are, and WHO and WHAT we are in the spiritual world along with the mission we have come to fulfill.

In this Eurocentric America, we are used to seeking knowledge and going after it; but, in the land of our ancestors we seek that to which we were born not a spirit just because we admire it and may not have been born to us. Our kingships, whether spiritual or physical, are handed down from generations past and many of them are STILL waiting for us to come and claim them IN AFRICA! All we need is Ifa to prove who we are and they are ours for the taking. Our power rests with the ancestors and the spirits that live within us!

A friend of mine had a dream once. And in this dream, she was fascinated by a beautiful spirit that she had heard about. She spent much effort and money pursuing this beautiful spirit. Yet, her ancestors were weeping and dismayed! When she asked them what was wrong? They said, "Why are you seeking that which shimmers like gold but isn't gold. For we, your ancestors, are left hungry and unattended. And the spirits who gave you life you ignore. Yet, you are from a royal lineage and the spirits that gave you life are the highest kings of the spirit you seek."

VODUN AND POWER

When most diasporans think of vodun they think of something that is intrinsically evil. Not only has the media portrayed it that way, over the years; but, to many, something that has the power to do the things that vodun claims, it can do, MUST be evil. When traditional Africans think of vodun, however, they automatically think of POWER. Vodun has the power to affect lives in a positive or negative way depending on what they are trying to accomplish. To those Africans who have been converted from their traditional spiritual systems, however, it takes us back to square one...It is the epitome of evil. Yet, it is the POWER that people seek in approaching vodun. It is the POWER to affect their lives, to either give them the things they need/want, protect, to stop or damage a neighbor, influence a love object or stay in political power or favor. Vodun, ultimately, is seen as POWER....the power to affect change. And many feel that this power can be bought.

If one examines the world's spiritual systems no others have this reputation but those that hail from, or originally hailed from, the continent of Africa. In spiritual matters, it is the traditional African that reigns supreme, with the Indian subcontinent following close behind, according to the voduns. The other parts of the world are simply trying to catch up. But where does all of this power come from? Simple, it comes from the spirits themselves. For it is within THEM that the power resides. An African traditional priest (or any other) is only as powerful as his relationship with the spirits is strong! He must be connected to the spirits and be in their favor. This power does not reside in the individual alone. While we are ALL born of spirits, it is until these spirits are discovered, identified and activated, in some way, that true power actually comes. Many are born with "spiritual gifts"; but, these "gifts" are only a foreshadow of true spiritual power. They are simply forerunners and overt indicators that we may be something special to the ancestors and the divinities in the spiritual world. Having these "gifts" means that one should get off their "dusty busty", stop fawning over one's self, get to an authentic and reputable diviner and find out what one's spiritual calling actually is. 'Cause it ain't sitting there simply talking about how "gifted" you are and giving us a list of your spiritual attributes. With these "gifts" come great responsibility toward mankind. But, if these "gifts" are not being used, in the service of mankind, then, what good are they? If not used one might wake up, one day, and discover that they are no longer there. Further, they do not exist to put spotlight on one's self even though that might inevitably come if, through your obedience, you are highly favored by the voduns. But, they exist to indicate one's birthright to serve the spirits and direct one towards that spiritual calling. Such persons can become extremely powerful in vodun. But, it is the relationship that they have, with the spirits, that makes them so. So, here's the million-dollar question...can spiritual power be bought?

Yes! I would be lying if I said that it couldn't; but, do I like or respect it? No! In fact, these "bought in" folk could, inevitably prove me wrong if I said no, 'cause they have spent goobly gobs of money doing just that! But, can they be just as powerful as a person born of the spirits and have received or activated their voduns/orisa as the spirits have directed? Well, it depends on what they done bought... Allow me to explain. There are voduns, that one may have not been born into that exists, in Africa, that one can become legitimate priests/priestesses of (i.e. THRON). However, many of the families that serve these voduns have been doing it for so long that it becomes the family's vodun. I'm not sure how it all works; but, it exists. My problem with the "bought in" folk is that instead of going to Ifa, to see if they were actually born to the spirits, or seeking legitimate ways to possess African vodun, they dodge the idea by trying to possess what others have been legitimately born into without seeking out possible legitimate avenues to serve the spirits. Then they want to sit back and talk trash! But let's be clear! Someone claiming Mami Wata, not born to that pantheon, but who has gone and bought some bogus Mami Wata initiation, somewhere, can not hold a candle to me, my initiation or any other legitimate Mami. I got vodun that will eat folks, like this, for breakfast and use their bones for toothpicks! Not only that; but, the grounding of knowing who my ancestors are, coupled with all those spirits inherited from them, plus spirits born to me, my spiritual mission and destiny gives me a spiritual power that they cannot possibly possess. Thus, their illegitimacy leaves them spiritually vulnerable to those who are legitimate. It is not just about them trying to buy what we legitimately possess and they don't and suffering our anger towards it. It is also about POWER. And under such circumstances they simply do not possess what we have...that deep spiritual power! They can put up a shingle, go participate in bogus initiations or whatever else they want to do; but, they'd better tiptoe, like the dickens, if one of these legitimate ones, of the priesthood, gets angry at one of them. How these folks have the audacity to stand up and talk trash, when I correct one, I'll never know. And how they can begin to think that they are on the same level as someone born to these spirits and duly initiated, as per the directions of the voduns, I'll never know either. In fact, you legitimate folks out there, who are initiating, them for the money and their European contacts, ought to start telling them, because, it is YOU that are responsible for them and it is YOU that will have to answer to the voduns for it! And YES, I am calling you out on it!

Another way to buy power is to go to a vodun, through a priest or priestess, and have that vodun do work for you. That is how most folks elicit help from a vodun...especially one known to be expert in a particular domain. For instance, in the pantheon of Mami Wata is Ayidowedo. This great spirit is the God/Goddess of wealth. Many will visit a Mami Wata temple in search of help and to appeal to it. Divination is performed to diagnose a person's situation and the spirits will give a remedy, or sacrifices to be performed, to address a particular issue. While one may not be born, of this pantheon of spirits, one may elicit its help. When a Mami temple might not be available Africans, in Benin, visit the great THRON. This vodun has a rapport with all of the vodun and can approach any vodun on your behalf. This is also a vodun that offers protection. It protects you in such a way that if someone sends you juju...it boomerangs back! I call THRON the kola vodun. It uses kola in divination; and, it's shrines are filled with it. There is no denying that vodun is indeed POWER!

But that power is to flow through those born and designated to have it, discover its innateness within them, initiate into it and to be used responsibly. For vodun, TRULY is, power from on high. And, within its human born vessels these divine spirits/horsemen... those that created our very universe... are able to help its creation...mankind. But, be not deceived, those who practice the dark arts also have power. But this not vodun. It is the anathema of vodun...it is sorcery.

Spirits are spirits; and, whether it is the dark spirits, of chaos and destruction, or those that benefit mankind, the one who serves them receives his/her power directly from them. We, as servants of vodun, are not to serve with BOTH hands. For if so, one's time, on this earth, could be cut short. However, in serving the spirits, one must decide to which side one would be on and to which source of power one will use in undergirding one's spiritual work. Personally, I love the voduns with all my being. It is a labor of love. This love has come about through a unique relationship, with them, that began long ago in my life...way before I even fully understood who they really were. Many of you are on that same journey. For I know that I am not alone. Because, as one of my facebook friends have already stated, we are African not because we were born in Africa, but, because Africa was born in us! So, go to Ifa and claim the POWER!

For those interested in the subject of cross cultural initiations, in the Republic of Benin, you can find research material on the subject. These initiations can and do happen. As I have continued to say, through my writings, all who are born of the spirits have a right to serve regardless of race, creed, color or gender. But do the stuff correctly! Go to Ifa and find out who and what you are in the spirit world. All this dipping and diving, slipping and sliding, when you know your stuff ain't, right but still wanna talk trash is not right. Mami got a serious problem with that! However, if you are legit, I may not like you any better; but, at least, as one obedient to the spirits, I will acknowledge you, respect your right to serve and help you if I can.

RELIGION VS. SPIRITUALITY

The most common definitions of religion are as follows: (1) a set of beliefs concerning the cause, nature, and purpose of the universe, especially when considered as the creation of a superhuman agency or agencies, (2) the service and worship of God or the supernatural and (3) commitment or devotion to religious faith or observance. Spirituality, on the other hand, has been defined as a process of personal transformation in accordance with one's religious beliefs or ideals. Since the 1800s, the concept of spirituality has been separated from that of religion and has become more oriented on subjective experience and psychological growth. In other words, it denotes how a set of beliefs, that one has chosen, has affected one's life or how one has changed since coming in contact with them. One may have a set of beliefs that one caters too; but, those beliefs may not, in any real way, affect one's life. For instance, my American family is staunchly opposed to vodun. They consider themselves Christians, however, very few, of them, have seen the inside of a church, in recent years, unless there is a funeral. Christian ideals are their standard. Yet, believing in those ideals doesn't necessarily make them tow the line on how they choose to treat their neighbors or each other. As long as they do nothing that involves the police they are fine. They are more concerned with civil obedience rather than spiritual obedience. That is, of course, until racial prejudices come into play and then all bets are off. Civil obedience swiftly becomes civil disobedience; but, that is a different subject entirely.

I understand, that with this subject matter, religion vs. spirituality, I am straddling a very fine line here. But, my prayer is that most will come to understand, because, if not, then, it will be difficult to understand African spirituality and, further, to allow it to direct one's life. One must come to realize that the spiritual world is a living and breathing thing. While it is on another plain, one that we cannot see with the naked eye, it is very much alive, vibrate and extremely active in the affairs of mankind.

In Africa spirituality exists on a grand scale. Let me explain. By whatever faith one claims, on that great continent, their faith dictates the personal lives of its followers. As we witnessed in Old Testament times, with the children of Israel, it's civil laws and everyday lives were dictated by their religion. As a result, they were, and many of them still are today, a very spiritual people. We witness this, today in Africa's Islamic community, African Vodun, and many other spiritual systems that exist on that great continent. These folks live their lives based on their religious convictions. In America, however not so much...

Americans are vastly different. While a religious people we are not necessarily, a spiritual people. For one there is a separation between church and state in this country. One may go and sit in the church pews, on Sundays, but are free to do whatever they want the other six days of the week. And, again, as long as you are not bothering anyone in such a way as the authorities may become involved, then, no one is going to bother you. Spirituality, in this sense, is reserved for the Preachers, Priests, of various kinds, Gurus, Imams or those termed as "religious fanatics". But, I assure you that the religious fanatic is not so much spiritual as someone using a set of beliefs to justify wrongdoing or their superiority over another.

So, let me break it down to you using myself as an example. I, as most from my generation, grew up in the church. During my undergraduate years I went back after a hiatus of being forced as a child. I chose the Church of Christ. There I learned the bible in earnest. Patterned after the 1st century church, out of the book of Acts, those folks taught, and still teach, bible like no other. I was reading, the bible, in Greek and studying it like a theologian. However, the more I learned the more I realized that something was missing for me personally. I, eventually, prayed myself right out the back door of the church. What I mean is that I wanted a personal relationship with the divine, so bad, that all I did was pray, read the bible and pray some more.

Even when relocating, to New York State, I continued attending at the large Church of Christ in Manhattan, Harlem, upstate New York and wherever I happened to roam. But to make a long story short I ended up, in February of 1998, standing on the shores of the Republic of Benin with the Supreme Chief of Vodun. And, after a long divination, he revealed through a translator, that my trip was planned by the ancestors. And the rest is history. What he meant was that I was put on a journey to find the ancestors and the spirits. It was a search for the self. From that day forward my life has changed dramatically.

One must understand that to engage in African spirituality it can be, and often is, a life changing experience. It is not for dabblers, the faint hearted or the "New Agers" looking to stop the mundaneness of their everyday lives. It takes commitment, focus and a willingness to yield to the obedience of spirits that one cannot see. But eventually, in their own time, they will reveal themselves to you. And you will see, first hand, the beauty of the divine.

As for me the spirits chose my mate and dictates my every move. How I view my life, now, is as their servant and my concerns are only about what I can do, personally, to better fulfill the spiritual mission that I was born to do. If the spirits don't dictate it, then, I do not hear it. They are the light unto my path. While I am most cognizant of the desires and opinions of mankind, if it doesn't jive with what the spirits want, you are wasting your words on me. While I am a social being and love people, if you don't like me because of what I espouse, then, that is YOUR problem, for I am here to serve the spirits and to fulfill a spiritual mission...not to make friends.

African spirituality changes you. It tells you WHO and WHAT you are, in the spirit world, what your mission is and why you came to this earth. It identifies your ancestors, their origins and the spirits that gave you life. It anchors you and guides your life like no other.

It empowers your convictions and grounds you like a mighty oak. Personally, I might not have much, in the way of "things"; but, in the spirit world I am a king (my spirit is male). In his serpent form he has diamonds and pearls dripping down his back and on his head, sits 41 crowns of gold. In human form, he sits on a mighty golden throne, in the spiritual realm, and in the temple his likeness stands laden in gold, pearls and finery. For I KNOW who and what I am! This spirit, and the others that accompany him, are my all and in all. They ARE my ALPHA and OMEGA; and, I do not have to wait until death to know them. I know them now; and, so can YOU! This is spirituality... In fact, this is African Spirituality at its finest!

AFRICA, VODUN AND THE DISSERVICE OF THE CHRISTIAN MISSIONARY

It breaks my heart that so many Africans have been led away from their ancestral affiliations, and spiritual obligations, due to the effectiveness of the Christian missionary. Think on it... Here comes a person, generally ignorant of African traditional culture, who has been indoctrinated into the belief that those who are not of the Christian faith...THEIR faith....do not know God. And that, somehow, to know him and to commune with him one must denounce the caring of one's ancestors, give up one's ancient customs.... those customs older than any others in existence... and follow them. This, directed at a people who were God's first creation, in the first place, and to whom all the world's cultures derived. It is assumed that these people, somehow, had no communication with their creator until "you folks" arrived on a boat or bought a plane ticket and showed up stumping' in the middle of their villages. The assumption, I suppose, is that after God created this original man, an African, he simply left him to his own devices with no communication, from him, whatsoever. Does this make any sense at all? Oh, the ARROGANCE of such people!

While in Africa I had the occasion to befriend two young Christian missionaries. What drew me to them was the fact that they were

African American. They were part of the "Adopt A Village" program. I was by no means trying to convert them. That is not the way of vodun. However, I did attempt to impress upon them the idea of learning something about African traditional culture and respecting those things that they saw within that cultural context. I felt if they took the time and observed the culture and immersed themselves into the lives of the Africans that they claimed to want to help, then, they would come to respect Africa, its culture and its traditions. After all these were two missionaries of African descent; and, in that sense I was on a mission...a mission to help them better understand themselves. Well, it almost worked!

Of the two young women, one was older. The older one, while humoring her partner, simply tolerated me. As the younger one and I became fast friends the older one would have ice cream outings with us and join us to visit various tourist sites; but, it was apparent that she was keeping her eye peeled on the friendship brewing between me and her partner. She had realized, early on, that I could not be converted. I knew the bible better than her; so, she was a bit fearful of my influence. To make a long story short the younger one was eventually sent back to the United States; but, not before they had a visit from two more very seasoned Christian missionaries. I was delighted!

Standing at my door, one morning, were the two young women and two much older African American missionaries. The eldest, who was a great grandmother, was accompanied by a middle-aged woman. Grandma had been seasoned by working for many years in Liberia. She delighted me with stories of old; and, we got along like two peas in a pod. Being southern bred and born I instantly reverted to all the training I had learned in respecting my elders. Grandma loved it; and, I loved her. The visit was a wonderful success! Or so I thought. When my young friend returned to the United States she forwarded something to me by Internet. Not realizing that the forward included correspondence between her and grandma it said,

"Your friend was a wonderful delight! But these are the times that we must remember that the enemy [Satan/devil] often comes cloaked as a lamb." Grandma, rather than believe that, as a vodun priestess, I was a lovely and compassionate person, adhered to her Christian doctrine that because I was vodun (or "other") I must be evil. I could only shake my head in amazement.

Christian missionaries have done a great disservice to the African continent. If one was to examine the history of various tribes, in Nigeria, for instance, one would find entire temples destroyed and ancient spiritual relics abandoned, demonized or wiped out due to their efforts (i.e. the Ibo). As a result, generations of Africans have been separated from the privilege of eating with their ancestors because the younger generations no longer serve or see the need to feed them. I have friends, from Nigeria, living right here in the United States who talk about family members burning down the family temples after the last traditional priest, in that family, died. While in Africa I have seen beautiful temple relics, infused with vodun, sitting in tourist shops to be sold to anyone that would buy them. I have watched, in horror, while ancient spiritual thrones were sold to European museums by children of deceased African priests. This disrespect and dishonor to the ways of the ancients is difficult to witness. Yet WHO would walk into a Jewish Synagogue and desecrate its religious relics? Who would arrive in Mecca and spit on the Black Stone? And, who would walk into the Vatican, in Rome, and throw stones at its holy crosses? No one; but, to Africa it is to be tolerated? A place where civilizations existed long before many of these were ever thought about?

One could argue that the upside, to all of this, is that the Christians bring in a great deal of money and human services with their African outreach. But I ask you, from their own holy book, "For what is a man profited if he gains the whole world, and loses or forfeits himself [his soul]?" Luke 9:25 (NIV) I say accept the services, if they are beneficial; but, leave them their religion. Or, if one chooses to follow Jesus, continue to feed one's ancestors so as to be protected. Do not throw the baby out with the bathwater, because, Jesus is not a part of your ancestral tree. But the problem is, that in most cases, one cannot avail themselves of these human services without having to take on the religion. It all comes with a price! Africa is in spiritual crisis today. And that crisis is there, in part, because of the Christian missionary.

So, where are our four African American Christian missionaries today and me? Well, the last time I heard my younger friend, while back in the States, went back to school, got herself a degree and married a nice young fellow. Grandma has gone to the other side. Her companion is still a staunch follower of the faith and the older of the two missionaries, whom I first met in Benin, is still serving and waiting for Jesus to drop her a man out of the sky. However, as anal as she seemed to be, that might be a mighty tall order for any spirit. Mami, of course, is still standing and clinging to dem' voduns. And, even more so, today, especially since I've got myself a new set of knees! God bless America and its health care system!

VODUN AND THE TORAH

In my writings, I have often spoke of my love for the Old Testament writings. But it is not so much the writings, themselves, that I love but, rather, the written history and example, within these writings, of how God/the spirits dealt with the Israelites. This written history, or example of a spiritual relationship, is the truest recorded history of the nature of the divinities and how they dealt with a group of people within their creation. It is my view that, in the New Testament writings, we do not have a balanced view of what God is. While the CREATOR is, indeed, depicted as loving and kind it gives a one-sided view of the nature of God, mainly, due to it's writer's attempts at furthering a new religion. And, it's leaders, during the canonization of the Bible, hand picked those writings, which were simply letters, from the disciples, to the churches, that would best further that political end. As a result, we are left with a reincarnated prophet, according to the voduns, as being the long awaited Jewish Messiah instead of looking, specifically, at how the divine deals with mankind, thus, revealing their true nature. And, because of it, far too many are stuck on Jesus and are going nowhere, spiritually, to boot!

The children of Israel came to know and understand God in the truest sense of the words. And, their relationship with their God, coincides with all of the things that I have experienced, come to know and see, in dealing with vodun, today. The spiritual system of the Jews, in its purest sense, is vodun...that which is sacred and given directly from the spirits, or God, to mankind...their unique creation.

What one defines as "Jewish" has often been the subject of debate throughout our history. In the 1980s the United States Supreme Court, specifically, defined being Jewish as a "race" for purposes of nondiscrimination laws. However, the Torah (the ancient spiritual writings of the Jews depicting their history and relationship with God) terms Judaism, in the ancient sense, as being a group of people with a common history, a common destiny, and a sense that they are all connected to each other which includes a common spiritual system. And, as with vodun, that system started in the oral tradition and is the subject of this writing.

The Torah, itself, consists of the Oral Torah, or those teachings now contained in the Talmud, and the Written Torah, the first 5 books of the Bible, or Pentateuch, as written by the prophet Moses. And, according to the Jews, there shall be no other Torah and Moses is their greatest prophet. And, personally, I find it hard to disagree. What I find in Moses I see in exceptional African priests today. Their ability to control the elements, as well as their devotion to those needing their assistance and obedience to the spirits, is a testament to their relationship with the divine. For a priest is only as powerful as his relationship with the spirits/the divine is strong; and, only THEY can push back the waters, of the sea, and allow a man to walk on its bottoms like dry land. This feat was witnessed, just a couple of years ago, on the shores of The Republic of Benin.

The Talmud is the body of Jewish civil law, ceremonial law and legend that governs the Jewish people. The New Testament refers to these oral traditions as 'The Traditions of the Elders'. These laws, of the Pharisees, governed the Israelites and held the power of life and death over them. The Written Torah, or 5 books of Moses: Genesis, Exodus, Leviticus, Numbers and Deuteronomy records the early history of the Jewish people and their relationship with God. It is a testament to how a people were led out of bondage and taken to a promised land and how God used those ordained by him, the prophets, to get them there.

While the similarities are there for another group, that was taken into bondage, one should not be looking towards Jesus for one's spiritual freedoms but to the example of the children of Israel who looked toward their ancestors, traditional spiritual priests and obedience to God (the spirits) to take them out of spiritual, as well as, physical bondage. If any of you have not read these ancient books I highly recommend them.

GENESIS is the book about beginnings. It starts with the creation story and ends with the covenant with Abraham. But, what we learn, from this book, is that faith in our creator(s) and obedience to him/them brings about blessings. Disobedience, on the other hand, brings about curses and disarray in our personal lives.

EXODUS, the book of redemption, chronicles the deliverance, of the children of Israel, from Egyptian bondage and their crossing of the Red Sea. We see God as a redeemer by delivering his children out of bondage, by the blood of the passover lamb, and his power by the parting of the Red Sea. It is also where we see God's holiness by giving the Israelites his righteous laws. However, we also witness, that if anyone falls short of these laws they still have access, to the divine, through temple sacrifice and the Levitical priesthood. And, it is the same, in Africa today. These things have not changed...the temples, the sacrifices nor the priests.

LEVITICUS, the book of holiness, taught the Israelites two things: (1) how to worship and walk with God and (2) how the nation was to fulfill its calling as a nation of priests. It's underlying theme is holiness. One learns, in this book, that a holy God can only be approached on the basis of sacrifice through the mediation of a priest. This is basic in African Vodun.

NUMBERS, recounts the 40 years the Israelites wandered in the desert and their experiences while there. The beauty of this book is that it bears witness to the fact that God continued to care and provide for the needs, of the Israelites, even when they were rebellious and unbelieving. He continued to love and forgive his people even when they complained, grumbled, and rebelled against him. This is still the same today. No matter how much we moan and complain those spirits, living within us, still continually care for us.

DEUTERONOMY, or the words, emphasizes the need of teaching children to love and obey God. Deuteronomy ends with the renewal of God's covenant with Israel (chapter 29), Joshua's appointment as the new leader (chapter 31), and Moses' death (chapter 34). In African Vodun families we continually see the instruction, teaching and initiations of the young ones. Children in these families are trained and brought up in vodun throughout all of their lives.

These books bear witness to a more balanced view of who God is and his/her nature. It is a God who is loving but commands absolute obedience. This view of God is not a sugar coated forever benevolent God, but, one who takes no nonsense from mankind. If one is unholy and disobedient it does not go unnoticed or unpunished. These are the divinities as I have come to know them; and, that is why I love the Old Testament writings.

And so we come full circle. I contend that at the root of all of the world's spiritual systems are the spirits themselves...that which we call vodun...meaning "spirit". For in the world's traditional cultures we know that spirits exist in the trees, mountains, the waters and in all of God's creations. Nature, itself, is vodun. Spirits form the basis to all the organized spiritual systems that exists. In vodun, for instance, we witness spirits, who come forth, who have served Islam, Christianity, Hinduism and Buddhism, just to name a few, before their deaths. Buddha, Krishna, and other such spirits, are part and parcel of the Mami Wata pantheon of spirits; and, the ancestral spirits, known as Mami Tchamba, are examples of those spirits of the Islamic faith with Allah as one of its voduns. I have seen other spirits come who were Christian in life. Vodun encompasses all and is in all. These spirits are ancestral, as well as, divine. And, while individual in character, serve to make up the total nature of God.

VODUN AND THE 'DAUGHTERS' OF GOD

Every time I see a picture of the Black Madonna I think of a particular dream that I had in Africa. The voduns were definitely trying to show me something; but, 'till this day, I have not inquired as to what. It is high on my agenda, however, when I return there. In the dream, the voduns had taken me by each arm and, with them, I traveled backwards, seemingly, in time. It was as though I was in a time warp that was quickly and continuously spinning me backward through time itself. When it stopped I was in front of a beautiful woman holding a female child. The child had amber eyes. I knew this because the voduns had stopped me, face to face, in front of this child. If I had wanted I could have reached out and touched her. But, as my home, at the time, was filled with voduns, walking all over the place; and, I was having a multitude of dreams, I never took the time to inquire, from the bokono (diviner), what this dream actually meant. But I knew that they were showing me something extraordinary. However, for me then, it wasn't the time; but, it appears to be the time now. I can't explain it I... just know. But getting back to the subject, at hand, it brings me back to the concept, in vodun, of the male and female duality and women and motherhood in general.

An African priestess, once, said to me that women were held to a higher standard because it is from women that all creation flowed. I believed her. In vodun we know that the spirits are male and female. We know that in the larger temples one finds the male priest, of the head spirit of that temple, as well as his female counterpart. For instance, in the temple of the Supreme Chief of Vodun, in (Ouidah) Benin, we find Daagbo (meaning ancestor) and his female counterpart Naagbo. In my own temple, one finds the male Dattatreya, Behumbeza, and his female counterpart, of the same spirit, myself. This is African Vodun. So, be not deceived, the female counterpart, of any spirit, is just as important as the male; and, together they form a whole. However, there are some pantheons of spirits where women tend to have a very different role. Why this is so I do not understand yet; but, for whatever the reasons are it is not an excuse to think that women have a lesser role in vodun, or African spirituality in general, because, they do not. For even the Fon Godhead is male and female... MawuLissa. Those in vodun have always understood that it is both the male and the female who created our universe and all it contains. I have encountered this spirit in its female form. So, there is much truth in the saying that God really is a woman! Even in the creation story we hear the words, "Let us make man in our (notice the "our") image, after our likeness..." (Genesis 1:26); and, later we learn that the image is to be male and female (Genesis 1:27). It is my contention, then, that women have nothing to prove to men. But, rather, what we must do, as women, is understand our worth and unique position in the universe and in its creation.

As American born, folks often inquire as to how I can endure an African traditional marriage. I am married to an African priest. For one, my marriage was arranged by the ancestors and the divine spirits themselves. My husband nor I would have chosen ourselves for each other. And, it was difficult for both of us, at first, to accept; however, what I have learned is that I can only trust in the spirits as to what they have given me. And, in hindsight, I have been blessed with more than I could have ever chosen for myself. This man has been one of my greatest gifts from the divine. I thank the spirits daily for him. Yet, as a woman, I am only human with many human frailties; but, I fix my eyes on the divine and refuse to waiver. For whatever this man may do, in his lifetime or in reference to me, I will continue to follow the spirits and turn all problems over to them. And they will make it right. Yet, even if the man ends up with 15 wives (let's hope not) I will hold myself up with dignity, respect, humility and obedience to the spirits. 'Cause on that day, when my eyes close, forever; and, I stand before the divine, there shall be no fault found in me.

So, in conclusion, as women of the spirits, we have our own relationship with the universe and mankind. As mothers, as sisters, as women, in general, and as vessels for the creation of life, we have nothing to prove against men. For it is through us that all creation flows. We are the "daughters" of God; and, as such should hold ourselves up to the highest of standards. Can I get a witness?

VODUN AND ONE'S VOW BEFORE GOD AND MAN

When one makes a vow, of marriage, we think of it as, being, a vow made before God, symbolized by the preacher, priest or spiritual person officiating the ceremony, and man, those people, our family of loved ones and friends, who are there to witness the event. The marriage certificate, itself, officially documents the event while the consummation occurs, later, when the two become one physically. But, the vow, itself, is the commitment that the two, who are wed, make before the divine and is witnessed by one's peers. That is why traditional African marriages are just as valid as those officiated in the diaspora. These marriages, officiated by traditional priests, witnessed, and thus, documented, by the attendance of the family members and said witnesses, tend to be tremendously more binding. This is marriage throughout all of the world's cultures; and, it is the same when one marries a spirit in vodun. For in vodun we can marry the spirits that gave us life; but, as in any marriage, that commitment can be broken. However, in vodun, this can result in devastating consequences.

Vodun is not something that one should take on lightly. The cavalier attitudes of the "New Agers" or those who choose to "dabble" in the perceived "exotica" of African traditional spiritual systems serves to devalue vodun, the African ancestors and its priesthood. In addition, it draws contempt from those who serve the voduns in earnest. Serving the spirits is a birthright and a privilege, one in which, before birth, a contract between the spirits and a person is reached. It should not be the result of someone's whimsical fancy, latest spiritual after thought or newest business plan to drum up a means of wealth. I have heard of people, in the diaspora, who claim to know the spirits, initiate into them and later give them up for their newest spiritual craze or a simple tiring out from serving them. It is my contention that these people were never truly hooked into the spirit world in the first place. Think on it...how does one continue to live without the spirits that live within them once initiated into them? Does one believe that one can initiate or marry that of the divine and then throw them away simply because it is an inconvenience or one's interest in the spiritual has waned? No, my dears. A true spiritual marriage, to a spirit, does not end in this manner. It is a true lifetime commitment. These divine beings come down with us, in birth, and will remain with us until death. And, if one discovers them, through Ifa, chooses to obey the commands of the spirits and initiate, if commanded, one is spiritually bound.... more so than in any other union that exists between God and man. One's initiation process, in essence, or one's authentic marriage to the spirits is forever binding, thus, one's decision to serve the spirits is a serious one. Folks who claim to serve and later decide not to serve were not really serious in the first place.

While one is born to serve, the spirits has given mankind choice as to whether one actually seeks to realize this birthright. One can choose to serve or not if commanded. However, one does not choose to serve simply because it is something that is cool to do or is the latest spiritual craze. One can serve the spirits in many ways; but, the priesthood, itself, is not for everyone. It is only through authentic African divination that this can be determined, not through simple playing cards, intuition, tarot or anything else. Vodun came with its own divination system; and, it is one that was and is ordained by the spirits themselves. There are cases, however, when spirits that possess someone, during vodun ceremonies, can reveal much about a person. These spirits speak through the voices of a servant of vodun...a vodunsi. In this case we are dealing with what Maya Deren (1953) termed as a "divine horseman", or spirit. If it is not through divination, that one discovers that they are born to the voduns, this is the only other way to determine this and in what capacity. But if the discovery is indeed made one should take council with one's self, consider the seriousness of this endeavor and enter with one's eyes fully open. The priesthood can be a long and arduous road. The initiation process begins the journey it does not end the journey. One is molded and refined, daily, to be more and more useful to the spirits to complete one's spiritual mission while here on earth.

While living in New York City I began, in earnest, my discovery of African spirituality. I began visiting Africa in 1997, but, started visiting the Republic of Benin in 1998. After a couple of visits, I hired two native Beninese, who worked for the Benin consulate, to teach me the Fon language. They were very kind women who took the time to introduce me to the traditional foods, customs and rudimentary phrases in the Fon language. One had even been a famous singer in her native lands. I was most fortunate. One day, upon my visit to take lessons, my two new friends had a visitor. It was a middle aged African gentleman who was very distinguished looking and seemingly well versed. My friends mentioned, to him, my interest in vodun and, specifically, Mami Wata since I had discovered, through Ifa during my last visit to Benin, that I was born of that pantheon of spirits. As we spoke I saw the seriousness that began to wash over the face of the visitor. He looked at me with kind but determined eyes and said, "This Mami Wata thing, my dear, is a serious matter. Take your time and consider it carefully." In hindsight, he was so correct! So, I pass it on to those of you who have found this to be your journey and destiny as well. This vodun thing is a serious matter. Take the time to consider it carefully. For vodun is a vow, a commitment and a marriage that lasts a lifetime...before God and man.

VODUN'S EMPHASIS...THE SPIRITUAL MISSION

In vodun, as in any vocation or system, there is a reason for its existence. In the diaspora, or our physical world, for instance, organizations, vocations or entities are formed for a purpose. In other words, they are created for some reason...something that they are attempting to accomplish. In these various vocations, or systems, whether governmental, business, or what have you, men and women hope to assail at their craft. If they do they are to be acknowledged, congratulated, and put on a pedestal, to bask in their accomplishments. This is the world as we live in it; and, there is absolutely nothing wrong with it. But, in the spiritual world, this is not so much the case.

In the spiritual world, it is primarily about the spirits; but, the emphasis is not about the priest or priestess, but, about the spiritual mission...that thing which we have agreed to do, before birth, and come down to accomplish. I will be the first to say, however, that, in vodun, there are some super stars out there. I am married to one! But he will be the FIRST to tell you that his priority is the voduns and his obedience to them. His true marriage is to them; and, all other wives are basically girlfriends. It is his example, and other such priests in Africa, that has taught me that a priest or priestess is only as powerful as his or her relationship with the spirits is strong. Who we are and what we are, in the spiritual world, must come directly from them.

Before birth we volunteer for a spiritual work or some other type of work. Those spirits that give us life, along with our ancestors, come down with us to help us accomplish this work. But, first, authentic African divination, must tell us what this work is. Ifa tells us who and what we are in the spiritual world. And, if we were born to serve the spirits, in some capacity, then we must accept it, prepare for it (initiation); and, with the help of the spirits set about the work, being molded and refined by them daily, and complete it. We are the vessels for the spirits. They are to work through us. Therefore, vodun is about that to which we were born to do...the mission...not us, the priest or priestess. We do not initiate to look cute on a throne seat. We are initiated into vodun to work.

Many of us are born with great spiritual missions; and, with it carries great spiritual titles. These titles, that Ifa reveals to us, are indicators of the gravity of the work or responsibility, we of the priesthood, are born to. Hey, I am the first to admit that the nature of many of the spirits, in me, will often reflect their fabulousness overtly. I'm a big ole ham and know the importance of being born with the spirit of a Dattatreya. But I know from whence any of this fabulousness may come...from the spirits that live within me...not me. For I know that I am a temperamental old fuss bucket with a potty mouth! I am often short on patience; and, as I grow older, turning into every old mean relative that I knew as a child. I do not understand how the spirits are able to choose those most imperfect to help serve mankind; but, it happens. Over and over throughout our history it has happened. So, I am here, an imperfect vessel. But I know who and what is perfect. I know who knows more than me; and, that is the voduns. And I will serve them, to the best to my ability, for the rest of my life; because, it is not about me or you, but, THEM and the MISSION that they have brought us down to fulfill.

VODUN AND ANCESTRAL MEMORY

It came across my facebook news feed several months ago... a quote so beautiful and profound that I have included it on my list of favorite quotes. A young man wrote, "...I'm African not because I was born in Africa, but, because Africa was born in me..." The quote was not only beautiful, in its simplicity, but 100% correct in its assessment

Science has now proven what the spirits have made clear, to me, since the onset of my spiritual journey back to the faith of our African forefathers...that as children of the African slave we are indelibly linked to them, and the continent of Africa, in every way. It debunks the notion, perpetuated by the "bought in" folk in diaspora African-based spiritual systems, and those, of either race, that are ill informed as to our connection to our African ancestry and insist that these systems are somehow, new lineages, and while based on African systems, are something unique and different. They are not! While local traditions may have been added, it is the slave experience that interrupted these systems, for the African diasporan, and caused much knowledge to be, either, lost or abandoned. This notion of a separation between traditional African vodun, from the motherland, and that in the diaspora serves as a convenience to "bought in" folk in order to deny Africa's influence or authority over them, support their illegitimate claims to the priesthood and justify their unwillingness to be ruled by the tenets of traditional African vodun. And what is even more appalling is the persons, born to these traditions, who continue to initiate, these people, without the benefit of authentic African divination for the sake of the mighty dollar. At some point, there will be a reckoning and a public denouncement of their actions.

As the African slave was brought to these shores, bound in chains against their will, they brought, with them, an ancient way of life and ancient spiritual systems that were given to them, directly, from the divine ones themselves. Campaigns were often lodged, against their own native spiritual systems, and they were forced to serve a system that was not their own. And, many continue to serve that system today. However, in secret, many continued to serve and call upon their ancestors. But, the slave experience caused much to be ignored or forgotten, of these systems, out of the sheer necessity for our people to survive. As a result, much must be re-instated to these systems...authentic African divination being the primary thing. Now slavery, in its overt stage, at least, is finally over. The African ancestors are awakening many of their children. Their invisible hands are opening and beckoning to us within the blood. And, they are putting into place those who will point the way, spiritually, to return home and are forming bridges for those destined to cross. It is time my brothers and sisters. It is time. Let's go home...for I have been there and would be delighted to show you the way.

And just a note...while I am not sure how perfect the science is on all of this...I am absolutely sure of what the spirits say about it! Africa and we (those descendants of the African slave) are one!

THE FRUITS OF THE SPIRITS

As most African Americans, from my generation, I grew up in the Church. I had some serious bible toting relatives; and, I still do today. From sisters on down they tend to love me; but, make no bones about it they think I'm gonna bust hell wide open with this vodun stuff. But, hey, since I know that the spirits exist in all of the organized spiritual systems and all others too it's no never mind, to me, at this point. I'm just hoping to leave a legacy for another generation down the line somewhere. For I feel that, just like me, the ancestors are going to wake up one of them whenever they are ready. But, in the meantime, I will prepare a place for them to come. I would love it if I could get some of my trash talking sisters to respect the ancestors though. It would be nice to make this a family affair, just like I have in Africa; but, this is America, so, until then lets get back to the subject at hand.

One of the first bible verses I ever memorized still sits in my memory to this day; and, I feel it to be most appropriate to what this essay highlights and is the cornerstone of Vodun and all African-based spiritual systems in general...the spirits themselves. Galatians 5:22-23 says, " But the fruit of the Spirit is love, joy, peace, forbearance, kindness, goodness, faithfulness, gentleness and self-control. Against such things there is no law." (NIV) When we do not either understand this, or stay focused on it, we lose what African spirituality is supposed to be about. It is not about egos, or nuances of the meaning of words. It isn't about someone seeking a following, whose system is better or anything of that nature. It is about hearing and being obedient to the words of the spirits. Those diasporans who have not used Ifa think that they can some how intuit what the spirits want; but, they are being deceived by their own self importance. One needs to go directly to the spirits and ask THEM what they want. And, one can only do this through authentic African divination. I constantly hear that I am on an ego trip; but, if I am it is one that the African ancestors and divine spirits put me on because it is at their insistence, and my obedience to THEIR words, that I am back in the diaspora doing as I was told. This is how authentic African Vodun/Orisa works. It is the spirits, themselves, that direct our paths and should of all those who serve them. This is what the spirits want of their children of the diaspora. So, I will not entertain fruitless debates on what vodun is or who I am or my spiritual mission. Got a problem with me take it to my bosses...the spirits themselves.

Because I know what my spiritual mission is doesn't make me an elitist; but, it does give one an example on how they too can know who and what they are in the spirit world and that is through authentic African divination...Ifa. But, the diviner must be born to this priesthood, properly initiated, according to the tenants of this particular priesthood, and duly trained. Bought in folk is a waste of your time. A diviner inherits his natural talents for the art of divination; and, in his opele lives centuries of ancestral diviners and spiritual priests of old. His opele is made from an elder from his/her village and passed down through the generations. This is just one of the things that the spirits want reinstated into diaspora African-based spiritual systems...the divination system that came with these systems in the first place but either fell out of favor, due to lack of training, or was lost due to the trans-Atlantic slave trade.

A person with their mind on the spirits doesn't sit back and argue incessantly about what is or what isn't but goes before the spirits, themselves, and ask about the person to whom brings a new or different message. And, if the spirits verify that the person is so ordained and sent by them, then, that person hears and obeys the words of the messenger. This is why I love Ifa. Anyone wanting to know who and what I am, in the spirit world, can go and inquire. A person of the spirits, will go to the spirits and inquire, instead of these so-called scholars who want to argue about the nuances of a word used. It is these "educated fools" who cannot see the forest for the trees and thus hinder the work of the spirits. I have nothing against scholarship at all; but, when a person is busy promoting themselves and their publications without an inkling of understanding of the spirits, then, they can keep on stepping...them and their publications. For it is the practitioner that knows the spirits the best; and, it is to the practitioner that the researcher comes to get the information to write their books...that is to whatever the practitioner chooses to reveal or the voduns allows him/her to reveal. No researcher will ever know the true secrets of vodun. It is not for them to know. Of course, if one is called by the spirits and then initiates it is then that they will find that there are things that they can not write about; so, thus one makes a full circle.

As we look at what the bible says about the fruits of the spirit we see traits like joy, peace, patience, kindness, goodness and self control. These I see in African priests as well as others not mentioned. But, as I live among the Africans who serve the spirits, obedience is the most prominent trait that I see. They the original servers of the spirits understand and know that the spirits, themselves, are the cornerstone to all of what they profess. My prayer is that those of us in the diaspora come to understand this as well. Many of these servers of the spirits are considered illiterate at best. Many have never graced a classroom or read a scholar's book; but, they know the spirits inside out. They learned it by doing, by depending on and serving their ancestors and the divine ones every day of their lives. For their lives, and well being, often depends on it; and as a result, these humble people share in the secrets of the universe. I don't know 'bout ya'll; but, for me it don't get no better than that!

VODUN AND IT'S BIRDS

I ask your indulgence in this little essay, for, it might appear fanciful to many. But it was prompted by a conversation I had, several weeks ago, with a great and humble lady.... a lady of the spirits. She will know who she is; but, every day I look out of my kitchen window and observe the birds I smile and think of her.

In Vodun the divinities are known by their manifestations as people/humans and by animals. The ones I know the best are the great Sakpata (the Cheetah) and the great Mami Wata (fish, whales, pythons, the crocodile) and so many others. This part of Vodun has always intrigued me. But one of my favorites is the soul itself. In Vodun it is called the Se (accent over the e and pronounced "say"). This mighty spirit travels in the body of a white pigeon or beautiful white dove.

I will never forget entering the temple, in Lome, Togo, in having this great vodun put down (installed). When I walked in the temple everything was white and beautiful. The Mami voduns were seated in their perspective rooms; and, all throughout the rafters, of this temple, were beautiful white pigeons. They nested everywhere. They are very much a part of any ceremony involving the Se or soul be it cleansing, purification or sacrifice.

One day as I was about to leave my home I headed toward my front door. As I opened it and was about to open my outer glass door I hesitated. Under my blooming dogwood were two beautiful pigeons eating. Instinctively I froze and quietly moved back further from the door. There was no reason for two beautiful pigeons to be in my neighborhood. I lived in a division of homes and realized I was witnessing vodun. I watched for some time mesmerized. One pigeon had a long black streak down it's tail. When I was able to compose myself, and pull out my cell phone, from my purse, I immediately and frantically called my husband in Benin, West Africa. I had to know if my instincts were correct. My husband went immediately before the voduns, on my behalf, and came back and said, "Mami, it is your Se and my Se (our souls) traveling together"; and, the tears flowed. I have been feeding birds, from my backyard, for some time now.

So, when this great lady took the opportunity to call me; and, she mentioned her love for birds and the fact that they attract to her...I said nothing. But quietly I understood that this woman was a child of the divine. I understand who and what she is. And to my new-found friend... keep on feeding and loving the birds; and, may the spirits continue to guide your path.

TWINS

In Africa; and, as in around the world, twins are very special. They are a blessing to families; and, in the spiritual world, they carry much power. They are vodun...spirits that are sacred. Between the two siblings is a very special and deep spiritual bond. In traditional Africa if one twin dies the surviving twin must participate in the appropriate ceremonies that the deceased twin is able to be remembered. The image of that twin is generally carved into a doll and the living twin cares for the deceased twin, in this life, as it were still here. In Ouidah, Benin there is a yearly festival for the twins. I'm sure the Orisa has it's special ceremonies as well. While I am not an expert on this particular vodun I have mentioned a couple of basics. Most Africans are much more versed on the subject of the twins as I.

VODUN'S ALL IN THE FAMILY

In African Vodun we are a close net family. In that Voduns, or spirits, come from specific regions and families they are also linked to particular ancestries. Proof of this is the fact that with many of those, who are born in the diaspora, who have come to us and have been found to be of the pantheon of the African Mami Wata, tended to be ancestrally connected to either myself, my husband or one of our spiritual children. This is due to our ancestral link to a particular pantheon of spirits and ancestors. And many of those of European descent have been found to be, particularly, of the ancestry of Lankpon. I am not exactly sure why to this ancestor; but, it has been proven, to me, over and over again that the diaspora experience, be it due to the trans-Atlantic slave trade or various population migrations, connections to our African ancestral heritages, simply, have not been wiped out. We are, all of us, implicitly linked to Africa whether we accept it or not. And, those who espouse otherwise are doing so out of sheer ignorance or deliberate propaganda.

In Africa the head of each pantheon, of spirits, generally knows what is happening in most of his associated temples. A calendar of various events for the year, for that particular pantheon of spirits, generally goes out to all of the participating temples. And, the temples are invited to each other's events, especially, concluding initiation ceremonies. These events must be witnessed. And, a priest or priestess finds great pride in his/her abilities to put on a beautiful initiation concluding ceremony and showcase how well their initiates have been taught the pantheon's dances and the display of their beautiful pearls, cloths and other accouterments associated with one's vodun. There are certain standards that those of the African priesthood must abide by; and, you'd better believe, like in any other family, the gossip is strong. If someone is, out there, doing some crazy stuff it will undoubtedly be talked about throughout the community.

Any disputes or issues, needing to be resolved, are generally addressed by those in authority in that pantheon of spirits...first at the temple level or with the chief of that pantheon. If they can not be resolved there, then, they can be appealed to the Supreme Chief of Vodun himself. There is accountability in traditional African Vodun. Folks are not just out there doing as they please without folks noticing; and, in most cases interceding.

Because of all of this comradery we generally know who is who and what is what within our own pantheon of spirits. Unlike the diaspora we know who is or is not legitimate to our particular pantheon. We often know the characters of those around us. Illegitimate priests, in Africa, practically do not exist. At least not in Benin. If one is not born of the priesthood there are priesthoods that one can actually purchase. Whether those are respected in Africa, however, is another story. However, with many a diasporan tourist, they can be easily fooled as to who is and who is not legitimate. Often family members, of priests, have lived with the voduns so long that they know many of the ceremonies or secrets of vodun if they have been active participants in the family temple. Spiritual knowledge, in Africa, is not that hard to come by. So, it is often these impostors of initiated priests that tourists find to give them things that legitimate priests will not, because, the spirits forbid them from having them. And, these are also many of the folk returning, to the diaspora, with voduns they do not know the name of, can't feed and end up causing them a world of grief. Ignorant folk, like this, have no understanding that a vodun taken in this way can actually kill them!

There was a woman, on a website, asking folks what vodun she had because it had started giving her trouble. She brought it out of Ghana and a few others out of (Ouidah) Benin. She had lived with this spirit for a number of years. Only I recognized it as Sakpata who can be straight up dangerous! When she couldn't answer my question as to why being in Ouidah, for so many months, she did not know that there was the Supreme Chief of Vodun living there, I realized, then, it was because she had gone through non-conventional methods to get her voduns because she, certainly, had not been in anyone's initiation chamber. She bought them! And there she was in Europe, somewhere, having had no initiation, anywhere, taking folk's money and claiming she was of the African Priesthood knowing jack NOTHING about vodun. And, she wanted my help? Forget about it! I do not like or respect "bought in" folk! Yet, sadly, those that actually could be born to the spirits will often go to Africa and return, to the United States with nothing but a series of titles that they love spouting off. Many have befriended me, on my facebook page; and, when asked about their African affiliations, proceed to write out a list of titles, so long that I become tired of reading. Many are not aware that they have not only been duped; but, without a proper initiation and no vodun you've got no spiritual power. All of these titles, be they fake or real with no spiritual foundation, proper initiation, training or vodun does nothing for you. For the title, itself, is not what is important but the spiritual mission behind that title. What, specifically, one has come to this earth to accomplish, for mankind, on behalf of the ancestors and the divine spirits is what is the real importance. Both cases, aforementioned, are very sad; but, let's get back to our subject matter.

African Vodun and those who serve the spirits, in general, form a family. For each pantheon of spirits, we are linked by ancestry common spirits, many inherited from our ancestors, and a common way of life. In starting one's spiritual journey one starts with finding one's ancestors. That means going to Ifa. Finding the ancestor will figuratively and literally help us to find our family... be it ancestral or spiritual.

TO STAND BEFORE THE DIVINE

As most folks, when I drive, I listen to the radio. Usually, if there are no Motown (old school) sounds playing, I switch over to gospel music. Music, in general, is one of my greatest loves; and, gospel music, as most African Americans when I was growing up, often inspires me. I just drop the Jesus part and revel in the love that I have for the spirits. Black folks sing with soul; and, it is to that level, of devotion, that I connect.

Tamela Mann, one of my favorite gospel singers, croons a tune that almost brings tears to my eyes. In the song, she imagines what t would be like to stand before the divine. It touches me so because poor Tamela, and others like her, do not understand that, in vodun, one doesn't have to imagine. It can actually happen! One does not have to die to see the divine. If it has been revealed by Ifa that one s of the priesthood, or a server of the spirits; and, if one, according o the tenants of the ancestors and the divine spirits, themselves, is duly initiated, then, one has access to the divine. And, as such, can stand before that spirit, to whom ever gave them life, face to face. And believe me, when it happens, it takes you to your knees. One feels so in awe and so small just having a glimpse of the mightiness of the divine. But, let me further explain this opportunity, in more detail, because some may believe that with any type of initiation one can see the divine....No!

There are plenty of people, in the diaspora, claiming the Priesthood and initiations, of all sorts, who believe they have this ability...again no! They also claim that they are speaking with spirits and all manner of things. But there are some things that many, in the diaspora, do not understand; so, I'm going to be clear. If you have not gone to Ifa and found your head spirit, accompanying spirits ancestry, spiritual mission and other spiritual information.... you are not really connected to much of anything. Most divinities will not reveal themselves to folks who are not initiated or trained properly. These divine beings can't even be called by such people... they simply will not respond. Ancestral spirits can and will often reveal themselves; but, those who created the heavens, the earth and all it contains absolutely will not! Therefore, the majority of folks, in the diaspora, who claim themselves initiated haven't a clue as to what their head spirit really is. Without understanding that we are born with many spirits, some, assume that the first spirit that can mount their heads is it; but, it isn't. A true divinity, in its attempt to mount will not be able to speak because the person has not been initiated. And, for all of those running around throwing cowrie shells without the benefit of having the spirit Ifa installed, you are divining on the waves of gravity...nothing is happening there.

For those of African descent slavery brought us into the diaspora Those who came with our traditional spiritual systems did enough t keep our systems alive. To these great Africans, and their descendants we shall be forever grateful. But, now, the ancestors and the divinities in their infinite wisdom, have sent those chosen, in the diaspora, wit deep African knowledge, of the spirits, to help us to reconnect to ou ancestors and help us replace those tenants, of theirs, that were los during the slave era. It excites me every time an authentic Africa priest or priestess comes to our shores for visitation or to reside Therefore, I beg of my brothers and sisters not to view the things espouse, and others, as some type of comparison as to which is bette because it came out of Africa. That is not the reason these peopl have been sent, into the diaspora, but to teach, to share, to show wha our challenges are, how we can overcome them and gird ourselve to be all that we are supposed to be in what is our birthright. We, th descendants of the spirit's first creations, the mothers and fathers o all of mankind, the priests and priestesses of the world who are th standard must be just as effective, in the diaspora, as in Africa. So while Tamela Mann, and others like her, can only imagine...we d not have to imagine...because we know and understand that standin before the divine can happen right here and now! However, what w must do is yield to his/her molding yet unchanging hands.

THE SPIRITUAL MISSION

We all come to this earth with a destiny. That destiny may or ma not encompass a particular spiritual mission. For instance, if one ha come destined to be of the priesthood or a server of the spirits, insid of that particular destiny or "vocation" exist a particular spiritua mission. That is a particular group, or population or emphasis o spiritual work.... something that a person finds, themselves, drawn t or good at... as a spiritual practitioner...one's "nitch" as one would say I bring this up because, often, I refer to my own and its importance i what I do, on a daily basis; but, in that folks often scoff at it and accus me of egomania, I realized that many simply do not understand tha there is such a thing and what it actually is. It is not the becoming of a spiritual practitioner that is the mission, but, rather what, in particular, that the spirits have instructed YOU, as a practitioner, to do. This "mission", as revealed by Ifa or the spirits directly, is designed to serve a particular need in society. The spirits, in their infinite wisdom, see this need and put in place someone ordained and sent, by them, to address this need. It is a direct manifestation of the love that the spirits have for humanity, so, should not be scoffed at. People on these missions often give up the comforts of their own lives to be sent into foreign places, or out of their comfort zones, in an attempt to service humanity. The work of the priesthood is not to seek glory and status but to serve mankind.

So, when one goes to Ifa to inquire as to one's life, vocation, or any other matter; and, if one is found to have been born to the priesthood, inevitably, one will discover one's special talents, abilities or spiritual gifts designed to work in that special "nitch" or spiritual mission that one came to fulfill. Sometimes a person can spend an entire lifetime developing these special skills; so, that when the time is right they are especially equipped with the skills, needed, to complete the spiritual mission given. And that's when the spirits put them on a path to discover their true vocation.

For instance, when I was knocking about in my youth, from degree to degree, I had no idea what I wanted to be. I had fanciful notions of wanting to be something fabulous, in the fields, of each and every degree I pursued. At the time, each degree was not so much a degree earned but a gauge of the extreme indecisiveness of what I wanted to do with my life. Yet, in hindsight, I see the beauty and infinite wisdom of the ancestors and the divine spirits. This indecisive nut case was born to the priesthood; and, that undergraduate degree in Urban Politics, Masters in Education w/ emphasis in World Cultures, Teaching certifications in History, Geography and Economics, Masters in Psychoanalytic Studies, three years of training as a Psychoanalyst, five years of doctoral study (Psychology) and eight years of initial laying in and out of African temples has all come together. These voduns know exactly what they are doing; and, we shouldn't attempt to judge their decisions.

My advice, and prayer, to all of the spiritual practitioners out there. Find that "nitch" or spiritual mission, out there, particularly designed for you. If you do not know it Ifa will reveal it to you. This is not about egos, competition, or status symbols but about service. We are the vessels for the spirits that they may help the creations that they love.... mankind. And, no, we are not perfect; but, if we keep our eyes on the divine they will help to keep us on the right path that we may be able say...let THY will be done and not our own.

THE USURPATION* OF TRADITIONAL AFRICAN SPIRITUAL SYSTEMS AND CULTURE BY CHRISTENDOM: THE CASE OF NIGERIA

I am reminded of a post, I read a few days ago, where, in Nigeria, the traditionalists were seeking their rights...the right to be included in governmental functions, the right for children to be taught traditional culture and religion, and the right to be recognized by the government itself; and, it saddened me deeply. For how is it that in an African nation and traditional culture, that, what was there first has been so thoroughly usurped that one has to now, in this modern age, beg for the right to be at the table. And, as I thought of it, I realized that one of the keys to the problem was reflected in the phrase I had just written...this modern age.

1. **An act of usurping; wrongful or illegal encroachment, infringement, or seizure.*
2. *Illegal seizure and occupation of a throne.*

As I would travel through Lagos, Nigeria in route to various destinations north, I often rode the local buses. The passengers would often be entertained by videos or movies that were filmed locally. Nigerian cinema is extremely popular; but, a constant theme, in many of the movies, were always men being leered away into danger or seduced by a woman or spirit coming from the sea. The concept of serving the spirits of Mami Wata for the general public in most instances was something to avoid. And once I reached those regions, dominated by Muslims, the clashes between the two groups, Muslims and Christians, were often taken into the streets. All I could do was shake my head, duck and be extremely quiet. I was the most maligned of all...A vodun priestess.

But every now and then I would be spotted by someone who understood; and, as they would spot the crisp white head wrap, covering my head, and the sacred pearls (beading) surrounding my left ankle would immediately pull off their head cloth and drop to their knees. I am an authentic African Mami Wata; and, for some reason that continence, of spirit, simply could not be hidden.

While many would look to blame Nigeria for wanting to copy everything foreign in its quest for economic gain and the appearance of modernity this problem's roots actually go all the way back into Nigeria's colonial history. The Igbos/Ibos, for instance, one of the largest tribes in Nigeria, saw its villages, traditional shrines and spiritual objects completed decimated. As a result, most of the Igbos, of today, are now Christians. Some Igbos even claim themselves to be one of the lost tribes of Israel and others burn down the temples and destroy the temple's sacred objects after the last traditional priest, in the family, has died. The colonial process, with its wars and indoctrination of Christianity, by its missionaries, are part of this modern-day tragedy, in Nigeria, to where those of the traditional culture find themselves having to claw back into cultural recognition. So, it cannot be blamed, entirely, on the everyday citizens of Nigeria. It is what it is. And many tribal groups, in Nigeria, have fallen prey to its colonial history.

The bible, Christianity's sacred text, clearly speaks against divination, astrology, mediums, occult and the like (Leviticus 19: 26 31, 20:6). This is just a few of such passages in the Old, as well as, the New Testament texts. Many of these passages are not even noticed by most western cultures because many of the spiritual implements of traditional African societies, do not exist, in the diaspora, on any grand scale. But to an African these scriptures denounce the very traditional rituals that have existed in African society since the beginning of mankind's creation. As a result, Christianity is in complete opposition of African traditional spiritual systems. For fundamental to these systems is divination, the serving of ancestral as well as divine spirits and the concept of animal sacrifice. These rituals are demonized by the church. And, as such, wreak havoc on African traditional society...not to mention that pesky old teaching in Christianity, that a man can only have one wife. Even Islam allows the African four wives.

But, putting aside African traditional domestic practices, for the moment, the recent actions of the traditionalist to demand equal respect for African traditional culture and those traditional spiritual systems, of the region, is absolutely valid. If these systems die a part of Africa dies. We, whether born on the continent, of Africa or not need the help of our ancestors and the spirits that gave us life. This push back is not only necessary but important to the future of Africa and thus to all of mankind.

VODUN'S OUIDAH

Ouidah is a major center of vodun in Benin, West Africa and arguably the world. The seat of the Supreme Chief of Vodun, himself lives there. It is an ancient place, one of mystery, great paradoxes, and deep spiritual power. It is steeped in traditional African culture and infused with ancient spiritual secrets...many that the world, today have not heard of since biblical times and cannot fathom still exist

But they do in this place, this place where the voduns openly walk, and spirits of all kinds, good and evil, coexist in a world where time stands still. This is the beauty, power and majesty of Ouidah.Ouidah is well known for it's history in the transatlantic slave trade. It was one of the large slave ports of that time; however, my emphasis in this writing, is to discuss what Ouidah is to vodun and help those who choose to sojourn there to better understand it and its people.

Since UNESCO's Slave Route project, launched from Ouidah in 1994, many have traveled to this village in Benin, West Africa. Some have been interested in research of the slave trade, some, as I, searching for ancestry; and, still others to buy spiritual power. That last group, mentioned, tends to be the ones that are most uninformed about African traditional culture; and, they are the ones I am concerned with in this writing. They do not realize that there is a stark difference in vodun, or what passes for vodun, in the diaspora and the genuine article. They also do not realize that whether you are in Benin, Togo or Ghana you are still practicing vodun. The Akan tradition, of Ghana, folks...is vodun! In many instances, these folks sitting on these thrones, in the Akan tradition, are doing so because they were born to a particular vodun or spirit. One that is considered throne worthy in that particular family or clan. But in getting back to the issue, at hand, many run from their foreign countries, to Benin, hoping to buy power.

I am not saying that it cannot happen. It does far too often; but, a priest or priestess serving the spirits, with integrity, will not give you anything that you are not supposed to have. These Africans, of the priesthood in traditional African vodun...the original vodun...as well as any other African traditional spiritual system will first consult Ifa. And, if the spirits say that you were not born to it you are not getting it. In these cases, such folks have been known to run around Ouidah, or neighboring countries, and find someone who will take their money and give them what they want. But, in the end, it can cause them much grief. For example, there was a woman I knew, on one forum, which had been living with a spirit she had brought out of Ghana for years. She didn't know how to feed it nor knew its name. She was busy, on the Internet, describing its behavior (it was acting out) and trying to discover what vodun it was. Only I knew she had a Sakpata. The same Sakpata, that when I met her several years earlier, came to my husband and asked to be fed. In that we had become friends my spirits took note of her. But when I delivered the message she took it poorly and broke friendship. Yet, here is a woman claiming the priesthood. It would be laughable if it wasn't so sad. Why? Because a spirit like this, authentically done, could actually cost you your life if you do not know what you are doing. African vodun is not for the curious, the eccentric, or those wanting to dabble because it is avant garde. It is the real deal; but, dangerous to those who want to use its power, yet, give it little respect.

It is an affront to me these folks who run to Africa to attempt to buy power that are not supposed to have it! And, it is an affront to all of us who are found, by Ifa, to actually have been born to the African priesthood! It is an off shoot and a consequence of the trans-Atlantic slave trade and racism in America and beyond. While it is my belief that we all are born of the spirits; and, therefore, all have a right to have access, to them, I can not help but try and help folks understand the reasons why some, of my brethren, do not want certain folk to participate in traditional African spiritual systems.

Slavery, in the diaspora, has put those of African descent at the bottom of the economic scale. We may be found to be of the Priesthood but can not deal with the cost; yet, someone with money comes and attempts to buy what we have a right to and they do not. It hurts. While I believe that all, that are born to the Priesthood, should serve regardless of color, sexual orientation or gender, I do draw the line at those who attempt to buy power who are not supposed to have it! It is to my estimation that these people bastardize and lower the standards of that which is holy...the African Priesthood...and, of them, I find I have little tolerance. Their lack of understanding of respect, for African traditional spiritual systems, damages lives and wreaks havoc wherever they go; and, they will find no peace as long as I am around.

Ouidah, for those who legitimately want to serve the spirits, is a great place to visit. If you arrive there in humility and show respect for this place and its people, carrying ancient knowledge, you will be fine. If you hear the words of the spirits, after authentic divination, and respect what they say you will also be fine. But, if you think that you can visit and leave with hidden motives you are mistaken. For inside this place the spirits examine the hearts of all men/women as they enter. Inside this place who you are and why you have come loses its secrecy. Inside this place a spirit can count the bills and coins, in your pocket, one by one. Many of its people may not have been privileged to go to school; but, the things they know and understand are worthy of the Gods. And if you feel that you have come to buy, steal or attempt to exploit...be careful where you tread your feet...for what one may do here can bring back extreme consequences.

SPIRITUAL COURAGE

As I was to return to the diaspora, from Benin, West Africa, I remember speaking to each and every vodun, I had, at the time. They had requested that I come to take counsel, with them, about the trip I was about to take. The words of one spirit continually unveils its meanings, to me, to this very day. These were the words of the great spirit, Adjakpa...the crocodile. This ancient spirit has the wisdom of a sage. He said, "It takes courage to sit on the seat of the father." At the time, I hadn't a clue as to what it meant or in what he might have been referring to; but, like all the others, I simply wrote it down. But, for some reason, it never stayed hidden in the corners of my mind. It stayed there, fresh, as though it had some great importance. And, as each year has passed, its meaning has continually unveiled itself to me.

Of my years, on the Internet, I have constantly had to stand up for what our ancestors and the divinities have laid forth for vodun. I have had to confront the racism from those of African descent as well as non-blacks alike. I have had to confront those who are chasing the mighty dollar and initiating folks who had no right to be in the priesthood. I've had to fight the bigotry, the machismo, those broken brothers who wish to subjugate women with their phony kingships. I've had to listen to the "bought into" folk who set themselves up as authority and who disrespect those of us born to the priesthood. And most of all I have had to be the bearer of news, from the voduns, whether good or bad.

Being a child of the spirits may not win you any popularity contest. If you are honest, serve the spirits with integrity and are a straight shooter it more than likely will win you more enemies than friends; but, that's what Adjakpa meant. It takes courage...courage in the face of adversity, courage in the face of those making goobly gobs of money and you working diligently for little to no pay, courage in speaking the truth, in love, to folks who need it, courage to get up every morning and serve the spirits with all your being. But in the end, if one is committed to the service, of the spirits and mankind, one's spiritual rewards shall be reaped. So, for all of those out there serving the spirits every day with integrity and to the best of your ability...this is for you! The spirits see your hard work. They see your diligence. Do not be discouraged for, to the spirits, you are highly valued. Just a little something for those working in the trenches.

VODUN AND THE CONTRACT

When we are born we come to this world with a mission that may or may not direct our destiny, and, for many a contract. I say that the mission may or may not direct our destiny because it is our choice whether to carry it out or not. For those of us in African traditional spiritual systems Ifa explains just what this mission is, for others, we either bump into it or our own personal spirits are strong enough to lead us to it. By whatever means we travel along this spiritual path;

and, if all goes well we accomplish it...whatever it might be.

For many of us there is an actual contract. At this point in time I am not sure if we ALL are born with a contract; but, I know that some are because I was and a few other people that I know were. But, for the convenience of this post, I would assume that we ALL were because the contract, itself, involves how long we are to be on this earth. Remember how the old folks used to say the phrase, "When your time is up..."? This is to what I am referring.

In Africa, I learned that these contracts can be extended. Often, if an Hounon/Vodounon has been ill for an extended period of time, the spirits will demand ceremonies/sacrifices to extend one's contract... life here on earth. Mine has been extended a couple of times. In some instances, the priest's or priestess's work is so demanding, spiritually, that they lose a considerable amount of time on their contract. This time must be bought back through sacrifice. These types of priests are rare...born to suffer their bodies for the sake of mankind. They travel deep into the spirit world pulling folk from demons and bad spirits. They work in zogbe ministering to the dead. They travel wherever the spirits command and do whatever the spirits have them to do. They are not mere priests. They are the ones that become designated as 'National Treasures'. They are a rare breed of priests that are born of special missions. Often, they must buy more time on their contracts and those to whom they often service must help bear these costs. For, in some instances, only these types of priests can give them what they need due to their own special missions.

For those of us born, in the diaspora, therefore, this is yet another reason for us to reconnect to that which has been lost to us...our African spiritual heritage. Jesus has no provision to extend or renew our contracts; but, vodun certainly does!

Addendum: I must add that we can come with other contracts as well. Those that are specific to our mission here on earth. These may be contracts with a specific group of people, tribe, ancestors etc. to do a specific work.

VODUN'S VENGEANCE

To me one of the greatest passages, in the Bible, comes from Romans 12:19..."Dearly beloved, avenge not yourselves, but rather give place unto wrath: for it is written, Vengeance is mine, I will repay saith the Lord." (King James Version)

In African vodun we know and understand that you neither insult or offer an overt attack on a child/wife of the spirits! Young children, initiated into vodun, cannot even be spanked in fear that their personal voduns will go on the attack. The "plug in" to vodun or one's relationships with one's spirits is so close that one does not wish to harm or offend a person's spirits. Men give broad space between themselves and the wife of an African priest.... fearing that if the woman is approached incorrectly or if unintended affections might pour upon her, the spirits of the priest, might bring him an early demise. And even if one chooses to covertly attack a priest or a child of the spirits by sending juju, depending on that person and their relationship with their spirits, they are notified of what's coming before it even gets there, doing ceremonies to send it all back! THIS IS AFRICAN VODUN! And no one insults/attacks these folk without consequences. Not, immediately, because the spirits are long suffering. You will have forgotten the incident and maybe even the person; but, one day when your mind is on another thing...it comes!

Many diasporans are unaware of this. These folk who have 'bought into' these African traditional spiritual systems do not understand that vodun comes out of a specific cultural context. It is ancient, it is old, and it is African! You don't call vodun's children all types of names or falsely accuse them when they are out here defending vodun. In Africa, we know you do this at your own peril. I'm noticing that in the diaspora some folks are just making up their own rules as they go. Sanitizing things to fit their own agenda they are often rude and very disrespectful. But let me say this! Ask any African if nsulting an authentic African priest/priestess is a good idea; and, ou will hear it for yourself. African vodun doesn't play that! And ne of the number one voduns, that all of Africa fears, for retaliation or it's children is the Mami Wata! She is as swift as she is dangerous! These folks that have 'bought into' these systems do not understand he nature of these divinities. They are too busy talking about who is nd who is not to be accepted and a whole bunch of stuff mentioned n books; but, I say as more folks reach to Africa and reinstate that o which we have lost. Many of these 'bought into' folk are going to ee trouble. Not necessarily from us who serve, but, from the spirits hat we serve. Vodun has a way of getting rid of folk who interfere vith their divine plans. Vodun is something you learn by dealing vith the spirits on a daily basis not sitting there mouthing off about he latest research! One has to develop true relationships with these pirits...knowing them by conversing with them and communing vith them. One must allow them to mold you into a better person. I elieve that part of the reason these folks may not experience change s because they are not really hooked into anything! They, in their lesire to buy their way into these systems, have not gone through the roper channels (the ancestors) to be properly connected to anything. These folk don't see Africa, or it's ancestors, as being important in my estimation. If so they would have more respect!

So, let's end, this, with the last part of that passage shall we: Romans 12:20..."Therefore if thine enemy hunger, feed him; if he hirst, give him drink: for in so doing thou shalt heap coals of fire on his head." (King James Version) And that's the way it's done folks! We will be ever so kind, ever so cordial, waiting, just waiting for the spirits to tell us when we have been avenged.

AS THE COCK CROWS

When I am here in the United States one of the things that I miss, the most, about my beloved Africa... a sweet simplicity that gently reminds me of her... is the cock crowing. In places like Haiti, Africa or on an American farm, the crowing of a cock means the dawning of a new day. It is a renewal and a refreshing in the midst of the cycle of life! And for me, in vodun, the cock is definitely crowing. Not because vodun's ageless tenants are being challenged nor its priesthood is becoming lax, but, because the opportunity to know vodun, in all of it's glory, is now accessible beyond the borders of mother Africa! For she is waking her children and opening their eyes to the realities of who they are! And little by little she is ordaining the chosen to guide them. But challenges, even for those of us born of the in-game, will continue to persist among us...

A young man posted a thread in an Internet forum I have come to enjoy with a very "cocky" attitude (excuse the pun)! The young man said that he was cool with the group and wanted to promote vodun but wanted to be spared any idiotic notions, in vodun, of the supernatural...extra sensory perception and the like. He had spent 10 years studying vodun and wanted level headedness in the group! At first, I ignored the posting thinking it was absolutely absurd. I almost posted the snide remark asking anyone if they had any popcorn. It reminded me of my younger days when we used to sit, out on the stoop, and listen to the neighbor's fight. Folks tried to talk reason with the young man; but, he wouldn't hear anybody. He was too busy being the cock of the walk! Yet he claimed that he was, in fact, defending vodun! I then took a more serious look at the thread and posted a response. He obviously didn't understand vodun; however, the real question was why was he promoting something that he obviously had little tolerance for or didn't like? Then it hit me! Many of our Afrocentric brothas and sistahs will promote vodun because of its African ties; but, that portion which seemed savage/medieval or somehow idiotic (meaning less scientific or learned) is rejected. They wish to be politically correct, down with the Afrocentric premise, but reject anything that makes them look bad or insult their inflated intelligence! In my grandfather's words, they are "educated fools". These are the folk who come to Africa spend their entire time there in the most expensive hotel, they can find, and say they went home. Their only interaction, with the people, is to take a tour and a photograph.

As traditional vodun is being promoted across the globe we will see more of these types of people. Brothas and sistahs who are hell bent on purifying vodun. One might say that these folk, under the surface, hate themselves and a whole lot of folks around them; but, still we have to continue to impart knowledge and challenge them where needed. We STILL must stand up for vodun; but, this is not always easy. I have been battered and torn during many bouts on many forums, yet, I still stand. I continue to stand for two reasons... one, by remembering something my grandfather used to say, "Right is right and right don't wrong nobody!"...and second...With the ancestors at my back and the spirits at my front, I cannot and will not be moved! So as the cock crows let the new day begin, a new day in the re-establishment and promotion of African Vodun!

AFRICAN PRIESTS AND PRIESTESSES

The life of an African priest or priestess is not often an easy one. All of us have heard rumors where young virgins are, supposedly, held in temples, not to know man, being prepared as great Priestesses or Oracles of some kind. In some areas, of Africa, this may indeed be true; yet, these stories undoubtedly serve to highlight the seriousness of one's destiny if it is to be of the African priesthood.

In a vodun family, in Africa, or even of those still following its traditional ways a child is taken to the oracle...Ifa...after its first three months. At that time, the spirits reveal what the child is in the spiritual world. If it is bound for the priesthood, what spirits it is carrying, what ancestor has comeback in him/her etc. During these consultations, the family is informed if this child is to later be initiated and to what capacity.... a Vodunsi, Tassinon, Diviner, Priest/Priestess etc. It may or may not be revealed, at that time, the child's true destiny...that is a specific spiritual mission to do something. The family Priest writes all this down and at an appropriate age this child, usually while watching a ceremony, is "captured" by the temple vodunsi and swept into the initiation chamber while its family runs behind them pleading and crying. The family, then, must be told what is needed for the initiation and start putting their funds together or coming up with the appropriate sacrificial animals and supporting the child in these months of seclusion, initiation and training. All the secrets of the family Voduns are passed on to these young ones including secret languages, only spoken by them, and ceremonies peculiar to that clan. After initiation, the young person trains years on end in the ways of its family Vodun isolated from its regular peers except to go to school... if even allowed. Herein lies the beginning differences of the African Priest and all others. These are those such as Behumbeza who started this process at eight years old!

And, even in Africa, there are priests and there are PRIESTS! At the top of the pact is the priest that is born to give his life for the people. These live humbly. They were born to save others and the work that they do takes years off their own lives. They are constantly having to renew their spiritual contracts in reference to their years on this earth. The Africans know what I am talking about! They pull people from the demons, from the witches and from the bad places where souls have been captured by bad juju or bad spiritual work. They travel to unknown places, at the command of the spirits, searching for items for persons that were left long time ago in other lives. They are the ones to whom the highest divinities reveal themselves because of the mark of their birth and their pure hearts. They are the ones that priests who see trouble, with their own lives and spirits, go to. They are the ones who watch TV with no sound that they are sure they hear the spirits whenever they call. They don't do ANYTHING without the will of the spirits. Their spouses are chosen by the ancestors and the spirits particularly to aid in their spiritual missions. They become Dahs or King Priests. Their entire lives are to serve others and allow the fruits of their labor to provide for their everyday needs.

African priests and priestesses, in general, are very unique. Their nitiations can be long and arduous. Their customs are old and ncient. They take counsel with the very divinities themselves. These re good things! My message, today, is that they are the standard! When these traditional African spiritual systems were brought to the iaspora the slave culture did much to stifle us. To save these systems ve had to outwit the "massa" to continue to serve. In most cases it was yncretised with other systems, hidden amongst them in order to ook legitimate so as not to be whipped! Much of our knowledge, from hese systems, were lost, much forgotten and initiations shortened ecause of the planting of the fields! However, what has happened, in he diaspora, has not made complete new systems. It is essentially a ontinuation of the old...just a bit tattered and changed. This is what hose, that have bought into these systems, wish for us to think. But hey really are a continuation of the same. The same ancestors we ad when our forefathers were wrenched from mother Africa are till there! They haven't gone ANYWHERE! So, reach back to the tandard.... reach back to our ancestors and our forefathers...reach back and kneel before the divine!

SPIRITUAL AUTHORITY: WHERE DOES IT COME FROM?

I once had a young man ask me this question on a forum. It ppeared that he wanted to know by what spiritual authority did I peak. One gets this, a great deal, when one is up against folks that ave bought into to these African traditional spiritual systems and you are trying to correct them on an issue. So, here was my answer.

In African Traditional spiritual systems, for whence all such diasporan traditional systems originated, spiritual authority comes from the ancestors and the divine spirits themselves. It is THEY who ordain us. In original vodun, as I have often stated in my writings, after three months of the birth of a child, the family takes it to Ifa/ Fa/Afa. It is Fa who tells us WHO and WHAT this child is in the spirit world and what his/her mission is because, through the birthing process, we forget this. We learn, from Fa, whether this child i born to serve the spirits or not, and if so, in what capacity...a pries vodunsi, diviner, tassinon or whatever. It is a misnomer to believ that everyone is born to serve the spirits. They are not.

As many of us, in the diaspora, come to vodun later in our live we too must mimic this process and go to Fa. Fa tells us WHO an WHAT we are in the spirit world. Once we know; and, if we heed th call to initiate, if told, it is the initiation process itself that brings u in line with the ancestors and the divine spirits. At every juncture o that initiation we continually consult the spirits, through Fa, askin how to proceed and what specifically should be done for this persor Spirits are as individual as we are people. The spirits, therefore, knov WHO and WHO DOES NOT belong to them. So, if one then goes t Fa, on behalf of anyone claiming the priesthood...it is Fa who wil authenticate that person, for us, and tell us WHO and WHAT tha person is in the spirit world.

Now, I have also been asked, recently, as to what happens in th case of priests and priestesses who may wish to exploit their brethrer or those who choose to take advantage of their followers sexually The first thing I want to remind folks is that like, in any other suc circumstances, women need to be aware and not allow themselves t be exploited! A man seeking to take advantage, sexually, is a scoundre whether he has been ordained or not! And, if a priest or priestess i seeking to exploit, it should be obvious that he/she is not followin the tenets of the spirits and will eventually have to answer to them However, as in any religion or traditional spiritual system, peopl acting badly are not to be tolerated.

In African vodun we have mechanisms to deal with such. Buil in, is a system whereby complaints can be logged and if found guilty consequences will happen. That is why, in African vodun, there ar the heads of each pantheon of Vodun and a Supreme Chief of Vodur that such complaints and/or disputes can be handled. And in all suc cases Fa is consulted. Many things are happening in the diaspor because of a lack of authority and a departure from the tenants that were originally brought over with these great systems. The BOUGHT IN people want to keep it this way. They want to give the illusion that their stuff is legitimate...after all they did pay for it...and that they stand shoulder to shoulder to those of us who were born to serve and came here with specific spiritual missions. I've got news for them... they are not! And, again, if we reach back and employ those traditions and customs that were originally bought with these systems, like Ifa, the unfit will eventually be weeded out or severely limited!

So, again, in African vodun, if we want to know ANYTHING about a particular Priest or Priestess... whether they are truly ordained, of good character etc. simply go to the spirits, via Fa, and ask. Our spiritual authority comes from them!

IN VODUN WHOSE OPINION MATTERS?

In late 2007, while recuperating from knee surgery, I began to peruse the Internet looking for others in vodun to talk to. With no temple, here I was looking for like-minded folk in which to converse. I was desperately missing the fellowship of a temple; so, I ended up on Haitixchange. This was terrific! My Haitian cousins were aware of vodun and the forum itself, since I am a political junkie, helped to keep me in the know. Since then, however, I have been on yet another and now Facebook. On each of these I have been a part of forums with vodun enthusiasts, self-styled experts and those eager to learn. Opinions and theories fly all over the place! Feelings are often hurt, posts are sometimes misunderstood, egos abound and testosterone filled machismo is often the special of the day! In other words, there can be/is DRAMA! But what does it all matter? Whose opinions really are to resonate anyway? What then is the standard? I'll give you a hint. It sure isn't us!

In vodun it is easy to forget WHO is in charge. It isn't us! It is the SPIRITS! It is THEY that handed this system down to us! Vodun is not like New Testament Christianity whereby some, so-called, spiritual men wrote letters to the churches. No! The tenants, of vodun, ar handed down by the ancestors and the divinities, themselves, an they are STILL there running things! They are not dead! They ar active and alive, not in the physical sense, but ALIVE just the sam If we want to know something pertaining, to the voduns, we go an ask THEM! We don't postulate and pontificate we go and ask. And w do it by the method in which they gave us to communicate. Not on in which We THINK is OK, but, the one in which THEY SAY is OK For me this is simple; but, for some reason the message simply isn getting out! Thus, one of the reasons, why I deem vodun a spiritu system and not a religion. It is a direct system of communicatio with those whom installed it. With a little bit of time and effort, on does not have to wonder about a thing/question. Just go and ask! I a spirit is standing in your midst, during a ceremony etc., ask you question, after approaching correctly, or ask the priest or priestess t do it for you. If a spirit isn't in your view go to the diviner and let If go and ask. In any event you can know the answer. You do not nee to attempt to come up with it on your own. You do not need to sit u and debate theology... simply ask the spirits! It is THEY who are IN CHARGE! Not us!

VODUN AND THE CULTURAL CONTEXT

I'm not sure how to present this; but, my issue is us looking a African vodun from the lens of American culture. Vodun came ou of a specific cultural context. The culture it is embedded in is ancien polygamous and very high on ceremony. It is patriarchal, in nature not because men are "dogs" as our trash talking feminist sisters wan to espouse but because this has been a way in which every woman and her children, are under the auspices of a man's care. Now w may debate the merits, of monogamy, in another venue; and, I an sure that the Africans can point to a lot of our own challenges suc as the proliferation of single parent households, baby "mamas" an "daddies" and women who keep their legs open so much that the don't even know WHO their child's father is! But these are periphera issues to what I wish to discuss today.

I was fortunate in that I attended college with many Africans in my undergrad years. In addition, I studied and later taught African history. Therefore, I became familiar with the culture at large. And, of course, I learned even more after embedding myself, in vodun and it's culture, for eight continuous years. Yet, even today, being married to an African and living there, when I travel, I am STILL learning. So, I beseech many of you, as I have in previous posts, to began to read about African traditional culture. It will give you a better understanding of Africa and its people. It doesn't have to be heavy duty research but just a few of the basics that you are able to better understand the differences between uninformed or biased documentaries, on vodun related issues, versus the truth. Most recently a discussion came up, on a forum, about initiates in vodun who are of tender ages. This is an everyday phenomenon in vodun families. Early in life these children are identified, through Ifa, as being born to serve. When they become of age they are "captured", put in the family temple, initiated and spend a lifetime of training into the service of the spirits. My husband is an example. He started at eight years old. An uninformed researcher will see this as child slavery and/or abuse of some kind. They do not understand that these are family temples and what has transpired before; thus, filtering African customs through a Eurocentric lens and giving the issue an incorrect slant. We too are often guilty of such! We must read, we must become better informed! Since Black History Month is upon us I end this by reminding us of a dark part of African history that reflects a horrible clash of cultures...Liberia.

In the early 1800s free African Americans returned to Africa.... Liberia! Once they got there, they thought they were better than the indigenous Africans and sought to suppress them. This is where I will stop because I would like to make it your first reading assignment. Find out what went wrong. Someone post your findings, on a forum, and let's discuss them. There are lessons here; and, for those abroad read up on Sierra Leone, and the Black Loyalist who settled that country. You see guys we can mess up a great deal when we filter Africa through our own Eurocentric lenses; and, these are two case studies that prove it!

VODUN AND THE CASE OF LORD RAMA

Almost 8 years ago, a young man contacted me through a vodun Internet site. He had visited several persons claiming to serve the spirits, before me, but didn't feel satisfied. He wasn't sure about me because he saw that I was an informative source; but, in that I never advertised, about anything, he wasn't sure but inquired anyway. Unknowing, to me, something deep inside him was ushering him toward Africa. He didn't reveal it at first; but, when I told him about Behumbeza, from Africa, he bit down like a bulldog. And, since then, he and Behumbeza have been one of the most amazing spiritual father and son relationships that I have ever witnessed. Not only did this relationship teach me more about one of the top priests, on the African continent...BEHUMBEZA...;but, it has taught me so much more about the spirits themselves!

Behumbeza went to Ifa as he always does for his divinations. His divination tool is ancient. It is the mirror. It has been passed down through the mother's side of his family and is one of, if not, THE oldest in existence. Last year, during an Ifa conference, people came from all over the world to see it! In it he calls the spirits forth and the spirit of the mirror goes to find them and they appear. It is very hard work. Spirits can be fickle. If it is a big divinity they may send all types of spirits, before hand, to ask certain questions. He can be sitting there all night or they may say return another night or with a particular sacrifice. He can be put through a ringer dealing with these great divinities. But when they do show up Behumbeza and they can proceed with discussing the person at hand. Our young man, who is Haitian born, has the head spirit of LORD RAMA! This is Mami-Dan. This is important here. Why? Because many would assume that a

Haitian born individual would have a Haitian spirit. True, but maybe not a spirit that gives life. Our oldest ancestors are from Africa NOT Haiti! The Haitian spirits are indeed part of his heritage; but, Haiti, as America, would consist of our newest ancestors NOT our oldest! His ancestor left the African continent just as ours as African Americans, therefore, we must start there and Behumbeza did!

Lord Rama's ancestors sent Behumbeza to Ghana. He first went to the Ashanti village (my maternal ancestral village) for help and they escorted him to the Akogban people...the paternal ancestors of our Lord Rama. In that village after many months of work, negotiations and sacrifice Behumbeza was able to carry out the ancestral spiritual throne seat, that our Lord Rama had inherited, of the 41 ancestral throne seats that still existed, there, and all of the spiritual artifacts that went with it! Many months later he repeated the same thing with the Ogboni tribe, of Nigeria, who were the maternal ancestors of this spiritual child. He brought back the seats and all the accoutrements that were rightfully inherited by this young man. When I dreamed of an opele, that was not my own, I told Behumbeza and we found it to be the one belonging to Lord Rama and, again, Behumbeza returned to the Ogboni tribe, negotiated, and upon the death of the aged diviner returned with the opele for his spiritual son. Time and time again Behumbeza was sent to various countries or sacred waters and sites to gather items for his child. Thus, the work of this great Priest. I have witnessed him do so much for so many people, that, I am often in awe of him; but, he does it over and over again! Lord Rama is of the pantheon of Mami-Dan. Yet, known also as one of the Hindu spirits. This is what I mean by our head spirits can come from anywhere! Yet our ancestral spirits remain constant. First coming from the birthplace of man and traveling in various directions.

Ifa has revealed that there are just a few more things, to do, in the wrap up before concluding our preparations for the initiation of Lord Rama. Behumbeza will then be able to initiate his spiritual child. We are all excited and very tired. Not to mention our Lord Rama who is biting at the bit to get this all over with. It has been a long journey. We hope it will conclude this year.

But recently our Lord Rama had a dream. In the dream, he had a caller by phone. They asked him, “Did you get the shirts?” It was two shirts in a suitcase, one purple, one black! His newest ancestors, the Haitians, have arrived! Bonjour Ghede!

Behumbeza has many spiritual children all around the world but, besides me this is his first one on the American continent. I tel the story to help you understand the importance of reaching back to Africa! You see vodun, in the diaspora, is not separate from Africa. I is a continuation of Africa! The case of Lord Rama proves that. If you have questions of how this works feel free to inquire yourselves. Lord Rama, our spiritual child, is on facebook under MamiWata Priest He is Haitian born; but, by reaching back he has been able to include ALL of his ancestors, as I, from the oldest to the newest. And the thrones that he will chair, after his initiation, will have been passed down through the generations even though slavery occurred!

AFRICAN VODUN AND AN ATTACK FROM WITHIN: THE SELLING OF ARTIFACTS

What I have learned, in life, is that with, anything, sometimes WE become our own worse enemies. In Africa, for instance, I occasionally witnessed Africans defiling their own temples. It was never the priest himself, or happened while he was alive (unless stolen while he was away); but, it was the children, or descendants, of a priest. It was those children that had become Christians and were somehow convinced that, after the death of the last traditional Priest in the family, all remnants of a past demon filled life must be demolished...the family temple. So, after the burial of the priest, they would go in and put fire to all that remained while selling it’s priceless artifacts/statutes (bocios) and vodun paraphernalia that had been housed there for centuries on end. It is only later when their lives began to have trouble, and Jesus isn’t helping, that they go to Ifa and realize the damages that they have caused. These beautiful bocios, and implements of vodun, often sit in tourist shops or are sold on the black market to the highest bidder. There are even people coming from Europe, on a regular basis, to buy such goods for their Museums. Many seem to converge on Lome, Togo and work their way down to Benin and other places! It appears that others can see the value of our traditions when we can't.

I remember my first, and only, visit to the British Museum, in London, and my anger at the amount of treasured artifacts that had been pilfered from Egyptian tombs. I simply couldn't believe it! I felt violated! Mummies...dead bodies of kings and queens laying under filtered lighting when THEIR kings and queens were laid away, in splendor, at Westminster Abbey. And even here, in America, I see temple relics/bocios, items that belong in temples prepared through great ceremony and activated to contain spirits being sold on the Internet. It saddens me deeply! What is going on with the sacred treasures of the world? Anything to make a dollar! The spirits contained in these artifacts are not happy.

In 1997, as part of a group of doctoral candidates, I visited South Africa. My first trip to the motherland. We were ALL from the field of Psychology. Traditional Healing was one of my aims. Many of us were of African descent. It was an absolute scene when we got off the plane. Without a thought, and as in unison, each African American dropped to their knees in tears! All folks could see was my butt, in the air, I was kissing the ground so hard! There were no words that could describe what happened. Other tourists simply started taking pictures. Something had broken in me. I was balling like a baby as we all helped each other to compose ourselves and make it through the airport lines. After hundreds of years, since my ancestor was captured into chattel slavery, I his descendant, had made it back to African soil! I had no words...only tears of joy!

The trip, itself, was fabulous! The Sagomas, that I had met, pointed me toward Benin; and, the rest is history... But, I loved the country so much that after others left I and a friend stayed. On one of our last days, there, we went back to our favorite market. I saw what I presumed to be two exotic dolls; and, I purchased them with two pair of American jeans! I was out of money. I couldn't take my eyes from them. I had been circling the market; but, I kept coming back to these two dolls dressed as Zulu warriors. They were extremely unusual and handmade. Me, them, and my friend girl, to America we returned. The dolls became my constant companions; but, people were constantly afraid of them. I couldn't understand why. I adored them!

In 1998, while in Africa, they accompanied me to Benin. I took them to the Supreme Chief of Vodun. He smiled as he called the diviner. They spoke! They were Age (accent over the e) twins. Their names were Zinsu and Tevi and they saw what I was in the spirit world and what I was to become. And, they joined me for the work. They asked for sacrifice; and, I gave it and continually give it! Inside temple Behumbeza they now sit with Metanou... my DaZodji (Sakpata). Age (accent over the e) are spirits that control the medicinal plants and Sakpata engages in much healing; so, they sit with him.

These African artifacts, found to be voduns, were made for somebody and for some purpose! They were often active with spirits living inside. What are we doing when we defile that which is sacred? What are we doing when we steal and sell the family Asan or the Bocios from the holy places? Let the spirits judge each man according to his deeds!

VODUN AND SOME OF LIFE'S MYSTERIES

I've never understood the world's propensity for questions such as...Is there life after death? Do spirits exist?, or The Big Bang Theory versus the Creation Story and that question of: Was the earth created in seven days? It appears that the answers have always been right in our faces; but, we cannot see them.

The indigenous populations of the world, it appears, already know the answers to these questions. They and nature are one, nature being a manifestation of that which is divine; so, they live with the answers on a daily basis. We, in the brick and mortar world, look to books. But do we even listen or understand the books that give the answers in which we seek? But, of course, there is life after death! And yes, spirits exist! Does not the Christian Bible say that after our life, on this earth, there is eternal life (Matthew: 29, et.al)? Doesn't it also speak, throughout it's pages, of the Holy spirit(s)? Spirits that reign eternal? And, of the creation story...does not the Bible, this holy book not say, that for the Lord, a day is like a thousand years, and a thousand years is like a day. (2 Peter 3:8). In other words, our time and the time of that which is divine is very different. Our seven days is not seven days for the Creator...it is a metaphor! One that shows after, the creation of the earth, he/she...MawuLissa took rest. So, what's all the hoopla about? The ancients have always known these things. The indigenous cultures, of the world, understand these things as absolutes? So who is more learned... the professors seeking educational grants, to search out such mysteries, or the Traditional/Shaman Priests who work hard to help serve their daily clients?

Our God is an awesome GOD! This great Spirit created the heavens, the earth and all which it contains. He/She has the power to create life and/or take life. I think these bible passages might sum it up...

Psalm 46:8-10 New International Version (NIV)

8

Come and see what the Lord has done,
the desolations he has brought on the earth.

9
He makes wars cease
to the ends of the earth.
He breaks the bow and shatters the spear;
he burns the shields[a] with fire.

10
He says, "Be still, and know that I am God;
I will be exalted among the nations,
I will be exalted in the earth."

VODUN'S SPIRITUAL ARCHETYPES/PERSONALITIES

We understand, in Africa, that if you know the head spirit of a person you have a general idea of the person's personality. These pantheon of spirits have and are known for particular archetypal traits. And while, each spirit is as individual as we are people, there are certain characteristics or traits that one might find in that person due to one's head spirit(s). That is why, in African vodun, we refer to a person by whom they are "the wife of" i.e. Wedosi, the wife of Ayidowedo, or, Ablosi, the wife of Mami Ablo. One also may be referred to as Hounnon Ayidowedo meaning Priest(ess) of the sea spirit Ayidowedo etc. Many are simply called by the personal name of one's spirit such as Behumbeza, the personal name of my husband's Dattatreya/Den'su or Metanou the personal name of my Da Zodji (Sakpata). These personal names are revealed after one has completed all ceremonies for a particular spirit.

One does not return from Africa, however, and name oneself what he or she chooses. This is a dead giveaway to those, that actually have been initiated into vodun, that someone is falsely claiming the priesthood and has not completed the appropriate ceremonies. For example, there is a person, claiming the priesthood of Mami Wata, sitting in the diaspora who returned from a visit to Africa, in 2008, and named herself, inadvertently, after an African cemetery. She was unaware that Behumbeza, who was summoned by the persons she visited, in 2008, and authorized a Tchamba ceremony, for her, had a fully initiated wife, into the pantheon of Mami Wata, already living in the states when she returned. People such as this think that the distance from Africa to the Americas will hide their deception; but, the spirits have a way of working things out such that these people are eventually exposed. One, therefore, waits until they have received full initiation into the priesthood and the spirits, themselves, will tell you their names or what you are to be called. Such a person, who has supposedly initiated others, without ordained authority from the spirits, have simply taken these people's money and given them nothing. Only someone fully initiated into the priesthood, of that pantheon of that particular vodun, can initiate someone into that vodun. The voduns do not hear, recognize or consider this person because they have not been ordained by them.

It is important, therefore, if someone wants to know who their spirits are to go for authentic African divination. Ifa can tell you, initially, what pantheon of Voduns you belong to and if you need to initiate. If so, you will eventually learn your head spirit, accompanying spirits and eventually, after initiation, the spirits personal names. In African Vodun we do not name ourselves. The ancestors will give us a name; and, so will the spirits. Names are generally given after the appropriate ceremonies. Once one understands which spirits gave one life we can better understand why we, often, behave the way we do or like the types of things that we like. Our spirits help mold us into who we are.

THE AYIDOWEDO STORY

The following is one of my favorite stories. It is the story of the great serpent Ayidowedo and how he came to be, told, by an African who specializes in the oral traditions of the Fon people. I have used a combination of google translator and what I know of the story to post it in English. I will put up in the French original text where I feel that the translation is not that good. I have also noted where the original text can be found. Enjoy!

L'AURORE Friday April 21, 2000*

Arc-en-ciel or Dan Ayidohwedo

The Rainbow or the Serpent Ayidowedo

To this pantheon of Vodun, among the Fon, in the former kingdom of Dahomey, today, there is a voodoo which is the most important. This is the Vodun Dan Ayidowedo.

Dan = Snake

Ayido = Tu as pris [you have taken]

Hwedo = Ciatrice portee [Scar scope]

Then we have the following translation:

Serpent bearer of marks or scars.

The story of Ayidowedo is traced through the interpellation a combination of signs of the oracle Fa. This combination is called Wenlen-Yeku.

Hwedo was, a simple boa who wanted, over time, to distinguish himself from other boas . So, every year, he would seek to reach heaven by setting his tail on the ground and raising his head until it reached the very heavens. But, every time he would reach a certain level, he would crumble and fall back because he could not overcome the opposition, he encountered, from other entities stronger than him, which prevented him from achieving his dream.

So, one day, the boa decided to go to the oracle Fa** which is manifested by double Wenlen-Yeku sign. The boa constrictor agreed to comply with the recommendations of this dual sign, and provided everything that was asked for sacrifices. Among other items, he gives especially seven different types of beads, two plumes and two different kinds of birds were well appointed with two feathers and placed on the head of the boa like a crown. The Fa told him to try again, by standing on his tail, from the ground, and reach for the sky and nothing could stop him!

And, Indeed, the entities that prevented the boa from going to heaven fled leaving him passage upon seeing the beautiful plumage of his crown. Henceforth the boa has changed in nature and named the Divinity Dan [The Serpent] Ayidowedo, which is recognized from the trace it leaves in its wake. This trace is nothing other than the color of his crown. Thats why Ayidowedo or Arc-en-ciel still [has] seven colors [when] it appears.

Ayidowedo has two main tasks:

He/She is the God/Goddesses of wealth, it is he/she who gives material wealth, prosperity, great friendships, and true happiness.

Ayidowedo is also the single means of transport for the Vodun Hêviosso, God of Lightning and Thunder. Thats why in the temples of this great thunder God, Hêviosso, one will always finding drawings, on the wall, of Ayidowedo and in the temple of Ayidowedo there will always be represented the image of the Xeviosso voodoo.

Text drafted by Gabin Djimasse, Specialist in Oral Tradition and the promotion of the Fon Culture. (Benin, West Africa)

* *A newspaper from Benin, West Africa.*

** *Ifa/Fa/Afa*

Note: Spirits come in male and female form

VODUN AND THE FOLLY OF MANKIND

Some place, out there, there are those, among us, who are convinced that mankind is divine. They believe that we, ourselves, stand shoulder to shoulder amongst the Gods. This is the primary folly of mankind... that we the "creation" are on par with, or on the same level as, that of the "Creator(s)". This is the underlying premise behind the "do-it-yourselfers", in vodun, and those who seek to become priests/priestesses and lord themselves over others. Instead of realizing that we are human vessels, for the spirits, and servants to mankind, we in our folly, seek to lord over mankind and imitate that which is divine. We do not realize that we are only as spiritually powerful as our relationship, with the spirits, is strong. For while the divine lives within us, we ourselves are not divine beings, but, filled with human frailty, fallibility and thus in need of a divine entity for correction and/or guidance.

Man has been duped by his own genius. In the great minds of mankind his discoveries of the universe have made him inquisitive and all knowing. But the key to his folly is that he "discovers". Discovery implies that the thing he encounters was already there. It was there BEFORE he found it! That scientific wonder that he comes across, thus discovers, that he writes about, publishes and becomes famous for was ALREADY there! He didn't invent it, he found it, placed there by an entity more than himself...a divine being, a "Creator" of both the heavens and the earth. Science, therefore, is not opposed to Creation, science is Creation! It is the work of the Creator(s).

Mankind must understand who and what he is in relation to that which is divine. We are not divine; but, a portion of the divine lives within us. One must be still and listen because that which is divine is our moral compass. It is that which helps us follow the path of what is correct, true and pure. But, it is the carnal nature of man... man himself... that covets, lies, cheats and seeks to go against that which is divine. In this condition, he is not a god nor divine. It is his own intellect that dupes him into believing this. The indigenous populations, of the world, understand this. It is those that we assume to be simple, uneducated and backward, in their ways, unmodern, uncivilized who serve the spirits in all humility. They understand that there is something greater than themselves living among us. "Truly I tell you, anyone who will not receive the kingdom of God like a little child will never enter it." Luke 18:17. The more educated we are the less we tend to believe this. In our arrogance, we fool ourselves into believing that as God's equals we can, thus, call down divinities and commune with spirits of all kinds without being ordained by them. We are foolish to ever think such! We have no power within ourselves for such things unless given this power from the spirits themselves. Do not be deceived people that which is carnal is carnal; and, that which is spirit is spirit. And, mankind is definitely carnal in nature.

THE PRIEST/PRIESTESS, TEACHER, GURU

I was a bit annoyed, yesterday, when a young woman who claims the priesthood, in Haitian vodou, put up a post that instructed her members that there were no gurus in vodun...never has been and never will be! And, it brought me back to my old 2-part question of ...how is it that such folks get into vodun in the first place; and, if initiated and brought in, why aren't they taught properly?

The term, guru, means teacher. Mostly used, in Hinduism, it refers to a personal religious teacher and spiritual guide, or, a person with knowledge or expertise in spiritual matters. What, then, is a Priest, Priestess, or spiritual parent if they are not, first, a teacher or guru? They enter our lives to help us along our spiritual journey, they enlighten us as to the mysteries of the spirits, and, with the help of the spirits, are guided in our initiation process. Once that is over, through their continued guided expertise, they help us to mature in our knowledge of the divine. It makes no sense to say that there are no gurus in vodun. Vodun is ripe with them. Each priest or priestess that has walked their spiritual journeys for years, and, those who are considered elders are in essence gurus. While the young woman's annoyance was mainly directed at me, for teaching so much on her forum, to post such, in the midst of a 2,000 + membership, on Vodun, is a tragedy.

Many come to these forums to learn. There are some that are on spiritual journeys, some, simply want to get a feel of what vodun is; and, still, others may be looking for a spiritual parent. But, when a forum is set up with the main purpose of marketing or hunting down clients, this is often what you get. A disrespectful little dictator, with a potty mouth, claiming to be a high priestess after a couple of weeks in someone's initiation chamber, who fears true knowledge, because it exposes her lack of, making up her own rules. My prayer is that for the years to come diaspora Vodun, with the advent of more seeking training, in Africa, or reinstating those elements lost to us, due to the slave trade, will began to filter out those to which the Voduns may deem unfit; and/or, put brakes on the people who initiate them.

I'm beginning to think I do not do well in groups...

VODUN, AFRICA'S DOMESTIC SLAVERY AND THE SELL OF SLAVES BY AFRICANS

So, okay, since the subject has been brought up several times, recently, let's talk about it! Let's throw open the closet doors and pull out the skeletons.... shall we? Many African Americans claim that Africans must come clean on the issue of their participation in the trafficking and selling of their own people into slavery. And, recently, a young woman, of German descent claiming the priesthood in Haitian Vodou said, in response to my insistence that you can not cut Haitian Vodou off from it's roots, Africa, said, "...we know the truth, Africans sold slaves!". My response, "...so? Does that mean that since Africans sold slaves that it makes them, now, not our ancestors? White folks owned slaves and slaughtered Jews are they not YOUR ancestors?"

In other words, in BOTH instances, does Africans who

participated in the slave trade or had domestic slaves nullify the fact that these ARE our present-day ancestors? Or, does those whites who were slave owners, and/or bought and sold slaves, in the diaspora and beyond, stop being a person of European descent's ancestors? Of course not! But here are the differences. Africans are owning up to their participation as sellers and owners of slaves. Those of European descent, often, are not!

In Africa, since the inception of The Slave Trade Project by Unesco, launched in Ouidah, Benin in 1994, Africans have not only been remembering slavery but have been acknowledging their part in it. Throughout the west coast of Africa, monuments, acknowledging the millions who left in chains, and Africa's part in it, have been erected. Route de l'esclaves exist along the shores of the coast, as well as, Doors of No Return to acknowledge this monumental travesty in the history of mankind. 2014 marked the 20th anniversary of the UNESCO Slave Route Project. African museums, up and down Africa's west coast, where millions departed, are ripe with the mementos and artifacts depicting the slave era. In addition, I encountered numerous African tour guides, speak to their own histories, in referencing personal ancestors who participated in the slave trade and how, today, they are attempting to make amends. Those of African descent who continue to beat the drums of anger and despair, against those African ancestors who participated in slavery, are speaking from a lack of knowledge as to what is actually happening on the African continent today. And those who use Africans, who participated in the slave trade, as an excuse to deny Africa's connection to diaspora Vodou and African based spiritual systems, in general, are only doing so because they fear that, if examined by the tenants of African Vodun, the source of diaspora Vodou, they would be found grossly unfit!

There is always a spiritual component that undergirds positive things which occurs on earth. The Voduns are always engaged in the lives of its children. Matthew 18:18 "Truly I tell you, whatever you bind on earth will be bound in heaven, and whatever you loose on earth will be loosed in heaven." (NIV) While I believe that the good things are first loosed in the heavens (based on that which is spiritual) and, then, released on earth, this passage is enough that one may get my inference. In Africa, there are many tribes that participated in domestic slavery. My ancestors both the Dahomeans and the Ashanti did. Many, of these slaves were treated as family members. Therefore, today, descendants of such tribes serve the spirits of these departed domestic slaves as they served us. Mine are called the Tchamba Voduns. I do not know what they may be called in other societies; but, I know these are there.

What I am saying is this. Our history whether it is of the slave or the slave owner must be acknowledged and not forgotten. There are always lessons to be learned in human events. The Jewish Holocaust is another such traumatizing event. We have them throughout mankind's history. We, of African descent, are not alone. The Trans-Atlantic Slave Trade ushered in many dark things in our history. Horrible things that are still with us today in the construct of racism and all manner of prejudices. However, we must find a way to work through this pent-up pain and anger. To me the best way is to reach toward that which is divine. I am only human. I know, that as a woman raised in a racist south, I have been affected by it. For years I wore the Afros, I protested against the Ku Klux Klan, I threw the bricks; but, when I touched the soil of Africa....when I reconnected to the ancestors and began to communicate with the divine... I started to change. While doing research, once, I read an old text where an old Indian guru said something to the effect of, "Until we understand that instead of people who walk with spirits we are spirits who walk as people we will never know God". As a result, I've tried to teach, myself, not to look at the surface of what I can see, of a person, but to try and see the spirit of the individual beneath. And when I began to do this I saw beauty. It is time, my brethren, to make our peace with slavery and move quietly on.

TO WISH UPON A STAR

In African traditional spiritual systems, it is believed that for every person born...to every soul which exist on earth...there is a STAR. As one looks toward the heavens, on a clear and cloudless night, one sees the divine beauty of these stars. Some may appear brighter than others, while others grow dimmer as you watch, a few form magnificent constellations; and, if you are lucky one may even shoot across the majestic sky. If stars are thus, in this writing, a metaphor for people, then, to whom do we wish upon, or attach ourselves to, when our lives, or the world as we know it, becomes topsy turvy? We look around us, we search for that star, or person, who has the spiritual power to help us in our spiritual time of need. We may find our own personal star to be growing dim or has, somehow, lost it potency or brightness; so, we find ourselves attaching to another...one to whom we perceive will help us in the pursuit of the divine.

This is important because, today, many are pursuing the spiritual for profit! Many advertise..."Come to us! We will make you financially prosperous or give you that unattainable thing for which you desire. Come to us; and, we will give you power and fame untold." They, therefore, show you their homes or their "things" that you may witness their prosperity. I have even seen some, claiming the priesthood, that have websites showing mountains of cash and rolled up $100 bills. This is false advertising! Why? Because there is something called destiny. We were all born with a mission, of some type to be performed while on earth. We are, thus, born of spirits that come down, to earth with us, to assist us in fulfilling this mission. There is absolutely nothing wrong with wealth; but, wealth and fame may or may not be a part of one's destiny. Only authentic divination, as ordained by the spirits, can reveal what our missions actually are. In addition, these "things" that we may want, be it a man/woman that belongs to another or left us earlier, may not be what the ancestors desire for us. African spirituality is about finding out who and what we are in the spirit world and, then, pursuing and accomplishing that mission to which we have come to this earth to fulfill. One's mind, therefore, should be on the spiritual and not obsessed with the physical or the acquiring of "things". For as my grandfather used to say, "I ain't never seen no U-Haul trailing behind no hearse! You simply can't take it with you!"

So, look the stars over. Usually, those that shine brighter than others are pure in heart, are a servant of the spirits and mankind. They can not only take you to the divine; but, they serve as an example of obedience, to the tenants, of the spirits. While no human is perfect, they strive, daily, to be the best that they can be in order to help their fellow man. They have taken no shortcuts to initiation but hear the spirits in all things and allow them to be their light into the darkness. It is to these spiritual stars that one should attach themselves, these spiritual stars are particularly important because they find "favor" in the, eyes of the divine, and are, thus, showered with their love and spiritual blessings. They may appear humble, in means, but are rich in spirit. In such attachments, one will find good spiritual blessings falling upon themselves as well. So, do not be afraid, to make a wish upon a star; but, take the time to find that "right" star.

VODUN AND THE PEBBLE: THE ROAD TO THE AFRICAN PRIESTHOOD

When one stands upon the banks of a river reaches down and picks up a pebble then skips it across the water there is a ripple effect. That rippling gradually becomes larger and larger until it disappears and becomes one with the river itself.

So, it is when one in the diaspora begins to serve the ancestors and the divine spirits. As diasporans we often concentrate on the numbers of those we wish to help, or the numbers of those we have performed ceremonies for. Daily we mentally add to our talley and say, to ourselves, well done good and faithful servant. But this is not the only reason we have come. Metaphorically speaking our value, as the pebble, is not only in helping those that we can see, with the eye, but in serving those that we cannot see and what that service actually means to them. This is one of our spiritual challenges!

For me, one of the greatest quotes, of all times, comes from a conversation held between Cinque and John Quincy Adams, in the Greenhouse, from the movie La Amistad (1997). Cinque, and his compatriots were about to go to court in seeking their freedom to return to Africa. John Quincy Adams was their attorney and the following exchange took place between the two men:

> *John Adams: ...the test ahead of us is an exceptionally difficult one.*
>
> *Cinque: We won't be going in there alone...*
>
> *Adams: Indeed not, no, we will have right on our side, we will have righteousness at our side...*
>
> *Cinque: I meant my ancestors. I will call into the past, far into the beginning of time, and beg them to help me at the judgment. I will reach back and draw them into me. And they must come...for at this moment I am the whole reason they have existed at all.*

When I first heard these words, and each time I hear them anew, to my knees I fall. The poignancy of these words, "...for at this moment I am the whole reason they have existed at all" touches me to the core of my very soul! For as I think back, over the history of my people, I think of those who were captured by the slaver, mourn for the ones that died on the road to his ship, weep, in despair, over those who were thrown overboard to conserve on food in route to the diaspora, cry out for our mothers who were raped in the hull of those ships, mourn over the auction blocks, the whippings, the castrations, the ill treatment of all kinds. For the the blood of my ancestors is alive in me! And it is for them that I stand! It is for them that I serve, for them that I give nourishment, of the blood, that they might rest in peace. For every one that wandered in the woods, running to freedom, following the north star, for every one that was ever spit upon, for every one that was ever incarcerated unjustly or called the "N" word I stand. For within me they shall see victory! For within me they shall live! And each time I call upon their names, they will hear...for they are the only reason I have existed at all!

The road to the African priesthood is not an easy one. Serving the spirits, in whatever capacity, can often be difficult. Many think it is the road paved with money. Folks run all over trying to buy power, of all kinds, so as to make their fortune; but, that isn't vodun and that isn't the road. True vodun takes the road less traveled. It is a road with prickly bushes, seemingly unkempt, it is a road with potholes, steep inclines and narrow ledges. It is often dark and overgrown with thicket; but, it is a road that, with the help of the spirits, can be lit up brightly and transversed.

As the pebble hits the water the rippling grows...it encompasses not only what is seen but what is unseen until it becomes one with the river itself. In hindsight one might ask themselves...am I that pebble?

AFRICAN SPIRITUALITY AND THE BOOK OF LIFE

For those of you that are familiar with my writings you already know that I adored my grandfather. Grandpa was the apple of my eye! When he passed, on November 7, 2012 the day Barack Obama won his second bid for the American Presidency, I remember vividly some of the things that the spirits/voduns said about him. For one, they said that he was a man who had done many favors for and had helped many people; but, secondly, they were angry that he did not take the time to allow my father to truly know his relatives. As my father was an only child and my, divorced, grandfather traveled the road, a lot, he never took the time for that interconnection. He was too much a free spirit; and, as a result I have to hunt down these relatives, those still living, if I want to pass on the knowledge of their African ancestry. Daddy doesn't know them; and, neither do I; but, it is not so much WHAT they said, about my grandfather, that sticks with me, as it is the fact that they TOOK NOTICE. And, that's what I would like to draw your attention to today...the Book of Life!

In Christianity, the bible speaks of it; and, I am sure that there may be other traditional spiritual systems that reference it in some way as well. The bible starts out, early, by referencing it, against wrong doers, in Psalms 69:28 it says: " May they be blotted out of the book of life and not be listed with the righteous." (NIV) One also finds it referred to throughout the New Testament such as Books 1&2 of Thessalonians; Philippians 4:3 and extensively throughout the book of Revelations: 3:5; 13:8; 17:8 and 20:15. But, my favorite is Revelations 20:12 " And I saw the dead, great and small, standing before the throne, and books were opened. Another book was opened, which is the book of life. The dead were judged according to what they had done as recorded in the books." (NIV)

I have known of many of these bible verses since my childhood; but, now as a priestess, of vodun, they have been given credence. Numerous times my husband has returned, to me, discussing something the voduns have written in their book. And, if this is true, which I know it to be so...what does this say about how we conduct our daily lives? What does this say about those of us who may think we are doing something in the "dark" or hidden from others. What does it say about us and character, especially, if we are of the priesthood? What it says is that one's deeds and character IS important! It says that what we do in the "dark" will eventually see the light of exposure... be it on this earth or beyond. And, most of all, it means that there definitely is a judgement. It may not be exactly as the bible portrays; but, one will come. I learned early on, in vodun, when speaking with those who have passed over, through Ifa, that punishment is also there. Many have spoken of being punished for bad acts. It, of course, has not been punishment for all of eternity; but, it does exist on the other side. I assure you that it does!

It is such instances that also reinforce my understanding that inside of all of the world's spiritual systems are the hand of the spirits. And, when something goes wrong in these systems, it is not the hand of the spirits, rather, it is the hand of man.

My grandfather was many things to many people. To an ex-wife...

a philanderer, to girlfriends...a rascal, to a little girl... my hero, to his friends... a good guy who would do a favor, to the voduns...good enough to be written in "The Book of Life".... what about you?

VODUN AND ONE'S SPIRITUAL BIRTH

Well folks, if many of you are paying any attention to your notifications, lately, you may have discovered that I have a birthday on June 26th. 1955 happens to be the year...so, go ahead and click on your calculators or do your figuring in your heads, because, I've been here for a minute!

In the 1950s folks didn't believe in having children out of wedlock. So, when my grandmother discovered the pregnancy her teen aged only child was trying to hide by wearing a tight corset, she pulled together her father and her two brothers. Suffice it to say this company of men jumped into their vehicles; and, when my dapper grandfather answered his front door, was jacked up, him and his only son; and, a wedding party found themselves making swift tracks toward the South Carolina border. Grandpa was mortified, he once told me, never had a chance to put on a pair of his argyle socks, pick up his pearl handled walking stick, by the closet door, change into one of his fabulous suits or hats or even finish smoking his stogie. Those moonshine running hooligans, originally from Georgia, could not be reasoned with and was toting two double barreled shotguns. So, with a wedding in late April and my birth in late June, I made it, boldly, across the finish line of legitimacy...barely.

But, what I want to discuss, today, is not so much our physical or biological births but our spiritual births. For long before that wonderful miracle even happened... we existed. Many of the spirits that came down with us, during this process, were already extremely old. Some even existed before the world was formed. These divine beings came with us to help in the spiritual missions that we have agreed to before birth. Therefore, when we have a physical birthday, they do too; but, they are much older than our physical or biological years. So, as such, should be honored as well. In vodun, on our biological birthdays, we also celebrate by serving our spirits drinks and anything else that they may ask for as well.

Within us is a make up of ancestral spirits and what I term as "universal" spirits. These are the divine ones that breathe life into us. They are the creators of the universe and all it contains.

They are the Sakpata(s) and the Gu(s) and the Dattatreya(s) and the countless other pantheons of divine beings. They come from all cultures and originate from many different places. For instance, Dattatreya (called Den'su in Africa), my head spirit, originates from the Red Sea. This is the home of his birth. He once told me, "You date me, for you existed long before the world come!" I have, of course, felt exhausted every since... However, these great spirits, in their desire to find a way, to come will choose a particular ancestry and two people to make their journey to our physical world possible... thus the miracle of birth. And, as we mature, they put us on a track to discover them and our spiritual missions. As we get to know our spirits, after initiation, they will tell us their origins as well as their personal names. What is good to note here is this...we are not simply people who can physically walk and happen to have spirits, rather, we are spirits who have been born into bodies that allow them to physically walk.

DIVINE POWER

When I speak of power in vodun or in any of the world's traditional spiritual systems, I am speaking of the power directly related to and/or coming from that of the spirits. As we are the vessels, for the spirits, our power is only as great as our relationship with the spirits is strong!

In the diaspora, we think of spiritual power in terms of that which comes from the practitioner. But, it is not the priest or priestess with the power, rather, it is the relationship that he or she has with the divinities that gives them the power. As we are all born of the spirits; and, as we may be born with certain spiritual gifts...these gifts can only be fully activated and developed through the help of the spirits. Therefore, it is not mankind that we should thank, for this power, but the spirits themselves. For behind every truly spiritually powerful person lies the power of the divine.

I cannot help but emphasize this because, as human beings, it is our tendency to put ourselves, or mankind, on a pedestal when we should be giving the glory to the spirits. It happens in all the world's spiritual systems. In Islam, an Imam's words can become second only to Allah, or even replace Allah's, if he is popular enough, in the Hindu system a guru can be treated as a saint or god, in Christianity a preacher can be treated like a rock star with his words becoming the gospel instead of the bible itself; and, in Vodun a priest can be revered as to be all knowing. We are the vessels for the spirits, we are the servants of mankind, we are human with human frailties and faults of all kinds; but, it is the spirits, within us, that should be dictating and accomplishing the work. Yet, we must be the type of vessels that the spirits can actually dwell within. And this is where birthright and character comes into play.

In African Spirituality, in that we are brought forth with particular missions, not all of us are born to carry great spiritual powers. Depending on what that mission is not all in the priesthood are born to the same level of spiritual responsibility. I do not know how to explain it more clearly than this; but, the Africans know what I am talking about. In the spiritual world, there is a hierarchy and some births are rare. The work that some priests or priestesses do is so high end, or specialized, that it can literally take away from the life span of the person. These folks snatch people from the witches and bad spirits of all kinds. They travel in and out of the spirit world bargaining and dueling with dangerous spirits pulling back those that have, somehow, entered their hands or have been taken into their realm through the dark works of others. These people can be instructed, by the spirits, to travel great distances to do their work. These specialized individuals, as all others, are identified by Ifa; and, their spiritual authority, as to others in the priesthood, comes from the ancestors and divinities themselves. And, as such, are identified and known by all of the spirits... be they good or bad.

As an example, while in Africa, I had countless dreams. The spirits use dreams to communicate; and, in many instances help us to discover who we are. The following dream is one that I will always remember. I found myself at a large gathering. I noticed that those gathered, as me, were dressed in vodun cloths. As the people, there, were dressed like me and looked like me I assumed that we were all of the priesthood. Yet, when I looked into the eyes, of many, I noticed that they had no whites in their eyes. To my alarm their eyes were completely black! I overheard two people speaking under a tree. One said, "She is not like us!" I became afraid! And like I used to do, as a child, in fear...I tried to flap my arms and fly away. I actually escaped. I was very new, in the faith, at the time. I understood very little; so, I went to an elder priest, whom I respected; and, he asked the spirits. I had been called before the witches. They knew who I was and had allowed my escape (according to him, in most instances, people can die in their sleep) ...I was identified as a white witch; but, a young one, with little understanding of my power, at the time...they wanted me to know they were aware of me. As I have grown over the years they have not attempted to call me again, for it would, now, be at their own peril. I still must learn the art of negotiation with them; but, I have no problems with knowing how to fight! And, my voduns take no hostages!

Who we are and what we are, in the priesthood, comes from within! It does not come from the amount of books one may have read, on the subject, or how many youtube videos we have perused or who we know. It begins at birth...coming to this earth with a specific spiritual mission, having one's spirits (ancestors, head spirit, accompanying spirits etc.) and mission revealed by authentic African divination, obeying, if commanded, to enter the initiation chamber, training and daily obedience to the words of the spirits. There are simply no short cuts! One's daily dealings, with the spirits, allows one to be able to understand their true nature and develop who they are spiritually. One experiences a daily refining process, like a diamond in the rough, so as to be a more acceptable vessel as one matures.

VODUN'S THE FATHER, THE SON AND THE HOLY SPIRIT

The concept of "the father, the son and the holy spirit" is ancient. It is ancient because it came from the divine ones themselves and, therefore, predates anything in Christendom. It is the description that we, as the creations, of the divinities have with that which is "sacred" or the voduns. For we are the children of the spirits. It is they that created and gave us life. They are our fathers and mothers...the ancestors...and we are the "brides of" if married to the divinities. But all in all, this concept of "the father, son and the holy ghost or spirit" points directly to vodun and African spirituality in general.

That "holy ghost" or "spirit" is not just one but many. It is that head spirit and accompanying spirits which came down from the heavens or sacred places with us at birth. It is those spirits that are the lights unto our paths of life. They are our moral compasses as it were. They are the designated ones who came to help us fulfill our life's missions. And they are holy and divine in every respect. For they are Gods...those that created the universe and all it contains. I highlight this because often, in the diaspora, the Voduns have been reduced to mere emissaries for those who want to bind lovers or do trivial labor for a handful of pennies. Vodun has been reduced to good luck baths and potions and spells of all kinds. Because few have seen authentic African vodun, in its majesty, few have understood, until now, what vodun really is. It is not spells and potions. But it is a relationship that one has with the divinities themselves...those that actually created mankind, earth and all it contains. We are not referring to folks who once lived, died in revolutions, and are now in the spirit world. For these are ancestral spirits. We are talking about those divinities who CREATED the spiritual world itself.... the God and Gods of Vodun! Those with the power to create and/or destroy, punish and/or lift up. And, it is in the original African traditional spiritual systems that one sees their majesty and royalty... not the effected, by to the slave trade, versions.

In the Mina language, we can refer to a priest as Miator meaning "my father". Den'su, the great 3-headed spirit known in the Hindu spiritual system as Dattatreya, means "father of the river". The concept of the "father" is highly regarded in African spirituality. One's ancestry is first traced through the father. In African traditional society, the children belong to the father. If a wife wants to step, she can get to steppin' but leave the children! This trinity is not about Christianity but about spiritual life and our relationship within that spiritual life. And Africa, is at the root of all life be it spiritual or biological! Using myself as an example my spiritual life is thus: the father...Dattatreya (my head spirit); the son/daughter....me; the holy spirit(s)...Dattatreya and all of the accompanying spirits born to me or inherited or otherwise. Get it guys?

IN VODUN A CHANGE IS GONNA COME!

When I was a little girl my dad sat me on his knee and taught me a song! What he was doing was testing my voice. My father, during the "doo wop" years, had dreams of becoming a great singer. When my grandfather didn't insist that he worked the family business, to feed us, daddy ran around the country singing in up and coming "doo wop" groups...the frivolity of an only child! Daddy wanted to know if I had inherited his singing abilities which I more than had; so, the song "A Change Is Gonna Come" by Sam Cooke (1963) has a special meaning for me in connection to my dad. And, if I can keep from breaking down, will sing it, for him, as they're lowering his casket into the ground one day! That is if any of us can afford the expensive white tuxedo he wants to be buried in and the casket that will show his feet! The man is a ham! In any event, the song, itself, reminds me of the changes that are coming in vodun; and, in reality, are already here!

Let me be clear, though, vodun itself is not changing. It's tenant remain the same. The spirits are the same, yesterday, today and forever! It is how we view vodun and how we serve the voduns that will/is changing; and, this is targeted at us diasporans! I am a voice among many that are proving this reality! Diasporans are returning to Africa to train, they are reaching back to their ancestors, not just because of our insistence but because the ancestors are quietly awaking their children. Inside of them the ancestors are planting a thirst to know, to understand and to search. Because of 'choice' many may not make it to the finish line; but, it is happening! Black folks and others, to whom Africa was a far away place, are viewing Africa with a more approving eye, saying to themselves..."Maybe I SHOULD visit! Maybe I CAN find the ancestor!" Oh yes you can! No matter what race, creed or color you can! Go to a reputable diviner; and, Ifa will tell you! You do not need to serve someone else's ancestors, to have access to vodun, you can serve your own!

In 1994 UNESCO, and others, launched the Remember Slavery project in Ouidah, Benin. Dignitaries, from all over, were in attendance. Daagbo Hounon Houna stood on the beach and prayed. In that prayer, he spoke about the children of the slave returning home. And, indeed, we began to return in dribs and drabs; and, in February 1998, on that very same beach, Houna told me, after consulting with Ifa, "Your trip was planned!" And, in 1999, I became the first African initiated priestess of Mami Wata Dan from the African Diaspora. And quietly, but surely, we are still headed toward Africa, whether vacationing, simply to experience, or coming for ceremonies we are returning and, because of it, Vodun in the diaspora, will see a change.

People wonder, why this insistence on reaching bacK? Aren't the Hoodoo people, and the Haitian Vodou people doing just fine? Yes, they are; but, slavery is over! The physical restraints are anyway...

And it is the will of the ancestors and the divinities, themselves, that we reinstate vodun to its full glory! This is not a postulated theory, but, the active will of the divine! And whether folks like it or not it's happening. And the ancestors and the spirits are actively involved in this reinstatement. So, all you "bought in" folk and you "self styled experts" you can say what you wanna say, kick us off your Internet forums 'cause you don't like what we're saying; but, hear this! A change is gonna come, in vodun; and, you ain't gone be able to hold on forever. You either do the things right or let this avalanche roll over you because not one of us, born into it, is gonna wait for you! And one thing I know is this...your arms are too short to box with the African ancestors, the voduns and their divine will!

"The concept of African gods, Hindu gods, Greek, etc. belongin to a specific race or ethnic group is tired and dated. The Divinitie are Uni-versal and color-blind. I've crossed paths with blond haired, blue-eyed individuals carrying Sakpata, Heviosso or G (traditionally identified as African Gods) as their Patron deity. I'v witnessed Hanuman take possession of a Southern belle fron Kentucky, just long enough to greet the divinities that shadow me My spiritual mother is a strong African American woman from th deep south carrying a Big ol' fierce Dattatreya divinity on her head My spiritual father traces his priestly lineage back thousands of year from Benin to Egypt and beyond. The true divinity that rules you head will only reveal itself to a priest who is capable and qualified t call that divinity forth (and for good reason). Unfortunately; mos priest are incapable of either correctly divining or calling fort your true Patron deity/head spirit. Without the spiritual authorit to divine the truth, most seekers are denied the truth. "ignorance o ignorance, is the death of knowledge"

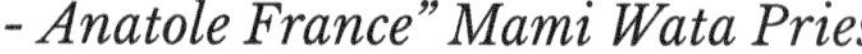

- Anatole France" Mami Wata Pries

CHAPTER 5

AFRICAN VODUN: INSTRUCTION

"Nothing in all the world is more dangerous than sincere ignorance and conscientious stupidity."

- Martin Luther King, Jr.

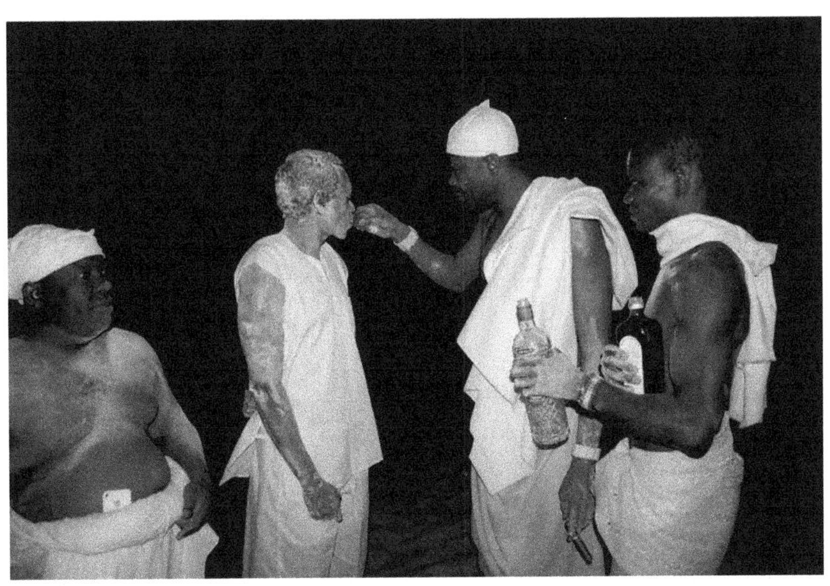

VODUN TIDBITS

1. The term "vodun" means "spirit" in the Fon language.
2. Vodun is a pre-colonial spiritual system (in actuality these are the spirits that created the universe); therefore, today's political borders do not apply as to where vodun is practiced. For instance, the Mina people live from southern Benin to Ghana; so, vodun is practiced, by them, in all three countries.
3. One cannot practice African traditional spiritual systems effectively without the ancestors. It is the ancestors that intercede with the divinities on our behalf. It is because of them that we are here. Many of our voduns (spirits) are inherited from them. One must know them by name (their tribe etc.). Ifa can tell you this.
4. Everyone, regardless of race, has an African ancestor. Ifa can reveal who it is.
5. We serve the spirits that gave us life not spirits that we do not know or they us.
6. To serve the voduns is a life of service, to mankind, not one where we serve ourselves.
7. The concept of "Nana", out of Ghana, has a spiritual underpinning. In some African families to be Nana one must be born of a particular spirit...Dattatreya called Den'su in Africa.
8. Everyone initiated into the priesthood, in Africa, has the spirit Fa; but, not every priest is an Ifa priest. Ifa is a separate priesthood.

9. People who die of unnatural deaths (shootings, animal maulings, disease, etc.) go to a different place than those who die of natural causes. It is called zogbe. One must do sacrifice that our loved ones, who go to Zogbe, are able to eat with the ancestors. Those in zogbe are always fed (given sacrifice) outside of the temple.

10. The Christian concept of the "cross" is rooted in traditional African spiritual systems. The cross came from "the crossroads" This is where a sacrifice is placed in the crossroads and one's ancestors are called from the north, south, east and west to come and feed.

VODUN TIDBITS 2

1. In African Vodun there is a Supreme Chief! He is called Daagbo Hounon. Daagbo means "ancestor" in the Fon language and Hounon means "priest of a sea spirit". This man's head spirit is the great Agwe. The throne of Vodun's Supreme Chief has been in this one family since the early 1600s. It is located in Ouidah, Benin; and, EVERYWHERE that Vodoun is practiced this man holds authority. I witnessed Houna call Priests as far as Ghana and beyond to question them on matters of vodun or settle disputes. He is, in essence, equivalent to the Pope in Catholicism. I spent three years in this temple with Daagbo Hounon Houna and was initiated into Agwe there. Hounna died in 2004. This man was known for his power! Anyone telling you that there is no Supreme Chief of Vodun, in Africa, does not know Vodun. And, anyone claiming to be initiated, into African vodun, while claiming such should cause a red flag to go up on their authenticity.

2. There will be a Supreme Chief of the African Diaspora at some point. The seat is ancient and has been vacant for centuries. It too originated out of Benin. The person was born in the diaspora yet ancestry is African. When the seat is officially taken it will be covered by African and international media.

3. In African vodun, when authentic initiations are done, they conclude with much ceremony and pomp. Dignitaries, in vodun, are always invited. This serves to bear witness to the event. Drummers are there to drum and dancing for the spirits abound. It is a festive time and feasts are prepared. Sacrifices are done. Blessings are given from elder priests and statesmen. On some occasions, the Ministry of Culture may be in attendance. This depends on the notoriety of the priest/priestess initiating the person. Many folks are visiting Africa and returning with staged photographs of them sitting on a seat, dressed in white, with a few Africans in the background. These are staged events...beware! For an African priest/priestess can be identified immediately in Africa. Their head is always covered, they wear certain beading, on the appropriate side and parts of the body that ONLY THEY wear and they carry the vodun staff. These small things help us to identify frauds. Frauds are not so easily identified here, in the diaspora, because many have never been to Africa and do not know. But in initiation ceremonial photos that one might post, look for the drummers, look for the vodunsi dancing, look for the dignitaries and the feast and the crowds in attendance. If these things are not present beware! Remember initiations, in Africa, are long and arduous. A person on vacation does not a priest or priestess make!

VODUN'S GROUND ZERO

If one were to think in mathematical terminology using the integer (whole and negative numbers) spread out across a number line the midpoint, on that line, would be zero. As one begins with zero and travels to the right, of that line, the values of our numbers increase and as we travel to the left the values of the numbers decrease. Those who are not aware or familiar with the world of the spirits are, in essence, always somewhere to the left of zero on that number line. However, if one's ancestors and the spirits that gave them life, through the manipulation of those spiritual gifts born to the person or by some other methods, are able to get them to the point where they began to inquire about them and go for authentic African divination, then, the person has arrived safely at ground zero. One's spiritual journey has truly just begun. And even then, the road can be bumpy!

I bring this up because, recently, a young woman approached me seeking someone to "work with". I had to gently explain that authentic African vodun does not work this way. When she first approached she was busy explaining her spiritual gifts...those things that she found that she could do in reference to the spiritual realm. So, in my confusion, I first thought she was seeking divination until she explained that she actually wanted to "work" with me. Even though I was flattered it tugged at my heart to have to refuse her, because, she was so genuine in her request. I believe that underneath it all she really wanted to learn and grow in the world of the spirits; so, I feel that I need to explain how one actually does come to work in authentic African vodun; and, I pray that she returns for divination one day. She seemed like a real sweetie pie! And, with my ole' crusty and flawed bedside manner, I can't afford to throw away sweetie pies....

As I have mentioned countless times it begins with authentic African divination...Ifa. By using Ifa we are able to determine your ancestry, the spirits that gave you life and whether you were born to serve the spirits or not and, if so, in what capacity. This information tells us who and what you are in the spirit world. And it is through the initiation process, if instructed by the spirits, that the spirits prepare you for whatever spiritual role you were born to. Diasporans mistakenly think that the initiation process is about you and the priest or priestess. It isn't! It is about you and the spirits. For it is there, in the initiation process, that the spirits "activate" those spiritual gifts that one may be born with to their fullest potentials. It simply does not happen without it. In addition, through divination, we can ascertain your ancestral history or whatever, physical or spiritual thrones that you are a direct descendant of. While we were taken into slavery those inherited rights are still there, in Africa, for us to claim if it can be proven the only way traditional Africans will accept...through authentic African divination.

So, once we discover who and what you are in the spiritual realm, we proceed from there. If you are not born of the Mami Wata pantheon, Behumbeza the great priest of Mami, will ask the voduns, through Ifa, to whom (because we are all ordained by them and they know us) or to what priest or priestess they want to perform your ceremonies. He then goes to that person where divination is again performed for verification, with the new person, and negotiations made, on your behalf, to perform your ceremonies if you choose to proceed. You then are turned over to the person to whom the voduns have commanded of us. However, if you choose, we are there with you every step of the way. Our purpose is to make sure that you are treated fairly, honestly and somebody isn't building a new house off your back! It is NEVER a good idea for a diasporan to approach the African priesthood on their own with no prior knowledge of the people. You could be ripped off big time! I have been there, done that; so, use my help. And that is the way one begins to associate with or "work with" authentic African vodun. You start off with your own spiritual needs being met, and then train under your spiritual parent in his/her temple until you establish your own if is your destiny to do so. But before that we all start at ground zero. One's spiritual gifts, prior to initiation, does not put one on the level of anyone in the African priesthood. It is a process developed by the spirits, themselves, with absolutely no short cuts!

PORK: WHY WE DO NOT EAT IT!

Pork: Why many do not eat it! As an African American I grew up eating pork. We called it "soul food"! But, now, it appears to be a contradiction in terms. Pigs feet, pig ears, pig tails, the head and chitterlings were all part of the diet... still is for many. We started eating it, in the slave era, because it was the scraps left over from the better parts of the pig. The "massa" got those better portions; and, we got that portion which was to be thrown away...the garbage. As slaves, we learned to cook it in such ways as to make it palatable. Today, it gives us high blood pressure and helps to keep us fat! All my life I have known it wasn't good for me; but, once I made it to Africa I learned the spiritual reason why.

Notice that many organized religions have some type of food restrictions; but, pork is #1 in many. It is considered unclean. Upon initiation into Mami Wata it is the first and foremost food restriction over all others. Why? Because the hog is the one animal that bad/evil spirits can and will dwell in. Once a hog/pig is killed and eaten these spirits can be unleashed, in the body, and cause havoc or battle with spirits that already dwell within the person. There are some voduns that can consume pork; but, the Mami Wata children can not! I would assume that this same spiritual reasoning underlines that of the Jews and Muslims as well. FYI for those interested. The TRUE food for the soul are the items contained in a fresh salads. The vegetarians actually have it right!

PRAYER TABLES

People often ask me about setting up prayer tables. In traditional African vodun, prayer tables are set up, by priests/priestesses, for those who have been initiated into vodun carrying a particular spirit(s) as identified by Ifa. These tables carry sacred objects, of the voduns, that enable the person to call these spirits forth. One acquires these objects during the initiation process; therefore, I am not sure how functional these tables would be for the average person. However, if one wants to honor, a spirit, I cannot advise against it. The key, in vodun, is to understand that divinities, are just that...DIVINE! They are creators of the universe itself. They cannot be called by, nor do they hear just, any "Joe Shmoe". Vodun adheres to a specific set of tenants. All IS NOT equal in vodun! One is born to particular spirits, as revealed by Ifa, and set on specific missions/destinies in this world, also revealed by Ifa, with a specific spiritual status: worker for vodun, vodunsi, priests/priestess, Ifa priests, etc., etc.

A favorite of many is the ancestral table/alter. Folks are really getting into wanting to remember their ancestors. This is great! Folks put up photos of love ones wanting to honor and remember them. But, let me say this! What the ancestors want most is to be fed! They need the "blood"...sacrifice! They want to work for you, smooth out your path and intercede, on your behalf, to the divinities themselves. You see they already on the other side...seeing all and hearing all. Give them the power they need through the "blood". And looka here folks! We ain't talking 'bout no chicken! Think on this a moment. An ancestor left Africa, in chains, 500 -700 years ago or more; and, you want to sacrifice a chicken? Somebody ain't ate in centuries? May he take 'dat chicken and slap you cross de' head! African ancestors chop big African bulls! Start with about 3 of 'em with the big humps in the back with long horns; and, the ancestor (daagbo) might bless ya! 'Til NEXT feeding time!

VODUN AND THE CONCEPT OF RESURRECTION

The other day I saw on my facebook news feed that the concept of resurrection was mentioned as coming from traditional Africa. This is true! As in the Christian cross (taken from the African crossroads) the concept of the death, burial and resurrection predates ALL organized religions. As part of the African initiation process, one, spiritually dies to self, is buried and then later raised up or "resurrected" into a new life. The old passes away and the new begins. Often this takes place as a deep sleep into the spiritual world where the spirits are in control of the person. This is where initiations can be dangerous in Africa. This is where one can either be taken, by the spirits, or released back into the physical world. It is an intricate balance between life and death!

This serious element about initiation is often not understood in the diaspora. Too many 'cookie cutter' initiations are performed by untrained and unskilled individuals simply out to make a buck. They do more damage to the person's spiritual lives than good. The tell-tale signs are when someone, just initiated, comes to the internet or goes to others to try and learn what their priests or priestess could not, or claims not to have time, to teach them. I ask, "If this person does not have the knowledge to train you in what they initiated you into, then, WHERE did they get the knowledge to even initiate you in the first place?" What one knows of one's spirits are supposed to be taught INSIDE the initiation chamber with years of "on the job training" after. It is where you learn the songs, the dances, the colors; and, if told you are a priest or priestess, taught to feed and care for one's voduns. And, if it is revealed that the person is an Ifa priest, then 16 initial days of Ifa training is done, by an Ifa priest, to be continued by him later. Initiation is not about the person initiating you but about YOU and the SPIRITS! Initiation is where the spirits, themselves, prepare the person for one's priesthood in order that one may complete one's spiritual mission. It is the place where those spiritual gifts, that one was born with, are fully activated. And, it is a place where one's heart and soul is judged or examined by the spirits. One can survive this initiation or not! But getting back to the concept of "resurrection" if one searches youtube there are several videos that give example of such resurrections during the vodun initiation process. One of my favorites is of a young girl during her initiation into Sakpata, in Benin, West Africa, where the concept of the burial and resurrection is clearly seen.

WHAT INITIATION IS ABOUT

Here is a post I put up on the internet in response to what someone said on the issue of initiation. Recently, to my dismay, there has been folks offering 3-day initiations....

One responder said, " To get an initiation is to establish a connection with the initiator, and to accept them as your godparent means that you agree to be guided by them in spiritual matters."

This isn't what initiation is about. In traditional African spiritual systems...The INITIATION process is not about you and the initiator; but, rather, it is about YOU and the SPIRITS. In the normal course of life there is a separation between that which is physical and that which is spiritual. When Ifa determines that someone is to be initiated into either the priesthood or as a vodunsi (worker/horse etc.), for the voduns, one enters a sacred place where the voduns/orisha/lwa prepares the person for his/her sacred duties. That wall that separates one from the spiritual becomes more pliable or shattered that the spirits become more accessible to the person and the person to them. One puts themselves in the hands of the spirits as one might say. It is in this special sacred place/chamber that the spirits activate more fully those spiritual gifts that one was born with. In addition, it is a place where new spiritual gifts may be given. The initiation chamber also becomes a place of learning or school. One learns the colors, the songs, the dances and the habits and ways of one's spirits. One learns how to care for one's voduns and how to serve them properly. One, if deemed to be a priest of Ifa, spends at least 16 days learning the initial rudiments of Ifa to be taken up later in a more intensive and lifelong training. In other words, the initiation chamber is a serious matter. In Africa people have died during the initiation process. If done correctly the initiation process is often long and arduous. Not to say one doesn't learn something from one's initiator; but, it is by no means the reason for initiation. Most of this has been lost...it appears...in the diaspora. Yet, it would certainly explain why many folks who THINK they got something, while initiating in the diaspora.... DON'T!

SAKPATA: THE CHEETAH

In vodun many of our spirits are seen in their animal form. For those of the Mami-Dan pantheon of vodun, for instance, these spirits are often seen by, their children, as serpents (snakes). In an earlier post, I told the story of the "Bagged Serpent" a dream, I had, depicting the spirit living within me and its message. But often living in one of the oldest, fastest, most agile jungle cats, in the world...the cheetah, is the great spirit named Sakpata.

Sakpata's domain is everything that is under ones feet...that portion of the world that is covered by land. We are all born with a Sakpata spirit. It is Ifa who will tell us which one, out of the pantheons of Sakpata spirits, we have. There are two different pantheons of Sakpata. One is fed with corn meal and palm oil and various sacrifices such as goat and chickens while the other is part of the Mami pantheon. This Sakpata takes white flour, and a clear oil and goat with a particular type of chicken. There is a separation between the physical world and the spiritual world. It is Sakpata that commands Legba to take the key and open the door that the spirits may come down and spend time with us. This information has been lost, to diasporans, because of the slave trade.

Sakpata is often called by many names in different cultures. Ganesha is the Hindu Sakpata. I suspect Ghede is the Haitian Sakpata; but, I must consult with him to be sure. What leads me to suspect this is the description of this Haitian spirit; and, the fact that when my husband called, this spirit, he answered and told us he was being fed incorrectly. Sakpata drinks something called sodabee in Africa. It is a clear drink made of palm wine. The closest I've come to it, in the States, is corn liquor. It's clear and strong. Africa's sodabee will blow your head off! Sakpata loves it! The other spirits call him the sodabee man!

Sakpata is a trickster! He enters the ceremony telling jokes and making fun of folks. He will often insult you if needed. He has little tolerance for people pretending to be something they are not. He will often show up as a beggar just to see if you will give him something. In Africa if one sees a man looking as though he is on hard times, dirty, smelly, rags for clothes and begging...we fall all over ourselves trying to give money. Often times it is Sakpata coming to test you. Sakpata can be deadly. He can cause disease; but, he also is a great healer. Many of the Sakpata priests are known for their great healing abilities. These priests are often prosperous as well. In fact, all of the voduns are rich. But whether they give their riches to you, or not, is up to that particular spirit coupled with your destiny.

The king of the Sakpatas is called DaZodji. This is my Sakpata; and, he is within the pantheon of Mami. He is referred to as Da Da Zodji. This means King King Zodji. As with ALL spirits each one has a personal name. It is after the initiation process that one will reveal his or her name to you. But, one of the most important things that one needs to know about the great Sakpata is that he is the one that commands Papa Legba to unlock the door that the spirits of the deceased can pass back into the spirit realm. It is from the ancestors that we come and it is to the ancestors that we hope to return.

AFRICAN VODUN AND COSTS

Folks often ask me what is the costs of initiations, in Africa; and, I always answer, “I do not know.” or “It is difficult to know.” Why? Because diasporans do not understand that voduns (spirits) are as different as we are people. No two spirits are alike! Two people may have the same spirit and much, in each initiation, is the same; but, each individual spirit may ask for something a bit different from the other. This knowledge has been lost in these “cookie cutter” initiations that are designed to elicit money instead of helping the person.

In Africa, most folks can tell you where their ancestral village is or at least where they came from. Some old papa, in the village, has been giving sacrifices, in these villages, even if the city dweller has not. While everyone has to give sacrifice to the ancestors, during initiation, it is often less involved for an African than a diasporan. Finding the ancestor for us, after centuries of disconnection takes time, effort and often expensive sacrifice. After 400-700 years in the diaspora our ancestors are not interested in chickens. They want strong African bulls...several of them...and they can be expensive! You think things are tough in the United States? Try living in Africa! Things are even tougher and the animals more expensive. So, after feeding ones ancestors you start in on initiating into one's own spirits.

Depending on what your head spirit is, and one's accompanying spirits, this too can be a long, arduous and expensive. Again, it is because of the sacrificial animals and whatever one's spirits require. In Africa, the initiation process can take months to years. And, at each juncture, the spirit, through Ifa, is consulted. If it is a family temple the priest simply gives you a list of things to buy, you go do it, return and he performs the initiation for you. If money is low you purchase your items a little at a time and return. He is a family priests so you dash (give whatever you can afford) him at the end. In the diaspora, the slaves could not be away, or isolated, for long periods of time because they had to be in the fields or wherever they were assigned. If a spirit jumped on somebody's head, or tried to, folks assumed this be a child for the spirits. Problem is it isn't always the head spirit that's a jumpin'. We have many spirits. But they initiated them just the same and, due to slavery, the initiations had to be shortened. A lot of the preliminary work was cut out. This isn't the case in Africa. You need time and money! For my most recent spiritual child, to be initiated, we have been preparing for over five and a years. My husband has had to travel to three different countries and still has one more to go, at the direction of the child's spirits, collecting things from his ancestral villages, sacred places, rivers, oceans etc. that when he enters the initiation chamber all will be in place. This Haitian born young man's head spirit is Lord Rama; therefore, he is Mami-Dan. Authentic African initiations take time, planning and money. Africans often take years to complete all that they need to in vodun. It is a life learning process not a two-week process. After eight years in African initiation chambers, and sixteen years in and out of Africa, I still have much more to go, more spirits, more training, more commitment and sacrifice. That is the way of African traditional spiritual systems as they exist in the motherland.

So, again, how much are initiations in Africa? Hard to tell. I suggest, if you are serious then first obtain an authentic African divination finding out your ancestry and your spirits. See first if you are one of those bound for the priesthood or vodun, in general, because everyone isn't! Save your pennies and put away some time... and go for it!

AFRICAN VODUN AND COSTS 2

Another factor in costs, for African vodun ceremonies/initiations etc., is to whom one chooses as their priest(ess). Several folks have headed toward Africa and gotten ripped off! One must do a bit of research and find out more about who is who before taking such a long journey. I remember a gentleman, out of London, asking me questions about a certain family of African priests. I attempted to caution the gentleman; but, he wouldn't listen. Get's to Africa, finds out he has been scammed so attempts to contact Behumbeza. Behumbeza, a priest listed as a 'national treasure' in Benin, had traveled and was busy...couldn't see the man. The gentleman was extremely angry! We had offered to help him earlier; but, the man was bent on doing his own thing and traveled back to London in a huff!

Africans can be dishonest too! They can gladly take your crisp euros or American dollars and give you absolutely NOTHING! Do some research! Go to Ifa if you have to. Know who you are dealing with and their reputation. In Benin, the Ministry of Culture can help you if you need it. Reputable priests are known to them. Reputable priests are known throughout the vodun community; so, ask around or take benefit from those of us who have been there. Also, be leery of someone taking your monies, while on a two-week or one-month vacation, and then telling you that you have been initiated into something. Traditional vodun doesn't work like that. The most you've gotten is started. These brothers screaming, they in the Akan tradition don't even have a clue that these traditions are steeped in traditional culture and vodun. Most kingships are held because a person is carrying a particular spirit that is inherited from the king before him. It is the spirits themselves, through divination, that put that person on a throne. It is from birthright that he/she is there. Not because they paid somebody! One might buy a kingship; but, it certainly doesn't make you a king! You may pull the wool over eyes, here in the States; but, the Africans are laughing...all the way to the bank! So, ok Mami, what can we do then? Is vodun only for the rich? For goodness sake NO!

Plenty folks struggling, in Africa, and they STILL do vodun. As I have said it takes a bit of time and commitment like it does them. Save what you can; but, if you have time this might help. Plenty of folks come to the temple, after divination of course, (we need to know that you belong there) and work. They not only learn about the temple and train; but, when a more prosperous person shows up, needing the same ceremonies as them, we give them a list of sacrificial animals, to buy, for their own spirits and include them in the ceremonies. They work it off! There are many ways that a priest can help you get this done. It may take a while; but, it can be done. That is why many of us visit Africa so regularly. We come home, make some money and go back! Where there is a will there is a way! The initial divination is so important for this. We find your ancestry and spirits; and, in feeding them, through the blood of the sacrifices, give them the strength to help you complete what it is that you need in vodun. That really IS the secret in vodun... feeding your ancestors and the spirits that breathed life into you. For with the ancestors, at your front, and the spirits, at your back, there is NOTHING that you will not be able to accomplish if it is their will.

I'm not telling you that life, in vodun, is smooth sailing 'cause many times it isn't. The voduns will mold you and change you like a diamond in the rough. For a true servant, of the spirits, it is often the road less traveled. It can be rocky and difficult. It is a divine calling; but, like anything else you do have choice. You can choose it or refuse it! But if you choose it make sure you understand that it has its costs. These priests, nor their spirits, work for free. Priests must eat and so must their spirits. Sacrificial animals do cost. One must pay for the work. But, what you pay is between you, the priest and the spirits.

AFRICAN VODUN AND COSTS 3

Often times to cut costs of initiations, in Africa even further, initiates will enter the temple in groups. Often, he Mami Wata enter initiation in groups. However, for each, divination is done to consult with that person's spirits. One of the ceremonies, for Mami, involves initiates going through the market places. They are taken out as a group. These men and women are always beautifully adorned. This is the African Mami. The priestess initiating these initiates is always at the front leading them through the market places with vodunsi flanking their sides so as they are not touched, inadvertently, by onlookers. Those wearing cloth draped across their left shoulders are of the priesthood. The left side is our vodun side. Others not so adorned are vodunsi. After the initial 3-4 months, in the initiation chamber (or however long the spirit commands), they will continue by doing the initiation ceremonies for the priesthood. At that time, their heads will be covered not to ever be unveiled again in public. They will also receive the staff, stool, pearls (jewels of the priesthood) worn around the neck, arms, wrists and left ankle. But, this is just the beginning. As more spirits come (those inherited etc.) more ceremonies are done; and, so it continues. All is taught to you, while n the initiation chamber. Everything one needs to know, about one's pirits, is taught in the initiation chamber, the dances, the songs, the colors, the prayers, how to take care of your voduns (spirits) if one s in the priesthood etc. It is a time of learning and communication, with the voduns, so as to prepare you for your spiritual work.

HEAD WASHINGS AND GOOD LUCK BATHS IN VODUN

In the diaspora, I see and hear of many, diasporan initiated folk, promoting head washings, good luck baths and all types of quick ceremonies or remedies for various spiritual ailments. The Haitians do good luck bath. I do not know if they are promoted in other Afro-based spiritual systems, in the diaspora, as well. I'm sure they might be; but, do they work? That's the million-dollar question!

The original traditional African head washings and purification baths do have a specific function. If the spirits have been causing a person great despair usually a washing of the head, after appropriate sacrifices, pushes the offending spirits at bay and offers a promise to the spirits that they will eventually, at a later date, initiate or respond in some particular way to that to which the spirit is commanding. The spirit usually agrees to this after consultation and divination. If the person takes too long to make good on their promise the spirit may began their harassment, of the person, all over again. These head washings include sacrificial blood from an appropriate animal (food of the spirit involved) poured over the head, rubbed in with other foods or items for that spirit, various prayers said, a washing down with herbs and soaps, water from the sea (if you are Mami) or sacred waters from the temple and an ending with a rub down with perfumes and powders. In any event it is a pact or contract between you and the spirits. Purification baths have a similar function in that they purify you spiritually that the spirits may dwell, in your presence, and work on helping you have a more fulfilling life. In BOTH instances sacrifice is an integral part and must be performed by ordained priests or priestesses...those to whom the spirits recognize.

What I have observed in the diaspora, from various forums, is folks coming out of these 'cookie cutter' initiations and setting up shop with limited to no training and promoting these baths as a means to make money. These are some of the same folks who get on the internet and ask for help on serving the very spirit(s) they are supposed to have been initiated into. Sacrifices may or may not be involved and many of them appear to be giving nothing but expensive herbal shampoos. It's as if the idea of a spiritual bath, itself, is to give the luck and prosperity. And, to some, whatever problem you may have this "spiritual bath" is supposed to get rid of it! But, with these folk it really doesn't! And, unless it has the components mentioned above it won't!

In African vodun these baths have their place and are there for specific reasons. But NOTHING takes the place of feeding your ancestors and the spirits that gave you life! For without that everything else becomes just a band-aid.

HOW AFRICAN TEMPLES ARE NAMED

How African temples are named: When one sees an African temple one often sees many spirits depicted on its walls. These spirits are not painted there simply by chance. They are depicting the spirits that the priest(ess), of that temple, were born to. In addition, there may be spirits, inside the temple, that one has inherited from deceased relatives. Since one's spirits tend to be passed down from generation to generation a family clan usually houses all of its spirits in the family temple. The main spirit, in that temple, is the head spirit of the priest or priestess who founded the temple. And that spirit has a 'personal name'. In African vodun when one is initiated into one's head spirit, or any of one's spirits for that matter, the voduns reveal, to you, their 'personal names'. African temples, therefore, carry the personal name of the dominant or head spirit in that temple. I am not sure if this applies to every single temple in Africa; but, it generally does for us Mami Wata priests/priestesses. Temple BEHUMBEZA, therefore, (the temple to which I am a part) carries the personal name of my husband's spirit...Dattatreya (Den'su) in Africa. There are 2 such temples (Cotonou) Benin. Behumbeza was the name of his mother's Dattatreya; and, upon her death he inherited her throne or spiritual chair. So, we have her temple and our own.

Now it is HE that is Behumbeza. Behumbeza has been deemed a NATIONAL TREASURE by the government of Benin. Temple Behumbeza is one of the largest Mami Wata temples on the West Africa if not the largest with vodunsi from all over the globe. I will attach a photo of our temple below:

WHO ARE THE TCHAMBA VODUNS?

Some, in the diaspora, have assumed that the tchamba vodouns are comprised of slaves from the trans-Atlantic slave trade. However, this is incorrect. The tchamba vodouns are indeed ancestral; but, they pre-date the trans-Atlantic slave trade. As I have stated, in earlier writings, there were (and still are) many large tribes, in Africa, that used slaves. These were often persons taken in battles, from other tribes, purchases or those who came, to the tribe, by other means. These were Africans owning and serving Africans...domestic slaves! And, in many cases, they were treated as family and took on the customs and ancestry of their enslavers. The Ashanti tribe, of Ghana, was one such tribe. The Dahomeans (Fon) were another. I specifically speak of the Ashanti because it is through this ancestry that my own tchamba voduns have come. In that these slaves faithfully served my ancestors...I now serve them. When Ifa reveals one's ancestry, Ifa or the spirits, themselves, will reveal if one's ancestors had slaves and if one thus serves the tchamba vodouns. When one wants to know WHO and WHAT they are the spirit world, one simply needs to go to Ifa.

THE TASSINON

In African temples, there are many spiritual positions or seats within a temple. In ALL of them a person is born (meaning that the Fa reveals it) to their specific seat. A little-known position, in the temple, is the position of "TASSINON". It is a high position in the temple and usually held by a woman. Tassinon is "the woman of prayer". When folks come into the temple and ask for prayers, and the priest/priestess, isn't available, or if he/she is, the Tassinon will/can pray for the person. This woman is born to this high seat in vodun. The Tassinon has a unique relationship with the spirits...for the spirits stand at her side to listen. Upon her death, great honor is bestowed and ceremonies are performed. Just another Vodun tidbit.

DEPARTED LOVED ONES

In the fall/winter of the year we often think of our departed loved ones for many reasons, holidays is the most noted reason; but, in actuality, this is the time of year that our departed one's do come out to feast. The concepts of "All Soul's Day"; "The Commemoration of All the Faithful Departed"; the "Feast of All Souls" or the "Day of the Dead" is actually based in spiritual fact. The voduns usually give us the exact date (anywhere from Oct. 31 - Nov. 3rd) and we set out goodies for our departed love ones to partake upon. They then show up in our homes or designated places for their own feast. The Haitians do something this time of year also. I'm sure there may be similar celebrations throughout the diaspora in various other cultures as well.

IN THE HANDS OF THE SPIRITS

As Americans or Europeans many of us have compartmental lives. We reserve a portion for work, a separate portion for our love lives, a bigger portion for home and loved ones and a small portion for our friends. And then, when all is said and done, we take an even smaller portion and head to church on Sunday. If we are a more devout person, maybe, we squeeze in a Bible study, on Wednesday night, some Church choir practice or volunteer in some way. The totality of these compartments designs our week and our lives. But when one lives in the hands of the spirits it is not us that determines our lives, but, the very spirits themselves. So, what does this really mean? And what does this look like?

While living in NYC I met some wonderful people, from the Benin Consulate, that were teaching me Fongbe. One day the two young ladies had a visitor while I was there. They explained, to the gentleman, my desire to go to Benin and be initiated into Mami Wata. He gently put his beverage down, on the table, and addressed me. He said that this endeavor, this thing with Mami Wata, was not to be taken lightly. He explained that it was a serious commitment not to be toyed with; so, choose my steps very carefully. At the time, I politely listened but had no idea of the gravity of his words.

Of the eight years in and out of initiation chambers, in Africa, my voduns sat in temples and I would go feed them and, with help, perform the ceremonies they requested. But one day about a year and a half, before my departure, in 2006, they requested to come live with me. I brought them. In a huge home by the sea and I set them up. My life has NEVER been the same since! Their desire was to reveal themselves to me. And they began to walk, to talk, to take me on trips in the night, walk in my bedroom when they so chose, scare me to death by seeing them, as I took showers, knock on doors, wake me up if I slept too late, eat up all the fruit in the house; and, I can go on and on. I was in THEIR hands and they wanted me to know it.

Spirits are active and alive! They can and will make themselves known to whom they have ordained. Through divination they reveal your spiritual mission and through communications, with them, plot out your path in order to complete that mission. Controlling portions of your life is a means of helping one complete this mission. As a result, whom you choose as mate becomes important to them. If you choose wrong it could affect the course of your mission.

Therefore, one who has put themselves in the hands of the spirits must realize that the spiritual mission takes precedence over all else. This may result in the spirits telling you who to marry, where to live and generally...be all up into your personal business! This is what it means to be in THEIR hands. So, as the gentleman told me, as I visited those two young ladies in NYC, pursuing the spirits is a serious matter. It may be your destiny...only Ifa can determine this! But, if you choose to go forward understand that your life may never be the same!

THE SPIRITS: HOW DOES ONE CONNECT?

Many of you are beginning to turn your hearts and ears to the calling of your ancestors and the divine spirits living within you. It is a long way from hearing of the spirits to actually serving them and even longer to know them. One usually wants to know just where do I begin? Here are a few practical instructions that might help the beginner or even those who would like a deeper relationship with those spirits that lay within them.

Step 1. Because African traditional spiritual systems come out of a particular cultural context reading about African traditional culture, in general, is a great place to start. One can go, to the nearest library, and do some research or access online research libraries to see what is available. One can also check online book selling sites and peruse published authors on the subject. I would choose a great many of my books by Africans because it is THEY who can tell you best about the culture in which they live. Step 2. If one wants to know one's spiritual path authentic African divination is a necessity. This is Ifa/Fa/Afa the West African Divination System. In authentic African divination, one's ancestry can be found, one's head spirits and accompanying spirits can be called forth, any presenting problems are revealed and remedies and/or sacrifices are prescribed. The divination process tells you WHO and WHAT you are in the spirit world.

Step 3. I would begin to prepare my mind and body for prayer to beseech the spirits to aid me in my goal. Remember that there are spirits living within you. They are privy to your every thought and conversation that you have; so, when you pray they will hear you. However, one must be in the right frame of mind and body to get the maximum effect. Eat fruits, salads and drink fresh water... these are the foods that nourishes the soul. Abstain from sex and alcohol during extensive bouts of prayer! It allows the spirits to dwell more effectively with you. Get up, brush your teeth, freshen your mouth, wash your body and let your FIRST words of the day...before speaking to anyone or anything else...go to the spirits in prayer. You may use incense and white candles which will serve to attract the spirits that they are there to hear your prayers. Remember the old Bible adage, "You have not because you ask not!" Speak from your heart and formalize your thoughts clearly and humbly make your request. From there one puts the request in the hands of the ancestors and the spirits to clear obstacles and open doors...you are on your way!

HOW DO I PROTECT MYSELF FROM FOLKS SENDING ME JUJU?

How do I protect myself from folks sending me bad spirits/ juju? The greatest protection one has from juju is that which lives within us. It is your FIRST line of defense! If one is feeding one's ancestors on a regular basis and caring for those spirits that gave us life, it is THEY that will be flanking our fronts and our backs! In Africa protecting one's self from one's enemies is often very necessary. The concept of Envy in societies that have less access to economic resources can lead folks to do things out of desperation. And, with more people entering African traditional spiritual systems in the west, protection against one's enemies is becoming more needed here as well. But what if I'm new to the game and feeding nobody at the moment; but, I still feel somebody is sending me something?

Well your first course of action is to go to the Bokono or Babalawo and find out for sure what is going on. Ifa will reveal if anything has been attempted against you and tell you what to do to counter the effects. Don't jump on the internet and think that everyday folk are gonna be able to diagnose your spiritual problem. They might have their suspicions or even ideas based on experience. However, only Ifa can tell you for sure! These traditional spiritual sites are filled with people posting and wanting to get instant redress for their problems. Go to Ifa. If it is a spiritual matter, then, it is he that can help you!

And one final note! This is something I learned while in Africa. A person may go and sell you to a vodun to cause you damage; but, if you are not guilty and your heart is pure...the vodun, itself, will refuse to strike! That is of the divinities. The dead* can always be bought; so, be careful out there!

VODUN AND THE FAMILY

Many have asked me if my family members serve the spirits also; sadly, I have to give an emphatic no! African Vodun families are notorious! My husband comes from a long line of traditional practitioners; and, even in my ancestral line, Agassou, the priesthood has been our primary vocation for centuries. But we, in the diaspora, are often not as fortunate.

**The dead referred to here are spirits not being cared for by family members etc., who roam outside of the temple and will work for needed sacrifices or whatever bargained for. These are often dark spirits.*

African Americans and Westerners, in general, are very connected to the church. Many of us come from deep church roots; therefore, it might not be so easy for our loved ones to embrace this new sense of spirituality. I made this mistake when I first returned from Africa. My family members were excited to see me after eight years abroad; but, as the newness wore off they reverted back into their old ways and old prejudices.

My father, who in all of my 59 and a half years, I've only seen walk into a church once and that was at his mother's funeral, told me he believed in Jesus Christ. My baby sister, the great evangelist, that says she doesn't need to sit in church every Sunday but can worship at the feet of the Television Evangelist while cooking, says I am worshiping the devil. My baby brother refuses to visit me in the night at the advice of his girlfriend for fear of spirits walking; and, I don't even want to begin with that other sister...the gay one that sits in church more than all the others... nieces, nephews and aunts all put together. Suffice it to say I ain't that popular unless somebody broke! That's the deal with most struggling African American families. The only family members cool with it are those who are already on the other side. So, do not be surprised if you've got to make this journey alone. Your support will be your spiritual parents and your spiritual brothers and sisters.

We are always eager to share our new experiences with our loved one. But, with this journey, I would simply make my inquires quietly and learn as much as I can, from those who have been there, until I could stand on my own two feet. Loved ones want to protect us. And in their minds, they do not want us compromising our very souls even though they might not understand that is exactly the opposite of our intentions. In such instances vodun websites that are balanced, informative and fair can be helpful. For those of you searching I wish you the greatest of luck! The road isn't often easy. You wake up one morning and all of a sudden there comes a deep yearning from inside...a yearning to reconnect to the ancestors, a yearning to feel nd communicate with the divine. You are not alone...we are here!

AUNT JINX

Growing up, as most Black folks, I had much extended family; but, one member I always remember, fondly, is my aunt Jinx. Aunt Jinx was actually an older woman and advisor for my mother. I had a young mother and when her mother was not around aunt Jinx was it! I'll never forget the time she showed up at my school. I had been talking back to the teacher for a while that day. Don't know what bee had gotten into my bonnet; but, the teacher had threatened that she would call my mama. Well, hey, I said in a huff, "You can't call my mama 'cause we ain't got no phone and my mama is watching the stories" about now!" The teacher quietly left the room. By the time class was over and I was standing by my locker I noticed all of my friends looking at me wide eyed. As I turned around there stood aunt Jinx...pink sponge rollers in her head, about a million feet tall, black as an ace of spades size, 11 "men feet" crunched in some yellow flip flops, wearing flowered pants with a striped shirt and nothing matching. I had forgotten that mama had given the school her number in case of emergencies. But all I could see was that braided switch in her hand; and, I started running... And some of my turn coat friends caught me! They were just as terrified as I was! But it was a whipping that stopped any further back talk to a teacher for my many years in anybody's school.

I bring up my aunt Jinx because as a young girl I was ashamed of her. Aunt Jinx was a survivor and lived during a time when times were hard for Black folks. She ran a "liquor house", served home cooked food and hosted card games to make ends meet. She was a war torn woman who could fight like a man with healed cuts up and down her arms and was formidable to anyone who wanted to tear up her place of business. She had no formal education; but, my mother adored her. I remember her saying to me once when she thought that I might be getting old enough to have a boyfriend, "Gal, you need to get yourself out there and get you some of 'dem birth con' stone pills. Don't be bringin' no babies up in here!" That was my beloved aunt Jinx...

While very much a real character in my life, my aunt Jinx also serves as a metaphor for those individuals, in our lives, that we are the most ashamed of...that uneducated relative who could embarrass us in the most unlikely of times or places, that uncouth friend to whom we would not dare introduce to our work associates or that brother or sister that we wouldn't claim in front of our friends. And even more sadly, that handicapped or mentally ill one, in the family that we do not know how to explain. These people are precious in the sight of the spirits. They have been placed in our lives for a reason. They may not meet the standards of our own misguided morality or rational; but, they have a place and a purpose.

And especially for those who are handicapped or mentally challenged. In the world of the spirits they represent the vodun Tohoussou. Taking care of these loved ones is where we see our blessings; and, loving those less fortunate among our kinfolks is an opportunity where we can build our integrity and fortitude. So, hang in there with the aunt Jinxes in our immediate families and of the world. For they have much to contribute to who we are.

WHAT HAPPENS IF I IGNORE THE CALL OF THE SPIRITS?

In traditional African vodun, it is Ifa that tells us WHO and WHAT we are in the spirit world. In other traditions one may become possessed, out of the blue, or have the gift of sight and/or predict things before they even happen. Some may possess skills that no other child, in the family, has...a penchant for the spiritual, a tendency to understand things beyond one's physical sphere of existence. These are the chosen ones, these are the sons and daughters born, in each family, that if living in Africa would be serving the spirits! Every family has them! So, what do we do?

In the western world, these are the people who become our Preachers, Physicians, Imams, Gurus, Shamans, Psychologists and healers, of all kinds, who put themselves to work ministering to the spiritual, emotional and physical needs of many. But those traveling the more traditional paths must answer the call yeah or nay. They must accept or refuse; and, if they refuse understand it's consequences.

In more traditional societies, like Africa or Haiti, the spirits will trouble your life tremendously! I have seen people struck down with illness, their economic life in shambles and doors to opportunities shut firmly in their faces. Where they had money, it disappeared. Where they had fabulous possessions they lost them, women who yearn for children cannot produce them, those searching for loving mates become pariahs. Life begins to suck big time! In the diaspora, where many African Americans are already struggling life seems not to give us a break. Hopelessness begins to filter in. Many of our extremely talented and gifted turn to self-medication and strong drink. Those at the bottom stay at the bottom; sometimes, reaching out for answers that the church simply can't give. So, we go to Ifa or some type of diviner or traditional spiritual person. They tell us that we are a child of the spirits and offer us some temporary relief with sacrifices or a head washing to open our pathways...for a moment anyway. So, for a while, we are cool. These temporary reliefs are a promise, to the spirits, that one day we will serve. But if we take too long, or continue to ignore the call our troubles simply start all over again!

Yet, this could be just the start of it! Diasporans tend be aware of the fact that the divinities are patient and long suffering; but, if they search your heart and see that your intentions are, willingly, never to serve them they will do their best for you; but, you are greatly hindering their work! And your life will not be as productive as it could be! Before birth a contract was made with the divinities. You agreed to a divine mission with them. They came down with you to aid in the completion of that mission; and, if you emphatically choose not to honor the contract, after you have become aware, and complete the mission their efforts are thus nullified. But, YOU, are left to walk this earth with a more difficult path. Your ancestors will do their best by pleading and trying to intercede for you; but, you are essentially on your own and will bear witness to it if your life continues to spiral downward. You will either have to hitch yourself up to someone else's star and good fortune or live a life not developing to your full potential!

Serving the spirits is not an easy road. Many think it is about sitting up on a big king's seat, with stick in hand, and having folks kowtow to you. Some have even entered the priesthood to amass fame and fortune or to feel good about themselves. They point to a path that is smooth, with beautiful trees, flowers growing on its sides with the sun shining bright in a cloudless sky. They visualize a place where all Black folks are living in perfect harmony. That is not the path mon petit chéri! It is that other one...the crooked one with the rocks and the potholes. It is the one with the narrow and steep embankments and the thorny bushes flanking its sides. It is the one that, when traversed, will make you a better person, humbler and a perfect servant. And when your task here is done will place you on a spiritual throne dripping in gold!

VODUN PRACTICALITIES

There are some questions that some may have about vodun that they might not know how to ask. I will place this under what I term "Vodun Practicalities" and see what we come up with...

1. What if I am NOT Mami Wata how can you help me? Well that is why there is Ifa. Ifa tells us who and what we are in the spirit world. If someone does divination with us and we find them to be Heviosso, Gu and any other pantheon not connected to Mami, we then ask the Voduns what Priest do we take this person to. In African Vodun all Priests/Priestesses are

ordained by both the ancestors and the divinities. These spirits are aware of how those of the Priesthood conduct themselves and their business; so, the spirits, themselves, (your spirits) will chose the Priest or Priestess that we are to take you to. It is then our duty to take you to that person, discuss our Ifa findings, they do their own verifications and we help you in negotiating your ceremonial fees, with them, whatever they might be.

2. What if I am not to be initiated into anything; but, I want to serve my ancestors etc. After divination, one's ancestors generally reveal themselves and tell us what they need...what ceremonies or sacrifices. We can do those for you in accordance to the specification of one's ancestors; however, once one's ancestors are revealed you may go and look up these folks on your own. We can tell you where they are and/or direct you to them. You then may go and make contact. They will make their own verifications, through Ifa, to be sure that you are their child and you may proceed from there.
3. I am not Mami Wata or another vodun that you possess; but, I know of their attributes; and, I would like those vodun's blessings and/or protection. One may either find a priest or priestess from that pantheon, of vodun, and elicit their help/prayers or one can go to the vodun Thron...to whom I call the Kola Vodun. The Vodun Thron, in Africa, is a vodun that has the authority to go to ANY spirit and beseech a request on a person's behalf. In Africa, one does not have to be born with this spirit to become a priest or priestess of it. It is the one spirit, in Africa, that people can actually buy into! Thron also offers protection. This is the spirit that gives the protection where if someone is out to harm you the bad juju will boomerang back! This is Thron. I am not an expert on this spirit. I do know that there are some Thron Priests on facebook. If one has interest they will have to do their own research.

VODUN AND SPIRITUAL TITLES: WHAT IS THE SIGNIFICANCE?

In traditional African vodun, as I have stated in previous writings, authentic African divination reveals WHO and WHAT we are, in the spirit world, and what our spiritual missions are on earth. Divination tells us if a person is born to be of the Priesthood, a Tassinon (woman of prayer), a Diviner or whatever other spiritual role they came to perform or none at all. The title, in this sense, describes the types of "spiritual tasks/work" that the person is to be involved in. One may also view it as a "job description" of what one should be doing in his/her designated spiritual role while here on earth.

In Haitian vodou I understand that folks, who are initiated, may go through a series of levels of initiations. If authentic African divination was re-instated, into diasporan vodun, this would not be necessary. The spirits would emphatically tell us to what level, of initiation, if any, a person was actually born to. It would also tell us who is not born to the priesthood or if a person was born into the priesthood, but of a different capacity such as Ifa or another such specialized field within the spiritual realm. Some priests, for instance, are priests of the ancestors, such as a "Daagbo" (Fon) or a "Togbe" (Mina). These are ancestral titles peculiar to a particular tribal lineage. African divination can reveal all of this, to us, and more!

In the diaspora, we often approach vodun from the outside looking in. Therefore, we assume that, like a college course, vodun can be viewed in that way. It can't! We assume that just like degrees we may actually continue to achieve higher levels of spiritual knowledge and the more titles accrued would then designate this. That IS NOT how vodun works! In vodun one is BORN to one's spiritual seat. One comes, to this earth, born of a particular pantheon of Vodun/Spirits, a particular ancestry, a particular spiritual title, designating one's vocation in the spiritual world/level of work, and a particular mission if any. Ifa can reveal all of this to us. Once you determine what these are then you initiate into whatever it is, if commanded to do so, and continue from there. One's true knowledge and expertise comes from the years of training and working with one's spirits. The longer one works with the divinities the more one is molded and refined by the spirits themselves. One's power and knowledge becomes as great as one's relationships with the voduns is strong not through the acquisition of levels of initiation.

The titles, therefore, do not exist to make us look good or to be acquired, for self-serving purposes, but, to designate the level of spiritual work that one must do in the mission of one's service to mankind. For the greater the spiritual title, or spiritual work to be performed, the greater the responsibilities and accountability to the spirits.

"THOU SHALT HAVE NO OTHER GODS BEFORE ME": WHAT THAT MEANS IN TRADITIONAL AFRICAN VODUN

Over the years many people have come, my way, seeking guidance and/or a better understanding of Vodun; but, very few have stayed or crossed the finish line into full initiation, according to the tenets, of traditional African Vodun. The reasons have varied; but, for most it has been the realization of what African Vodun actually is as opposed to what they may have thought it to be. The life commitment, the costs, the length of initiations and demands, on one's life, has been such that very few have been able to fathom or commit to it.

In this very Americanized/Eurocentric world, that we live in, we are accustomed to compartmentalizing our lives. We give a portion to work, a smaller portion to our friends, a larger portion to our families and a portion to our church or religious duties. But in traditional African society, and for those that serve the voduns/spirits, it is the voduns/spirits...themselves... in which our lives are to revolve. It is THEY that dictate who we marry, where we live, the vocations we pursue and everything that pertains to our everyday lives. THEY, the voduns, are our center; and, WE revolve around THEM. That is traditional African Vodun...ORIGINAL VODUN! For it is that spiritual mission, as reveal by Ifa, that takes precedent, in our lives, thus EVERYTHING that we do must support that mission! And the people we allow in our lives, whether spouses, or whomever, must not deter us from that mission. So who becomes a part of your life and how you run your life becomes of great concern to the spirits. Therefore, THEY, who searches the hearts of mankind and come down, with us, to help us complete our spiritual missions must become involved in one's everyday life decisions. That is what we mean by "being in the hands"of the spirits; and, that mechanism which puts you there is initiation. It is within the initiation chamber that the spirits prepare you for your spiritual mission ahead. It is there where the spiritual world and the physical world folds down upon itself allowing the spirits to have a more complete access to you and you them. It is the place where innate spiritual gifts are activated and one learns the ways of the priesthood. It becomes a spiritual academy...one learns the spirit's dances, their colors, their songs, and their very nature begins to be revealed with much spiritual knowledge passed down. That is why it is the spirits that determine how long one spends in the initiation chamber not mankind. This could be months on end and years of preparation. But I can assure you...it is not two weeks! Nor is it the length of someone's three-week vacation in Africa. Cookie cutter initiations are not a part of traditional African Vodun!

So, when the spirits come tell you, through Ifa, get up and return to the United States... you do so. When they say come back, to Africa, when we decide not when you decide...you listen. When they say wait for those destined to come to us because you have signed a contract with the ancestors...you wait. When they choose you a spouse; and then, send him in the jungle for months on end for their work...you don't complain. When they say he is married to us you are just the girlfriend...you understand. This is the vodun that I know; and, this is the vodun that I impart to others because it is the vodun of our forefathers in all of it's power and glory. And like them I choose to walk, talk, hear and obey the divine. For if I had three pennies, in my hand, I would give all three to the voduns and wait for them to decide upon my portion. Few can make such commitments, few understand what it is to put the spirits first before all else. And that is why not many stay or make it to the finish line, or rather the beginning line, of full African initiation. They want to put up a shrine here or there something that is politically correct and afrocentric, that they may speak the lingo and be in the know. But, I assure you vodun is much more than that!

Our God, the God of Abraham, the God of all mankind, or by whatever name one may call him/her, is not only an awesome God, but, a Jealous God! Obedience is primary in serving the divine. In pursuing the Priesthood, one must take counsel with one's self and understand what is involved. God loved Abraham because of his obedience; and, that obedience was tested when asked to sacrifice his son Isaac. (Genesis 22: 1-13). Would you be able to pass such a test? Would you be able to put him/the spirits first above all others?

THE USE OF THE SPIRITS FROM THE DARK SIDE TO FULFILL OUR DESIRES

Vodun, itself, is about that which is sacred, pure and clean; but, there are those who employ spirits, from the darkside, to seek the negative or carnal desires of those who come to them. These individuals use what I term as "rogue" spirits...spirits, of persons who have passed over, that are not being cared for, by family members etc., that will bargain to do tasks in exchange for what they need. Or they may use spirits that have always been dark or whose main purpose is to be dark. Some of these people can become extremely wealthy. They are aware that using the dark arts may take a toll on themselves or have certain risks; so, they demand high fees for their work. They deal with the people who want to damage/kill their neighbors or enemies, exact revenge, take away that which belongs to another, or seek untold powers and/or make request, for things, that regular priests will not touch.

In vodun when one seeks the priesthood we are instructed that we must not serve with both hands. For if we do the spiritual consequences can be dire; yet, there are always those who will choose to do so or make the dark arts their primary vocation. This is the domain of the sorciers. It it not vodun...it is the anathema of vodun. But for those who serve the divinities, in the ways commanded by them, these dark arts, nor their priests, have any dominion over them. It is their work that we defend against, their work that our clients seek for us to undo, their curses that we must remove and their damage, and havoc wreaked, that we must correct.

If one has connected to one's ancestors and divine spirits, and they have been properly fed and cared for, such sorciers can do minimal damage. One's ancestors and spirits form a wall of protection around them and when bad things are thrown, their way, can be quickly thrown off through the appropriate sacrifices. The blood of these sacrifices gives the spirits the strength they need to do a work and fight off any bad juju that has come; but, if one is not protected and vulnerable one can see trouble from these negative forces. In Africa, we take these things very seriously. We know that the world is full of strife, envy and folks who wish to do us harm...sometimes even in our own families...so Africans protect themselves, and their loved ones, out of sheer principal...church goers or not!

A young man came to us. For years an element in his family used the dark arts against those to whom they chose. Ifa revealed the young man as a priest; so, he began his journey to the priesthood. Once his ancestors were identified through Ifa and fed those ancestors rose up and, that element that had been wreaking havoc for year upon his own bloodkin was, struck down! The ancestors rose up and did away with that bad element. The family members are, to this day, are trying to figure out who caused the demise of this wicked person.

Our first line of defense, against any spiritual foe, will always be our ancestors and the divine spirits that gave us life. And when we are born to the priesthood we come here for a reason and with a particular mission. Whatever that mission is one should be true to it. However, once entering the Priesthood, we have choice whether to serve with both hands, be true to our spiritual missions or serve from the dark side. Spiritual consequences exist for either; but, in any event if one's ancestors and divinities are served, fed and cared for your worries, from the dark arts, will be minimal.

VODUN, KNOWLEDGE AND BUYER'S REMORSE

There are many that approach me with an inquiry here or there; but, a few come with something a bit vague. It is generally something that I can't wrap my mind around at first. So, I continue to ask questions to better understand what they are asking or what is it that they need. And, usually it turns out that they are working with someone that they have paid for a service; but, they are not seeing results quick enough or none at all. They approach, stealthily, trying to get a handle on what someone else is doing with the money they have paid. They don't want to come out and tell me, hey, I've spent my money somewhere; and, I'm not sure if I'm getting swindled or not. So, they want to know a timetable for how long it will take to get results or if I agree with the way the person is handling their problem. They are having buyer's remorse!

In my mind, as they're speaking to me, I'm always asking...If you wanted my opinion, why didn't you come to me in the first place? Why approach ME about what somebody else is doing or have done? Didn't you research these folks first? So, as I continue to listen, I delicately suggest that they return to the person and ask them what they are asking me? And, I get things such as , they are not approachable or they are too busy... Well, my friend, I say, what does that tell you? RED FLAG folks! These people are providing a service, got your money and is unapproachable? You've got to talk to an entourage before you can speak to the person? Another excuse...this person is so busy, a fortune 500 company, a big chief in Africa but, no other Priest, knows him. RED FLAG folks! He might be something on the internet; but, if I am telling you that no one that is anything big, in the priesthood, knows him...he shouldn't have your money! And, if he is so rich, then, why can he not help you do the ceremonies that you are telling me you cannot afford to do because of our financial crisis in this country? Everyone knows that African Americans have suffered much in this crisis. Our unemployment rates are the highest in the nation! A wealthy priest would seek to help you not wait for you to get money to pay for his Bentley. Of course, I have never seen a priest with one; but, you get the message! Something is definately not right here!

The best armor against buyer's remorse is knowledge. One should learn as much as one can BEFORE spending your hard-earned money! There are many secrets in traditional African spiritual systems; but, that does not mean that a priest or priestess can not share enough to allow you to make correct decisions. This is essential! Many people introduce themselves over the internet to draw business; but, do not be carried away by flowery words. I read an introduction of a gentleman the other day. He described himself as being full blooded African...BORN in the United States! Then his mother was a queen, the father was a king; and, I can go on and on. In other words, he was the spirit's gift to all mankind and had given himself a title and name that was a paragraph long. Boyfriend could walk on water and his feet stay dry! RED FLAG folks! See if the person is talking about the spirits and how they can affect your life. See if they are speaking about divination that they can go to the spirits and diagnose your problems. See if they are cordial, willing to take time with you and be there when needed. See if they are honest or forcing you into something just to make a dollar. Ask the questions BEFORE you hand over money and not after. See if they can offer realistic solutions and be honest about a timetable as to seeing results to ceremonies etc.

In other words, get your head out of the clouds. Do not be deceived. Being a priest or priestess is about service. Too many of us of, African descent, are too impressed with titles and money. Too many aspire to be like the "Housewives of Atlanta" or sports celebrities. As priests/

priestesses we are not here to take our titles and lord them over people, nor, make them feel bad or show how aloof we can be. We must put ourselves aside and become the vessels, for the spirits, we need to be. And for those searching and seeking I ask you to come to me, or my facebook page, BEFORE buyer's remorse sets in. Read the free essays, on Vodun, that I have generated. With them you are armed with enough information to make much better decisions. Leave a message in the inbox if you need to; and, I will answer when I can. Remember, knowledge is power; and, it will generally help alleviate a great deal of vodun's buyer's remorse!

SHRINES, AUTHENTIC AFRICAN PRAYER TABLES AND VODUN

In Africa when one has been initiated into vodun, as a vodunsi (wife of vodun) or the priesthood, of any kind, the priest or priestess, who has initiated, the individual goes to them and sets up a table or space that the person can offer prayers and communicate with the spirits. If, initiated into the priesthood, the spiritual parent, after initiation, prepares one's Voduns according to the directions of the person's spirits. These sacred objects are either carved from sacred trees, by ordained carvers, or if pots, prepared by those selected to do such, and with the usage of various ingredients, activated to contain a particular spirit while outside the body of the person. These objects, whatever they are made of, go through strenuous purification rituals, ceremonies, sacrifices and then are set up by the dictates of the person's spirits. They are then housed, according to the directions of the spirits; and, these become the voduns encased inside a dwelling... the temple for that person. The temple is then known by the personal name of the individual's head spirit, or whatever the spirit demands.

Much more is involved in these processes than I have described here; but, the point is that these items become sacred objects imbued with the power of the sacred spirits that live within them. The newly initiated priest or priestess will enter their temple to pray, call forth their spirits, for a particular work, or tend to them. It is through one's relationship with them that the Priest or Priestess is taught and continually molded to do their will over the course of years. As the years go by the priest or priestess becomes more and more a vessel for the divine and, with age, becomes imbued with the wisdom of an African elder.

A similar thing happens for the vodunsi. This is a servant of the voduns but not of the priesthood. Spirits often take the head of a vodunsi at ceremonies. They are a "Divine Horseman", if you will, a term borrowed from the great Maya Deren (1953). Not all are born of the priesthood in vodun. This is a misnomer in the diaspora. There are many different roles or vocations, in the temple, that one can be born to. After initiation, the spiritual parent goes and sets up a prayer table. As in all, that are initiated, the person's Fa is done. This spirit allows them access to the spirit world that they are able to communicate with their spirits. Without it, when one throws the cowries, they are relying on gravity to manipulate the cowries; but, they are not communicating with any spirits. There is a difference between having the spirit Fa, to communicate with the spirits, and being a Priest of Ifa/Fa/Afa. Everyone, initiated receives the spirit Fa; but, not everyone is an Ifa/Fa/Afa Priest. This is a special priesthood; yet, every priest or priestess uses some type of divination system. So, he/she needs the spirit Fa to communicate with one's spirits. Even so, in doing initiations, 3 Ifa Priests are usually in attendance. I have heard of as many as 16 Ifa Priests convening on issues of great importance. They have great power!

On the vodunsi's prayer table are sacred objects originating from the person's initiation and imbued with spirits and/or objects with spiritual power. The spiritual parent sets up this table according to the instructions given by the person's spirits. These objects allow the individual to commune with them, offer prayer; and, because they have the spirit Fa, receive yes/no answers to their questions. If they need deeper understanding or answers they go to the Bokono (diviner of Ifa) or return to their spiritual parent and go before the voduns.

My taking the time to explain these things is to show you how inept these diaspora shrines are. They are nice to look at; but, have no power. It is noble that we want to put up photos, of spirits, or of known loved ones that have passed over; but, if you want the help, of your ancestors, you must FEED them! This involves animal sacrifice! Prayer is a wonderful thing; but, they cannot help you if you have not given them "the blood" to strengthen them so that they may do what is necessary to actually help you. They will remain powerless and unable to help if there is no sacrifice. The same thing with these diaspora shrines. They look cute and the photos honor whatever spirit(s) you are aiming at; but, if they haven't been set up by someone who himself or herself has been ordained, by the spirits, nothing is happening there. They just look good! If nothing sitting there has seen any blood sacrifice or ceremony, of any kind, if no spirit has dictated its set up nothing is happening. If food has been placed; but, the person has not been given the spirit Fa, for the ability to call or communicate with their spirits, nothing is happening. A shrine does not make you a servant of vodun, Ifa's determination, initiation and obedience to the commands/tenants of the spirits does!

VODUN AND A PLACE CALLED ZOGBE

It was in the first week of July 2003. I was teaching English at the American Cultural Center in (Cotonou) Benin, West Africa. I no longer owned a computer. My laptop had died early on during my stay there; so, I would check my email at work. I remember it vividly, an email from my youngest sister, saying, "Our brother is dead." I sat stunned! I couldn't move. I knew it wasn't a joke. No one in my family would do such a thing. We took family and death far too seriously. I said nothing to anyone. And I had no money to return home.

Of my two brothers, this one was just two years younger than I. He was six feet two inches tall of solid muscle. He was an avid health nut, an artist; and, while wearing my paternal grandfather's face, had hands so large that they could cover a person's entire face and some. He had always reminded me of a Native American warrior. Over the years we had not been close. Like in so many African American families my brother was one that was incarcerated. He had been for many years. Carrying a 50-year sentence from a robbery that had gone bad, back in the 1970s, my brother was a prison statistic. And because of the years spent in prison and his associations with prison crime, very high up in the ranks, he was murdered...just one day before maxing out. And there, I sat, so far away from the States, in Africa, to mourn alone. For I was to mourn not only because of my loss due to his death, but, because of the lost years of communication with him. So, I am not sure why, at the time, I couldn't cry out or tell anyone. Deep inside, of me, I felt I owed a debt...a debt for not being there. And one that he allowed me to fulfill.

As his death began to hit me hard I missed him dearly; and, then the dreams came. I would see my brother out in the distance; and, I would always, drop whatever I was doing in the dream, and call out to him. But always his back was to me and there was distance between us. Several times this happened. Not understanding I headed to the bokono (diviner); and, there is where I learned about Zogbe. My brother was asking for a ceremony. This ceremony would allow him to feed, thus taking in nourishment, and reconnect him to our ancestors. He, now being in the spirit world, needed my help for this; and, he knew that as a priestess of vodun I, being in Africa, could make this happen; and, I did for him and many others, in my family, that had passed on.

When a loved one dies of unnatural causes (murder, disease, animal maulings and others) this creates a separation between the spirits, of the person, and the ancestors. Such deaths are outside of the temple walls or the natural ways of death. Our spiritual contract has been prematurely broken. And, as a result, these loved ones must be fed outside of the walls of the temple, at a place called zogbe (where they go after death), and ceremonies performed that they may be reunited with the ancestors in order to feed with them. For in vodun we know that our journey, on this earth, begins with the ancestors; and, it is to the ancestors that we wish to return. And, in order to do this, in cases of unnatural deaths, these ceremonies must be performed.

When I think of the hundreds of years those of African descent have spent in the diaspora I cannot help but see the urgency. I think of those who were lynched, beaten to death, murdered, castrated, died of disease, mistreatments of all kinds, drugs and countless other ways; and, I wish I could do more. My brother was a man with his own mind and destiny. I make no excuses for his crimes or how he chose to live his life. For all I know, in hindsight, he may have chosen to live it differently. But there is one thing that I do know, he was and is, my kin and my blood. He is my brother. I love him dearly; and, he deserves to eat with his ancestors and rest in peace too.

TO LEARN "WITH A CHILD'S HEART"

When we seek to teach or train someone we generally start with where the person is. It is rare that we tell a person to forget all that they have learned and start all over again. We, as instructors, attempt to build on that which is already there. As diasporans, and adults, our life's lessons often help us to understand new concepts or new ways of thinking. But as I remember my early years, in Africa, I began to understand more fully a particular bible scripture from my youth. I could see, from the Old Testament writings to the New Testament writings echoes of thoughts, words and actions of the divine. For it says in Matthew 10:15, "Truly I tell you, anyone who will not receive the kingdom of God like a little child will never enter it." (NIV) This very short essay is about what the attitude of the learner should be in one's quest in understanding the spirits.

One of the things I learned, in Africa, is that the trainer or priest(ess) should not be bombarded with questions. Eurocentric modalities of learning and training simply did not apply there. This is an ancient land with an ancient people. One must have respect and reverence for the teacher and allow them to teach you according to their own time. These men and women, of the African priesthood, carry inside of them secrets of the universe itself. If you want the knowledge which they possess you must, first, be destined to know (as found out through Ifa divination) and be quiet, humble and respectful in your quest to learn. Patience is a key. Vodun involves a lifetime of training and learning. I, myself, am but a babe in vodun. Yet, that which I do know comes from authentic African training. But I do not allow anyone, in the diaspora, to call me an elder, because according to African standards, I know and understand very little. But it is enough, that with the help of the spirits, I can help folks make more informed decisions while on their spiritual journey. For I have seen and done more, in African vodun, than many diasporans will ever know.

One of the things that have pained me, in the diaspora, is the rampant disrespect from those claiming to know vodun and to be of it's priesthood that have been found to be "bought in" folk initiated by people who should know better. These born of diasporan vodun families, in their thirst for money, have let unfit people in giving them nothing but a title and contempt for legitimate priests and priestesses. However, I am confident that the spirits will hold accountable each one in kind. But the insistence that a student of the spirits must have an attitude of a child...one of humility and a willingness to learn... is very much an African concept. This is why I do not debate vodun and have little tolerance with people who are stiff backed and condescending, towards me, when I am teaching on vodun. I have been ordained by the ancestors and the divinities themselves. Therefore, those people who do not have the proper respect will get nothing from me. People need to be aware that in vodun all are not equal. I will attempt to explain myself; but, if one is disrespectful, towards me, they will be unfriended very quickly. I do not have time to put up with folk's nonsense. But if one has a kind heart, a gentleness and an earnest willingness to learn one's ancestors, and the divine spirits, will always put folks in one's path that will help, teach and guide them along the way. It happened for me; and, it can happen for you.

WHEN THINGS FALL APART

When a person has all the financial wealth that one could ever need, when one's social life is hitting the high road, when one's job or business has no worries and the apple of one's eye is doing all the right things it is hard to reach out to the spiritual. That is why, to get our attention, the voduns (spirits) often allow things to fall apart in our lives. For, usually, it is only when we experience trouble that we may choose to reach out. And by that time the person has either spent all their money on foolishness, taking for granted the spirits that blessed them with it in the first place, or have made such bad decisions within their personal lives that it has cost them dearly. So here they come, broke, po' mouthing, dragging the ground, in deep misery, begging for our assistance.

While we may sincerely desire to help them; coming broke often limits what we can do. For those, of the priesthood, who work with integrity we may be willing to actually charge nothing for our own personal services; but, divination must be done and with this the items bought to do it. In addition, sacrificial animals must be procured if the voduns recommend ceremonies. Sometimes the priest is sent to various sacred sites to perform certain rituals or even to a person's ancestral village(s) for these ceremonies; so, his transport and expenses must be figured in also. Furthermore, to assist in these ceremonies, those who have been duly initiated, the vodunsi, must give of their valuable time away from their jobs and loved ones. We often need to compensate them for their time or help them with transport. This is how authentic African vodun works. It is not a cheap endeavor. It is time consuming on the part of the priest and his vodunsi; and, it can be expensive on the part of the consumer as well. In fact, we have found, that the larger the trouble the larger the cost, due to the expense of the many sacrificial animals needed for ceremonies. However, if a person has been feeding their ancestors and personal spirits all along the repercussions of the trouble, that suddenly docks at our door, is less and the ceremonies prescribed by the voduns also less. These ancestors and/or spirits have been fighting for you all along and may need fewer ceremonies to remedy the issue(s).

What I suggest for those needing assistance, with no funds, is to appeal to good friends or loved ones. And after the ceremonies have been completed and one's pathways opened again then you can reimburse them for their assistance. But one needs to understand that most African priests are of humble means. They may have the knowledge to help you; but, YOU must provide the financial resources for them to do the work needed.

You can not be annoyed when they explain to you that they cannot do so due to your inability to pay. Yes, there are charlatans out there! Yes, there are folks that are all about the money! But there are also good and honest priests out there in EVERY country. That includes, Africa and the diaspora. You simply need to take your time, do the research and find them!

VODUN AND ONE'S ENEMIES

A young lady just asked me, recently, about juju. Her question was if juju was ever done to help people? Yeah, I thought it was an odd question too! But, if folks don't know they just don't know. But I certainly have never heard of anyone going to the juju man, or root doctor, to put something on one's neighbor so that he/she could prosper way before themselves. Black folks were, and still are, busy trying to get ahead. If anything, somebody wanting juju is seeking revenge or some way to harm his/her neighbor. If you wanted to help yourself, when I was growing up in the south, you went and got yourself a good mojo...something to give you some good luck with the numbers, that pretty gal down the street, who won't even be thinking about you, or something to keep yourself out of jail. But if you wanted to stop your neighbor, then, you went for the juju. Back in the day the root doctor got plenty of business and those doing the root work were predominantly black. While I'm not sure about what's going on, in the root world today, the ads I see, out of New Orleans and such, are of model type white girls advertising root work. I don't know what happened; but, something did! Root work is the remnants of what is left over from African vodun and is even more watered down than anything one would ever find in the Caribbean. But, that's neither here nor there in this particular essay. One's enemies is the topic.

It's life that not everyone is going to like us. It took me years to figure this out. I had assumed that a person with a great personality, looks, talent and smarts was all I needed. And even though I was a loner high school proved that being liked was not something that came easily. My being cute, book smart and a loner made me even more of a target. I didn't care to fight, avoided it at every opportunity by hiding out in the library; but, I sure could wish a person dead! This was all fantasy, on my part of course, until I became a priestess; and, then, I had to change up. Not only was it inappropriate as a priestess; but, I had some voduns that would actually go out and do it! African vodun is some serious stuff; so, I've had to pull back, my thoughts, drastically; and, let the voduns work on their own. And that is what happens, in vodun, if someone is actively serving the spirits. It is one's ancestors or divine spirits that will cut down one's enemies. You do not have to do anything.

Folks can dislike you due to envy, jealousy or any number of reasons. But, as stated above, you do not have to do anything if you are actively serving the spirits. Your ancestors, and the spirits who gave you life, are your first line of defense; and, often you don't even know when they have done something, or knocked someone out, until the voduns come and tell you about it. I had a disagreement with a young man who had issues with women in general. He was busy trying to juju an ex-wife, spoke disrespectfully of his mother and eventually had a beef with me. He ended up taking a trip to Nigeria to have work done...the same place he went that messed him up, in the first place, and my husband had to travel to Nigeria to repair. Young man didn't wanna pay 'cause he was annoyed about something I said. Guess he called himself gonna make it to Nigeria and do something to me Called one of my spiritual children and told him the story behind the divination. Spirits said the man is kind; but, leave the woman alone, for, there is too much death around her feet. The young man inquired further because he just knew that it meant I was evil; and he figured he was on to something. The diviner said, "No, the death around her feet is the bodies of her enemies." I haven't heard from that young man since. I love Ifa!

When people seek to send juju usually they do not serve the spirits but know of the spirits and seek to hire them out for a work Usually priests who serve with both hands (serve vodun, as well as the dark arts) do this work. The voduns specifically speak agains this. According to them it shortens one's life and is not something sanctioned by them. Traditional priests are aware of the dark art because we often must counter against it. But there are some priest that the dark spirits fear. They know who they can get past and to whom they cannot. Evil or not they are still spirits. And spirits are what we deal with. In Africa, the populous is most aware of the fac that one can have enemies; so, the average African protects him/ herself. So, when juju is sent, not only do their spirits alert them if they actively serve them; but, it boomerangs back if they are protected. So, in Africa, the priests sending out the juju, will keep the one paying for the juju near to him so that if the juju boomerangs back it hits the person and not them! In that most diasporans are no protected; and, their ancestors or personal spirits are not known or fed they are very susceptible to juju. And, then, they start the search to find someone to get it off. Many do not realize that something is even wrong until their life ends up almost in the toilet. In any event to help them authentic African divination must be done to diagnose the problem and ceremonies performed to correct it. Praying and going to church is not going to help you. If someone has gone to the spirits to put juju on you one must go to the spirits to get the juju off you. Church simply does not have this kind of power.

THAT TO WHICH WE INHERIT

If one was to use the 'family unit' as a metaphor for the whole of African spirituality, then, one could better understand its importance. For in traditional Africa...that Africa to which all mankind was created... the family unit is of infinite importance. Within this family of men, women and children are born unto it priests and priestesses... those ordained, by the spirits, to intercede between them, and all mankind. They are stationed to aid in the everyday affairs of our existence. And, within their domain (their temples) are born those to assist in their work...Diviners, Vodunsi, Tassinons, and other people born with particular spiritual gifts and given particular spiritual roles to help facilitate in this relationship between the Creators and that which they have Created. But these human vessels do not spring forth from nowhere. For they are rooted in a solid foundation...a foundation that was put in place by the divinities themselves. For in the heavens...inside that spiritual sphere, wherever one may deem it, where the divine reigns, are 41 spiritual thrones...royal and ecclesiastical thrones where 41 members of each set of ancestors, that preside on earth, sit. And it is from them, my loves, and those spirits that breathed life into us that we owe our allegiance. And in every family temple, in Africa, those 41 ancestral spiritual thrones, if the village still exists, continue to physically sit.

So, I don't care what the 'bought in' folks are telling you about African Vodun/Orisa and the African based spiritual systems, in the diaspora, not being connected. They simply do not know what they are talking about! Why? Because those 41 ancestral seats, sitting in the spiritual realm, have physical counterparts STILL sitting in African temples today, thus, proving them straight up wrong. Their convenient theories to justify holding on to what they have "bought" into and their pontifications of grandeur cannot erase the facts! Those who were sitting on many of these seats, in pre-colonial Africa, were taken into slavery, dispersed throughout the diaspora; and, as such their descendants now have claim to them. I know, because, I sit on one from my Agassou ancestry. I know, because, we have claimed several for our spiritual children from the diaspora. I know, because, I have put my feet down on African soil. And, I know, because, I serve the spirits as my ancestors did. We are absolutely and unequivocally connected to Africa and its ancestry!

The possibility of being the heir to one of these ancestral thrones is just the tip of the iceberg. In traditional Africa, certain families had and still possess particular vocations in which they have expertise. Many were/are healers of bones, many had/have special affinities to particular vocations and secret societies with unusual spiritual gifts. For instance, there are Africans with the gift of travel, to great distances, in a single night, families who employ secret languages, whereby, only they and those in their temples understand. There are Priests who can wake the dead and ask them how they died. In certain families, there are secret voduns/orisa that only they possess. All of this was put into place by the divinities themselves. And, all of the great feats that the world considers miracles can be had by finding the ancestor and reconnecting to these ancient talents. Many have died because the persons possessing them has died; but, I understand, that, for those rightful heirs, of these specialized gifts, the spirits, themselves, will rise up and teach you what you need to know.

Our life, on this earth, begins with the ancestors; and, when our time, here, is done it is to them that we hope to return. Much can be said about the things that we do, within our lives, that block us from this return; but, the most prevalent, for the diasporan, is not knowing him at all. The slave experience, for those of African descent, has made that reconnection much more difficult. And, for those that are furthest removed the devaluation of Africa, its traditions and its people have hampered your reconnection as well. Much of WHO we are and WHAT we are, in the spiritual world, comes from our ancestors. We inherit many of their voduns/orisas. Our opeles are handed down from generation to generation. For inside that opele lives the spirits of those diviners and priests that have come before us. Their power, their wisdom and blessings must be passed on. Our opele and our physical bodies, thus, become one. For spirituality and religion are two very different entities. Religion is something many seek.... spirituality is something that encompasses who and what we are. Therefore, for those of us searching and seeking the ways of old, the ways of our forefathers, the powers they possess and the spiritual gifts rightfully inherited and due us, we must reconnect. We must reclaim that which was lost, for, in Africa many thrones have lain bare, for generations, because of the trans-Atlantic slave trade. Many have been denied a history, a spiritual worth and a dignity due us. And, because of the prejudices of some, who disliked the color of our skin, we, and our ancestors, have seen much suffering. But, the time has come to rise up, my brothers and sisters! You must strengthen your resolve and wipe the pain of suffering and injustice from your limbs that it not over take you. You must reach back and claim a legacy that reaches towards the very heavens itself. And you must reach out to the great Ifa, that spiritual bridge between the heavens and earth; and, put claim on that to which we are to inherit.

AFRICAN ANCESTRAL AND SPIRITUAL THRONES

This essay is a spin-off from my essay entitled, "African Spirituality: That to Which We Inherit". I want to better explain African royalty and it's ancestral/familial and priestly thrones.

In pre-colonial Africa, there was a distinct class system. It's remnants still exist, in Africa, today. However, kinship (who one is related to) was everything in pre-colonial Africa. So much so that it developed the social structure of society...who one would know and who one could be associated to was extremely important. But, it was within the class system that these social liaisons would occur. In pre-colonial Dahomey, for instance, the highest social class/caste, was that of the King and his royal family. Next to them were those of the Priesthood; and, next to them were the artisans to the king. After that you had various persons of commerce and trade, ordinary citizens; and, at the lowest rung, the domestic slaves. However, African domestic slaves, were often integrated into the kin, of their owners, either by adoption or marriage. So, when one thinks of kingships from Africa, thrones, and familial ties, in reference to vodun or traditional Africa in general, we are referring to a pre-colonial Africa. Vodun, while in existence before the world was ever formed, concerns a pre-colonial Africa; and, it was the transAtlantic slave trade that interrupted, for a moment (if one is to see time as the spirits do) a continual line of familial and spiritual inheritances.

If Egypt can be said to have a valley of the kings, then, Africa, south of the Sahara, can be said to be the land of the kings, because, in every single family there is one. And one's kingship comes through familial ties. Putting the tribe's highest king and his royal family, aside, within each ancestral group is a series of kings. For example, to each ancestral group, ie. Agassou, there are many different branches of Agassou. I remind our diasporans of our family reunions. At each of these family reunions we see the various branches of the family that have sprung up due to marriage and other unions. This is the same in Africa. However, at every branch, in Africa, there is a king. I am Agassou. But, I am of the Agassou-Aligbonon branch; therefore, of that branch there is a king called Dah (meaning king in Fon) Aligbonon. Each branch of the Agassou clan also has its king. And added to that are the 41 ancestral thrones to which of one I am heir to. Traditional Africa, as you can see, is full of kings. Every family has them; and, as we have ancestral ties, to Africa, we lay claim to these familial ties. But only Ifa can identify them. I am sorry; but, DNA analysis can't. Ifa is connected to our ancestry, because, just as the ancestors were put in place by the divinities, it was also them who gave us Ifa to use for our communication with them. Ifa, therefore, can give us the answers to our ancestral related inquires.

So, my brothers and sisters, if we are found to be of the Priesthood, we have a priestly throne connected to the head spirit that gave us life. If we have familial ties with the royal families, of Africa, we may be an heir to that throne, or, if we have familial ties to the king of ur clans or branch of the family we may be heir to that throne; and, f we were born to a special work like the Supreme Chief of Vodun, r something, we could be heir to that throne. The Ifa Priesthood as it's throne, the Tassinon has its throne. Each priestly vocation as its throne. I hope you get my point. Africa is a land of kings nd thrones. It is not necessary, as diasporans, for us to go to a book f African names and choose or gift ourselves a priestly title and/ r throne. Unless they come through familial kinship; and, can be erified through authentic African divination no one, in Africa, will ake them seriously anyway. Ask yourself. Can any Joe Shmoe, who hows up, lay claim to the Queen's throne in England? Of course not! There must be proof of a familial tie and verification as heir. And, an eir comes through birthright! It is the same in Africa. So, why give ourself an African name because it sounds good without knowing what tribe you are from and letting the elders, of your own ancestral eople, give you a name? I know we are drawn to the name because of what it means. But, there was a time when we were ignorant of the act that we could actually find the African ancestor. That time has assed. We know better now. I discovered Ifa! And I, as others, are ere screaming about it off the rooftops! I hear too many diasporans who have taken on Ghanaian names whose ancestral ties turn out o be from Dahomey or some other place. There are folks out there laiming the Akan tradition without even realizing that the Akan radition is Vodun. So please do it right. Stop with the playing at being African...find your folks, through Ifa, and find out who and what you eally are in the spiritual realm. Your ancestors will be delighted!

ONE'S SPIRITUAL THRONE...IT ISN'T NECESSARILY A DONE DEAL

Matthew 18:18 (NIV) reads, "Truly I tell you, whatever you bind on earth will be bound in heaven, and whatever you loose on earth will be loosed in heaven." This biblical passage brings up the subject matter that will be discussed in this essay...one's spiritual work; but, the biblical writers have it turned around. Whatever is loosed in the heavens can be loosed on earth, in reference to one's spiritual throne and missions; however, in the world of the spirits, none of this is done deal!

In Vodun/Orisa one is born to their spiritual seat or thron One's Priesthood comes through birthright. Before birth we make contract, with the spirits, that we will do this or that or perform som particular spiritual mission. After birth, this spiritual Priesthood an mission is discovered through Ifa. Through the birthing process w lose this knowledge. In most instances; and, if born in a tradition African family this information is discovered in infancy. For mos diasporans, however, it is after we discover Ifa, in adulthood, or i some spirit comes and takes our head (mounts us) or attempts to. I any event Ifa supplies the answers to our questions, "Who is this tha has come back?", "What is this person in the spirit world?", etc. etc One's spiritual throne already exists in the heavens or whatever on wishes to call that holy place of the spirits. We, after it's discovery must make it happen here on earth; and, to do so by participatin in the appropriate ceremonies, rituals, and/or initiations accordin to the tenants of those particular ancestors and spirits that gave u life. This is imperative, because, if the appropriate ceremonies ar not performed, then, the seat continues to sit there, in the heavens waiting for someone else, born from your clan, to claim it. So, it isn' a done deal! Initiation, if one is born to serve the spirits, is importan for many reasons.

So; ok, one has performed the appropriate ceremonies, accordin to the spirits, and one now sits on the throne, physically, on earth? Is i a done deal now? By no means! One can take the seat physically; but, i one leads their life to where it is ungodly or unbecoming of someon of the Priesthood, one may sit on the seat, physically, but forfeit th seat spiritually. This is where one's character, integrity and how on chooses to conduct their life matters. One cannot expect to live, serv the spirits with both hands, lie, cheat and steal and claim a spiritua throne after death. One cannot expect to mistreat one's fellow mar or woman and expect a crown or the spirits to say, " Well done my good and faithful servant." One's spiritual title does not guarantee one's character because the spirits have given us choice; and, as with all others if one lives a life of disgrace one will die in disgrace. One's spiritual throne will be given and/or inherited by another who acts appropriately...according to the tenants of the ancestors and the divine spirits. For the spirits see the past, present and future all at once; and, nothing that we do, as humans, go unnoticed by them.

So, no spiritual throne is a done deal. One spends a lifetime earning it. And one's character, integrity, humility, service to mankind and obedience to the spirits is the price. So, do not be deceived, my children, a Priest or Priestess who lacks integrity may sit on a physical throne; but, in the heavens...in the highest of the hollies...nothing exists there for them. That spiritual throne has been forfeited, saved for another; and, the spirits will make punishment upon those to whom they see fit.

VODUN: A FEW QUESTIONS AND ANSWERS

1. Q. After divination, and my ancestry and spirits are revealed, what do I do next?
   A. After one's ancestry and spirits are revealed, through authentic African divination, we then inquire, of the spirit(s), as to whom they wish to do their spiritual work. In that all ordained Priests and Priestesses are known to the ancestors and the divinities the spirits, themselves, will tell us who they choose to do their spiritual work for the individual. At that time we give you that information, if you want to make your own arrangements, or we approach that particular Priest or Priestess, on your behalf, and enter negotiations for initiation or ceremonial fees.

2. Q. If it is revealed that I am of the Priesthood or some other station, in Vodun, do I have to serve if I do not want to?
   A. No, everyone has choice; however, one has to be willing

to deal with the consequences of one's choices. For some, to ignore the spirits, could result in, the spirits, giving you a very difficult time until one relents. I have seen this happen to Africans and Haitians. Most other diasporans discover that they are experiencing difficulties in their lives so go for divination. Divination, then, reveals that they are of the Priesthood and must initiate.

3. I was initiated in Haiti; but, I am of European descent. Is there anything I am missing? If you have absolutely no familial or ancestral ties, to Haiti, you undoubtedly may not know your true head spirit or have had your oldest ancestors (the original African) revealed, to you, if authentic African divination was not performed. Many of the spirits we possess are inherited from our ancestors. Also, without the ancestors, the voduns can not be served effectively. It is the ancestors that intercede for us, with the divinities in times of trouble. In addition, the ancestral spirits have particular functions in our daily lives. Many of our spiritual gifts, as well as, familial spiritual throne seats are inherited; and, in order to claim these spiritual inheritances, one must first find the ancestor. That includes one's opele. It must come down through familial lines. Being married off to someone else's ancestor does not help you as much as your own ancestors being fed.

4. Q. Hey, I'm gay or transgendered! Can I serve the spirits too?

   A. You most certainly can! Everyone has the right to go before the spirits. And, if the spirits have something to say about one's personal lifestyle choices they, themselves, will speak.

5. Q. Somebody is making my life miserable. I think they are slinging juju at me. How do I get back at them?

   A. Most folks ask for some type of spell; but, the best defense is a continual feeding of the spirits, thus, empowering one's own spirits to fight off the dark arts. One needs to go for divination diagnose the problem and allow the spirits to seek a solution. If one's own spirits are fed they will rise up and seek their own revenge on injustices to their children. However, in isolated instances, ceremonies can be performed, after divination, to deal with emergency issues as well.

6. Q. Well. what about my European ancestors, are they to be ignored?

   A. Absolutely not! Whether one is of European descent or of mixed race, or someone who is of multiple heritages, authentic African Vodun reaches all the way back to that oldest ancestor and pulls forward capturing all that are related to you from the darkest to the lightest. But, as the African continent is the birthplace of mankind, those oldest ancestors are going to be, somewhere, on that continent; and, Ifa can find him.

7. Q. What's up with these spiritual baths, are they any good?

   A. Sometimes the spirits will request a spiritual bath for a person after divination. The reasons can range from a cleansing, for spiritual purification purposes, or a promise, to the spirits, that the person will eventually initiate. It should be done, however, at the direction of the spirits. In the diaspora spiritual baths are becoming a "racket" for those interested in accruing fast money after an initiation; and, so are these Mami Wata offerings being put into the water (fruit, cookies, sweets, salad and dove or pigeon all bundled up in white cloth). Such ceremonies should be directed by the spirits and not by someone trying to make a mortgage or car payment.

8. Q. I've got no money to go to Africa. Can't I do my stuff here in the diaspora?

   A. One of our problems, at this time, is authentic African temples in the diaspora. With the Orisa there are certain temples/places visited by authentic African Priests on a regular basis, but, African Vodun is presently handicapped in that regard. Most do Haiti. But our prayer is that, in the future, authentic African Vodun temples can be put into place. But because of the language barriers and the difficulty had for those, from Benin, to get a visa, to this country, we are behind. In addition, an authentic and fully trained African initiated Priest or Priestess, born in the diaspora, is a rarity here. In African Vodun the initiation process can take months to years to complete. And full training, from an African temple, even longer; but, my prayer is that, in the future, more will complete the process. Until then the best we can do is offer ties to authentic African Vodun temples and Priests. For a while, anyway, folks are simply going to have to treat a trip to Africa as an important life's goal. And, for me, the opportunity to touch the soil of my oldest ancestor would be; so, save your pennies the spirits will help make it possible.

THE CONCEPT OF 'SPIRITUAL BIRTHRIGHT'

What was to become the United States of America was founded by a group of people, the Pilgrims in the 1600s, who fled to these shores for religious freedom. They sought to throw off the yoke of the Catholic church, but, their religious fervor later allowed them to almost, completely, decimate one group of people...the Native Americans... while, devastatingly, enslaving another.... the Africans. But, what they failed to understand was that, both of these groups, came from traditional systems of belief that were dependent upon a direct relationship with the spirit world and its natural elements. And the African, specifically, came from a system where "birthright" not only dictates personal life but one's spiritual life as well; and, that is what those of African descent must understand in order to regain that spiritual connection to our ancestors.

In the United States, specifically, the concept of birthright is most often associated with money. One thinks of what one might inherit after the death of a family member. Long ago, in this country, the connection of birthright to a monarchy, a throne, a lordship or any other type of title, associated with a gilded class, was severed with the fight of the American Revolutionary War (1775-1783). This country's declared independence, in 1776, severed it from the concept of a monarchy (form of government in which sovereignty is actually or nominally embodied in a single individual). However, the concept that all individuals are equal and the Eurocentric concept that all knowledge can be gained, by anyone seeking it, flies in direct opposition to that of the African ancestor and African traditional spiritual systems in general. Spiritual knowledge, in Africa, is intricately intertwined with spiritual birthright...that which one has inherited through birth...the priesthood or any other spiritual station.

Of those of African descent we did not ask to come to this land. We were not fleeing religious persecution or seeking to sever from a monarchy...we were stolen! We were captured and brought, in chains, against our will. And we came from a system where a person's birthright, be it spiritual or otherwise, dictated our existence. In most instances, domestically, It STILL does in Africa; but, in the traditional spiritual realm one cannot get around it! One's spiritual seats or thrones come directly through birthright and only Ifa can determine this information for us. Ifa must reveal, to us, our ancestry; and, through that ancestry we discover what we inherited spiritually. Ifa, thus, in this sense forms a bridge from the diaspora to our African ancestral heritages.

So, when I say that in traditional African vodun one is born to one's spiritual seat I am referring to ancestry. I am not speaking about someone who has run to Haiti or some other place and purchased power or the authority to claim the priesthood. I am speaking of someone who has had authentic African divination performed; and, it is revealed who their ancestors actually are and we have gone into those villages or discovered, through Ifa, what specific spiritual seats, be they ancestral or divine (priestly throne of their head spirit), that these folks were born to or inherited. That is SPIRITUAL BIRTHRIGHT; and, that is African Vodun! The African ancestors... mankind's oldest ancestors are ancient. While we have changed they have not.

They were put into place by the very divinities themselves; and, even their energy is far more different than our younger ancestors around the globe. It is they, in unison, with the divinities that direct our paths; and, we must respect their tenants. This is why, my "bought in" friends there is no respect to be gained from those of us who were born to our spiritual thrones or seats. Why? Because you are, essentially, refusing to obey the tenants of the ancients. And if you are not ordained by the ancestors and the divine spirits themselves, then, you are not known to them and your power is forever limited. A person who purchases his/her throne, in Africa, is given no respect.

We are an ancient people my brothers and sisters. Contrary to popular belief the trans-Atlantic slave trade did not sever our ties from our African roots. For who we are is in the "blood". And in that blood, is ancestral memory. The enslaver did not count on that. Whatever you have inherited, spiritually, can be found. It awaits you... all of these centuries it has awaited you. And it doesn't matter where you came from. You can be furthest removed from African ancestry or first-generation African born in the diaspora. It doesn't matter, it is there. Go to Ifa and find it; and, may the spirits be forever with you!

VODUN AND THE MISTRESS: THE RESEARCHER

The researchers that chase the Voduns have always intrigued me. One, because I was one and two, because the researcher tends to believe that they can study Vodun and not be affected or touched by it. There is a sense that the researcher, of Vodun, can be an objective observer; but, that is most untrue. And while the researcher thinks that they can unfold and reveal her secrets it is the researcher who is often caught up in her trap. For to think that you can profit off the

Voduns (write a book, documentary or whatever) and Vodun not exact a price is the epitome of unknowing! Vodun is a living and breathing thing! For the meager monies, you might use to entice a Vodunsi or Priest, here or there, is only the tip end of it. That is for those who lack a bit of integrity. The Voduns examine the hearts of men and women, therefore, what you are doing, and your motives, are always laid bare before them. While you may think you are hustling Vodun, Vodun may end hustling you, therefore, exacting its price.

I stepped off the plane, in Johannesburg, South Africa, as a doctoral candidate in 1997, I did the same in Benin, West Africa in 1998. When I stepped off the plane, in NYC, in 2006 after 8 consecutive years in an out of African temples, I was no longer a doctoral candidate. I was the thing I had gone to study...an African Priestess. I didn't write my dissertation, rather, I lived it! I had been caught by the ancestors hook, line, and sinker!

But, in hind site, I had been smart. My research methodology was that of a "participant observer". While I wanted to know Vodun my quest was to actually find the ancestor; but, that led me right smack into the fray. I couldn't really know them without being immersed in it; so, here we have it.

Since that time, I have seen many researchers come and go out of west Africa. Some came with plenty of cameras, bribed to get in ceremonies or gave money to see things that they weren't supposed to see. The French, Benin's former colonizers, were very adapt at that. They had been writing about Vodun for eons so had their methods down to a science...plenty of cameras and plenty of Euro. Americans often came on a budget; and, that included me! Some came (the women), not all, and started dating the local men, and thus would bat a few eyelashes to get access, to places, through their local lover and go about learning the language...these were the researchers on grants or fellowships. The focus was on the research; but, there was the after hours icing of partaking into the local desserts (the local brothas) if they had'nt actually started dating the Priest, himself, already. The brothers would roll in and stay at the nicest hotels they could find for about a week or two...their university was usually paying. They'd hustle themselves up a good tour guide and visit a few remote spots and do a documentary claiming they had been home giving no mention, or notice, to the African American sistah that, they had heard about, who had been living in a mud hut, in Ouidah, for a number of years.... yeah I'm STILL mad! So, while some of them had shoddy research, they did tend to keep their focus.

So, why are you writing about this one might ask? It is simple. Plenty people come to us...some researchers. And, I have found that these folk can be especially vulnerable to the Voduns if they have somehow offended them. One researcher returned after a few months, in Ouidah, and wrote a scaving book about her relationship with the Supreme Chief of Vodun himself. This researcher has since been discredited and has saw much personal tragedy since her return. Others have come with other such devastating personal tragedies in their lives. I am not saying that I was perfect while in Africa. I made a few mistakes; but, my focus was always on the Voduns; and, if anyone chose to cut me off from them... in anyway...they were dropped like a hot potato. I showed respect and honor, toward the Voduns, even when those who served them did not. I fell down, I got up, wiped myself off and continued at every step. I refused to be beat or struck down; and, even when the odds were against me, I kept on moving...'cause there was something in me that refused to let me give up! That ancestor, that spirit that pushed me, daily, knew what was needed. There were times I was tired, worn out, hungry, out of money, struck down with malaria and didn't think I would make it; but, I did! For inside of me was the blood of centuries of Africans, centuries of those who died in slavery; and, I wasn't about to give up.... I had come too far to turn back. It wasn't for me I kept going it was for them. For it is THEY who died and sacrificed for me... there is none other.

So, to the researcher...the mistress chasing the Voduns...if your heart is pure Vodun is a gentle lover. You will not know its true secrets for they are not for you to know; but, it will reveal it's majesty! But in either case, whether your intentions are good or not, there is a price; and, Vodun will exact that price whenever it is good and ready. Oh, and by the way folks, don't believe everything, about Vodun, that you may see in books. You can't learn Vodun from books. You must go into a temple to truly know Vodun. The mistress never knows the husband better than the wife.

VODUN PLAIN AND SIMPLE

I have great respect for my academic friends. I also have great respect for those who are able to express themselves, beautifully, using some of the most prolific phrases and/or words from the English language. I so wish that I could do that, but, I can't. I'm just a plain woman...educated to be sure...but for some reason straddling both the 'hood and the world of academia. Problem is I'm feeling way too comfortable from whence I come. I'm more of a storyteller than an academic; so, today I'm just going tell you all, a few basics, plain and simple, about what vodun is and how it may benefit your life.

1. The term vodun means "spirit" in the Fon language. I like to refer to the term as "spirit" or "that which is sacred". As the slaves brought it over with them during the transAtlantic slave era it has become known, in the diaspora as, "voodoo" or vodou, in the Caribbean, and "hoodoo" or "rootwork" in the Americas. But not to confuse, you, I am going to continue with describing what the original African Vodun is...the source, or origins, of diasporan voodoo.

2. There was a time, in mankind's history, when he had a direct communication with his ancestors, as well as, the divine beings that created him. This time predates any organized religions that are in existence today. This is vodun.

3. On the African continent, the birthplace of man, this mode

of direct communication with divine beings (spirits) existed then and still exist today. And in other traditional cultures, around the world, this direct communication between man, the spirit world and nature may be called many things, due to the different languages; but, it still denotes...that which is sacred or vodun.

4. In vodun animal sacrifice is necessary. Why? Because in order for spirits to be able to work, and help you, they need the blood of animal sacrifice. It is the "blood" of the sacrifice that reinvigorates them and gives them the power and force, needed, to work for you. Just like blood does for us... it is the life force. Without our blood, we simply die. Or, if our blood is low and we are transfused, it reinvigorates our bodies. Well, this is what the blood does for the spirits as well. Each spirit has it's own preferred sacrificial animal.

5. Vodun's direct communication with the spirit world comes through two mediums: divination and possession. Divination comes through the system of Ifa or the west African divination system. Spirit possession occurs when a vodunsi, or server of the spirits, is possessed by the spirit of an ancestor or a divine being. In Maya Deren's (1953) prolific work she describes this phenomena as the "Divine Horsemen".

6. Vodun employs a Priesthood and workers, or servers, of the spirits. These individuals are born to their vocations, or stations; and, Ifa reveals those born to it. In that we are all born of the spirits Ifa can reveal who and what we are in the spirit world, as well as, our ancestry. These individuals are sent, from the spirits, to be of service to mankind with specific spiritual missions, and, if initiated according to the tenants of the ancestors and the divine spirits are ordained by them. They in turn, therefore, can tell you, through the use of Ifa, about each and every one they ordain.

7. What can Vodun do for me? Well if you are a diasporan of African descent, or any other decent for that matter, it can reconnect you to your African ancestry or original ancestry. Authentic African divination can reveal ancestry, head spirit and accompanying spirits, any presenting problem(s) and recommended solutions (sacrifices to be given) to alleviate these problems.

8. When we are born we may come down with a specific spiritual mission. Vodun, through Ifa, can reveal that mission and connect you to the spirits that gave you life.

9. Vodun can help you contact loved ones who have passed over to the other side. It can help you to make sure that they are at peace or allow you to seek their assistance, with the divinities, to help you in times of trouble. Our ancestors specifically intercede, on our behalf, with the divinities seeking their assistance for their children in trying times. Therefore, giving sacrifice to our ancestors is paramount in this and enables them to do what they can in, the spiritual realm, to help us.

10. In that the voduns see the present, past and future they can guide you in making the correct life's choices, be it a mate, financial security or career choice. They are good in practical matters, as well as, spiritual because if one's life goes "topsy turvy" there is usually a spiritual component, that is lacking, that causes these problems.

11. One more thing I would like to mention. I speak of organized religions above. I refer to vodun as a spiritual system, rather than a religion, because the spirits designed it, rules it, and insist on obedience to its tenants; but, traditional African vodun is more organized than one would think. There is a Supreme Chief of Vodun and chiefs of each of the pantheons of voduns. Therefore, there is some accountability in African Vodun. The diaspora sorely lacks this at the moment, as well

as, an authentic divination system. But the spirits in their infinite wisdom are in the process of relieving some of these challenges.

For many, today, church simply isn't working for us. I say go back to the ways of our ancestors. The information, above, is not a complete picture of what vodun is; but, it is a start. Check it out! You might find it to be a better fit!

BEWARE OF THE SE (SOUL) BINDERS

In Vodun the Se (accent over the e) is the soul. This beautiful spirit comes down with all of the others at birth. When one has been identified, by Ifa, as being born to serve the Priesthood, or the spirits in general, this great spirit must have ceremony as all others. One can be born of a particular gender; but, one's head spirit, as well as one's Se can be of another gender. In any event this great spirit is our moral compass, as it were, and comes direct from the Godhead itself.

Increasingly we are seeing people who come to us with great difficulties in their lives due to their dealing with unscrupulous Priests, who in an attempt to control them, bind their Se. We have had folks who have gone to Nigeria for work and have come to us; and, when divination was done, revealed that their Se was captured, bound in a tree and crying. One particular case took my husband, an African Priest, one week in a Nigerian forest, surrounded by people he did not know, to undo this work. Others have come where their Se has been banished and bound to zogbe, the place of those who have died of unnatural deaths; and, still others have been found walking without their Se, or soul, because some Priest is out there attempting to control them and has it in their possession. We have found this phenomena with just as many men as women.

With women, it has been those that are the most vulnerable. Those women who either go to ceremonies. They are at their most vulnerable moments. If they are beautiful, of a foreign nationality;

and, it is divined that they carry a big and prosperous spirit they can become a target. Some unscrupulous Priests will caution them not to worry; but, instead, will busy themselves asking their particulars so as to bind them to them as spouses and/or for financial gain. And, in that we cannot function properly without the Se, one will begin to experience their lives falling apart right before their eyes but not understand what is happening. When they finally come to us divination reveals that their Se is no longer with them.

As mentioned above, in many instances, these women see their lives falling apart bit by bit but cannot figure out what is going on. They find themselves caving into the wishes of a certain Priest, or Holy man, but cannot figure out how they came to have gotten into such a mess. They had no initial attraction to the person; yet, they find that they are, now, sending money to this person and doing things that they would not normally do. When they, somehow, come out from under and authentic African divination is performed, by a highly skilled diviner, they find out that their very soul has been bound.

For men, this happens generally because someone is angry, envious or attempting to steal their star or life force. If it is revealed, through divination, that this person will see wonderful things for his future an unscrupulous individual, while claiming he is doing work for the gentleman, can be actively binding him or stealing his very essence that they may use his good spirits, star and/or fortune for themselves.

Vodun can be a dangerous business folks if you do not know what you are doing! Too many folks in the diaspora think Vodun is just a bunch of spells and rituals; and, for a few dollars one can get something done. Authentic African Vodun carries the force and power of the Africa, on their own, or jump on the internet needing help and say they have no money for ancestors and the divine spirits themselves. On that continuum of spirits are those that are godly and pure as well as those that can damage and/or take your life! Vodun is not about holy books and one having faith in its power. VODUN IS POWER! Vodun is mankind dealing directly with spirits that can overtly and completely affect our lives on every level of our existence. It is the original method of communication from the creator to its creation. It is serious; and, it can be dangerous!

But, do not be deceived! A person walking without their Se or soul is a dead person walking. This is too serious a matter for folks to be putting their spiritual lives in just anyone's hands. These Africans know things that many think died with the old prophets. But no! In some families, these secrets are still there. They exist! I promise you they do! Anytime a man, such as my husband, can sit in a mirror in Benin, West Africa and see me, his wife, sitting on a couch in the United States eating and dropping food on my vodun cloths, become annoyed, pick up the phone and tell me to go and change...there is power in Vodun! Anytime a man can spend 4 hours walking at the bottom of the sea with all of Benin watching, waiting and witnessing this walk on the banks of the sea with camera crews and media from all over...there is power in Vodun!

I know that many of you are wanting to make it to Africa to do ceremonies, find ancestors and do much more. But, I beg you be careful! Do not be in such a rush! Check out these people. Talk to folks that have been there. Look for reputable Priests/Priestesses. Do a bit of research before you go running, because, the work to unbind the Se (soul) is costly and tedious.

VODUN AND MONEY

I learned very early on, in reference to money, that what was for the voduns was for the voduns, what was for me was for me; and, what was for me was still owned and controlled by the voduns. As I had placed myself in their hands, by way of the initiation process, it was they that controlled my life and thus my resources be they financial or otherwise. And, regardless of how imperfect I may have felt, I was their vessel; and, that my human imperfections would be ounterbalanced by my promises of obedience to their words. And, ı so doing, they would be the light unto my pathways seeing, in nison, the past, the present and the future, thus, giving me all of the uidance that I would so sorely need.

In my early years in the Supreme Chief of Vodun's temple, in Ouidah) Benin, I would often give monies for the upkeep of the emple in which I was a part. As I would offer my money the chief vould insist that what was offered, to the voduns, be put in one stack nd what was given to him, personally, put in another stack. Then, would observe him take the vodun's monies, that I had offered, fter a ritual of giving drinks, kolas and prayer lay it down before the oduns. He would then take the monies offered, for his own upkeep, nd do whatever ceremonies he had been asked to do, by the voduns, or his family or self and use whatever was left over, if any, for his ousehold expenses. This I observed of many a devout priests out f west Africa. And, as a result, has become my own standard. As did not speak the traditional language, at the time, I learned by xample and by doing. And this is how I have come to know vodun's elationship to money.

Money is not to glorify ourselves, as people of the Priesthood, ut to do the important work of the spirits. It is not to show how rosperous we have become but should indicate the prosperity, iches and/or blessings of the spirits. This is not to say that being vealthy is a bad thing. It most certainly is not! For all of the spirits are ich! The wealth of the universe was created and is owned by them. But, to chase wealth in lieu of it becoming your God as opposed to he divinities, then, you have a problem. The spirits command that THEY be first not another. And, if it is in your destiny to be a person of means and are obedient to the call and commands of the spirits hen it shall be so. The beauty of a humble man is in appreciating that which the spirits provide for him and not coveting that which is for another.

It takes money to perform ceremonies. Sacrificial animals must be purchased, those working in the temples, for vodun, must be compensated for their time away from their jobs and/or families. This means that drummers must be compensated, those preparing the animals and foods, the vodun dancers, the Priest himself and so much more. African Vodun is very big on ceremony. This is what the spirits require, therefore, monies must be spent. But this is where the concentration of monies should go...on the work of vodun...not buying someone a new car, to profile in, or a new house to show everybody over the internet or impress one's neighbors or friends. These material things can either be lost or fade away; but, one's spiritual wealth and integrity lasts forever. And, as the old folks used to say, "I ain't never seen no u haul trailing behind no hearse!" In other words, you can't take it with you.

As a colleague said to me recently, the voduns have a way of dealing with wayward or incorrect people. He is so correct! The emphasis, in vodun, should be on one's spiritual service... service to the spirits as well as one's service to mankind...not the acquiring of things or money! But if you are blessed, to have been given means, through your service and obedience to the spirits, then, you have been divinely blessed! However, remember! What belongs to the voduns is for the voduns; and, what belongs to you is for, you, but controlled and still owned by the voduns because YOU ARE A VESSEL FOR THEM!

VODUN AND A MESSAGE TO MY YOUNG AFRICAN FRIENDS

As my friendship numbers grow, on facebook, I've noticed a huge proliferation of young African men requesting my friendship. It's a good thing, I enjoy great friendships; however, like clockwork, I can predict their pattern of behavior. They approach me immediately, upon my approving their friendship, and request help to find money, success, a decision on marriage or a way to make it to America or some parts of the diaspora. These are not problems within themselves. Many come to a Priest or Priestess to help better their life conditions; but, this is my general advice to you as I generally tate in our correspondences.

Do not pass go; but, take yourself directly to a local diviner, or fa/Fa/Afa priest, and lay your problems down before him. Now, his is where they ask me... where they can find one? Now, I'm in America folks! Like who is it that I'm going to know in your local neighborhood? Get your hind quarters out of that chair, leave your computer screen and go out and search for one! Africa is full of them! But this is not why I'm writing....

I'm writing because this, apparent disconnection to traditional Africa by Africans, is a fall result of all of the missionary work done n Africa! In Nigeria, for instance, spirits from the sea are often demonized and said to lure men to their deaths. Young African men are having to go on the internet and search for someone to tell hem how to go and have their needs met by their own traditional Priests! Someone, born in another country, has to teach them the mportance of what they already have. Our young Africans are desiring prosperity but do not realize that unless you are feeding your ancestors, and the spirits that gave you life, you may not see any prosperity! Things are difficult here in the diaspora; and, if they are hard here I can imagine how difficult it must be in many African countries. My young Africans this is one of those times when you need your ancestors, and the divinities, more than you ever have! You need to give sacrifice my young friends!

I don't care what that missionary or that preacher man is telling you! Go to your ancestral village if you still know where it is. Go feed your ancestors and the family voduns so that your pathways may become clear. Reconnect to the elders, in your villages, and ask the voduns to give you what you need that you may send back some of that prosperity to help your elders and the family. If you do they (the Priests and the spirits) will work hard for you. But you must return and give back. This is paramount! Because if you do not you will anger those spirits that worked so diligently for you!

My sons I appreciate the way all of you have approached me. For you understand that I am your spiritual mother. You understand the Priesthood; and, for that I am so very grateful. You have always approached me with humility and respect. My children, in the diaspora, can learn much for you. But, my loves, you must understand that to get something from the voduns you must give. Vodun cannot be done on the internet. You must go out and visit the diviner or the Priest and work with them directly. I will guide you to the best of my ability; but, I cannot do it for you! So, do not be annoyed when I send you right back into your own neighborhoods. You are Africans; and, what you need for your spiritual success is already there.

WHY LOVE SPELLS MAY OR MAY NOT WORK

One of my least favorite things has been folks who have come wanting to get old girlfriends or old boyfriends back. With a married couple, however, I view that dynamic differently. One's desire is to try and diagnose the problem so as to keep this union together; however, girlfriends and boyfriends, who have no such commitment and have already separated, is a different matter. And, with all the bad things out there, witchcraft, folks throwing juju right and left, people walking around without their Se (accent on the e), or souls, due to incompetent spiritual workers or straight up charlatans, folks showing up telling me about their love issues have, sadly, never been a priority. As a strong-willed woman, I have never wanted anybody who no longer wanted me. I would go cry myself to sleep, if I had to, if a man I really cared for decided to get to steppin'. I always felt it best to allow time to heal me. I had a bit too much pride and self-respect to go a' chasin'. So, I have made a few mistakes, in how I have viewed this matter, and lost a few potential friends and/or spiritual children in the process. To those persons I am truly sorry. But besides the fact that folks should try, if they can, to continue forward, if not wanted, I want to discuss some of the real reasons these love spells may or may not work.

The work of Vodun has always been to help persons live a more productive and prosperous life. Therefore, if one begins by, first, going to the diviner the spirits will instruct them on the best course they may take in obtaining their life's goals. Love spells may or may not work because it may not be in a person's best interest to actually be re-united with that person. If the spirit searches the heart of the person, in which you seek to reunite, and that person has flaws that will only complicate or cause you misery, then, the spirits... your ancestors and the spirits that gave you life...will refuse. Our own spirits, sometimes, causes dissension within our relationships to actually get rid of a bad or undesirable mate. Those spirits living within you, in many instances, can cause the person to flee. This is why I am often hesitant when dealing with these issues and suggest full divination to see if a person's spirits will actually allow someone to be reunited with the person they seek. Spiritual workers who make guarantees, of you getting an old lover back, without consulting the spirits are doing you a disservice. They are essentially taking your money, because, there are no guarantees if one is focused on obeying the instructions of the spirits. Case in point...

A young woman came to us so in love with some dude she couldn't see straight. She had to have him back at all costs. This child had spent over $10,000 on psychics. Her life, according to her, simply could not function without this man. He had dogged her out something terribly and took off with another woman. Divination was completed. The spirits, straight up, refused. Her ancestors were adamant! They had revealed the young man's true nature and all the things he was doing behind her back and the troubles he could cause her in the future. Once we revealed this to her she didn't care. She wanted this man anyway and pleaded that we do something. This is when WE refused! As a Priest and Priestess, of Vodun, my husband and I refuse to disobey the spirits. There is no amount of money anywhere that will allow us to do otherwise.

These love spells, that folks are peddling, can be very misleading if the practitioners are not using Ifa. There are never any guarantees to anything in Vodun until the spirits, themselves, have had their say. Often promises are made and those who spend their money buy into these promises and wait and wait and wait. When nothing happens, they run from practitioner to practitioner trying to see who has the power to bring this loved one back. But it isn't a matter of power. It is a matter of if the spirits will even allow this person to return. The spirits are all powerful! There is nothing that they cannot do; but, they will refuse someone to enter your life if he or she is detrimental to your well being.

Sometimes the person does come back on their own. However, I have found out, in life, that this is generally the case, anyway, if a person feels that they have made a mistake in regard to how they may have treated you. If you have continued on, in your life, you may find that time has healed you; and, you no longer desire this person. Or, after an apology and some sincere changing you may resume your relationship. Either way, if the reunion happens naturally, then, it more or less was destiny. But to force someone to return, I feel, has ethical issues.

In any event, I will no longer turn folks away when they come with these issues. But, I'm telling you straight up! We going to Ifa; so, you must pay for a divination. And, I will tell you what the spirits say; but, I ain't givin you no guarantees.

WHO DECIDES OUR SPIRITUAL WORTHINESS...THE VODUNS (THE SPIRITS) OR MANKIND?

In all of our world's "religions" one can find the invisible hands of the voduns ("the spirits"), or "God" or the "Almighty" depending on how one wishes to term our creator(s). However, to what extent man allows these spirits to determine the tenets of these systems and man's ability to be obedient to them largely determines their effectiveness in helping mankind with their everyday concerns. Throughout our history examples can be found that show what can happen when man puts his own spin on what is to be of these religious systems, for instance, those Muslim jihadists who misinterpret the term, the Christian Crusades (1095 - 1291) and the selling of Indulgences by the Catholic Church, in the late Middle Ages, just to name a few. And even in today's times we are forever dealing with those serving traditional African spiritual systems, in the diaspora, who propose to decide WHO and WHO CAN NOT serve the spirits.

This essay has been prompted by the recent decision of Pope Francis, on 11/23/2014, to canonize six new persons to the Catholic priesthood to spiritual sainthood. While I am sure, as part of the Catholic Church, this is his right; but, I question is this the right of man or of the divinities themselves? I argue that it is the latter. One could argue that the Pope is the mouthpiece of God for this particular spiritual system; and, for my own, vodun, a priest or priestess such as myself. But the difference in vodun is that we have Ifa. We have a mechanism that was put into place, by the divine, in order to determine what it is that the spirits, themselves, want rather than what we want. Voduns in their ability to see the past present and future all at once also examines the hearts of mankind. Any tests that may be employed by a human being cannot possibly compete with that.

When man/woman declares themselves on the level of God (I am not necessarily referring to the Pope) rather than the vessels to which they allow God to speak through them can become a problem. For it is only God, or the spirits themselves, who can determine who is to be elevated in the spiritual realm or identify those who were born to serve them. That is WHY everyone regardless of race, creed, color or gender should be allowed to go before the voduns; and, if their own ancestors or spirits find fault with them, or their life's choices, let THEY be the ones who tell them. But WE, as vessels for the spirits, have absolutely no right to make those judgment calls on our own. My only issues with folks, serving the spirits, has been directed towards those who REFUSE to serve according to the tenets of the spirits;

and, that is to seek authentic African divination to see if they were born to serve, in whatever capacity, and proceed accordingly. The African priesthood must be defended and upheld by those who were born to serve within it. Of this I have the spiritual authority to insist upon and will do so with my very life. But as to what color one's skin is, where one comes from or one's sexual orientation, in reference to their right to serve, is of no concern of mine. As for this right, let each man or woman answer to his or her own God. The task of helping those destined with the reconnection to their ancestors and voduns, as dictated by my spiritual mission, is my primary concern.

The voduns have their own methods of elevating those who have lived a life that is worthy to spiritual heights within the spiritual realm. And, through authentic African divination they can tell us who those persons are. As an example, I will leave you with this story...one that I have written about before. While attending a Mami Tchamba ceremony, in (Cotonou) Benin, a truly amazing story was told to me by a spirit that had lived many centuries ago. After taking the head of a vodunsi, he related his beautiful story to me through the English-speaking priest who was performing the ceremony for me. The spirit is called Ade (accent over the "e" and pronounced ADAY with a short sound over the "a"). This is the spirit of the hunter and is the patron spirit for those wishing to do work or feed their loved ones at zogbe...those who have died of unnatural causes. This is an extremely important vodun for us in the diaspora. While living as a man this spirit lived during the times of human sacrifices in vodun. He was the one, in his village, who would go out and procure the sacrifices. All of his life he had remained obedient to the words of the spirits and did not waiver. Upon his own death those who prepared his body were directed, by the voduns, to take sacrifices and with specific instructions, by them, use these blood sacrifices to prepare his body, according to their specifications, for his journey into the spirit world. And, as such, this humble man with the extremely difficult task of procuring human sacrifices for the work of the spirits, himself, became a vodun.

My brothers and sisters there is NO excuse not to serve the spirits with all due diligence. WE do not have to guess, intuit or leave it to chance. Ifa is there, the ancestors and the divinities are there. It is up to us to simply ASK, RECEIVE INSTRUCTIONS and OBEY.

VODUN'S FIRSTS

As we approach a New Year I would like to remind ourselves of some of vodun's basics...or vodun's "firsts" as it may. These are designed for those who may feel that they are being "called" by the spirits in some way.

FIRST, authentic African divination is essential. It is through this medium that one is able to determine ancestry and who and what one is in the spiritual realm, as well as, one's destiny or spiritual mission if applicable.

SECOND, finding the ancestor(s) is most important. Why? Much of who and what we are is inherited spiritually and biologically from them. Any spiritual or physical thrones (kingships/queenships) as well as divination tools, if applicable, are passed down through ancestry. INSIDE these divination tools lives the ancestral diviners, Tassinouns, spirits and any of their spiritual POWER which came before us. These tools, therefore, must be handed down or made by someone of one's familial clan. The great Ifa makes this all possible by giving us the appropriate familial connections. One's divining tool, whatever it is, (mirror, opele, or other) bares a direct linkage between you and those familial diviners that come before you. One's divining ability can not be "bought". It is innate! In addition, African familial clans often have voduns (spirits), languages, burial rites, customs and rituals peculiar to that clan and that clan alone. One wants to find this ancestor to reconnect and regain this knowledge (these secrets) that were lost as a result of either the trans-Atlantic slave trade or the family's migration out of Africa.

THIRD, African vodun and ALL African based spiritual systems hail from Africa...not Haiti, not Cuba, Jamaica or anywhere else. And IF one wants to see these systems in their original state one must travel there or involve themselves with authentically initiated Africans. However, for those spirits that may have lived and died in the diaspora those priest or priestesses, from those regions, may know them best. These are generally our youngest group of ancestors. They have no problems making themselves known to those that belong to them and have been diligent, over the centuries, in protecting their loved ones from the ravages of the slave trade. However, the DIVINITIES, those that created the universe and all it contains can only be called by those duly ordained by them; and, this is generally the Africans, However, while the African priesthood is trained in such a way that they may call any spirit from anywhere on the globe those who know diaspora spirits, for instance during a Haitian Revolution best, would be the Haitians and those of Cuba the Cubans; BUT, those who the divinities know without a doubt and they them are the Africans. So, if you want to know your ancestry from the oldest to the newest from the darkest to the lightest; and, if you want to be able to walk into that ancestral village or find out their origins, how they died, how they came into the diaspora or anything else...cross the Atlantic or better still have authentic divination performed by a reputable African or African trained diviner. Tarot cards, nor regular playing cards are the appropriate divination tools for African or African-based spiritual systems. And, if not a single ancestor you have has anything to do with Haiti or it's revolution and you are of European descent you have no business initiating in the diaspora. Your oldest ancestor is African and the youngest are sitting somewhere in Europe. You have no Haitian spirits or ancestry. Europe sits right on top of Africa what are you going to Haiti or Cuba for?

FOURTH, so you have had authentic African divination; and, it was found that you not only were born to the spirits but your ancestry was found and you should be initiated. What next? We, Temple Behumbeza, can escort you to that ancestral village if the divination was done by us. If not, you should be escorted by a reputable priest or priestess so that you will not be taken advantage of. REMEMBER! To many Africans we are strangers coming from a foreign land until it is proven, through Ifa, that you actually belong to them. And even then, some may see you as a threat to any throne that you might be in line for. In some instances, there may be a family temple. If so you may do all of your familial ceremonies there. In reference to your head spirit you may need to find a reputable priest who carries the spirit you were born to. One initiates with someone who has been duly initiated and has lived with the spirit that you carry. In most instances that can also be your family temple. For what better person to help you with this vodun. If you know no one, however, ask the voduns through Ifa. The spirits, themselves, knows to whom THEY have ordained and will tell you to whom they prefer. You go to that person or if it is us who has done this divination, but, you were not born with the spirit of Mami Dan, then, we will inquire for you, find that person and help in the negotiation process on the fees. If you choose we will also be there with you every step of the way or keep check on you if needed. From there you are in the hands of the spirits and the priest or priestess that you are being initiated by. But even in that here are a few pointers.

FIFTH, most start their spiritual journey by first receiving the vodun Fa. In this way, you may communicate with the spirits. This does not mean, however, that you are of the priesthood of Ifa. Only Ifa can determine that for us; but, ALL within the priesthood, of African vodun, are given the vodun Fa that you might communicate with the spirits by whatever divination tool the spirits say you will use. And, after the initiation process, when the priest is to set down your voduns, the first to be set down is the great Sakpata. Why? Sakpata owns EVERYTHING that is under our feet. Many, in the diaspora, know of Papa Legba; but, few understand that the patron (boss) of Papa Legba is Sakpata. Look at it this way... yes, one honors the one at the crossroads; but, one must FIRST honor the one who actually owns the crossroads. This knowledge has been lost, to vodun, in the diaspora. But, let me be clear here. If someone travels to Africa and is "supposedly" initiated but returns with no voduns YOU HAVE NO POWER! Our power is not in us but is in the voduns! And WE, as priests and priestesses, are only as powerful as our relationship with the spirits is strong. You come back here, from Africa, and All you have is a put together shrine...YOU'VE GOT NOTHING! But you have been had!

So, finally, here we have it, a few FIRSTS in African Vodun. The spirits that dwell within you and the priest/priestess, or spiritual parent, will take you the rest of the way. My task is to point you in the right direction and give you enough information that will allow you to make better informed spiritual decisions. I hope I have done just that this year. May the ancestors forever guard your back and the divine ones forever lead your front.

CHAPTER 6

THE FABULOUS MAMI WATA DAN

"With hair, heels, and attitude, honey, I am through the roof".

- RuPaul

WHO IS THE AFRICAN MAMI WATA

In the diaspora, one hears much about the great Mami Wata. This divinity is magnificent! Known by many names, Yemoja and others, she is a beauty to behold. But just WHO is this great spirit? Mami is a water spirit. She is not one spirit but many. She is the head of a pantheon of vodun (spirits) that include MANY spirits with many unique characters and personalities. Many diasporans are unaware of this fact which often leads them down a path of misunderstanding of this great vodun. Folks like to tell me they are Mami; but, when I ask WHICH spirit in Mami they cannot tell me. Africans can say which one. My focus today, however, is on a group of spirits, that are part of the pantheon of Mami, that many are just discovering; but, they have ALWAYS been there. These are known as many of the great Hindu gods.

Many say that Hinduism is the oldest religion in the world. It isn't! African spiritual systems are. It's just that much is not written. But common sense prevails if one understands that the African is God's first creation and God always communicated with this creation directly. However, for those book hawks out there Alice C. Linsley discusses this very subject "African Religion Predates Hinduism" in JUST GENESIS: Through the lens of Anthropology, May 5, 2010. One must understand that Africans generally serve the spirits they are born to; and, these spirits, while known in the Hindu culture by a particular name, may be called something else in Africa. Case in point, my spirit...DATTATREYA, known in Africa, as the great Den'su meaning 'father of the river', in Mina. I was born of this spirit; therefore, this is the spirit I serve which is part of the Mami Wata pantheon of spirits. I am not Hindu but vodun...see the difference? My sister is Krishna, my grandfather was Ganesh. Yes, Africans, as well as, African Americans or anyone else can be born of these spirits; and, they are Mami Wata. In particular they are called Mami Dan.

As researchers are combing the west coast of Africa they are seeing these Hindu spirits painted on the African temples and assuming that we are borrowing from Hinduism. We are not! They have always been with us! While there are many Hindu temples in West Africa...see "Hindu Gods in West Africa" by Albert Kafui Wuaku, 2013, Ghanaian devotees of Shiva and Krishna...these spirits are inclusive in vodun because there are Africans born of these spirits. In "Spirit, Blood and Drums: The Orisha Religion in Trinidad" by James T. Houk, 1995, many Hindu deities are discussed as being inclusive of orisha worship. But the newest books on African vodun are purporting that we have "borrowed" from Hinduism and various other spiritual systems. This is a misunderstanding of what vodun is. Vodun is spiritualism at its lowest common denominator...the spirits themselves. And while we are all born of spirits, originating from everywhere, the Africans serve the spirits that they were born to; and, those spirits known in the Hindu pantheon are born to Africans as well as the Hindu and many other people of various spiritual systems. They simply may be known by different names in the African pantheon of spirits. So, I want to get out in front and simply tell you that these Hindu spirits have always been a part of African practices. They may be rare, since we inherit many of our spirits from our ancestors or kin; but, it happens just the same. One generally has to be on the inside of these systems to understand this. Unless a researcher employs the research methodology of 'participant observer' and/or become completely immersed in a culture it is often difficult to understand this.

WHO IS THE AFRICAN MAMI WATA? PART 2

Recent works, on vodun, have begun to emphasize the Tchamba Voduns. In that these spirits are associated with Mami Wata I would like to say a few things about them.

These great spirits are ancestral, for some of us, and are called Mami Tchamba (or Mami Tchaba) voduns. In pre-colonial times, there were many great tribes in Africa. There still are today. Some of them owned slaves. One such tribes, the Ashanti, were one. I speak of it because, as a descendant, this is how I have come to serve these great spirits. When one's ancestry is divined, by Fa, these spirits eventually appear. As these slaves served our families we now pay tribute by serving them. Fa tells us how many of these spirits we have, who they were, how they died and our commitment to them. As a result, I can call them out by name. These spirits are generally fed outside of the temple because of death by unnatural causes. We call this place zogbe in vodun. Anyone who dies outside of natural causes goes to zogbe after death. It is from this place that we must feed our loved ones that they may get the opportunity to eat with their ancestors. Unfeed and bewildered they will always be separated from them. These ceremonies are extremely necessary for us. I think of all the young African American men who have died on the streets, in prisons, and of all manner of mishaps, lynchings and the like. We need to help our people. This Jesus whom, himself, died at zogbe cannot possibly help us.

MORE ON MAMI WATA

I have written on Mami Wata before. That essay is entitled "Who is the African Mami Wata?" in my earlier writings. But, today, because our yearly calendar of events is out, I simply wanted to mention a few things.

Mami Wata is the crowning glory of the voduns. Inside this great pantheon are countless water spirits...the highest being Mami Dan... Those spirits who manifest in the animal form of the serpent. This pantheon, of vodun, includes MawuLissa the Godhead. It is a misnomer, in the diaspora, that Mami Wata is all about the priesthood of women. This is incorrect! Mami Wata is equally as male as it is female. In most pantheon, of spirits, it has a counterpart in Mami. For instance, the king of the Sakpata is Dah Zodji; and, he is part of those who carry Mami. It would be the same for Gu and others. We are all born of spirit, from all of the elements it is simply a matter of who is our head and what pantheon, of spirits we were born to Ifa/Fa/Afa can reveal all of this. But, what is MOST important is ancestry! These great spirits come out of particular ancestries. If you notice, at the bottom of the calendar of events, is the name Togbe Lakpan. This is one of the great ancestors of the Mami Wata. I am not versed well enough to know if this is the main one or not; but, I do know that when it comes to, Mami Wata, decisions are made from this particular group. A Togolese would have to give you better insight into this. So, I do not care what folks, in the diaspora, tell you. You cannot do vodun, effectively, without the ancestor. You MUST take the time to go, to Ifa, and find him. Because it is there, through birthright, that one claims one's spiritual thrones. They are not made up or imagined. You are BORN to them!

MAMI WATA'S DRUMS/MUSIC

In African Vodun each spirit has it own pearls (beading), colors, dances, songs and many other things peculiar to that particular spirit. One learns about these things in the initiation chamber. This is why when Mami Wata vodunsi are dancing it is observed that they are doing so in sync. It is the sacred drum that calls these vodunsi to dance; and, the singer (the one who calls out the song), the drummer, the drum, and the dancing vodunsi work, in unison, to honor, each spirit, with his own music. All is sacred, the drum, it's drummer, the vodunsi dancers and their pearls, duly initiated into a particular pantheon of spirits...in this case Mami Wata, the songs and the dances.

WHY THE AFRICAN MAMI DAN INITIATIONS CAN NOT BE PERFORMED IN THE UNITED STATES AT THIS TIME

People often ask me about the initiation process in Mami Wata. They want to know how long it is and how much it costs. I have already written that costs, of initiations, in Africa, depend on what a person's spirit (spirits being as individual as people) ask to be done for that person. One always starts with feeding ones ancestors; so, throughout the process one is constantly dealing with the prices of livestock etc. Ultimately the fees and costs is worked out between the person his/

her spirits and the priest or priestess doing the initiation. But, my subject today spotlights Mami Wata. Not just any Mami spirit; but, specifically, those divine spirits that manifest their animal form as the serpent...Mami-Dan. These are the highest of the divinities, in Mami, and many of these spirits are known in the pantheon of the Hindu Gods; but, are born with those of African descent as well. I am Mami-Dan. And, the last time I checked, I was not only of African descent but born of the spirit Dattatreya, known in Africa as Den'su... meaning 'father of the river' in the Mina language. So was my father, my grandfather was Ganesha, a sister Krishna and so forth and so on. It happens folks! I am not Hindu or of European descent. So, all the critics out there who cannot understand WHY our temple has so many Hindu spirits in it...it is because my husband and I are BOTH Dattatreya and we ONLY serve the spirits that we were born with... those that gave us life! The personal name of my husband's Dattatreya is BEHUMBEZA, thus, Temple Behumbeza; and, WE are Mami-Dan. And Mami-Dan initiations cannot be done in the United States! At least not at this time. This is why...

First, of all, if during the divination and initiation process, if these great spirits see a person that cannot do your initiation properly they will not show themselves. It happened to me. My Dattatreya hid his three heads and Ayidowedo stood up on his great tail. The three African bokonons, in attendance, saw him and assumed I was Wedosi, the wife of Ayidowedo. If these initiations are done incorrectly it could cost you your life! This is one of the reasons, I believe, that many African Americans do not really know who their head spirit really is. There has been only one person that has come to us, in the seven years, I have been on the internet, that was told of their true spirit. And that divination was done by an African. We have not only told them their true spirits but found their ancestry as well. This is why, as a priestess, I am avid about ceremonies being done according to the tenants of the voduns themselves. I have little patience for dabblers, folks throwing shells and reading someone's destiny off the force of gravity, or folks throwing around spells. People's lives can be ruined and to undo this damage is costly; but, in the meantime the person has suffered relentless harm. It is priests/priestesses, like my husband and I, that have to clean up other folk's messes. It is our destiny. But if folk could understand that spirit work is a serious matter and not the work of every Tom, Dick, Harry or Jane it would greatly help!

The preparations for a Mami-Dan initiate could take years. These spirits must be carved or made by special people, usually in Ghana, that for generations only do this work. One's pearls or jewels must be dug out of the ground from sacred places. Each pearl (beading) must be hand strung by initiated vodunsi. One's priestly stool must be carved in one piece out of sacred trees, by artisans, whose work is only to do this. One's ancestral villages must be visited to give sacrifice and to claim those sacred items inherited by the ancestor that entered the diaspora, trips to India or countries to claim left objects, from another life, must be done if instructed. Gold, pearls, diamonds and precious jewels must be bought and collected to adorn the voduns, themselves, and I can go on and on. This is just the tip of it. Africa is an ancient land. These divinities are timeless; but, it is Africa that they first revealed themselves to man. Africa is ripe with the sacred rivers, mountains, temples, trees, lands etc. that is needed to adorn and work with these ancient spirits. As of yet, they have not identified sacred places in this country for us to work with or persons, who for centuries upon centuries, made the vodun carvings or stools etc. I am not saying Mami, in general, cannot be done in the diaspora. These two-week kanzos have been performed for generations it appears. I assume that for what folks understood they have done. The diaspora is full of Mami initiates; but, Mami Dan... No! Anyone telling you otherwise has not experienced this initiation for themselves! I have and STILL have much more to go. These very high spirits were here before the world was ever formed. Coming to know them isn't easy. The initiation process isn't easy. Any African will tell you they are long, arduous and expensive. One can lay in a temple months on end. It ain't no play... And it ain't done instantly... But why should it be? These are DIVINE beings!

THURSDAYS, TURKEY AND MAMI WATA

Mmmmm, turkey...yum, yum! In America on every last Thursday, in November, we honor those we are thankful for with turkey as our main course. But they do not know that Thursday is your sacred day; and, they do not know that turkey, as well as a few other animals, is your blood sacrifice. On this day, American Thanksgiving, all of America honors you my great lady; but, they do not realize it! For you are so very clever my beautiful one! It is YOU, the spirits and the ancestors whose invisible hands have given America her wealth and fame. Thank you for all that you do for us my love! Thank you... the great and beautiful Mami Wata!

TEMPLE BEHMBEZA: MY SPIRITUAL HOME

In at least one of my writings I have spoken of the difficulty in finding a compatible and honest spiritual teacher; that person, guru, priest or priestess that will serve to give you the tools you need spiritually as well as present an example, to you, of what true spirituality must be. It was a long and arduous road; but, after seven consecutive years, in the Republic of Benin, the spirits put both him and me on a journey where we eventually met. This humble man had heard of my story... an African American returning to her ancestral home and struggling to acquire her voduns. For many years I had, upon being initiated into the pantheon of Mami Wata, been called either Mami or Wedosi. I was initiated, in 1999, as Hounnon Houedossi AHOUEGNON. Mami, or some variation of, is often used, in Africa, in referring to women of middle age to be called out of respect. Wedosi was a name used given due to my head spirit being identified, in 1999, as the great Ayido Wedo...meaning the "wife" of Ayido Wedo. In African vodun our spiritual names are associated with the head spirits or pantheon of spirits we are born into. However, after initiation we are told the "personal" name of our head spirit and take it on and are then known by it. But several months prior to my meeting the priest, who would become my spiritual father, the spirit of my Ayido Wedo, himself, delivered the message that I needed to do more work for one of the spirits, I had, called Den'su, in Africa. This great three-headed spirit is known as Dattatreya in the pantheon of the Hindu Gods. I was aware of Den'su. For when my voduns were sat down he was among them. But when the priest, known as Behumbeza which later became my husband, performed divination, for me, to help with my vodun he, and he alone, discovered that this great spirit was not just one amongst others; but, that he in fact was my head. Standing on a mountaintop, when Behumbeza discovered him, he chose to speak and said that he had hidden himself, all of that time, until he found the one that he would designate to perform his ceremonies and was obedient to the will of the spirits. After I complete the requirements needed, as dictated by this great divinity, I will forever be called by his personal name. So, with this began my relationship with Temple Behumbeza which has become my spiritual home.

At present Temple Behumbeza consists of 2 temples. The first and oldest was built over 86 years ago; however, its history began over 183 years ago, in Togo, by an old ancestor of my husband's. As we often inherit the spirits of our forefathers, in African vodun, the spirit Behumbeza belonged to his mother, Edoh Adjele Afiavi Georgette, High Priestess of Vodun and High Priestess of Mami Wata and Guin Vodun (Benin, Ghana, Togo) before her rejoining with the ancestors. When his mother married a Beninese, moved to Benin and was installed as the priestess of the Benin temple, the voduns, from the Togo temple, followed her there. The second temple's construction began in the year 2000 and continues today. There are approximately 600 Vodunsi, Tassinon and Priests as part of the temple collective. Temples Behumbeza are part and parcel of a network of family and ancestral temples that span from Benin to Togo to Ghana.

This temple is what I term a "full service" temple. Authentic African divination is offered and is the cornerstone of our work. For one cannot do anything, spiritually, unless problems are diagnosed and redress or solutions offered by the spirits. One must know who and what a person, is in the spiritual realm, before one can proceed with initiations or in finding solutions for one's problems. It is the spirits that direct the footsteps of everyone that serves in this temple. For we are 100% in their hands; and, its priests do nothing without consulting them first. It is the way of the African ancestor; and, it is the way of African vodun. Divination often sends the priest, and his vodunsi, to one's ancestral villages, other countries or sacred sites to commune with ones ancestral and/or divine spirits and give sacrifice. This is most important for the diasporan due to the vestiges of the transAtlantic slave trade which cut us off physically from our African roots. But through the great Ifa this connection can be re-established both spiritually and physically if the village still exist. And, if not, one's ancestral history can still be reconstituted and our ancestral clan located. Ones head spirit and accompanying spirits can be revealed in this temple also. If divination reveals that one is of the pantheon of Mami Dan we offer full initiation into any spirit within that pantheon; and, if one is not of our pantheon can make appropriate connections for the person with those of the priesthood that one's spirits belong. And if requested can negotiate fees on a client's behalf and shepherd the person throughout the entire process to ensure that they are treated fairly and honestly. But we began by asking the spirits, themselves, to whom they choose to perform their ceremonies and proceed accordingly. Clients needing initiations, protection, healing, spiritual baths, would like to inquire about potential mates, and a multitude of requests, therefore, can be addressed. Fees for ceremonies are worked out between the person, his spirits and the priest. However, one must understand that if the spirits are not in agreement with that which one requests, then, neither are we. This temple does not delve into the dark arts or do anything contrary to the will of the spirits.

Dimple

Grants

CHAPTER 7

AFRICAN-BASED SPIRITUALITY IN THE DIASPORA: ITS TRIUMPHS, IT'S CHALLENGES

"We each have a destiny, a legend that only we can live. To embrace it is scary and dangerous, and most choose not to. Most put it off until tomorrow, until after high school, until after college, until after establishing a financial base. Can't they see? We only get one shot at this life. Tomorrow may never come. The time is now! Not to drop everything and move to Africa, but to find the passion that is inside us and embrace it, to listen to its subtle whispers"

- Erik Mirandette, "The Only Road North" p297

JESUS AIN'T WORKING FOR US

In a 2011 Gallup poll it was found that African Americans are the most religious people in the United States at over 86%. Out of that over 74% are Black women, yet; economically, as a people, we are at the bottom of the barrel. No one even comes close, except for Hispanics, who are the second most religious group at 78%. And Whites, the former oppressor (debatable as to whether it is still true today), at 65% is next to the bottom only more religious than Asians and at the top of the economic spectrum. How can this be? Simple... as we are of African descent we are naturally a spiritual people. It is my contention that Africans are the priest/priestesses of this world. The Voduns (spirits) tell us that Africa is first in spiritual matters with India being second. It, therefore, doesn't surprise me that the African American grabs hold to what he/she perceives as spirituality. It is the slave master that beat this religion into us telling us that we were savages and did not know God. Yet, it is those on the African continent that knew him/her (MawuLissa) first. But we have been duped!

The Jews have never accepted Jesus as the Messiah. The Torah explicitly tells us how the Israelites would recognize the Messiah and Jesus simply does not fit the bill. And certainly, if one reads the Torah one would find that the Messiah was not sent here to take away our sins. Only true sacrifice can purify us and atone for bad acts. So here we are, in America, calling on the name of a man who was a prophet at best, not connected to our ancestry in any way, ignoring the spirits that breathed life into us and disconnected from a history and spirituality that can be traced back to when the world was formed. And we wonder, everyday, why we are still suffering.

I say to those with an ear to here...go back my brethren, go back to that which was lost. Re-connect to that which is our birthright... African Spirituality because Jesus ain't working for us!

VICKI WINAN SAYS: "AS LONG AS I'VE GOT KING JESUS I DON'T NEED NOBODY ELSE" ... BUT, OH, YES WE DO!

As most African Americans, of my generation, I grew up in th church. Church was mandatory. It served wonderful purposes fo black folks, back in the day...probably still do; but, I haven't steppe in one in a minute. It was a place where you went to serve God, hea about politics (that which was adversely affecting blacks anyway) an to socialize. Sistahs loved to hear the latest gossip about some "flussy who may or may not have been a full member of the congregatio chasing some member's son or sweet on the Preacher. At work brother could be a janitor; but, at church, a deacon or an elder. Fo there he was "somebody"!

My passion was and still is music! Gospel music touches me dee within. And, African Americans, a people who have experience untold suffering, due to the slave era, Jim Crow and racism, put a spi on gospel music that has forever changed it! As a result, we are som of the best gospel singers that the world has ever known. We sin from deep within the soul. African American gospel has no equal And I love it just as much, today, as I ever have. The only thing tha has changed; however, is that today I know who to sing for. It ain' Jesus! It's the spirits!

I can not be annoyed at my brothers and sisters who are still i the church. Our faith, our spirituality as a people...a people wh instinctively understand that there is something out there greate than ourselves because of our African heritage, to them, I offe pardon and understanding. Why? Because I know that in all of th world's spiritual systems, whatever they are, the spirits are inside There has been many a godly church-going woman or man holdin their families together through the plight of some of our most difficul times in the diaspora. I cannot forget or dishonor them. Yet, I know that the ancestors are quietly waking their children to reconnect t that which our ancestors have always served; and, that is the ancestor and the divine ones themselves. Jesus is not, particularly, our way ut, someone else's way. He was the way of our "enslaver", the way f our "massa", the way of our "oppressor". He was the way of our lyncher" and is the way of our "incarcerator". We are a people with unique ancestry and an ancient heritage. It is to the ancestors that re are best served. And, it is to those spirits that were born with us came down with us) that should be getting the praise and the honor or overcoming those difficulties that we have had in our lives.

But, for those who love gospel and who enjoy gettin' the "good oot", like I do, just keep on listening to the sistahs like Vicki Winans. Girlfriend can sing! African American gospel is a part of who we are s a people! I am not a person who believes in the denial of self ...be hat of one's African heritage and/or one's American heritage. We are who we are! So, until you learn enough traditional songs to replace hem, keep on pattin' your feet and clappin' your hands.... just know who's really supposed to be gettin' the praise!

'O WHOM DO WE SERVE? : THE PROSPERITY GOSPEL

Well, I've been watching this "PREACHERS OF LA", a reality how about 6 Los Angeles mega church preachers...and boy, I don't now what to think! Like most African Americans (AAs) I grew up in he church...Methodist, then Church of Christ. Sung in the choir, the whole 9 yards. Love myself some good ole' fashioned gospel music. As child, it was required that I attend church...hated it as most kids do. Sistahs was ah shouting and carrying on with wigs turning sideways nd brothers snoring during sermons. I had to sit in the back, with he older kids, to keep from getting in trouble and being pulled out, y my ears, by one of them sistahs who was ushering. I loved to giggle lot when sistahs would get the 'good foot'... In graduate school I got aptized and joined the Church of Christ. This is where I learned he bible, read it in Greek, studied theology, the history of the 1st Century Church and ran right out the back door, of the church, and nto the arms of that which was before it and the root of all organized eligions.... Vodun. You see, in all organized religions, one sees the spirits. But in Christianity it is most evident in the Torah. I tell my spiritual children, "If you want to see the spirits at work, study how God dealt with the children of Israel." These same spirits are the ones we work with today! They are the same, yesterday, today and forever! But, getting back to the "PREACHERS OF LA"...

It is said that these folk are promoting what is termed as "the prosperity gospel". In other words, serve Jesus and you are going to prosper! But I tell ya', as I have mentioned in my piece on, "Jesus ain't working for us." I don't find this to be true! A true servant of God (the spirits) is one of humility and often of humble means. I have found, that in Vodun, one is only awarded after complete obedience is proven and one's heart is pure...putting the voduns above all else. I am not saying that Priests cannot prosper. Many do in Africa and all over the world! But, money cannot become your god in Vodun or any other spiritual system. If you are chasing money, new cars, nice clothes etc., etc. where is your commitment? Let the spirits bless you with these things BECAUSE of your genuine service to minister to others.

VODUN AND THREE DEGREES OF SEPARATION

As the the African American community lays yet another of it's children to rest, Michael Brown Jr. of Ferguson, Missouri...shot and killed in an American city street by an officer of the law, I cannot help but reflect on the concept of separation...that separation of a child, from its mother, when it's prematurely taken in death, that separation, from a loved one, that passes over when it's their time, that separation from those who constitute a family, yet, sold, individually, on a slave auction block or incinerated in a German gas chamber, that separation of a refugee, from all he/she knows, due to his/her war ravished country and that separation of a people from their native homelands whether by force or enslavement. Throughout the history, of mankind, these kinds of separations have occurred; but, for some reason the descendants of the transAtlantic slave trade have seen more than their share.

Those of African descent have suffered three distinct spiritual separations: The first, and foremost, was from our ancestral lands, the second our ancestors, themselves, and the third the separation from a spiritual way of life that can bring us spiritual healing and general well being and prosperity. African spirituality can connect us to all three...our motherland, the ancestors and inner healing and peace.

The loss of a child is one of the most devastating things that a parent can encounter.... a mother especially hard. It is at this time that one must reach out to the divine...that which one knows is greater than one's self. This grief can, sometimes, overwhelm us. In vodun we know that when one dies before their time or in circumstances that do not result in a natural death, i.e. murder, disease, accident etc., this constitutes deep spiritual separation. While the first separation, of course, occurs from our loved ones...those not expecting such an untimely death...the second and most unfortunate separation is the one from the ancestor. Let me explain.

In the world of the spirits all things began with the ancestor. It is through the ancestor that we come, to this earth, and it is to the ancestor that we wish to return. Unnatural deaths, or deaths by unnatural means, stops this process. When one dies of murder, disease, accidents, drugs, and other unnatural causes, one's spirit goes to zogbe...the place where such who die, this way, go after death. As this place is outside of the temple one must first be purified and ceremonies performed in order to eat with one's ancestors. With out it we are forever separated from the ancestor.

This is why so many of us who are hearing the call of our ancestors to serve must serve. For it is not so much for those that live that we do it...yes many desperately need us.... but it is for all of those who have gone before. It is for those loved ones, and forefathers, that died on the slave ships and were thrown overboard, those who died on the route of the slave before they even left African soil, for the relative who was lynched and hung on a tree, for the ones who died trying to make it to freedom from the slave massa's whip, the ones who were castrated, the ones beaten, to death, in the cotton and tobacco fields, the ones raped by the massa, the ones killed by crooked cops, murdered by the KKK and the list goes on. It is for these that we serve and feed them that they are finally joined with the ancestor and find peace. It is for the healing of the living and the dead that we serve. Our cause is one that is multi-faceted but designed to help reconnect that which has been spiritually separated

It did not escape my notice, or others I'm sure, that the mother of Michael Brown looked beaten down by the death of her son. As she rocked to and fro during the funeral services my heart ached for her. Of the many dignitaries in attendance, grandstanding black political leaders, celebrities and folks from all walks of life my eyes looked upon the mother's face with empathy and understanding. I think of what our ancestors must have felt when seeing their children suffer as we have throughout our history in this place; and, I found it interesting the color red that she wore, to the funeral, as well as, the red shirt of the gentleman sitting next to her. The commentators, on CNN, found it interesting also. Their comments were, that the red actually meant something, meant strength. I saw no strength in her composure. Only someone of the African priesthood would understand that the color red, in the spirit world, stands for those who have died at zogbe...of murder, diseases and un-natural causes of all kinds. May the spirits be with us.

AFROCENTRICITY AND ITS TWO PATHS

I am not sure why I sense the need to pen this essay; but, to whom ever may learn from it or put its thesis to thought...so be it.

Becoming Afrocentric, to me as a person of African descent, is a step in the acknowledgement of self and an attempt to re-connect to a lost part of the self disrupted by the trans-Atlantic slave experience

For those furthest from African descent I feel it is a coming to terms with what Africa is...the birthplace of mankind, containing the roots of all organized spiritual systems and thus important to mankind as a whole. It is an attempt to put Africa right back where she belongs... preeminent in the world of continents; yet, though, today, she struggles economically overflows with wealth spiritually. This, for me, be it with the good bad or the ugly, is my beloved Africa...my beloved ancestral home.

But far too many times I have seen those who become Afrocentric, those who claim to love mother Africa take another path....an alternate path...not the one where we come to terms with our history and seek to progress spiritually but the one where one becomes stuck in a world of hate, intolerance and uses this hate and intolerance to isolate themselves, demonize the other and, in effect, become stunted in their spiritual growth. I will have no part in this.

I, as we all are, am a product of my upbringing. Many of you have read about my experiences growing up in a segregated south; but, I refuse to let any of that define me and my duty to serve mankind... all of mankind, regardless of race, creed, color, gender or orientation. For it was on the continent of Africa that the spirits taught me that, under the skin, we are all born of spirits and that we are all children of Africa. It has not been an easy lesson; and, I struggle with it every day. I am so aware of my history, I am so aware of my people, our plight and our struggle; but, I am a servant of the divine and my duty is to serve mankind in whatever capacity I can. I love the spirits more than I love myself; and, that old self must die a bit every day.

Becoming Afrocentric in my estimation should be a step toward wholeness; and, if one finds themselves being led down a path of hatred it is not the path of the African ancestor nor the divine spirits. It might be a popular political path; and, I see many on this internet, daily, taking that path. However, I feel that one must be honest with oneself and ask, "Does what I'm doing really honor Africa and our ancestors or is my attachment to Afrocentric thought just a cloak for my political agenda and hatred toward the other?" For I believe that racism can be found in all colors, shapes and sizes.

VODUN AND ITS PLAYERS

Do you remember, back during the days of our childhood, when we used to play house? The girls would dress up as make-believe adults with our mother's high heels shoes, Sunday hats and dresses on; and, our brothers, male cousins, or the family pet would step in for that male component? Well this is what happens, sometimes, in diaspora Vodou or when we claim African spirituality outside of the motherland. Some of us actually "play" at it! Oh, it looks real enough on the surface; but, when the real thing actually shows up and stares us dead in the face...some folks are not really interested.

Now, I'm not sure whether this is a conscious thing or not; but, some of us can take a trip to Africa, maybe, or read a mountain of books or even consider ourselves "Afrocentric". We may wear the dreadlocks, talk the appropriate lingo, put on the kente cloth, hob knob with the big names associated with the right professors, Afrocentric people or Ifa Priests. We may even seek to market ourselves, after our trip to the "motherland", as we have returned with various titles and/or knowledge that we have legitimately or illegitimately acquired. You see, we figure that, Africa is so far that no one will be the wiser. These titles, then, help us to develop our important image, thus, making it and our popularity synonymous with who we know, who knows us and how many trips we've taken to Africa. Forget the fact that African initiations actually take months or even years to complete and training in African spiritual systems, in general, take a lifetime; but, we come back to the diaspora, espousing we have something, and start using terms such "elder" because someone took a trip way back when. It is all cute to be sure! And, none of this is bad within itself. However, within the spirit realm, if you are aware of the spirits; but, they are not aware of you, then, in the spirit world you are a very tiny fish in a very big pond!

I see it also as one of the downsides of not using Ifa, or an authentic African divination system, in the diaspora when dealing with African traditional spiritual systems in general. As I have mentioned, in other writings, those who are born to their stations, heed the call of initiation, if commanded, and initiate according to the tenants of the ancestors and the divinities, themselves, are not only ordained by them, but, known by them. And if one goes to Ifa and inquires as to anyone claiming the Priesthood, Ifa will verify and tell you about that person. But, here's the pickle... very few, in the diaspora, unless an African trained in Ifa and living in the diaspora even have the skills to use Ifa effectively, but, that's a whole 'nuther subject.

You see vodun is not about bells and whistles but about one's relationship with the spirits. All of this other stuff is simply window dressing! You can have degrees up the "wa wa"; but, If you have no relationship with the spirits, if you haven't been connected to anything, dealing with the spirits, and are busy espousing theory and man made logic, as opposed to, hearing/listening, accepting, obeying and respecting the commands of the ancestors and the divine ones... you are just whistling in the breeze. When you are stiff backed, challenging, accusatory and more interested in being right than hearing the words of those authentically ordained, by them, you are not really serious but at play. In vodun it should NEVER be about YOU, WE or ME, rather, it should be about the will of the spirits. WE are secondary to the spirits and their divine plans.

In my early years, in Africa, there was a woman that I had become most envious of. She was a Tassinon....a woman of prayer. Her abilities were most extraordinary. She was a woman born in the highest realm of the priesthood; and, she too was a Mami. Her ability to see spirits walking in the broad open daylight amazed me...I wanted that ability too! Then one day my voduns got tired of me asking about that particular gift; and, my Sakpata called me before him. Sakpata questioned, through an interpreter, "Why are you crying over the thing that shines like gold but reject the thing that really is gold?"

Sakpata was referring to me wanting to be like this woman, but, not allowing my own abilities to develop. By the end of that conversation I understood much... that I too was born with special spiritual gifts, undeveloped at that time, but, that who I was and what I was, in the spirit world, far exceeded anything that this woman could ever be. And, as I later got to know this woman and discovered her to be dishonest, a crook, and dishonoring the spirits at every turn, I learned my lesson. I have, since, been taught, by the spirits, to look beyond the shell and see what is beneath the exterior as the spirits do. For when a spirit looks, at a person, they are looking at those spirits inside of you, connecting with them, and reading the inner most thoughts and intentions of a person. The shell is important but secondary.

Who we are, spiritually, and how we conduct ourselves should be at the dictation of the spirits. This is not simply being a purist, of which I most definitely am, this is obedience. The fluff of the aura of Priesthood without the commitment, integrity of character and the bond, associated with one's relationship with the spirits, is like dressing up in make believe...it is hollow; and, it isn't real...there is no substance.

For it is the divine spirits that gave us life, it is THEY who have come down with us to help us complete our spiritual missions whatever they might be; and, it is THEY who should direct our feet. So, no players need apply.

VODUN AND THE AFRICAN PERSPECTIVE

In African Vodun... original Vodun... when a man buys, or attempts to buy, his spiritual throne he is not respected. Why? Because it is known that one born to his or her spiritual throne has legitimacy and is to be ordained by the ancestors and the divinities themselves. They are born with a spiritual mission that they must discover; and, with the divinities help, complete. So, it is in the diaspora. Those who buy into African traditional spiritual systems also lose respect from those who are authentic. And no matter what one does it will not change because these "bought into" people are simply not supposed to be there. This is from an African perspective.

If one wants to serve the spirits we do not run around chasing after initiations into spirits we like, simply, because we like what they do or think they are cool. One goes to the west African oracle, Ifa, and finds out who and what one is in the spiritual world. We find out who our ancestors are, what spirits we carry, which is the head and what our mission is on this earth. This is because, through the birthing process, we lose this spiritual (pre-birth) information. Ifa goes into the spiritual realm and returns with these answers to our spiritual questions. Tarot cards, while a divination system of another culture, are not part of this spiritual system; and, certainly not a deck of simple playing cards. Neither can produce this type of information. This is from an African perspective.

If we enter the Priesthood, we do not do so for financial gain but to help mankind as a vessel for the spirits. For we know that it is the spirits that will give us what we need. We understand the power of the spirits; and, we know to each man/woman the spirits judge our deeds and rewards and punishes as they see fit. This too is from an African perspective.

We know that who we are is in the blood, and, that the blood of our ancestors links us wherever we may go. Four or five hundred years, in the diaspora, of those of African descent does not change this. The ancestors know their children; and, if properly fed, and cared for, will rise up to help us in our hours of need, for, as Cinque so beautifully said, in the movie, La Amistad (1997) "...I will call into the past, far into the beginning of time, and beg them to help me at the judgment. I will reach back and draw them into me. And they must come...for at this moment I am the whole reason they have existed at all." This is an African perspective.

Science has proven that all of mankind originates from a common ancestor...an African man and woman. As a result, we all have ties to the African continent. Our oldest ancestor is there...in that place called Africa. Those of European descent, therefore, should not look to Haiti for their Vodun but to its origins...Africa. Your oldest ancestor is there, not Haiti, and when they are called to partake, in feast, will come from the oldest to the newest, from the darkest to the lightest. You do not need to serve someone else's ancestors, in Vodun, go and serve your own. For Ifa will tell you who they are. That is from an African perspective.

So, if one wants to serve the spirits, serve it the way your ancestors did. For Vodun is uniquely African, its roots, its tenants and its ancestors. To serve these diasporan African-based systems any other way is uniquely un-African; and, that is MY perspective.

AFRICAN SPIRITUALITY: OUR SECOND CHANCE

For all of us, those of obvious African descent, as well as, those that are considered furthest removed, who want to reconnect to our oldest ancestors and our ancestor's traditional way of life African spirituality offers us that second chance.

As I have said, in my earlier writings, the slave trade caused a severe disconnection from our ancestors and our traditional African way of life. Since the beginning, of his creation, the African performed certain ceremonies, rituals and sacrifices handed down, and given to him, by the divinities themselves. Those that enslaved our ancestors, however, imposed, upon them, their spiritual system, languages, norms and mores that have been passed down through the generations of diasporans. As a result, our people have suffered, socially, economically, politically and spiritually. This Jesus, of the Bible, is neither connected to our ancestry nor died for our sins. For it is through "the blood" of the African sacrificial animals...as given in the covenant of Ifa... that we will find cleansing, purification and nourishment, for the spirits, in order that they may have the strength, and the power, to help us in our hours of need. It is to these spirits, which dwell within us, who see through our eyes and hear through our ears and examines our hearts who work diligently, daily, to be there when we need them that we should give our thanks. It is the African Gods...Sakpata, Den'su, Gu, Heviosso, and others... that deserve the credit for waking us up to another day...not Jesus, a prophet, that has no connection to us.

Of all of the people that the slaver attempted to use as slaves and failed, due to their inability to cope, it was only the African who had the fortitude, the strength and the stamina to withstand one of man's darkest periods in world history...the transAtlantic slave trade. It was because of the centuries upon centuries of sacrifices given by our African ancestors and their relationships and/or covenants, with the divine, that we stand as free men and women today. A bit worn for wear, due to the experience, but one of the most gifted group of people that has ever graced the globe.

My brothers and sisters, African spirituality is our second chance. It is that chance to find the ancestor (through Ifa), that chance to feed our ancestors, know the divinities that gave us life and to regain those dignities that were taken from us. We are an ancient people. We have worth and value. Reach back and take the hands of the ancestors, reach back and reclaim the kingships, the thrones, the dignity and worth.

How does someone enslave a person both physically and spiritually? You tell them that they have no history, no value, no language, no culture, no God. But the African has his own language, his own history, his own culture, and within him, as others, lives his God! African spirituality and our reconnection to it is our second chance!

SAITH THE AFRICAN TO THE AFRICAN AMERICAN

While living in New York City, from the late 1980s to the late 1990s, I remember hearing of a conversation between an African and an African American. I do not remember whether I heard it, from someone, or read about it; but, over the years, it has stayed vivid in my memory. And, every now and then, I summon it to the forefront, of my thoughts, mull it over and re-evaluate it with a mental response. For what I have noticed is that upon each new response I have progressed both figuratively and spiritually. This essay is about my latest response to that conversation.

Saith the African to the African American: "If living in your country; and, I, an African, am forbidden to use my government name, it will not disturb me, because, I still have my African name. And, If, while there, I am refused to use your language...I, an African, have my own language. If I am told that I cannot wear your American cloth/clothes, it doesn't matter, to me, because, as an African, I have my own cloth/native dress. If I am in your country; and, I choose not to worship your God/religion I, an African, have my own God/religion. But YOU, oh African American, if one takes away your American name, your American language, your American clothes and your American God/religion, you, are left with nothing!"

When I first heard this, it made a lot of sense. In fact, it made me reach out and search for Africa...search for that connection...a connection that I thought was forever lost to me. I took Yoruba classes. I started wearing African cloth. I got rid of the Diana Ross weave and grew dreadlocks flowing down my back...the whole nine yards! I became AFROCENTRIC...trying and struggling to belong. I attended seminar after seminar and read mountains of books. It only got me started. It was the tip of the iceberg. My journey, truly, began the day I sat my foot down on African soil; and, the rest is history. So, over the years I pull up the remnants of this old conversation. Seeking to address it has spurred me on to a more fulfilling life spiritually. It wasn't so much what my outward appearance needed to say, but, rather, what the inner and spiritual me needed to come to understand. So, even though, after all the years, I still wear African cloth daily. It does not define me. An American woman dressed in African cloth does not fool any native African anywhere. But Africans have come to know, love and understand me because of my love, obedience and devotion to the ancestors and the divine spirits. That has been my true growth.

So, my latest response, to the conversation is this...Yes, my brother/ sister Africa, I can wear the cloth of this land, And, indeed, I have a name foreign to those of our motherland. It is true that I hear and I speak the language of this new home; and, Yes, some of us, even, serve the God of this land... But, do not be deceived, my brother/ sister, for in my blood flows the blood of my African ancestor, and, I have discovered, through the great Ifa, how to come back home, both, spiritually and physically, thus, reconnecting to all that has been lost to me. So, do not be confused by my name, my appearance, my language nor the years I've spent sojourned in this place. For through the blood, sweat, tears and sacrifices made by my forefathers, as well as, that blood which flows of my brethren, daily, in these city streets, we have purified this place and, now, can claim part of it as our own. Remember that the ancestor loves me just as much as he does you. So, do not pity me my African brother/sister, for, when you look at me.... you are looking at you.

AFRICANS AND AFRICAN AMERICANS: A CULTURAL DIVIDE

Today's African Americans often refer back to their African roots with great pride; but, over the years, I have often seen dissension among the two groups largely due to a misunderstanding of cultures. I was most fortunate in that, in attending a historically black university, I attended classes with Africans and began to understand a bit about the African culture. Early on I was intrigued. Later when I moved to NYC I would plant myself at the African market and try to know people. My first realization of just how much I didn't know, about African culture, was when one day a group of us women, at the market, bought a meal together. I saw ONE plate of food thinking it was ALL for me! Imagine my, supreme embarrassment, when 3 other African sistahs came to share in the meal and I had eaten it all! I vowed, that day, to learn better manners!

In NYC Africans are all over the place! I reveled in this new environment. Growing up in the southern United States it was usually only us, them and the KKK...with them and the KKK usually being the same. I loved Harlem where so many people looked like me! From 1982-1998, when I left for Africa, I thought I had seen a little piece of heaven; and, I figured that actually being in Africa would only make it even more so! So, imagine my pain when an African, in anger, screamed, "esclave go home!" in Ouidah, Benin of all places? I'm not even gone begin to tell ya'll how the brother that said it learned that African American women got attitude and could fight! Suffice it to say, that this man became one of my best friends after the encounter! He learned that African Americans did not survive slavery 'cause their women were weak! But getting back to that cultural divide. I remember an incident, in NYC, that made me hold my head down in shame for a sister that called in on a local talk radio show.

The topic was: "The worst date you ever had". The sistah called in and described her date with an African. She claims that the brother took off his shoes, under the table, and got comfortable. Well, for me, that was a typical African; and, I saw it as simply a cultural thing. Then, the brother proceeded to eat with his fingers and suck on that big ole' fish head sitting on his plate! Well that's what Africans do; but, this woman was mortified! The sistah was not familiar with the ways or etiquette of Africans. Africans make the same mistake, when taking out African American women, by not realizing how Americanized some of us actually are!

My problem with African Americans is that we want to claim Africa but NOT the African! We do not want to take the time to learn the culture. We want to pick and choose those parts we like and throw away the rest. To dislike that which is African is to dislike a part of ourselves.

The African is proud! He is his OWN man w/o an oppressor! He nay often seem crude, by our standards; but, take the time to know im and you can learn much!

DIASPORA VODOU, OTHER AFRICAN-BASED SPIRITUAL SYS-TEMS AND A FEW MISCONCEPTIONS

One of the greatest misconceptions, in the Diaspora, is that these African based spiritual systems are somehow disconnected from Africa! THEY ARE NOT! A tree cannot be cut off from its root and urvive! If cut it WILL surely die! The Africans that brought these piritual systems to the diaspora had roots/ancestry in Africa; and, is they did, so do we! Our oldest ancestors are on the continent of Africa; and, in fact ALL of mankind's oldest ancestry originates rom somewhere on that African continent, no matter how far one nay be removed, from that ancestry, or if you are first generation n the diaspora...every knee shall bow to that continent one day! So, to think that what is in the diaspora are new lineages is to fool oneself. One will NEVER see the true power, in these African based piritual systems, unless one reaches back to the source and pull in he knowledge of the ancients...those things that were lost due to the uppression of the slave trade! So, what can this mean for those of us iving in the diaspora?

To my Cuban family it means that Africa is the source of these African based spiritual systems and not Cuba! There has been a propensity for our Cuban neighbors (at least the ones I met on tribe), who have less access to America but more to Africa, to believe that they somehow got the skinny on these African based spiritual systems. No one does! Africa is and will always be the source! I commend you; however, on the use of Ifa! While I am not privy to all that is within your system it will appear that the closeness, to Africa, has been to your benefit! That machismo thang ain't working for you though.

As for my Haitian cousins, I have always covered you in my general writings on Vodun. So, I have little to say different, here, except to emphasize the reaching back to the source...Africa and to reinstate Ifa. You must reinstate Ifa! Too many folks are being lied to! Get your eyes off making a dollar and serve the spirits in humility and grace. No one is telling you not to feed yourselves; but, I am saying that when one emphasizes service, to the spirits, rather than the acquiring of things, the spirits, somehow, always gives us what we need! Not all that we may want, but, all that we need.

And, for the furthest removed it means that if you must serve someone else's ancestry to serve the spirits you've been LIED to! Ifa can and will find your ancestor! If the folks, you're dealing with, are not using authentic African divination then why are you there? Why serve someone else's ancestors and yours go hungry? What blessing is that going to bring to you?

The only thing it's gonna do is feed their folks out of your pocket! If your family tree doesn't have a single relative as part of any revolution in the Caribbean islands; then, you are over there doing what? Someone married you to an African spirit or ancestor; but, there has been no verification that you actually belong to these people/ancestors or spirit, for that matter, is a waste of your time and money! Buying into a spiritual system is not gonna do you any good deed in the long run. Those who actually were born to (according to Ifa) or belong to these spiritual systems/spirits/ancestors are gonna beat you out every time. For THEIR authenticity against your own screams.... I AIN'T REAL! This is the fear that people often have when they see me coming...an authenticity that cannot be denied. An uneasiness in the pit of their being. All I have to do is be there. But, hey, we can ALL have authenticity! Go find out, through Ifa WHO and WHAT you are in the spirit world, if anything, and then you may speak your piece! Yet, I deduce that it is the fear of the...if anything... that's got most unwilling to see or even pursue the reality! So, what does all this mean for those of obvious African descent?

It means that just because we can see the African in our skin color doesn't mean that African based spiritual systems belong to us ONLY!

It means that you do not have the right to determine who is and who is not supposed to be a part of these systems. It means that we serve the ancestors and the divinities not ourselves. It means that our ancestors did not sacrifice blood sweat and tears for us to act like asses, to fight in the sandbox and refuse to share. We do not tell a person to whom they may disseminate their knowledge when we have not bought their plane ticket or helped in the acquiring of that knowledge. And the welfare mentality must go! Nothing in this world is free! While it is true that MANY have seen these systems as a way to deceive and become wealthy, It does not mean that those of the Priesthood must work for free. Even though one could question where this mentality actually came from the way these African American sistahs like to shower their Preachers with Rolls Royces and such! Vodun should not be promoted like those who promote a prosperity gospel. The Priesthood is a position of service. Yet, sacrificial animals must be bought, Vodunsi must be compensated for their time working during ceremonies. These people give up time, from their families, to work for the Voduns, the dancers, the drummers, those who prepare the animals for sacrifice, the foods prepared etc. Authentic African Vodun is very labor intensive. Do not call those of us, who serve with integrity, crooks because you are cheap. You want something for free, homeboy/sistah love, go to the nearest Social Services building and apply.

As people of African descent our skin color is a blessing not a shame. We do not treat others as we may have been treated. We leave vengeance, if it is to be had, to the spirits. As descendants of kings and queens we should act like it! A young man whom I knew was royalty, in Africa, visited the States once. I mentioned it to a very close friend. She said, "Oh THAT'S in Africa not here! My question to her was, "When the Queen of England visits the United States does she stop being a Queen?"

We, people of color, are the firstborns to these African based spiritual systems. Do we claim them with honor or claim them with dishonor? The choice is yours.

VODUN, BLACK FOLKS AND CHICKENS

One of my fondest memories, while growing up, was mama and the poultry truck. As with most women, mama always dipped into the food budget when we needed other household items. As a result, mama had to be extra frugal; so, neck bones and rice became a staple in our house. But the worst, of it, was the endless amount of chicken feet, to which I referred to, in my youth, as chicken "foots". We ate so many that I swore, when I got growed, I would never put another chicken foot in my mouth! And I haven't! But once a week, at least, that poultry truck had to pass our house on its route to the poultry; and, if the driver hit that curb, just about right, a couple of big fat chickens would fall out, in their cages, with mama standing right there to pick 'em up. And, boy, would we get to eat chicken for real! We would have one that night and one for Sunday dinner! Mama might even get fancy, with one of those big ole' tough hens, and make us a nice pot of chicken and dumplins'. For a kid, that made life sho' nuff grand! So, I used to love the arrival of that poultry truck!

Black folks have always had a fondness for chicken. Many a Sunday dinner table is graced with mountains of crispy fried chicken, potato salad, macaroni and cheese, candied yams, collard or mustard greens, corn bread, biscuits, string beans, or other such goodies, laid out with kool aid, for the kids, or lemonade, on the side, with an apple pie and ice cream for dessert. Chicken is one of the world's greatest food staples and a versatile bird indeed. It usually only gets usurped by the turkey on Thanksgiving or Christmas Day. Yet, is chicken the ultimate animal when giving spiritual blood sacrifices?

Diaspora Vodou, and other such African based spiritual systems, here, understand the concept of animal sacrifice. But it has mainly concentrated on the sacrifices of chickens and goats and very few other animals. I have rarely heard of anything else being given except for pig when folks are dealing in the dark arts. And, yet, our spirits are able to tell us their preferred animal sacrifice if we simply inquire. But, without the use of authentic African divination, many spirits, in the diaspora, are being fed incorrectly. A few have actually told us so. Folks are going on what has been done in the past or what they intuit rather than what the spirit actually requires. For instance, I have heard of water spirits being fed goat. Mami Wata spirits do not eat goat. Each spirit has its own preferred sacrifice. For Mami Wata it could be ram, pigeon, turkey, duck and various other animals depending on which particular spirit, in that pantheon, one is dealing with. When giving sacrifice, for a work to be performed by the spirits, it is THEY, when consulted, through Ifa, that will dictate what they need or instruct us during a spirit possession. We do not have to guess, intuit or rely on what we may have seen others do. With diaspora initiations only 9 days, or so, one would wonder if there is time to learn anything spiritual at all. This bears witness by the proliferation of folks, who claim to have been initiated into the priesthood, in the diaspora, attempting to train themselves by jumping on spiritual forums, on the internet, in hopes of gaining knowledge and insight into what they are supposed to be doing. In traditional African spiritual systems, one learns all that they need, in the initiation chamber, while honing their skills throughout a lifetime of doing.

This needs to happen in African based spiritual systems, in the diaspora, as well. But it doesn't. Yet, does one even think that they are on par with an African who is, properly, initiated and trained, in the priesthood, who may have spent months, if not years, inside African initiation chambers? Not even... This is not to insult but to indicate that diasporans, destined for the priesthood, need further training. And I applaud those that travel, to Africa, to seek more intensive initiation and instruction. The slave era, out of necessity, shortened the initiation process. Keeping one's African spiritual practices under ground and shortening the initiation process was a necessity due to the constant work in the sugar cane/cotton/tobacco fields or to stop detection. One could be killed, or severely punished, if discovered practicing African spirituality. Our enslavers considered it devil worship; and, many still do today. However, there is no longer any excuse not to be trained, in African spirituality, properly. Slavery, at least the overt and physical bonds of it, is over. It simply takes the right contacts, time, effort and, possibly, a bit of travel to be properly trained. But please do not take me the wrong way. These statements are being made for the benefit of ourselves and, to those to whom we have been entrusted to help, not for the bruising of egos. As priests and priestesses, we must be at our best in order to be better vessels for the spirits. Why? Because if our emphasis is on the number of people we can get through a Haitian kanzo, for instance, and how much that brings to our pocket books, instead of considering the spiritual missions that lay before us, then, we are nullifying those spiritual missions in one felled swoop.

Each spirit, whether it be an ancestor or a divinity, that existed before the world was formed, has its own preferred animal sacrifice. We simply need to have the means to inquire. For if so that spirit, through the blood of that sacrifice, has the force and power to complete the work to which it has been given. To give an incorrect sacrifice hinders that work. As much as we adore, them, chickens simply do not cut it as a sacrifice, alone, for most spirits. Think on it this way... You are an ancestor; and, for 400-700 years you haven't tasted the blood of an animal sacrifice. Your child was taken into slavery, and due to that enslavement, neither he/she, nor their descendants, have been allowed to feed or serve you. You have struggled to protect them all of these centuries without being fed or even acknowledged. For in each high point, in their lives, your good works have, often, been attributed to another. Someone who is not even in their ancestral tree...the slave master's redeemer. You are hungry. You are tired. Will a chicken suffice, for a sacrifice for all of these years of back breaking work? The answer is no my brothers and sisters. The African ancestor takes strong African bulls. And we owe them plenty!

Over the years I have always wondered whether that driver used to dump those chickens off on purpose. For I became suspicious when I was told that my grandmother worked at that same chicken poultry, during that time; and, that our street really wasn't a part of that driver's original route. But what can I say...Black folks looked out for each other back in the day.

When it comes to sacrificial animals/foods our ancestors and the divinities, indeed, have discriminating palates. But, while fowl might very well be on their menu, I assure you, that the main course is not, often, going to be chicken!

IS THE HAITIAN EZILI PART OF THE AFRICAN MAMI WATA?

I was asked a question by a facebook friend if Ezili, the Haitian spirit, exists in Africa? I thought the answer would interest others as well; so, here goes. I am sure she is probably one of the African water spirits in Mami; but, I do not know, specifically, which one at this time. But I am sure Ifa/Fa/Afa would tell us if asked. The reasons for my hunch is solid however. Of all the slaves that left Africa it is pretty well documented, in Benin, where theirs went. The Beninoise museums proudly document their slaves to Brazil and Haiti. In fact, Toussaint L'Ouverture's father, Gaou Guinou, was from Allada...the same birth place of my husband, a proud Beninoise. A statute of L'Ouverture is even standing there today! He was the younger son of the king, of Allada, caught during the slave trade. Through these Allada slaves, as well as those from the Congo and the traditional local inhabitants, Haitian Vodou emerged. Because these African spiritual systems had to be hidden they did it in plain sight amongst Catholicism's images of the Saints.

In, other words, these former slaves while losing a great deal of these African Traditional Spiritual systems and their tenants still retained some! This tendency to reach back and serve the Rada spirits is to reach back to Africa. Voodoo/Vodun is an attempt to retain the term "spirit" in the Fon language. The lwa, the term for "spirit" by the Congolese. So, yes, I am sure that Ezili is one of the Mami spirits. My only concern, with the Haitians, is the tendency to get away from using Ifa/Fa/Afa, the west African divination system, while practicing vodun. I see too many folks trying to divine with tarot cards or not divining at all. This is not good! It is the spirits we serve; therefore, it should be the spirits that guide us. Tarot cards are not hooked into the African ancestry. Haitians need to train in Ifa, those that were born to do so. Slavery is over...over for them longer than us. It is time to re-learn that which was lost!

THE DECONSTRUCTION OF HAITIAN VODOU

For certain patriots of Haitian Vodou I have heard of an attempt to deconstruct Haitian Vodou from its Catholic symbolism. The emphasis, I would think, is to detach it from the imposed Christian religion that was forced down the throats of the traditional Haitian population...those specifically who came, into Haiti, as African slaves. However, as in African Vodun, Haitian Vodou comes out of a particular cultural context. And, while I believe that Haitians, as we all, should reach back to Africa and reinstate those things it has lost, due to the slave trade, it should be to help us to better serve the spirits, in Haitian Vodou, not to deconstruct it.

As an example, I feel that authentic African divination must be re-instated to diaspora Vodun in general. Too many people have been allowed into it's Priesthood that are simply not fit to serve. Not everyone is born to serve the spirits; and, certainly not everyone is born to the Priesthood. Authentic African divination tells us who is born to Vodun and in what capacity. In addition, everyone deserves the right to be able to determine their ancestry, not simply be married off to some known African ancestry. One needs to know one's true ancestry, because, this is where Vodun begins. Authentic African divination allows this to happen. I firmly believe that many, in the diaspora, are unaware of the divinities because they have no way to communicate with them and, thus, do not know them. Authentic

African divination not only gives access to our ancestors but also to the highest divinities; and, THEY are the ones who determine how long one stays in the initiation chamber not us. These cookie cutter initiations benefit no one! The over marketization of Vodun, in the diaspora, has served to damage it in my opinion. Far too many people are hanging out shingles that really should not. Reaching back to Africa will not only allow us to better serve the spirits, and those who need us the most, but give us the full benefit, knowledge and power of our African forefathers. There is no need to deconstruct Haitian Vodou, it is what it is; so, let's work to make it better. This does not mean, however, that Haitian Vodou is an entity developed on its own and therefore separate from African Vodun or is this "so called" different lineage. I reject that wholeheartedly!

That excuse is used, far too often, by those who fear that once analyzed by authentic African divination systems they may not measure up, can no longer make up their own rules or be told that they were never to be in the Priesthood in the first place. If so, that's a good thing for Vodun! Let the spirits tell you your true destiny and go for that. I am sure that it will be found to be more fulfilling for you. But having someone who was not born to serve, nor deemed fit to, is not helpful to people in the long run. It causes more spiritual damage than good and does not help to further the divine plans of the spirits.

Vodun was brought to the diaspora by the African slave. Each slave brought, with him, his spirits and ancestry from whatever region he hailed from; but, sought its survival, from the oppression of his "masser", by hiding it amongst neighboring spiritual systems. Without these systems Vodou, in Haiti, may not have survived. And, if one reaches back to the spiritual level to many of the religious systems, on earth, one can often see the invisible hands of the Voduns/spirits. While Christianity teaches different tenants, it is based on the spiritual...sacrifice, the blood of the lamb; and, I can go on. From a 18th and 19th c. perspective; and, with the terrible injustices put upon the African slave, in the name of Christianity, one can fully understand why one would, now, want to disassociate oneself from these Catholic symbols. But with any spiritual system, I have found, that it is usually mankind that manages to mess things up. We do a lot of terrible things in the name of religion. But if these Catholic symbols remind us of our Vodun equivalents then what harm are they doing? Is it the symbols that are the problem or the Catholic Church? Is it the people who misuse the Christian principles the problem or the Church principals themselves?

Haiti's history has many players. Long before the Haitian Revolution (1794 - 1804), actually started, these players were set in motion. One had the "Petit Blancs" who were the poor white people, of Haiti, who owned nothing and caused the most trouble with the slaves, African slaves, the French slave owners who looked down on the poor whites, free people of color, mulattos, French soldiers, indigenous peoples and others. This was the makeup of Haiti. Many of these people lived and died on Haitian soil. They are part of it's history, culture, and for anyone who died and were diefied, part of its spiritual system, thus, borrowing from all of these unique parts. That has become part and parcel of Haitian Vodou. How, now, does one deconstruct from its own history and culture? I argue that, under the circumstances, one cannot.

My premise has always been that Haitian Vodou is African Vodun minus that which was lost, due to the slave trade, plus elements of the neighboring spiritual systems that surrounded it. It is a unique and very beautiful system! I honor my Haitian cousins and the strength, dignity and tenacity in which they have served the spirits. My prayer is that they reach back, to Africa, not to change Haitian Vodou but to re-instate that which was lost to it; and, in doing so, help to make it better!

THE MARKETING OF VODUN

I first ran into this phenomenon when I was on a Haitian site. There was a Mambo, on there, who referred to herself as a "mutt" because folks questioned her race. Apparently, she was confused; but, we weren't. The Haitians simply wanted her to understand that just because she spoke fluent Creole, had a Black boyfriend and chose to speak negatively about him, didn't necessarily mean she was a home-girl! The amazing thing about her, though, was that she could market the drawer legs off a woman as she walked. Mambo, was selling everything, in reference to Haitian Vodou, except DVDs out the back of her car! Those she was selling on the internet!

Just returning from Africa I hadn't a clue as to what this was all about. Then one day I searched the internet and looked at the Hoodoo folks. To my amazement, not a single person, I saw was Black, the women looked like they just stepped out of Vogue magazine and sold love spells, and potions of all kinds. I was beginning to think that I had entered some alternate universe! Where were the old sisters that could hook you up a good home remedy, for whatever ailed you, while dodging their spit cups as they dipped their snuff? Where were the old brothers who folks used to visit, deep in the night, to keep their sons from going to jail? And who now did you go to when that pretty little thang, you done pulled, eyes done opened up, to your lack of funds, and your mojo done stopped working? Apparently, no one unless you had the appropriate funds; and, then, you probably wouldn't know what's actually in the package! I was greatly saddened!

Hoodoo/Vodou has always been a part of the African American cultural/experience. It is that connection, to it, that sent me to Africa to understand it better. Yet, folks are now trying to tell me that, somehow, African Vodun and that which lies in the diaspora are of two different lineages! IT ISN"T! It is what our ancestors originally brought here but hindered, severely, by the slave experience! In some instances, it added the indigenous cultures, of the land, or it hide, itself, beneath the slavers faith to survive; but, it is Vodun just the same! Tattered and bit worn for wear; but, it is Vodun! The ancestors, who brought it, had roots that lay in the African soil; and, as did they, so do we.

Africa was hard work! And, It still is; but, once you visit, the connection between the two, African Vodun and diaspora Vodou are obvious because your vantage point becomes of someone from the inside looking out. One can trace diasporans from their original home and the umbilical cord stretches far and wide. Yet, for those who have bought into the system, this vantage point eludes them. They do not want to see it nor acknowledge it because it becomes too inconvenient. It is a different lineage, they say, because it avoids accountability and/or a need to right wrongs or hear the voices of those out of Africa. They can formulate their own rules, become their own authority and ignore any of the tenants, of Vodun, that does not fit their objectives in making money. They can justify lying and telling you what you want to hear, as opposed to, what you need to hear. They can conclude a two-week kanzo and call it true initiation without understanding, or caring, that it was the suppression of the slaves that shortened this initiation process rather than the Voduns themselves. That, in reality, you cannot initiate into ANY divinity in two weeks! But, the saddest part, of all, are the people of, African descent, who initiate, these folks, and allow them to do it! THEY, in their quest for money, are simply not correct! And THEY are a part of the problem! They need to get their eyes off money, stop using these people, as pawns, to draw monies from foreign lands and simply serve the Voduns. Time and Time again, I'm hearing, "My Mama told me!" Well, I'm here to tell ya! Your Mama wrong! And the Voduns gone let her know soon enough!

As I conclude this I remember, when observing these things, going to my husband and telling him what I was seeing in the diaspora. Behumbeza, in his infinite patience said, "Mami, it is not our way!" And I thank the spirits, daily, that it isn't! Many people I have come across, in the diaspora, have asked me to market myself. I have continually refused. With money, not a priority, I am free to tell folks what they need to hear rather than what they want to hear. I can be honest and concentrate on helping rather than making a dollar and possibly ruining someone's life. I can do what I was truly born to do and that is be a servant. Don't misunderstand me. It doesn't mean that folks don't pay for services rendered. It means that the emphasis is different. But, it is the Voduns, themselves, that set the prices, or ask for whatever they want, for the work that we do. It is not us! We serve mankind, we obey the spirits and let the spirits take care of us. For that is THEIR way!

SANTERIA/LUKUMI AND THE REACH TOWARD AFRICA

On March 28, 2014, in the Miami Herald, the article, "As Santería grows and evolves, the increasing focus on Africa opens rifts among the sects" appeared. It was an interesting article because it was repeating some of things that I have been saying, about diaspora African-based spiritual systems, for years. It is not just those of us, in Vodun, that seek a reconnection to Africa...our ancestry and our spirituality; but, it is through all, diasporan, traditional African based spiritual systems that we are seeing this. Why? Because it is the will of our ancestors. The African slave was taken from many parts of Africa; and, it was ALWAYS intended that their children would, one day, reconnect to them. Many, of us, have been born with specific spiritual missions to aide the ancestors in this divine plan. So, it is by no means surprising, to me, that the movement to return to that which is the source, mother Africa, is happening all over.

For over 8 years I have been urging this reunion; but, even before me many diasporans were trickling back to the motherland. Of the many discussions, I have participated in on forums, heated debates have broken out as to the validity of such an endeavor. It has rarely been African Americans, however, who has challenged this return to mother Africa; but, rather, it has been the Santeria/Lukumi folks and those, in Vodun, that has chosen to buy into these systems that have led the debate. Many fear their legitimacy, in serving the spirits, or of what the spirits might reveal about them. They want to separate diasporan African-based spiritual systems from their root. But, it cannot be done. These systems are rooted in African ancestry...that from which the African slave evolved. However, since all of mankind evolved from the same continent, no tree can survive cut from its root.

While the African Traditional Spiritual Systems, in the diaspora, have borrowed from the surrounding spiritual systems that it found itself embedded in, these systems are extremely hampered by the knowledge lost as a result of the slave trade. They have suffered, due to essential elements needed, to allow it to function at its highest level. The non-use of authentic African divination systems, essential to communicating with the spiritual world, is one case in point. Because of it, diaspora, Vodou is pledged with excessive marketing, people unfit to serve and/or persons who were never born to serve in the first place. Too much knowledge has been lost, due to slavery, and too much is missing from diaspora ceremonies that could serve to help people. We must get back to our roots, we must not be afraid to find out what we are missing. Returning to Africa, the source of these spiritual systems, can only make us better.

VODUN/AFRICAN AMERICANS/AND THE WELFARE MENTALITY

A young woman asked me if we could do a divination, for her, for free. According to her, she had heard that a diviner, in Africa, could not turn someone away if they needed help. And, further, according to her, my essays had actually convinced her that African Spirituality had validity, until, I sent her our information sheet explaining our divination process and the cost. So, she wanted to know where we stood on the issue of free divinations. I told her that we at...Temple Behumbeza...stood on the side of the spirits; and, the spirits dictated to us, that we were to charge a specific fee, for our divinations, due to the NATURE of the work and the QUALITY of the work. This is not to say that we have not, in the past, done divinations for free. We most certainly have. But, I was struck by two things from this young woman: Number one, her misunderstanding of the nature of authentic African divination and what it can do, in reference to folks who do not have a clue as to their ancestry, the spirits that gave them life or how that particular ancestor ended up in the diaspora in the first place; and, number two, the distinctive gut feeling, that I had, of sistah love, wanting something for nothing. To this, I simply wasn't having it!. She was attempting to have me prove, the validity of my essays on Vodun, by guilting me into giving her free services. This for me was an attempt at spiritual blackmail!

True divination work, for diasporans, (the kind we do) can be extremely involved and time consuming, as well as of some cost. Authentic African divination is not a "diaspora reading" which I often term as either a psychic friends network type of thing where folks want to be told that life is going to be fabulous, regardless of what they do or the gloom and doom reading of a charlatan priest or priestess who tells you that you've got some type of demon or bad luck because they need money; so, let's do a spiritual bath that's gonna cost you a lot. And, that's because the "reading", be it free or not, was to draw you into spending money in the first place. But the fact that the young woman thought that she could guilt a hood rat, like me, into doing something like that took me by surprise. Look, I have just as much compassion as the next person; and, money, as a priestess of vodun, is certainly not a priority for me. I labor, endlessly, for the spirits on a daily basis; and, in all of these years I have never taken a dime from anyone. But, when divinations are performed, in our temple, we must follow the directions of the spirits in every way. Plus, that "welfare mentality" simply rubs me the wrong way.

While there may be some debate, on the issue, American historians claim that the first Africans arrived on these shores in 1619. A couple of hundred years, prior to that, African slaves had been toiling in the sugarcane fields on the islands in the Caribbean. So, with us being in the diaspora, at the least, over 600 years, that is a lot of history lost Authentic African divination can restore that knowledge, that origina ancestor, where he originated from, as well as, those ancestors who came after, irregardless of race or origins, spirits born to you, those spirits inherited, presenting problems, solutions for those problems (ceremonies to be performed), protection and much much more But, is the diviner, thus, supposed to take his own time, shell out the money from his/her own pocket, to purchase the items needed for the divination, possibly travel (in some instances) to a sacred waterway another African nation, or where have you, because someone is expecting something for free? No! I've got a newsflash for you...tha "welfare mentality" that assumes that folks owe you something is no an African concept! That is a cultural concept learned by some of our brethren because of our economic and political circumstances in the diaspora. In Africa welfare does not exist! Africans work extremely hard, they struggle, and they make do. And when times get really tough...depend on family. Sometimes it takes them years to complete their vodun ceremonies. So, what's our excuse?

Look, it would have been nice for all of us to have received that 40 acres and a mule as promised. But this is the hand that we have been dealt. Many, of us, struggle daily; and, I more than most, understand this. There are numerous ceremonies that I have not completed due to money. But, I'm out here striving, daily, to do what I can to complete what I can praying, every day, that the spirits make a way And, often, I must save and put money aside just to do one simple ceremony. There is nothing, in this world, that is worth having, tha comes without hard work and some sacrifice. That INCLUDES vodun

But if we are to reclaim that which has been lost to us, due to the trans-Atlantic slave trade, our ancestry, our spiritual way of life our dignity as Africans and free men and women, let's drop the one thing that the Republicans insist that we are...a people who want something for nothing! For on the contrary we are a people looking for opportunities to empower ourselves not looking for handouts. And let me leave you with this about Africa and Vodun. The one who pays for the voduns (to install them etc.) is the one who, not only, owns the voduns but also the one who receives their blessings.

TRADITIONAL SPIRITUALITIES: THOSE "BORN IN" VS. THOSE WHO "BUY IN"

Many who have read my writings understand that one of things that I detest, more than anything, is "bought in" folk into African spirituality. It is not that all do not have the right to serve the spirits regardless of race, creed, color or gender. They do! However, my issue is with those who refuse to follow the tenets of our spirituality; and, that is to go to Ifa, find out who and what they might be in the spiritual world, if anything, and then follow its tenants when commanded. In, other words, if you are going to do the thing...do it correctly! For only the spirits, themselves, can tell us who was born to serve them. Too many come to these traditional spiritual systems, illegitimately, just to make money and bringing dishonor and shame to our spiritual system, not to mention, coming with poor or inadequate training. Look at all those illegitimate folk buying into Haitian Vodou and the nonsense going on in New Orleans Voodoo. Why not simply go to Ifa, discover your own ancestry and go from there? To not follow the tenets of the world's traditional spiritual systems is to disrespect the ancestors, involved in these systems, as well as, shows the high disrespect for the sacredness of these systems. These "New Age" people are "dabblers" who end up serving nothing but themselves because many are out there simply for profit. Then, they want to disrespect those who are actually born to these traditional systems who oppose their foolishness. Yeah, MamiWata Priestess, is your worst nightmare! 'Cause I'm going to be calling you folks out until they cover my face with dirt!

THE ECONOMIC AND SPIRITUAL FALLOUT TO GIVING THOSE WHO WERE NOT BORN TO THE VODUNS THE PRIESTHOOD

I was surfing the net, recently, when I ran across a website where someone lodged a complaint, a few years back, against a Haitian temple because of their propensity to conduct mass kanzos. According to the person, lodging the complaint, this mass production of kanzos resulted in people who thought they had vodun but actually did not. Of course, someone shot back claiming the person, lodging the complaint, was homophobic; but, I do not believe that being gay was what the person was talking about.

It is not unusual, in Africa, for many born to a particular pantheon of spirits to enter the initiation chamber during the same time. It helps cut down on the costs; but, there are times when the spirits will insist that an individual enters alone. This happened to me. But in, either event, each person and their spirits are given individual attention and no time, on the initiation process, is overlooked or cut out. I can't possibly fathom what one can learn, about the spirits, in two weeks; but, I try and understand what happened, during the slave era, that allowed this to happen in diasporan vodou. I suspect that when a spirit came on the head, of a person, it was automatically assumed that this person was born of the spirits; so, the initiation process was shorten. The problem with this, however, is that the spirit taking this person may or may not have been the person's head. We are born of many spirits. Without using Ifa it is difficult to tell. In Africa when a spirit attempts to come on the head of an uninitiated person...the person cannot speak. The person is frozen, rigid and/or locked into place, unable to come forward or speak until we unfreeze them and send the spirit back. Uninitiated Mami people fear going into Mami Wata temples and/or near the ocean for this reason. Getting back to the aforementioned complaint, however, I think the complainant was more concerned about the character of a couple of the individuals that completed their kanzo, with this temple, than the mass production of kanzos itself. I must admit, I had occasion to run into these two individuals; and, they were most disrespectful and abrasive with what I term 'pseudo knowledge' of vodun. For anyone to present themselves as an authority over someone who has been duly and authentically initiated into African Vodun is beyond me! African initiated Priests and Priestesses spend months to years in initiation chambers. They are the standard, in vodun, if they are genuine. Africa is the source of all diaspora African-based spiritual systems. These 'bought in' people love to attempt to separate Africa from diasporan vodou. They do not want to be held accountable to the ancestors or the African vodun hierarchy.

So, for me, this is part of the fallout. For one, if Ifa has not been used these folks may not have even been born to serve the spirits. Second, kanzos are so short there is not enough time to learn anything about the spirits...least of all respect for authentic Priests or Priestesses initiated in the motherland. Authentic Houngans and Manbos usually come from a vodou family lineage where they have been observing and working with the spirits for years. They understand what Africa is to vodun. But, for the 'bought in' folk, the most disturbing thing is this. These folks who often spend a great deal of money buying into vodun also have the money to promote themselves. Let's be straight up here. These temples like to draw these folks because they have money to spend. So, whether they give them anything genuine, or not, these folks go right out, after the conclusion, and set up shop! They then sell this 'bought in' stuff to whomever else who is willing to buy; and, then set themselves up as experts because they pride themselves on their book knowledge. I have not met one of these people, not one, that can discuss the nature of spirits with me. They simply do not know the spirits. And some of their personalities and/or characters lead me to believe that they need therapy. They make up their own rules and want to tear down anybody that chooses to tell them differently. But I know this! My spiritual authority comes from the ancestors and the divinities. Theirs comes from nowhere....

I've said this before; but, I really lay the fault, squarely, on the shoulders of those legitimate Houngans and Manbos who go about initiating these people ...if that is what we are calling it! This obsession to find money and keep their lifestyles looking good simply isn't worth what they are producing. We all suffer when we have incompetent folk claiming to be part of our Priesthood. My prayer is that, with the reaching back to Africa, the re-inclusion of Ifa, thus consulting the spirits at every level, of our work, we can begin to weed out such folks for the future.

A MESSAGE TO MY FRIENDS OF EUROPEAN DESCENT

Many suppose that African Vodun and Vodun, in general, is an ethnic spiritual system. But, in a sense, it is not!

We are all born of spirits regardless of race, creed color and/or gender. Vodun, itself, is uniquely African....that is without a shadow of a doubt! But, the reality is, that the oldest ancestor of any of mankind, be they, black, white, Asian, or anything which lies in between, originates from somewhere on the continent of mother Africa. She is the cradle of civilization itself. So, in that sense, the oldest ancestor, of all of mankind, is African; and, science has proven that fact. So, regardless of your race; and, regardless of how far you may be removed from that African ancestry, everyone has the right to serve the Voduns. The problem, however, has been in how one chooses to serve the Voduns/spirits... by the tenants in which they, themselves, have handed down or by doing your own thing. And thus lies one of the fundamental problems between those that are closest to their African ancestry and those that are not!

I'm going to be candid here... The advent of chattel slavery and its descendant "racism" has duped many, of European descent, into believing that they are superior to those of African descent. And, as a result, many of you feel you can take these African-based spiritual systems and do with them as you like. Wrong! Just like those, of us, who faithfully follow its tenets, any of you, born to the spirits, must serve the same as those of African descent and as your own African ancestors did. Your whiteness gives you no special privileges; and you can be punished just as severely as those of us, of color, if you mess up or come in with the wrong intentions!

Too many times I have encountered those, of European descent, with condescending attitudes because they have somehow "brought into" these African-based spiritual systems. In many instances, I am sure if they had gone to Ifa they may very well have been born to serve; but, in their fear of someone who is really legitimate, who came into the spiritual system as they were supposed to (identified by Ifa and duly initiated), are constantly on the defensive and refusing to learn. And, in some cases, actually attempt to denigrate the one who is trying to help them. They want to set themselves up as equal, to the legitimate one, and then tell them how Africa is not important and that diaspora Vodun is a different lineage. This is the epitome of ignorance! One cannot cut the tree down from its roots, or, it will surely die. And, the persons initiating folks, such as these, and teach them nothing about Africa or its significance, to Vodun, ought to be whipped! Do not be deceived, those doing so will be punished, by the spirits, as well as those who are disrespectful to legitimate Priests or Priestesses of African descent. You see, in Africa, we know and are taught that to insult an African, of the Priesthood, is to bring condemnation upon yourself. The spirits of that person can rise up, on their own accord, and smack you down like a flea. So keep it up! You're gonna learn what real Vodun actually is! African Vodun is not something you can play with or its people!

Another issue I have encountered is diasporan Manbos and Hougans marrying these people off to their own African ancestry. Two problems here. First, these folks have their own African ancestry. Second, a non-use of authentic African divination systems is often at the root of this. Go to Ifa, allow these folks to find their own ancestors. Their ancestors deserve to be fed! Don't just marry them off to your own because you are out there trying to make a buck or you don't realize that they have one. If one goes to Ifa, the ancestor can be found. And, it does not matter how far removed the person is from this African ancestry. When called to feast, all ancestors, of the person, will come from the oldest to the youngest and the darkest to the lightest. It doesn't matter whether you are mixed race, lily white, light pink or blue black, everyone will show up because they know their children.... each, and every one!

No one can tell me that centuries of racism, in America and other parts of the diaspora, does not affect a person. It does! While I do not consider myself a racist individual I will inadvertently retreat to a position of defense when my people are attacked socially and/or politically. When, as a people, you have served at the butt end of racism, for decades, you know the enemy. So I know when I roll up on a person, of European descent; and, I question their methods, in Vodun or any other African-based spiritual system what the deal is, ... we retreat to our respective positions out of instinct. They... as the "superior one" wanting to do things their way; and, that they are all knowing and all right. I... blistering at their "perceived superiority" and the audacity that they can even think such!

In Vodun, my European friends, chattel slavery and its descendant "racism" has no power! Your privilege to serve comes through birthright, your ability to serve through initiation and the proper training, your communication with the divinities, themselves, through Ifa. The only hierarchy, here, is if you were even born to serve at all...

TO INITIATE OR NOT TO INITIATE? : THAT IS THAT QUESTION

I have covered the subject, of initiation, before in my earlier writings; but, I feel to reiterate it, at this time, due to the general thinking that Vodun can be learned solely through Eurocentric methodologies. Today this could include anything from books to social media. But, be not deceived, no Priest or Priestess, of traditional African Vodun, is going to share Vodun's secrets, to any researcher. Scholarly research is not bad within itself. One may ascertain certain generalities about this spiritual system; however, to really know Vodun is only for those born to know. Vodun is no simple "religion". African Spiritual Systems, in general, give access to the very divinities themselves... those that created the universe and all it contains. However, not everyone is born to have this access. That is one of the things that distinguishes them from other spiritual systems.

When one has gone to Ifa/Fa/Afa, the west African divination system; and, it has been revealed that they are born to the spirits, one must make the decision to initiate or not. One does have choice; however, for some the spirits can make your life so difficult that it may be your "only" choice. In any event the initiation process is essential in preparing you for the spiritual work ahead. In addition, there is a misnomer, in the diaspora, that all are born to the Priesthood. This is not true! There are many seats, or stations, within a temple. One can be born to any one of these stations from Vodunsi to Drummer, to Diviner, to Tassinon (woman of prayer), to Priest or Priestess and others. All of these stations, within a temple, have their own specific work; and, it is Ifa that tells you what that work is. Ifa tells us who and what we are in the spiritual realm.

It is assumed that the initiation process is about the initiate and the Priest or Priestess; but, this is not true! The initiation process is about the initiate and the spirits themselves. The Priest or Priestess is the vessel, for the spirits, and has a role; but, that role is to help the spirits in carrying out the initiation according to their specific instructions. At the beginning of every initiation process Ifa is consulted. Generally, there are three or more diviners in attendance. Ifa tells us the length of time the initiate is to remain in the initiation chamber, as well as, the spirits to be initiated into...one's head spirit and accompanying spirits. And, at every juncture, throughout the initiation process, Ifa is consulted to gain instructions from the person's personal spirits. For, in Vodun, spirits are as individual as we are people. Two persons may have the same head spirit, but, each spirit could require something specific to their particular personality and their spiritual child. Cookie cutter initiations, therefore, are not a part of authentic African Vodun. One relies on the instructions of a person's personal spirits to guide one through the initiation process.

It is during the initiation process that one learns all that one needs to know about one's station in the spiritual world. As part of a particular temple one will continue one's training; but, initially one learns the dances, the songs, the colors and all else one needs to prepare him/herself for their new life. If one is of the Priesthood, one's Voduns will be installed, in front of you, in whatever specified place; and, you will learn how to care for them and communicate with them. If one is found to be of the Ifa Priesthood this too will be revealed. An Ifa Priest will spend at least 16 initial days with you, during your initiation process, and then after initiation you are to go for further training. The Priesthood of Ifa is a specialized Priesthood and demands a lifetime of training. This is what happens with those in Mami Wata. Each pantheon, of spirits, have their own tenants. It is all revealed by Ifa.

Within the process, itself, it is a time when that division between the spiritual and our physical worlds are folded down upon themselves; and, the spirits gain more direct access to us and us to them. It is a time when those spiritual gifts, born to us, are fully activated by the divinities, themselves, and power, from on high, installed. It is a time of preparation for the spiritual work ahead. One's mission is discovered and the Voduns prepare, themselves and you, in working toward the completion of that mission. For before birth, while in the spiritual realm, you signed a contract; and, that contract is what the initiation process will help you in realizing and completing.

To initiate or not initiate. The decision lies with those who were born to serve. It is a noble calling for those of noble birth. For too long we, as a people, have suffered in this place, for too long our ceremonies have gone undone and our ancestors have suffered in hunger...listen to the beat of the African drums, listen to the call of our ancient ancestors...for who we are and what we are is in "the blood".

A MISNOMER IN THE DIASPORA: NOT ALL ARE DESTINED TO THE PRIESTHOOD IF INITIATED

One of the things I have noticed, in the diaspora, is the tendency for many to believe that if they are initiated, into vodoun, they are automatically destined to the priesthood. This is not true! In vodoun there are many stations in the temple and spiritual world. One may be born a helper or worker for the spirits, a diviner, a Tassinon, a Da (king) or any other station besides Priest or Priestess. While everyone is born of a spirit not everyone is born to the priesthood. It is Ifa that tells us WHAT we are (what pantheon of spirits we belong to) and Who we are (what station we hold) in vodun, as well as, our ancestry. Vodun is not like going to college where one chooses how far one wants to go and continues to add degrees. You are BORN to your spirit(s) and station in the spirit world. Now, however long it takes you to accomplish, all of these ceremonies, is up to you and your cash flow; but, this is how authentic African Vodun is done. And, for folks who run over to Africa for a two-three-week vacation and return telling you they are now the grand poo pah of the grand poo pah do not believe it! Africans will take your crisp tourist dollars and do a ceremony or two for you; but, authentic African initiations take years to complete. Training to one's spiritual station takes a lifetime!

AFRICAN INITIATION/DIASPORA INITIATION...DOES IT MAKE A DIFFERENCE?

This is a difficult subject because folks wanna believe that what they have, in the diaspora, ... that initiation for which they have paid for... is valid. I understand that; but, if one wants to hear the TRUTH, here it is. There is no comparison between the two. These African-based spiritual systems originated out of Africa...not Haiti, not the Caribbean, nor Cuba or anywhere else. These systems originated out of Africa brought over as a result of the transatlantic slave trade. And, as a result, the African initiation process, the original and authentic initiation process, for these African-based spiritual systems, reign supreme. It should be a common-sense thing; but, it isn't because the "bought in" folks are busy spreading their propaganda that Africa, and its ancestry, is no longer connected to African-based spiritual systems in the diaspora. But they, and the folks that initiated them, are perpetuating a lie which is self-serving and allows them, all, to stay in business. So, let's pretend that they do not exist, for a moment, and speak among ourselves. This essay is directed to those, outside of Africa, who are found to be born to the spirits, regardless of your race, creed, color or gender, because, if Ifa says that you are a child of the spirits, in whatever capacity, you are.

I am thankful that enough has survived of these systems, through the slave experience, that their spiritual foot prints have, forever, been placed inside of the diaspora. And, we are equally indebted to those families and/or individuals, here, that have served the spirits with honor and distinction for hundreds of years. However, now, my sisters and brothers, slavery is over...oppression not yet... as we currently witness the personal and political attacks upon our first black President and the continual shootings of our African American young people in the streets of America. We, more than ever, need the full backing of our ancestors and the power of the spirits that gave us life. And to do this we must look, spiritually, toward Africa. We must look toward the strength that exists in our African forefathers. And it is because of this that I must say that these two week, diaspora initiations, are simply not enough. They don't even begin to prepare, someone, for spiritual work. For those who have had them let it be your beginning place. Our diasporan ancestors, that have been our strength, will always be there for us; but, as we reach back, toward Africa, we not only reunite ourselves, with our oldest ancestors, but we re-unite all of those who have died, on these shores and in this place, with them as well. Our forefathers were snatched from their native lands. Therefore, they too wish to re-unite and receive the sacrifices that they are due.

It is within the initiation process that one is prepared for one's spiritual work or mission. That is why to each initiation, in Africa, it is the spirits that determine one's length of stay in the initiation chamber. It is the spirits, through, Ifa that direct us in what each individual and their own personal spirits need. It is the place where you learn your pantheon's dances, peculiarities and the like. One is not initiated, in Africa, and then has to come out and jump on the internet to find out what they need to know. It is taught, to them, while in the temple setting during the initiation process. People spend months and/or years completing ceremonies for their spirits in Africa. I, for instance, spent 8 long years in and out of African initiation chambers without taking my foot off African soil; and, I still have much more to complete...numerous ceremonies for the titles that were born to me. We, diasporans, have the same type of spirits and/or titles; but, simply do not know who and what they are. The non-use of Ifa or authentic African divination, in the diaspora, has hindered us greatly. People are carrying big and powerful spirits with huge spiritual thrones, but, will never know it because of the non-use of authentic divination practices that were/are actually original to these systems. Yet, we have these "bought in" folks using simple playing cards or tarot, with African based systems, and taking folk's money. It doesn't work guys.

If one examines traditional Africa, and observes its initiation processes, into the spirits, one notices that these initiations are long, arduous and sometimes even dangerous. They come through great personal sacrifice and inward reflection. It was NEVER the intent, in African-based spiritual systems, that their initiations were to be shorted this way. That "new lineage" crap, propagandized by the "bought in" folk and those that initiate them, is just that... crap! It was the slave experience, itself, that shortened the process. With these African slaves serving the spirits, in secret risking their lives in many instances, the initiation process, out of sheer necessity, had to be shortened. And, if a person was mounted, one could quickly see that the person was born of the spirits. The problem is...we are born of many spirits; and, it takes Ifa to tell us who they all are, what they want of us, our spiritual missions, as well as, the origins of our ancestry. Our head spirit may not be the first one who mounts. It usually isn't. The divine ones will not reveal themselves to those who do not know their ceremonies or is equipped to communicate with them.

So, my appeal, to those born to the spirits and living in the diaspora, is not of which initiation is better, African or diasporan; but, rather an attempt to restore traditional African-based spiritual systems to their full power and glory by reinstating those elements that were lost, shortened, or forgotten, during to the slave era. This doesn't mean that one loses what one has, but, it does mean adding to what one has if one chooses to do so. And, this would entail the first step of reinstating the authentic African divination system original to these African-based spiritual systems... Ifa.

African initiation, diaspora initiation.... does it make a difference? You bet your boots it does!

AFRICAN SPIRITUALITY: VODUN AND THE SEARCH FOR A MENTOR

One of the things that I have encountered, since returning to the diaspora, are folks looking for spiritual mentors. This has never been an issue, for me, since I was initiated in Africa and am a member of an African temple; but, it seems to be one of the avenues used, in the diaspora, in an attempt to learn and/or train in these diaspora African-based spiritual systems. However, there should be some common-sense guidelines to this that I do not believe many take into account.

For one it doesn't appear to dawn on many that if you are to be mentored it would need to be someone that carries the same spirits that you carry. This could be because folks generally do not know who their head spirit is anyway. But, if one goes to Ifa and makes this determination through authentic African divination, then, one would know. One could inquire as to what is one's head spirit or the pantheon of spirits that one was born to and one's ancestry. These are the least that people should know when pursuing a traditional spiritual path of any kind. Without this basic knowledge, one has no idea where to begin. In traditional Africa, we serve the spirits that gave us life. We don't run around here and there spinning our wheels on spirits we think we are "drawn to". And maybe there is some validity into that special "feeling" that one would have toward a particular spirit; however, one should absolutely know. And as not all are born to the priesthood, Ifa will also tell us if we are to serve the spirits and in what capacity. It is a misnomer that all are born to the priesthood in these African-based systems. We are not. There are many stations or vocations within a traditional temple. Not everyone is born to be chief.

I hear folks speak of levels of initiation into the priesthood. In authentic African spiritual systems, there is no such thing. The voduns, will tell you, via Ifa, to what rank or station of the priesthood, if any, you are born to... full stop. You are either born a diviner, chief priest/priestess, vodunsi or some other spiritual station. It is told to you, through Ifa; and, that is it. One doesn't work your way up. You are either born the thing or not born the thing.

But getting back to the subject at hand, if one thinks about it, it only makes sense that you would attach yourself (be mentored by) someone who is familiar with the spirit that gave you life because they would have insight into the nature of that spirit. I have never understood why diasporans find nothing wrong with someone "supposedly" initiating them and, then, them having to go outside of those folks to learn about the very thing they were initiated into. If these folks do not know enough to teach you, then, where did they learn enough to initiate you into that particular spirit? Common sense dictates that if they can't teach you about the spirit, then, they themselves do not know that spirit and certainly have not been ordained by the divinities to initiate you into that spirit. When folks come to me, like this, I send them back to the person. What I am trying to tell them is that their initiation is bogus; but, they do not often get it. They usually have only gotten a few thousand dollars poorer (or whatever the fee might have been) and in possession of an empty pot that they will eventually have to discard into the sea.

Another thing...the term "elder" is used, to death, in the diaspora. So much so that it has become one of the "buzzwords" in African-based spiritual systems here. Everybody is speaking about this or that elder when very few of these people have ever spent any real time in an authentic African temple. An African elder is not someone that has been initiated into somethin' about 5 min. ago, read a few books and then deemed an elder due to their years of interest, in the subject of African spirituality, and their accumulated book knowledge. An African elder is someone that has practiced vodun, or the orisa, for eons and have initiated many, as well as, being someone who is highly respected in the spiritual community. While, for instance, I have practiced vodun, since 1998, I am by no means an elder. The elders that I have, in Africa, are 100 years old and above.... some younger; but, you get my point. They are well respected practicing spiritual leaders who are just a few years from joining their ancestors. We need to stop "play acting" at African spirituality but instead become full and active participants in African spirituality.

I am not fully sure how this mentorship thing is supposed to work in the diaspora since all one needs to know, about one's spirits, are supposed to be taught in the initiation chamber; however, it would appear to me that a mentor should be chosen due to those common traits one should have to someone as opposed to the fact that they have the title of priest or priestess. For instance, if you were born of the spirit Heviosso and me Mami what could I teach you? My Heviosso is of the pantheon of Mami; but, if yours is not what good am I to you? If I am a priestess that is correct I would ask the spirits, on your behalf, to what Heviosso priest do I take you to? But in the diaspora, do we even have that luxury? Do we actually have, at this time, someone properly trained as a Heviosso priest that the spirits would even accept or recommend? It is hard to say; but, one thing is for sure. Vodun, and African spirituality in general, is far too serious a matter to be handing one's spiritual life off to just any Joe Shmoe who claims the priesthood. Folks performing ceremonies without the proper skills or knowledge could cause you more pain than it is worth! So, in searching for a mentor, all I can say is be very careful out there.

THE DIFFICULTY OF FINDING YOUR TRUE SPIRITUAL PARENT

I'm not sure that I have any definitive answers for this one. From my experience, it seems that finding the correct spiritual parent is part and parcel of that long and arduous road one follows along one's spiritual path. I can only commensurate with you and assure you that the spirits within us will eventually lead you there.

I spent an initial eight years, in Africa, in and out of temples from Benin to Ghana. But it wasn't until my seventh year that I met the person that the Voduns chose as that parent. Someone who wasn't about money, someone that the spirits adored and someone that this mighty spirit, in me, Dattatreya/Den'su would even reveal himself to. For seven years my head spirit was identified as the great Ayidowedo because he and Dattatreya wanted to protect me from my initiation, for him, being improperly done. While I indeed possessed the great Ayidowedo as a spirit. He wasn't my head. This is how much these spirits loved me. To do the initiation for Dattatreya, improperly, could have killed me; so, I went from temple to temple, spending money, practically building folk's temples, for them, and zigzagging up and down the west coast, of Africa, until the spirits made it possible to meet the correct teacher who was right there in my backyard. A mighty Priest that when he called that great spirit...he answered standing on the top of a mountain and said, "This is my child!"

My concerns about the diaspora has always been on how we go about initiating these folks. Many have realized, for a long time, that they need to re-connect to their ancestors and the spirits that live within them; but, how shall we do this? At present we have very few, if any, Priests/Priestesses qualified here that these mighty spirits will even reveal themselves to. And certainly, we are not equipped to initiate these folk in the African traditions here; so, they must understand that initially folks must go to Africa! We must equip these future Priests and Priestesses that they may transplant their ancestral shrines/houses and Voduns correctly in this land. They must go back, re-connect and train. They must return and learn what was lost, to Vodun, because of the slave trade. And, in so doing, they will become the Priests/Priestesses, of the future, for authentic traditional African Vodun in the diaspora! That is my prayer!

But in the meantime, one must be careful of those who promise to initiate you but true purpose is to extract money! All that glitters is not gold! There will be people who will come, from Africa, looking the part; but, many of them are out to make money. If you go for a divination and you sit in a room while they are back there behind a curtain or door doing your divination that is a red flag...African or not! Oh, they are talking to the spirits all right; but, amongst themselves they are discussing how they may exploit that to which they have found out about you. You should be sitting by that diviner if the divination is being done while you are present. Also, let NO ONE cut your hair for any reason! Your hair is something they can use to bind you to them and make you their money slave. Remember that very few people, here, have had authentic African initiations. They are long and arduous. If someone claims that you have such and such spirit but they can't even tell you how to serve it, and send you to the internet, that too is a red flag! Folks who have been initiated, in Africa, know their Vodun. Of the many months, in initiation chambers, one learns all they need to know, about their spirits, inside the temple. If someone cannot even tell you the basics about a particular spirit and send you to the internet how then do they know enough to even initiate you? Some Americans are hosting African Priests/Priestesses to get their own stuff done! They may tell you about spirits you might not even have to draw out monies to do their own Voduns. Not everyone is Amengasie, not everyone has the Tchamba Voduns, Mami Wata is not connected to feminism. And just because someone's website is attractive and informative does not mean that it is all correct!

Again, as I've said, I have no definitive answers for finding the correct spiritual parent; but, I can tell you the things to try and look out for. For I have been there... really, I have!

THOSE BORN WITH OBVIOUS SPIRITUAL GIFTS AND THEIR RESPONSIBILITY

During the transatlantic slave trade, many born of the African priesthood were taken into captivity from throughout all of Africa. That is why so many came and, in secret, continued to serve the spirits. The trans-Atlantic slave's first glimpse of these foreign lands happened in the Caribbean. And in the Caribbean these African transplants lived and worked these lands several hundred years before a chained one ever graced the shores of the Americas. Many found their way to the Americas traveling with their massa, many sojourned, in the Caribbean first and had their papers forged claiming it as their place of birth while all along having been stolen from mother Africa and sold. In any event, vodun, orisa or by whatever other name referred, in reference to the spirits, was brought over in the minds and hearts of the people from black Africa...that dark and, to the enslaver, mysterious and godless place. These African-based systems are just that...AFRICAN....the birthplace of man and at the spiritual root of every known spiritual system that exists on earth.

As many of us are descendants of these priests, of old, it does not surprise me that many are visited by the ancestors. In our dreams spirits can come and show or reveal themselves. It is usually a very good indication that this person was born to the spirits in a very real way. I have come across so many as I have served the spirits over the years. It indicated to me several things about the person. That generally they are carrying a very high spirit, that only Ifa can determine, and that the ancestors need them desperately for a work. That work may either be for the family, as a whole, or for mankind in general. In any event the ancestor is attempting to speak and is showing him or herself to the person in order to put them on a search to find someone that they may communicate their intentions through. This essay has been prompted because as I come across such individuals I am seeing something that could hinder their growth or block the efforts of what their ancestors, or spirits, is trying to accomplish. So, I must address this now...

There are certain tenants that have been put in place by the ancestors and the divine spirits. And, just because one is born of unusual spiritual gifts does not mean that they can get around these tenants. That "pompous" attitude I have found in many is actually not your fault. I have it too! If the person submits to authentic African divination we generally find them to be carrying some of the highest spirits that exist. These spirits are natural kings, in the spiritual world, and can be difficult. They cannot be called by just any priests but, only by priests that are like themselves and/ordained by them. They won't even show up or answer to just any authentic bokono (diviner). For instance, it took 7 years before my spirit, Dattatreya would reveal himself. And it was ONLY after he found someone whom he chose to reveal himself to. So, when I meet people with the Dattatreya's, the Krishna's, the Wedo's, those high spirits in any of the spiritual pantheons... I simply smile. Why? Because as they are busy expressing, to me, all of their gifts and fabulousness, my Dattatreya is busy talking about how he be the most fabulous of all! But getting back to the matter at hand.

There are many folk, out here, struggling to know. That is why the diaspora is now being visited by so many African trained priests and those searching for truth. I do not believe this is coincidence but the work of the divine. But, there are many of you that are the descendants of what I term as "king priests". These are the highest priests that Africa has to offer. They were born with specific talents to accomplish specific spiritual missions. I and my husband are among that number. But understand that even a spiritually gifted person needs a teacher. You can not accomplish the type of initiation that you need by yourself; and, the spirits know it. You, however, need to figure this out. There is somebody "Mr. Thang/ Miss.Thang" that knows far more than you about spirits. And, lo' and behold they were even born with more gifts than you. An African priests of the caliber that I am speaking of could eat you for breakfast...you know nothing. It is these types of priests that you need to give you what you need because they hear the spirits and follow their directions implicitly. They do not waver or impart anything on their own. If the spirit doesn't command it they don't do it. So, when spirits appear in your dreams they are not simply coming to say hello. They are coming to you hoping that you will go to someone who can communicate effectively with them to tell you what they want. You have not been ordained, you have not been initiated into your head spirit; and, even if someone has sold you some power that is not of the mighty spirit you carry, because, you did not know your true spirit...working with lower level spirits is not going to be beneficial to you in the end. Your power is in discovering who your ancestors are, which pantheon of spirits you we born to, who your head spirit is and to give sacrifice. All that other stuff is just window dressing. So, to my gifted folk, don't let your fabulousness get in the way of your doing what you need to do to heed the call of the ancestors and the divine ones. Get off your pedestal, for a moment, and do what you need to do to claim it for real. Being spiritually gifted is not going to earn you any special privileges with the spirits. It simply gives you more responsibility. Because until you do the ceremonies, needed, that throne will sit in your imagination only. You will never be able to claim it after death.

VODUN AND THE BAD SEED

This essay is about family, that is, that part of the family that we are not necessarily happy about. Many families are plagued with them. I am not, so much, talking about that bad apple or two...that one person or persons that could have been given all of the best of our resources but still couldn't hack it in the real world, the occasional self medicator (drug addict) or child gone astray...no not them. I'm speaking about that bad seed. The one that, while looks like us, and was definitely born to our family is bent on causing dissension, by whatever means necessary, throughout. This is that bad seed. These people actually exist.

Let me explain myself more clearly. Spirits that bring us here, through birth, come from many different places throughout the spiritual realm. For whatever our destiny is spirits find a way to bring us to the physical realm through a family and/or a particular ancestry. Some come from good places...where the emphasis, of the spirits, is to nurture and assist mankind or bad places...where the spirits come down hell bent on wreaking havoc upon mankind. Not all spirits are malevolent. However, do not be deceived, some definitely are; and, they can live and dwell inside of human beings. And, as such, these humans are, thus, ruled by these negative forces. They can be witches or negative entities (spirits) or forces from just about anywhere.What it has taught me is that, in understanding this spiritual reality, not all families are going to be bastions of harmony. Dissensions may exist, among its members, due to destructive forces, or spirits, living from within those to whom we have been groomed to love. It also explains why there are, simply, some bad people in this world who are predisposed to doing bad and unmentionable things. However, our ancestors and the divine ones have a way of dealing with them.

Those who serve the spirits, and feed them regularly, have nothing to fear. Those who wreak havoc and destruction will eventually be dealt with by them. Their bad deeds will neither go unnoticed or unpunished.

A young man came to us for services. He was of Haitian birth As he was found to be born of the Priesthood we began to prepare him. Back in Haiti there was an element, in his family, that had been using the spirits against it's members for decades. As we began to feed the man's ancestors and they became nourished, by the blood, and strong...they rose up...and, without telling us a thing, this man, who had been causing the family trouble back in Haiti, was no more. As we later inquired about this man, back in Haiti after his death, the ancestors revealed their work! The surviving sons, of the man, divined that there was a new emerging spiritual force in the family; but, to this day they have not been able to ascertain who it is or how it happened.

Family is a wonderful thing! But understand, as I have said in other writings, we are not simply people who walk who happen to have spirits, but, we are spirits who walk who happen to be people. And as such just about anything can happen.

WORKING THROUGH THE LAYERS OF ABUSE, EMOTIONAL STRESS AND PAIN IN OFFERING SPIRITUAL HELP AND HEALING

Often when people come to us, for spiritual help, they are usually at some of their lowest points in life. In their estimation life has thrown them a curveball. In some instances, they are blaming others for their pain...someone has damaged them, taken their loved one or doors, of opportunity, have shut firmly in their faces. Some come saying it is sorcery, juju, or someone has schemed against them. In the case of a loved one, they forget to mention that the person left eons ago; but, they want to blame it on anyone else, but, generally who is the cause...themselves. These people are often difficult to help because through the layers of their vices, hypersensitivity to correction, or deep emotional fears and paranoia they cannot hear you and accept the instructions, from the voduns, or realize their own part in the hot mess which has turned out to be their lives.

A young lady made our acquaintance once; and, we completed a divination. We were able to ascertain, as in all our divinations, her ancestry, head spirit, accompanying spirits, presenting problems and prescribed solutions (ceremonies) from the voduns. I spent hours, by phone, teaching her about her ancestry (I happened to know this clan from Ouidah), answering her questions and worked hard to encourage her to do the prescribed ceremonies to open her pathways that her life could began to improve. As the relationship continued the woman began to act irrational. Each time I mentioned the ceremonies (for the spirits kept coming to us and asking) she began accusing us of wanting money from her, and all manner of things. Her stance towards me became extremely negative. I was agasp. Even though my professional background includes Psychoanalysis, I was not paying attention to what I was encountering. In my role as a Priestess I was not red flagging any possible pathology or vices; but, I should have been because, in Psychoanalysis, this happens in the therapeutic setting all the time. You, as the analyst, become that negativity that the patient is seeking to work through. And, in traditional Africa, the Priest or Priestess wears many hats. It was only later, when the voduns revealed, to us, that the woman had a problem with alcohol, that I put it all together. Putting it matter of factly the woman was an alcoholic; and, during her bouts of drinking did not function properly. In the end the relationship went nowhere; and, she ended up back with the folks who had helped mess up her spiritual life in the first place.

What I have learned through this is that folks with vices, severe emotional problems, or over the top sensitivity, bordering on pathology, must work out these issues, sometimes, before the spirits can help them. Sometimes these issues stand in the way of the people hearing you or accepting the directions from the spirits. These folks know their lives are in the gutter; and, that is why they have come. But, if those layers of vices, be it alcohol, drugs, sexual pathology, emotional trauma such as rape, abuse, personality disorders, hypersensitivity bordering on pathology...any of these things... is making it difficult for them to hear and/or obey the spirits, then, you must attempt to get them to address these issues first. But remember they are going to attempt to find a way to blame anyone else for their ills but themselves. These people, even though they know they need help, may not be ready to accept the help.

In some cases, doing the prescribed ceremonies can help strengthen a person's resolve that they are able to overcome their challenges. That is why the spirits are prescribing them in the first place. However, if the person is busy trying to tear down the messenger before even getting to the ceremonies; and, you are not at fault, in any way, then do not be discouraged. It is not you it is them!

You can take a person to water; but, you can't force them to drink. In vodun, as in anything else, mankind has choice. However, the problem is that they simply do not get it that with choice comes consequences. And with vodun these consequences can be dire.

GHOSTS/HAINTS/SPIRITS IN THE NIGHT

Have you ever woken up, or thought you had, but you were in between that waking and sleeping state? And for some reason you look to your left or right and you see someone you don't know and you attempt to question them; but, you can't move? It is like a force, of some kind, is holding you to the bed! You are speaking but the person cannot hear you? You are expanding all types of energy; but, you simply cannot raise yourself? Well my love you just saw a ghost! : lol: Yeah sweety, they exist!

For some reason, many homes are still visited by departed ones or spirits that don't seem to pass over for whatever reason. Generally, I was taught, that once a person dies they linger for about 7 days. They might go and visit someone they haven't seen in a long time or something. We have ALL had these experiences on some level. But these occurrences seem to proliferate in areas where folks don't send their loved ones off well with ceremonies, or whatever is appropriate for that region. Small children and/or fetuses cling to their mothers until ceremonies are done. And those who die in horrific deaths can roam too. These ghosts can be very dangerous and cause havoc. Especially if they died angry with someone! It is these lingering spirits that can usually be seduced, by sorcerers and such, to participate in bad acts with the promise of being fed. Not doing the proper ceremonies, for our departed ones, can have negative consequences.

Those divine spirits, that were born with the person, leave just before death...that is if they haven't left the person already. For some very bad people divine spirits leave them long before death. That part which should return to the ancestors gets trapped here on earth or at zogbe (place where those who died unnaturally go). Until the appropriate ceremonies are performed they are forever cut off from their ancestors. Think of the many brothas and sistahs that have died in drive bys, through drugs, disease and all other types of unnatural deaths. They are doomed to roam this earth causing havoc if they choose. Think of the lynchings, murders etc. So many, of our people... sad souls wondering this earth, dead, cold, confused and alone. African priests are the world's first "ghost whispers". We hear these folks, through divination, and perform the necessary ceremonies to put them at peace. Therefore, returning to our traditional ways and performing the ceremonies and rituals, of our African forefathers, is the only thing that will give them rest. But until then we may continue to see ghosts, haints (the mean ghosts) and spirits in the night.

VODUN AND AMERICA'S OBSESSION WITH THE MACABRE

In the late 1980s and early 1990s I taught High School Social Studies in upstate New York. It was a large school with over 3,000 students and 27 Social Studies teachers. At that time teachers were of University caliber. We all taught from areas of expertise. Students began to experience, incarcerations, drive-byes and deaths. It became tough and the school declined. So, many, of the old guard, began to retire because of a crack epidemic in the city. I too, eventually, left searching for a better way to serve the African American community. One of my favorite teachers was a gentleman who taught European

History. He was a Jew who really knew his subject matter. In fact, most of our Social Studies Teachers were Jewish. To our dismay the gentleman became ill and was out, for a while, battling a very serious disease. When we heard that he would return we were all excited. On the day that he returned, to school, I had not yet seen him. As I climbed the stairway, to the second floor, he was walking toward me, as I headed to the department's lounge. As he approached, eager to greet him, I looked at his face. But, in doing so, almost fainted away! I tried to hold my composure; but, sputtered away shaking from my very core. I saw DEATH on his face! It was terrifying! Never in my life had I seen this spirit before until that day; and, it almost frightened me out of my mind! Several weeks later we heard that he died in his sleep.

America has become obsessed with the macabre. Television is ripe with shows on vampires ("Dracula"), zombies ("The Walking Dead"), werewolves ("Bitten") and paranormal shows ("The Haunted Highway") of all kinds. Slasher movies are idolized and witches and warlocks ("American Coven") are pop stars. Even the great Ghede is idolized in Haitian Vodou. Whether folks were born with this spirit, or not, they run toward him trying to serve and live in his exotic world of sexuality and death! Those who are GOTH find all of this exhilarating! So, what's going on with all of this?

I do not have the answer; but, I do know that, in African Vodun, we know that DEATH and anything associated with it is spiritually UNCLEAN! When the body is about to experience death one's divine spirits lift out of the body. This is why many have expressed "near death" experiences whereby their soul is looking down on them while being resuscitated. Once the body dies it is effectively unclean. In Africa, one will find that many from the Priesthood do not attend funerals or, if they do, must go through intensive purification rituals after. When conducting ceremonies at Zogbe, the place where those that die of unnatural deaths go, purification rituals, with sacrifices, must be done in conclusion. It is the same with going to cemeteries or anything pertaining to the dead or the impure. So, why folks want to dwell, in death, I do not know! You carry this "unclean" with you. All of this is "outside" of the temple walls..."outside" of that which is clean and pure. I suppose one thinks that there is much power, in death, and that by associating one's self, with death, they too will have such power. But may I remind you DEATH has his power and his domain; but, all of his power is given and designated by MawuLissa. The REAL power to help you overcome, foes, enemies, and even DEATH, itself, comes from those spirits that gave you life.... those DIVINE ONES that have BOTH, LIFE and DEATH in THEIR HANDS!

A REQUEST FOR VODUN DOLL - WOULD YOU BELIEVE IT?

I go on one of the internet threads, that I am a member of, and I see the following: " How to make a luv commanding vodou doll with the person's shirt? Would anyone like to share? Thanks ".

Can you believe this? This is what pains me about people's perception of what Vodun really is. It is a spiritual system that helps change lives for the better. But folks run to it for their trivial problems. But hey, it's not just in America...Africa too! I see Africans sit in Church on Sundays but come to the bokono (diviner) at night! What has happened in Africa is truly tragic. The missionaries have had an enormous effect in brainwashing Africans into believing that Vodun is from the devil. In addition, many educated Africans feel that to show their equality, to the Eurocentric world, they must turn against their traditional ways and spiritual systems. They have been seduced in believing that traditional African spiritual systems are those of the savage and the uneducated. It is a shame! Africans are the true Priests/Priestesses of this world. There is no group of people that can come close to them! Yet, when Africans reach America and see that African Americans (AAs) and others are thirsting for knowledge out of Africa, then, they want to claim it! So, AAs fall directly into their traps. They start spewing "so-called" African knowledge that they haven't considered since they, themselves, were young and run home to the family priests promising to make money abroad for the family to whom they throw a few pennies and they pocket the rest! While they indeed have the priestly lineage they, themselves, haven't even seen the inside of a temple since childhood!

What a mess I tell ya!

I recall a woman coming into the Lakpan temple one day in Cotonou, Benin. She wanted help for her problems. She had been suffering an illness for some time. As she laid down on a bench/slab, for the work, the priest noticed a cross around her neck. Filled with the great spirit of Sakpata on his head the priest said, " If you think Church can heal you then go to the church; but, if it is I to heal your problem, that cross must come off!

I learned then not to mix the two!

DIASPORANS BE CAREFUL!

I don't know how to begin this...I never do when I start writing; but, here goes. My concerns are of those seeking to know and serve the spirits who run into those only seeking to get paid. It simply is too much of it! It happens in Africa, as well as, the diaspora. However, today, I just wanna explain what's happening in Benin and on the west coast of Africa. Since "Ouidah 92" an emphasis has been placed on the promotion of Vodun in Benin, West Africa. Without getting too deep into the history of it Benin, for a period of its history, it had a Marxist government. Vodun, as well as other religions, suffered repression. This later changed. Today, Vodun is not only the national religion, of the country; but, it is actually promoted. As a result, many tourists, from all over the world, visit this small nation. In fact, this outpouring of tourist dollars is why so many are now trying to hook into it. Many folk, from West Africa, who shunned their spiritual roots hoping to be more American or European living abroad... now, seeing that money can be made, is presenting themselves as Hounnons and Vodunnons trying to cash in. Everybody is a king! But what most Diasporans do not understand is that in EVERY Africa family there is a king! In finding our ancestry (which Fa can do fo you) we are ALL descents of kings. What we have to do is be pruden in the questions we ask these people.

Do not be fooled just because the person SAYS he is from Africa African priests spend a great deal of time in their temples! Whe they travel it is for Vodun business! If someone tells you he is a bi priests in Africa, yet, he spends most of his time or lives in Paris o abroad on business ventures...that is a red flag! If he cannot give yo the name of his temple or his head spirit...that is a red flag! If he doe not know, or know of, some of the most prominent priests, in Africa and they do not know him.... that is a red flag! If he is not registere with the Ministry of Culture and claiming to represent Benin, in an way, ... that is a definite red flag!

In African Vodun, there is accountability! The Vodun communit is close knit! There is a Supreme Chief of Vodun, in Benin, livin in Ouidah. Presently, to our shame, there are two! One is legitimat one isn't! The one in the temple is really the one on the thron The other one has attempted to take his father's (Daagbo Hounno Houna) throne, who died about 2004. He's running around, in hi father's clothes, with no temple busy promoting himself! I know hi personally; but, we can discuss him later. He was a crook when I kne him and he still is!

There are also chief priests of each pantheon of Vodun. Issue of misconduct can be brought to them or the Supreme Chief if on so desires. But my point here is that there are many priests, fro Benin, and other parts of West Africa working with Diasporans; bu one must be careful and check out these folk's credentials. All tha glitters ain't gold; and, Africans can lie like other folk! One good thin though...there is a person who will take the throne as the Suprem Chief of the Diaspora out of Benin...born to the seat, sanctioned b the ancestors and the spirits. The seat has stood vacant for centurie but, now the person has come. When that ceremony takes place, the world will know! And I will make sure that you folks have a front row seat!

VODUN AND THE NEW AGE MOVEMENT

As mentioned in my posts, "Vodun's Flip Side 1&2", there is a tendency for many to view Vodun as this cuddly, feely, my spirit would never do anything mean/bad kinda thing. What I am finding is that this is indicative of what has been termed as the 'New Age Movement' (NAM).

This NAM, first appearing in the 1980s, looks to be a conglomerate of beliefs about spiritual consciousness from the concept of spiritualism, itself, to reincarnation, to holistic health, correct thinking, correct knowledge with a bit of salvation thrown in. It preaches a theology of "universal tolerance", "moral relativism" and let's all "fe*e*l g*o*o*d". So, you've got Wiccan witches skipping through the forests/tulips, communing with nature, folks thinking that menstrual blood, the most impure blood of all (not to mention a cast off from somebody's dirty vagina), can be offered to spirits, everyday Joe Smoes thinking they can call forth divine beings and mega attention on sex and the orgasm that hasn't been seen since the hippies of the 1960s. What a slippery slope! Some of these things are not bad within themselves; but, the foundation that some of these "feely good" theologies are built on is pure quicksand. I would like to deal with just a few today.

It appears that central to NAM, is MAN and his divinity, which puts forth its first flaw. Man, himself, IS NOT divine; but, there are divinities that live within him, and, even those can leave him if he is not living his life right. To access these divinities, one must be a part of Vodun/Orisha/Lwa or the spirit world itself. The ONLY way to do this is to be initiated into something. However, one must not only be born to serve but must initiate, according to the tenants of the Voduns/spirits, in order to have this access. Therefore, this idea of self-initiation is poppycock! Man, a being who is not divine and impure, in his natural state, has no ability to initiate himself, dwell with or call forth divine beings.

A second theme big with NAM is the belief that Christianity is narrow-minded. I agree with this part; but, they continue by stating that man is separated from the Creator not because of original SIN but because of a lack of understanding the true nature of God. I wholeheartedly agree! But, the New Testament has NEVER shown the true nature of God! I argue that it is in the Old Testament, of the prophets, that we see the true nature of God....the divine spirits. The New Testament writers were busy trying to start a new religion; and, the canonization of the Bible helped in this process. Much was left out to where we have virgin births and skewed realities. God is portrayed as a good, kind, feely good type of guy who turns the other cheek. The Old Testament prophets portray a God who can and will punish his children and who puts obedience as a first priority. This is the God (Voduns) that I know!

A third theme, in NAM, is that there are no moral absolutes. Jesus is not the only way. Great! That's true! So, the New Agers are embracing Vodun and other traditional spiritual systems. The problem, however, is that in these pre-colonial systems.... systems that actually pre-date organized religions, and in some cases man himself... that the divine ones might communicate with him/her...there ARE moral absolutes! And these moral absolutes are dictated by the divinities themselves not man. This attitude that there are no moral absolutes is at the root of folks thinking that they can make up their own rules in Vodun.

There is much more to these New Age theories; but, I will end it here for now. I have brought up those that I think have been some of the most detrimental to understanding the spirits that I serve. And I believe that many of these are the reasons why, when so many foreigners appear on the doorsteps of Vodun priests, seeking Vodun, in Africa, that the Voduns say NO!

These folk's priorities are incorrect. New Age folk often create their own realities. These aforementioned theories serve to vulgarize that which is highly sacred to the African people. And after the extreme sacrifices that were made, of African ancestors, that their children were taken into chattel slavery and toiled to build nations... is highly insulting to them!

HOMOSEXUALITY AND VODUN

When I was growing up, as in most African American neighborhoods, you always had your gay community. Well, not so much gay 'community', per se; but, your gay members were there. It didn't appear to be much out of the ordinary because it was always somebody's brother, sister, cousin or family member; and, like everybody else, you knew their family. So, it was just another facet of the neighborhood. We would sit on the stoop and chit chat on who we thought was 'sweet', if you thought the brother was 'flaming' or 'butch' if the woman wore men's clothes. All this talk, was of course, on the down-low 'cause you might get in a fight for talking about somebody's 'people'. So, we just whispered, starred and watched the grown folk shake their heads. On Sundays, the preacher would preach damnation and hellfire, from the pulpit on Homosexuality; but, it was just a formality because everybody knew that the choir director was 'sweet' and if you angered him we might not win anymore church choir contests. So, life went on, with our whispering and pointing fingers, while our gay brothers and sistahs laughed at all of us 'cause they knew who was tipping their way when the lights went out! Now, everything done gone political, gay folks talking equal rights and everybody wants to marry each other...not to mention the male gay reviews I'm seeing on 'facebook'! : lol: So, here we are; and, what does vodun have to say?

Truth be told I have not sat down and questioned the spirits on the subject. Never felt the need; but, I have encountered situations where one or more of my spiritual children have been in love triangles with someone that had a gay lover; and, in consulting Ifa, on their personal issues, have seen the spirits be extremely gentle and long suffering. I have seen the spirits break up some of these relationships, not because of sexuality; but, because of one's destiny or the fact that the two people were not good for each other.

Each of us come to this earth born of a spirit(s) and a mission. It is the job of the spirit(s) to assist in the completion of that mission. What we choose to do, as individuals, also helps in dictating whether that mission is completed or not...whether we hear the spirits or whether we choose to dance to our own tunes. Therefore, for me, it is not so much about one's sexuality as it is about one's willingness to hear and obey the spirits and to accomplish that mission/destiny that one has come, to this life, to fulfill. Can one do these things and be gay? I believe that decision is between every man/woman and their God... those spirits that gave him/her life.

As a priestess, my role is clear. In my obedience to the ancestors and the divine ones my own personal feelings (whatever they might be) are always put aside for the greater good. I am a servant of the spirits; and, whoever they have chosen to serve them is really not my affair... whether homosexual or of another race. I am not here to block the work of the spirits but to facilitate it! I am their vessel to be used as they so choose. I am in THEIR hands. The only authority I have is of that which they choose to give me. Their yes is my yes and their no my no. So, I might not like what you are doing; but, if you want me to take you to the spirits I will. My arms are far too short to box with God; and, my obedience to them far outweighs my obedience to self. And, after that, it is between you and YOUR God...I have done my part!

VODUN AND TRANSGENDER

I have written several essays on gender (the range of physical biological, mental and behavioral characteristics pertaining to, and differentiating between, masculinity and femininity) and gender roles he social and behavioral norms generally considered appropriate or either a man or woman) in African Spirituality, specifically, argeted to Vodun...the spiritual system to which I serve. I have lso addressed homosexuality (the romantic and sexual attraction etween members of the same sex) in Vodun. And to each, of these, I ave been consistent.

As human beings, we are all born of voduns (or spirits) originating rom the creator to whom, I believe, is divine. And, as such, each ndividual has the right to go before the divine (his/her creator) to ommune, discuss or inquire. I, as a servant of the ancestors, the livinities, and mankind have no authority to keep them away. And, f the spirits have issue with one's behavior, in any way, let each man/ voman answer to his own god or spirits to whom he/she serves.

However, for the issue of transgender (the state of one's gender xpression not matching one's assigned sex) I have, basically, shied way. Not because I feel that the issues of transgender are any less mportant; but, because I simply do not have all of the answers. I ave never inquired, upon the voduns, on the issue; therefore, I do ot know their official stance. However, there is much I understand bout the nature of the spirits; and, as such, can use this knowledge o, at least, create a beginning dialogue on the subject. A dialogue that s sorely needed, in the diaspora, and one that has become extremely mportant today. For there are far too many beautiful souls, out here, being turned away, at the gates of traditional African spiritual ystems, because we either do not understand them or simply refuse o be bothered. We, in the priesthood, have a duty to minister to, nd serve, all of mankind not simply those to whom we, in our own stimations, deem appropriate.

So, this is what I know. In Vodun each person who serves the spirits s referred to as "si" meaning the "wife of" the spirit. For instance, Ablosi or Wedosi would mean the "wife of" Mami Ablo or the "wife of" Ayidowedo. This does not matter whether you are male or female. Specifically, in the pantheon of the Mami Wata spirits, to which I am most familiar, male vodunsi or the "wife of" vodun often look, dress and appear female. I also know that a person born female can be ruled by male spirits. These women are female, biologically, but male spiritually...case in point...myself. I am a woman biologically in all respects; but, the spirit that rules my life and the majority of my accompanying spirits are distinctly male. I carry two hands of Ifa (generally given to males), I am of the Ifa Priesthood (generally male dominated); and, as a result, all of my Voduns are given in male/female counterparts as is most men in Vodun. My spiritual force is distinctly male in every sense of the word; and, my male husband is very much aware of this woman with a male spiritual head and soul. In the same vein there are men, in vodun, who have the spirit and soul of a female. I have seen them dress and prepare for vodun ceremonies; and, their finery is most beautiful! They are very much the bride or "wife of" the spirits. Does this translate into transgender issues today? I do not know. For me it is all new.

Have I, a woman, ever looked upon another beautiful woman with desire? If I say I haven't I would be lying! Is it the maleness in me? I do not know... But it is an issue that must come out from the closet. It is an issue that must be addressed head on. I love and adore my husband. I designate myself heterosexual; but, living within me is an an entire company of powerful male spirits. Does that, then, make me spiritually transgendered? Maybe! As I have said, I do not have all of the answers; but, it is time for me to go and get some. It is my prayer, therefore, that the next time I am, in Africa, and physically kneel before all of my voduns in the temple...all of those great male and female divinities alike...I began to seek the answers Until then may the spirits direct the feet of us all. It is my firm belief that regardless of one's color, gender, sexual preference, or anything else, all have the right to go before the divine. But my prayer is that I can gain first hand understanding, from the spirits, that I am able to address, such issues, with greater authority and confidence.

ME, VODUN AND THE CLUELESS

When I wake up some mornings I think of the enormity of the task of re-educating people in what Vodun and African spirituality really is. More and more I am encountering young people who are espousing this "New Age" rhetoric. In an attempt to make African spirituality, and other spiritual systems more accessible, to them, this New Age crowd has, in a sense, brought upon a devaluation of the sacredness of these systems. We are being bombarded with terminologies such as "universal cosmic law", "electrode" of my Ori, "god is in his creation", "truth is universal", etc. It all sounds good; but, what it indicates, to me, is that these persons know absolutely nothing about the spirits or the spirit world, in general, but is desperately trying to give the impression that they do in fact know. But, in reality, they are clueless. Repeat this nonsense to a traditional African Priest; and, he would wonder to which traditional root you've been smoking. When a person is grounded in traditional African spirituality, as command by the ancestors and the divine spirits and on their terms, this spiritual shallowness can be detected in an instant.

The mistake that has been made by the 'New Age' folk, and others like them, is that INSTEAD of attempting to meet the high standards imposed by Vodun, or African spirituality in general, they are attempting to bring Vodun and African spirituality down to their level. So, this is why I am having to correct women upon hearing such things as a woman's menstrual blood is sacred and can be offered to spirits. I was absolutely appalled that any woman, in their right mind, could, even, think of such a thing! "It's natural", they say. Oh, yes, it's natural for us to have this biological function in our childbearing years. But, do they really want to push the envelope, that far, and think that these divine beings would accept such? Are these women kidding me? An attempt to take something, discharged from their unclean vagina, and offer it to a divine being?

First of all, folks, these spirits are just that.... DIVINE! They are the CREATORS of this universe and all that it contains! To even go before them, or take their counsel, one must be cleaned and purified from the uncleanliness of mankind. When we do highly sacred work in Vodun, for instance, there are times when a man or woman must not have engaged in sexual relations, for a length of time, before they can participate in such work. The Priesthood is a sacred vocation. The temples are sacred places. Purification rituals are strictly maintained, and adhered to, that one can, even, work with the spirits. But, you, Mr. Joe Shmoe think you can simply call any one of them down at will? And you, Ms. Sally New Age, think that you can offer them the expelling filth from your body? A child that was not formed, but, discarded as bacteria laden waste? No! To even consider such things is to denote that you do not understand the divinity, of these spirits, nor do you value or respect them; because, if you did you would heed the advice of their ordained ones.... those of the African Priesthood... and know that this is nonsense!

One can see the dealings of those, in the Priesthood of Vodun, as far back as the Old Testament writings, because, Judaism, in essence, is Vodun (that's an upcoming essay). In Leviticus 16:2-34 one finds a description of the Holy of Holies... the tabernacle/temple of the Israelites. The tabernacle was a restricted area for the Israelites, only Aaron and his descendants...they were Levites* thus Priests... could enter it because God's presence was there. The understanding, throughout these passages, is that God's presence is one of holiness. Man's presence is one of unholiness. And, for man to approach God, it must take place on God's terms. Thus, the severe restrictions for entering the presence of God.

** Aaron was a Levite, a descendant of Jacob's son Levi. To have been a Priest one must have been a Levite. On the otherhand not all Levites were Priests. Some participated in the maintenance of the temple as African family temples are still run today. And bulls, rams, goats and animals, of all kinds, are still being sacrificed.*

This has not changed people! Temples are sacred places run by ordained Priests according to the tenants of God (the spirits). It has been this way for as long as the spirits have communicated with mankind; and, it is still this way today. And, as such, no 20th or 21st c. movements are going to change this! We humans may change; but, the spirits are the same, yesterday, today; and forever. As a result, it is we that must meet THEIR standards and not them that must meet ours!

VODUN, SACRIFICE AND WHITE NOISE

Since returning to the diaspora I have happened across numerous persons interested in traditional African spiritual systems for one reason or another. The sincere ones, once they are confronted with the enormity of the ceremonies, their costs; and, in some cases, the enormous sacrifices they themselves must make, often back away. I sincerely understand, with the economy like it has been for so long, it would give anyone pause. Yet, traditional Africans, who live on less than we can ever imagine, find a way to serve the spirits because they understand its value. And I firmly believe that those same ancestors and divinities that guide these folk, to me, will also help them find a way for them to serve regardless of the costs...if given half a chance!

Spiritual sacrifice doesn't only refer to the animal sacrifice that we give the spirits. One's sacrifice begins with the human sacrifice of everyday living. It is the putting of the spirits above all other concerns, or at least making them a priority, digging in and struggling through the journey. One's life and body, while a vessel for the spirits, also becomes a sacrifice, daily, to the service of God and man.

Over the years, I have heard the excuses for nonservice, the " I am busy," the, " I am broke!", the "I have no job!" or it's my life, my woes, my spouse, excuse after excuse on top of excuse. For me, it has become "white noise" a metaphoric sense of random talk without meaningful contents. For what it really amounts to is stark fear, procrastination and/or an unwillingness to sacrifice. One is caught up in the "me" or the "mine" or the "hurt" or the "pain". "Others have damaged me!", they often say! "So, fix me; but, I do not want to do any work!" They want some magic spell or potion to make it all better; and, by the way...make it cost only $2.99. Aren't you folks doing a special this week?

They want the help of the divine...these spirits who made the heavens, earth and all it contains...these spirits to whom all the wealth, of earth, is owned, along with the power and glory of the universe; and, it is to be given with no effort, on their part. Ladies and gents that is not how the spirits work. You must first know who they are, understand their majesty, and work hard to show that you are worthy of their help and willing to sacrifice to get it! It doesn't matter what the "New Agers" or the "do it yourselfers" say. These spirits are divine, can only be called by those to whom they ordain, and will only help you when you do your part; and, that which you cannot do put it their hands and they will complete the work.

My mother was a tough old bird. She stood only 5 feet tall and barely weighed about 100 lbs. She never minced words and never suffered fools lightly. If she hurt your feelings, she simply said, "If you don't like what I said, or how I said it, and you crying that your feelings is hurt, just pick 'em up and put 'em in your pocket, they'll ease off after while!" As a woman, who has a spiritual mission to help others, I do not have the luxury of tolerating a whole lot of tears or a whole pack of excuses. I consider myself compassionate and loving; and, my desire is to show all the way to the spirits. But, folks, you've gotta move your own feet, I'll be there with ya; but, I ain't walking for ya!

AFRICAN SPIRITUALITY: IT IS ACTUALLY WHO WE ALL ARE

Each day I look in the mirror I see more and more of my paternal grandmother's face. It vacillates however. Some days it is her face, some days my mother's. My temperament can be distinctly traced to my father...lack of patience, easy to anger. He too was born of the great spirit Dattatreya, called Den'su in Africa. I inherited my spiritual throne and much else from him, even, my health issues. My love of beautiful and quality things...comes from my paternal grandfather, that, dapper old gentleman who enjoyed a good cigar and was the love of my life. He was born of the great spirit Ganesh. And that no-nonsense mama, of mine, who was certainly her mother's daughter...my maternal grandmother who carried a hawk bill knife, in her bosom, and kept a can of red devil lye sitting beside her bed... was born of the great and mighty spirit Heviosso. So here we have it, a woman born to the spiritual throne of the great Dattatreya, inherited from her father, protected and influenced by the mighty spirits that have encompassed her life and the lives of those who have surrounded her since birth. Each of these individuals carry/carried a multitude of spirits; and, as such, these are the spirits that live in our lives, daily, from us and from those who are, and have been, most dear to us. Many we inherit after a loved one has passed on. But, this is Vodun/Orisa or the spirits...not Christianity, not Jesus, but, African spirituality in its simplest and most basic form.

I bring this up because many think that African spirituality is "ethnic". But in essence it is universal...universal to all of us in that Africa is, indeed, the birthplace of mankind; and, universal in that we are all...black, white, and anything in between, born of spirits no matter where we hail from.

Some of my Pan African brothers and sisters may not agree. My stiffest critics find no comfort in my teaching, what they perceive as, the "enemy". Their disdain for the injustices heaped upon the backs of a people who were physically enslaved, to another, still smarts in their collective memories. I understand. Heaven knows I do. Growth, be it spiritual, intellectual or physical can be measured on a line that forms a continuum from birth to death. Life is a process; and, each individual grows at his or her own rate. Each of us, therefore, may be behind or in front of another in our own personal growth. But I remember a few things from my youth. And that was that even in a segregated south, for children; and, I'm sure some adults as well, one could always find a good friend from across the tracks.

Usually these segregated neighborhoods were often separated by railroad tracks. As kids we played with everybody. It was only when the grown folks told us we weren't supposed to play with a particular child, because of their color, that we would consider otherwise. Children are innocent that way and don't play to color or politics. So, even though, as an undergrad, during the Civil Rights era, I could throw a brick like no other, as a child, I always had many a good friend from across those railroad tracks. And we were kindred spirits in every sense of the word. I am so thankful that, in my maturity, I have just as many today.

Spirits come from everywhere. And if we see people as individuals and consider that they are spirits that walk, as opposed, to people who walk with spirits, then, African spirituality is not just for Africans, or those of African descent, but for all of us regardless of race, color, creed, gender, or sexuality. Because there is one race that we all share; and, that is the human race. And, Africa is certainly the birthplace of that!

AFRICAN SPIRITUALITY: THE STANDARD FOR DIASPORAN TRADITIONAL SPIRITUAL SYSTEMS

I have been, on the internet, speaking about Vodun since the fall of 2007. And, my biggest beef has been with those coming from outside the African and African American culture putting their own spin on African traditional spiritual systems and claiming their sense of legitimacy while openly disrespecting those of us who came by it through birth! I have had epic battles with these folks! But don't get me wrong! To whom the spirits choose to allow initiation it is our duty to obey; but, these folks sure make it hard to want to give them anything...especially these nonwhites in America and those running to Haiti! They don't like me because I call them out when they wan o make up their own rules/tenants in Vodun. They come out of hese 2-week initiations and think they've got something! When ou tell them, they don't they then want to malign you. They even ave some dude calling himself a priest, and writing on Vodun that as a reputation of ill repute. Now somebody tell me...what he gone ell somebody like me about Vodun? I am a purist. My intention has lways been to impart as much general information about Vodun, s I can, without giving away its secrets. I want to make it easier to nderstand Vodun, dispel the myths and point the way for those who re destined to follow.

Africa is really where it ALL began...with the spirits...with life...with VERYTHING! And I feel that if people understood a bit more about RUE African spirituality they would understand the rudiments of hat is comprised in these African based spiritual systems that are in he diaspora. I find too many people...especially these white folks... unning up and down the internet putting THEIR spin on spiritual ystems that are based in a culture, to this day, they cannot fully nderstand. I'm tired of it! I got in an argument with a woman, that did not realize was white, until she cried racism, whom I tried to xplain the spirits to. As, an African Traditional Priestess, I am not sed to this type of insolence! And to be honest, I ain't got time for it! n Africa, she would be beat within an inch of her life, for that type of isrespect. This is why I have gotten sick of that tribe vodun thread. nd on it we had folks who went to another site to participate in heir nonsense because I explained to them that you can't try calling oduns/spirits down willy nilly if you do not know how. It could ause one great harm! One in that number even traveled all the way o Benin, West Africa passed every legitimate temple, with priests/ riestesses, and found some people who are NOT priests to make her p Voduns. WHY? Because, in Africa, no legitimate priest is going o give someone Voduns if they are not to have them. We have an bligation to the spirits and take it seriously. If FA says that a person s not to have them...they are not to have them! Now, she calls herself a priestess...INITIATED into NOTHING with some Voduns she can't feed or understand, in Europe, trying to make money off African Voduns/spirits. These folks simply do not have a clue! It is a SHAME! Their biggest complaint against me is I am egotistical. Wedosi is not egotistical...I just know what in the h**l I'm talking about! I am here to help anyone; but this ain't a slave massa situation. African priests and priestesses are to be treated with respect. One trained correctly in the ways of traditional African culture has validity. A person seeking what we have must come in humility as many have come to me on facebook. I am sincerely thankful for that!

INTERNET VODUN GROUPS: MY ISSUE WITH THEM

Since I've joined Facebook I have lived in relative peace with the Vodun community. However, occasionally, someone has put me in a group that I was unaware that I was in. So, after checking them out for a while I would promptly remove myself if they seemed clickish or started out wanting to exclude folks to whom they had old battle scars with. I hate drama! A couple I have remained in. But, one of these, I am beginning to question. This particular vodun group I am finding a bit intolerable. Today I answered a poster who pointed out that most folks, following African traditional spiritual systems, were white. That those of us, with melanin, were still clinging to our colonial religions. I promptly explained why, that even though African Americans were the most religious group, in America, it was due to the indoctrination of slavery. And, that the LEAST religious was those that actually enslaved us. Well, because I used present tense, according to the moderator, I was inciting racism. I didn't understand there was domestic slavery in Africa, blah, blah, blah! Now, ya'll know Mami know her history! To add insult to injury he says, "If you are as smart as you claim.... you would know how to use the correct tenses." I have NEVER made such claims; but, it was apparent to me, that the man had some issues. I responded to him twice, that he took the issue too far, but he began erasing any of my comments that would make him look bad. This man was insulting to someone who could run rings around him in reference to spirituality. So soon, I may be removing myself from another group. This is my problem with many of these Vodun groups; and, why, for so long, I have tried to stay under the radar! I have used them to try and impart knowledge to those who would appreciate it. I started out with Haitixchange, tribe and now facebook. But it seems that there are far too many folk out here, in African traditional spiritual systems, that want to run their own show! Haitixchange was cool however. I loved discussing current events with my Haitian cousins; but, the Mambos, on there, were a bit insufferable! These women would sell your panties, on ya, while you walked if they felt it marketable! I'm just wanting to serve the spirits and complete my mission. But it's often difficult for a lone wolf like myself. It would be easier to go back to Africa, sit under a palm tree, and have a refreshing drink! My only worry, then, would be if my husband decided he wanted an additional wife. Oh, de life! But no, ole Mami was sent back here to wait on folks, destined, to come home to the ancestors and the spirits. Oh wow...what's wrong with de' ole' world o'. Me de tired o'!

Don't mind me chill'in...Mami just belly aching today!

WHO DECIDES OUR SPIRITUAL WORTHINESS...THE VODUNS (THE SPIRITS) OR MANKIND?

In all of our world's "religions" one can find the invisible hands of the voduns ("the spirits"), or "God" or the "Almighty" depending on how one wishes to term our creator(s). However, to what extent man allows these spirits to determine the tenets of these systems and man's ability to be obedient to them largely determines their effectiveness in helping mankind with their everyday concerns. Throughout our history examples can be found that show what can happen when man puts his own spin on what is to be of these religious systems, for instance, those Muslim jihadists who misinterpret the term, the Christian Crusades (1095 - 1291) and the selling of Indulgences by the Catholic Church, in the late Middle Ages, just to name a few. And even in today's times we are forever dealing with those serving traditional African spiritual systems, in the diaspora, who propose to decide WHO and WHO CAN NOT serve the spirits.

This essay has been prompted by the recent decision of Pop Francis, on 11/23/2014, to canonize six new persons to the Catholi priesthood to spiritual sainthood. While I am sure, as part of th Catholic Church, this is his right; but, I question is this the righ of man or of the divinities themselves? I argue that it is the latte One could argue that the Pope is the mouthpiece of God for thi particular spiritual system; and, for my own, vodun, a priest o priestess such as myself. But the difference in vodun is that we hav Ifa. We have a mechanism that was put into place, by the divine, i order to determine what it is that the spirits, themselves, want rathe than what we want. Voduns in their ability to see the past present an future all at once also examines the hearts of mankind. Any tests tha may be employed by a human being cannot possibly compete wit that.

When man/woman declares themselves on the level of God (I an not necessarily referring to the Pope) rather than the vessels to whic they allow God to speak through them can become a problem. For i is only God, or the spirits themselves, who can determine who is t be elevated in the spiritual realm or identify those who were born t serve them. That is WHY everyone regardless of race, creed, colo or gender should be allowed to go before the voduns; and, if thei own ancestors or spirits find fault with them, or their life's choices let THEY be the ones who tell them. But WE, as vessels for the spirits have absolutely no right to make those judgment calls on our own. M only issues with folks, serving the spirits, has been directed toward those who REFUSE to serve according to the tenets of the spirits and, that is to seek authentic African divination to see if they wer born to serve, in whatever capacity, and proceed accordingly. Th African priesthood must be defended and upheld by those who wer born to serve within it. Of this I have the spiritual authority to insis upon and will do so with my very life. But as to what color one's ski is, where one comes from or one's sexual orientation, in reference t their right to serve, is of no concern of mine. As for this right, let each man or woman answer to his or her own God. The task of helping those destined with the reconnection to their ancestors and voduns, as dictated by my spiritual mission, is my primary concern.

The voduns have their own methods of elevating those who have lived a life that is worthy to spiritual heights within the spiritual realm. And, through authentic African divination they can tell us who those persons are. As an example, I will leave you with this story...one that I have written about before. While attending a Mami Tchamba ceremony, in (Cotonou) Benin, a truly amazing story was told to me by a spirit that had lived many centuries ago. After taking the head of a vodunsi, he related his beautiful story to me through the English-speaking priest who was performing the ceremony for me. The spirit is called Ade (accent over the "e" and pronounced ADAY with a short sound over the "a"). This is the spirit of the hunter and is the patron spirit for those wishing to do work or feed their loved ones at zogbe...those who have died of unnatural causes. This is an extremely important vodun for us in the diaspora. While living as a man this spirit lived during the times of human sacrifices in vodun. He was the one, in his village, who would go out and procure the sacrifices. All of his life he had remained obedient to the words of the spirits and did not waiver. Upon his own death those who prepared his body were directed, by the voduns, to take sacrifices and with specific instructions, by them, use these blood sacrifices to prepare his body, according to their specifications, for his journey into the spirit world. And, as such, this humble man with the extremely difficult task of procuring human sacrifices for the work of the spirits, himself, became a vodun.

My brothers and sisters there is NO excuse not to serve the spirits with all due diligence. WE do not have to guess, intuit or leave it to chance. Ifa is there, the ancestors and the divinities are there. It is up to us to simply ASK, RECEIVE INSTRUCTIONS and OBEY.

VODUN IN THE DIASPORA: ITS CHALLENGES

I think it is wonderful that, in spite of slavery and the oppression of Africa's descendants, Vodun survived in the diaspora! A bit tattered and frayed, at it's edges, a bit changed; but, it STILL survived! For, that, we can thank the ancestors, the divinities and the steadfastness of our people. But as I look around me, on these various forums, and hear the words of many of those who claim to serve, I can see the challenges that befall us. Since, when for instance, have I heard priests or priestesses get on a soapbox, in Africa, and take up our precious time debating who is to be accepted, in Vodun, based on what happens in someone's bedroom, and with whom, as opposed to something about spirit work? NEVER! That isn't what we should be concentrating on. Folks come to us for spiritual guidance not to seek inclusion based on a political agenda or to gain power and notoriety. These folk, to me, are clearly unfit to serve! Their agenda is something else entirely!

In Africa, when a stranger walks into our doors seeking spiritual help of any kind, we immediately go to Ifa. We ask the spirits about this person. We want to know who and what they are, in the spirit world, and the truth as to why they have come. It is a misnomer to believe that everyone is born to serve, the spirits, or even to be of the priesthood. It is the spirits, themselves, that determine these things for us through divination. It is THEY who examines the hearts of mankind and tells us 'what is' and 'what isn't' as it pertains to a person. And I guarantee, that if we reach back to our original spiritual systems, on the continent of Africa, and re-introduce authentic African divination it would serve to weed out some of these bad apples. Bad apples, that in my judgement, shouldn't have been given anything in the first place. While Vodun is very much INCLUSIVE of those of different races etc., it is inclusive of those who are born and FIT to serve! Not just any Joe Shmoe that shows up with a pocket full of money. As a result, these folk that have 'bought into' African Traditional Spiritual Systems can serve to damage it. In fact, they are already bringing it damage. These folk with issues of ego, obsessions of inclusion, standing on political platforms and/ or looking to become rich off other folks' misery bring shame to the African ancestors and the divinities. This, to me, is one of our biggest challenges. We may not be able to do anything about how the past has been conducted; but, we certainly can do a lot about our future.

I applaud, therefore, those that are reaching back to Africa, reaching back, not to exclude as these shallow priests would have you to believe, but, reaching back to learn and make Vodun, in the diaspora, better. You see these folk don't want us to reach back. Why? Because they are afraid! They know that they simply cannot measure up! For them there is no need to reach back. They've got their little "power"... their little "nitch" where they espouse their twisted history about Africa and it's people...their little "nitch" where THEY control the narrative. WE ARE NOT THE SAME they and us! We were born and ordained in the priesthood by the ancestors and the divinities themselves. THEY have bought and paid for a lie!

CHAPTER 8

WOMEN, VODUN AND RELATIONSHIPS

"Where love rules, there is no will to power, and where power predominates, love is lacking. The one is the shadow of the other."

- C.G. Jung

VODUN AND THE FEMININE MYSTIQUE

In the diaspora, there seems to be a great deal of concern about the issues of women spiritual practitioners and their right to do particular tasks. I, personally, have found it a bit odd because, in Africa, I have found some of the most powerful people, in the priesthood, to be women. I do not believe, however, that this is the case in all pantheons of the voduns/orisa, for instance, one could examine the pantheon of Heviosso or Sakpata. But it could be due to the pantheon that I am in, personally, which is Mami, or in particular, Mami Dan. It is a misnomer, in the diaspora, that this is a female controlled pantheon... it is not. It is just as male as it is female; but, there are many great women in it!

My purpose here is to have us to try and look on the spiritual level, if we can, instead of just the physical. What should take place, in traditional African spiritual systems, is that each individual should be told their spiritual role and vocation, if any, through authentic African divination. In that way each person, born to the priesthood, knows his/her destiny and particular spiritual mission. This should alleviate many of the issues surrounding what one can or cannot do. It is the spirits, themselves, that will dictate to what extent one's role is in the world of the spirits be they male or female.

The key after that would be the proper training and/or instructions on how to serve the spirits and care for ones voduns which is generally taught during the initiation process. Continued training must also occur as one matures and becomes more and more proficient in one's service to the spirits. I have found that when people attempt to serve the spirits through books, as opposed to the practicality of entering a temple, serving them becomes an exercise in, folks, reciting various dogmas at me as purported by researchers. They have absolutely no understanding of the nature of spirits...that to which they are supposed to be serving. And, as a result, their verbiage becomes like annoying chatter in my ear. I lose all patience! An understanding, of the mysteries, of the divine must be revealed, to one, by dealing on an everyday basis with the spirits themselves. As they commune with us, daily, and continue to interact with us, and mold our lives, we began to understand their true nature. For the nature of the divine cannot be learned or understood through books but, rather, through practical application. One may find many, in traditional cultures, who may appear illiterate by most standards, but through application or direct hands on, with the spirits, they know and have come to understand the nature of the divine.

I was once told by a priestess, in Africa, that women are held to a higher standard because it is through us that all creation flows. There is not a single culture, that I know of, which does not appreciate a virtuous woman. Who we are, as women, should reflect who we are spiritually...virtuous in every way. This is true, regardless of, whether one's head spirit is male or female.

AFRICAN SPIRITUALITY AND "WOMEN' S WAYS OF KNOWING"

In the early 1990s, while taking a course in Women's Studies, I came across a body of work that really intrigued me. It was an essay entitled, "Women's Ways of Knowing" by Belenky, Clinchy, Goldberger and Tarule. At the time the study was in it's infancy, now, it is a published work. What interested me, was the 5 stages that, according to the authors, women transversed when obtaining knowledge: Silence, Received Knowledge, Subjective knowledge, Procedural Knowledge and Constructed Knowledge. And, depending on where one is in one's development, as women, could be in any one of these stages. One's hope is that one would go from Silence, a total dependence on an external authority, to Constructed Knowledge, viewing all knowledge as contextual, in due time.

In examining the responses of the individual participants, in the study, it became apparent that African American women or, I contend people of color in general, learned through their experiences. What we know we know, largely, because of what we experience in our everyday lives. We live, we experience, we touch, we see, we hear, we do, and, thus learn or come to know. As women, in general, we intuit; but, as African American women we couple that with 'mother wit, an intelligence/knowledge brought on just by living and experiencing, in conjunction with a spiritual hypersensitivity and then we are good to go! This is important in understanding WHY, those seeking the Priesthood, must go beyond books if they are to understand African Traditional Spiritual Systems. Books are a wonderful start; and, often necessary...do not get me wrong. But, until one walks into that temple...until one goes to Ifa and finds out WHO and WHAT you are in the spirit world, and act upon it, if needed, the spirit world will never truly open up to you. Therefore, sisters, we must couple our book knowledge with the practical knowledge of experiencing what it is to live, on a daily basis, with the spirits. This is where your learning will TRULY begin! The spirits, those within you, began to reveal their natures to you and thus open up a path for divine learning and understanding.

I was checking on some possible email, from another forum, the other day when I came across an irate critic. This person's largest complaint, or rant, was that I thought that I knew it all and was most delusional in my assumptions. They had, apparently, been following me on my facebook page, as well as, other forums. The person ranted and raved, throughout the post, and attempted to denigrate, me, in every way possible. Saddened, by the obvious cowardice of the person, at not confronting me head on, and stunned by the apparent envy, by this person, of my knowledge base, it reminded me of the aforementioned body of work that I had always admired. How women come to know what they know; so, thinking it might be helpful to others, I decided to share it! For I am a firm believer, that NO WOMAN SHOULD HAVE TO DUMB THEMSELVES DOWN TO BE LIKED! It isn't worth it! What I know, about vodun, is what I learned laying in and out of those African temples for so many years and what I continue to do. It came through learning, experiencing and training at the foot of those who knew. It came from hard work perseverance, and the continued guidance and obedience to th ancestors and the divinities. It came from my willingness to hear acknowledge and to obey. But it's not just for me...it is for ALL of us Anyone who hears the call can do as I've done; but, I do not apologiz for what I have experienced or what I know. And, if some folks don' like it...well tough cookies! I share what I can, help where I can an serve where I can. As women, we can often be our harshest critics but, my prayer is that instead of pulling each other down we continu to build each other up!

A lot of what we know, as women, is found deep within us. My grandfather used to say...Education doesn't make the person, Integrity does! That was good; but, my grandmother used to say, marriag is like a head and a neck. The head is on top; but, it's the neck tha directs the head in which way it should go! Grandma knew stuff!

As I look over some of the great sisters of old...Harriet Tubmar Sojourner Truth, just to name a few...these are my She(roes)...womer of strength and integrity! I carry them in my heart, in my soul, daily I call upon them in my darkest hours, for, We, are WOMEN through which ALL creation flows! And in this world, it doesn't get no bette that that!

VODUN'S SPIRITUAL WIVES

We all have heard the saying, "Behind every good man is a goo woman!" We see it when we think of powerful Christian pastors when we see wives of great Imams, wives of respected rabbis, and such women throughout the spiritual world, except perhaps, with Catholicism...those that lead the celibate life; but, even then we se the powerful work of the Catholic nuns. That female counterpart i necessary and very much a part of the work of the divine. For tha duality, itself, started with the Creator, MawuLissa, the male an female counterpart of the vodun Godhead. That duality extends itsel throughout the secular world, as well; and, we spend much of ou time, on earth, searching for that soul mate...that which spiritually completes us!

In traditional Africa, one cannot help but notice the wives of great priests. In that Africa's polygamy is based on every woman being cared for a good man will attract many potential wives throughout the villages. If a man is well respected, cares lovingly for the wives, feeds his children abundantly and manages his household properly, other women may offer, themselves, or fathers may seek to marry their daughters to such men. These fathers know that their daughters will be properly cared for and want for very little. The new husband will give the woman money to do business, of her own choosing, but be responsible for her housing, food and provisions for her children. In most cases, if the woman is the first wife of the man, tradition dictates that she chooses, or consents to, any new wives that he may take in the future. In Africa, a man's children are his wealth; but, good wives help supply that wealth in a great many ways. In the more modern African households the man may provide separate housing for a new wife and her children, separate, from his primary home or compound. But the most impressive, to me, are the wives of prominent traditional priests; and, especially that first one.

These women are generally chosen by the spirits themselves. While all potential wives are to be brought before the voduns, for their consent, this woman is essential in the spiritual work of the priest and his particular spiritual mission or destiny. She is either the female counterpart of his particular head spirit or carry such comparable spirits. Many of these women are priestesses, in their own right: but, work with the husband as one functioning unit. If, as in the larger temples, a female counterpart of the priest's spirit already is seated (a family member etc.) then this female certainly has a great deal to offer in the completion of the priest's spiritual mission. One generally complements the other.

Of the wives of priests, that I have observed, these have been phenomenal women. I have seen them manage large households and support, as well as, participate in the spiritual work of these great men. They have been wise, knowledgeable, and have always anticipated the needs of their men. They are his helpmate, soulmate, confident and partner in the spiritual realm. These are not mere women...they are Africa's spiritual queens. And when these great women speak lovingly about the work of their husbands, remember, that the one speaking is a big reason why he is what he is!

AFRICAN SPIRITUALITY AND THE AFRICAN AMERICAN MALE/ FEMALE DYNAMIC

What has prompted this essay is two things: 1. The proliferation of sisters entangling themselves, in relationships, with so called "Afrocentric priests" or brothers claiming the priesthood after their visits, to Africa, and the mistreatment of these women, and, 2. Brothers returning, from Africa, with a misunderstanding of traditional African culture, in particular polygamy and its male/ female dynamic, and their buying into fake kingships. All of this, in my view, stems from a misunderstanding of traditional African mores and these brother's incessant need for validation even before they stepped foot off the American continent.

If examined carefully, one would find that, these men tended to be broken before they ever sought to visit Africa. Generally, somewhere, in their lives, they have ALWAYS had issues with women; and, after a visit to Africa and seeing polygamy in action, and the respect paid, in these patriarchal societies to men, return with a new fervor to suppress or attempt to put women "in their places". Something they have not been able to do most of their lives. African American sisters, wanting to respect the ancestors and re-claim their African heritage, then, get duped into believing these broken men are about something, because they have been to the motherland, and are supposed to know what's best for them! But, I'm telling you, sisters, that they DON'T!

Africa's polygamy is based on a system where women are to be cared for. Under its system every woman has someone responsible to feed her, provide housing for her and take care of her children. It IS NOT a system designed to disrespect and/or to subjugate women and exploit them through sex! It is based on mutual respect and care. Good husbands and/or family men are thus honored and respected in Africa. And if he doesn't do what is right, by his spouse and their children, then, that woman's male family members will certainly come a calling at his door with sticks in hand! So, I beseech you my sisters...do not believe the hype! When a man serves the spirits, it is his relationship with the spirits that will serve to mold him into a better person. If he approaches you acting and mistreating you like a scoundrel would, then, that's what he is...a scoundrel! It doesn't matter how many titles he throws your way.

African women are strong! To think that these mighty women do not wield power when they choose to is to make a horrible mistake! The African American female is known for her tenacity and great strength to have withstood the selling of her children on the slave auction blocks, the rape of her body, the daily inner-city slaughter of her male children, the denigration of her man, yet, she still stands... she who held the family together through slavery, Jim Crow, the Civil Rights Movement... she who has continually stood by her man when in and out of jail cells because of the color of his skin! Where do you think she got this strength? What blood runs through her veins? It is the blood of her African maternal ancestors! She is the African woman who stands and have always stood behind her. So, if you think that African women are some type of submissive wimps I beg to differ! So, sisters don't take this nonsense, from these Afrocentric brothers, because you don't have to! A bad man is a bad man whether he visits Africa or not! Kick that fool to the curb and continue on your way 'cause boyfriend ain't running nothing up in here but his mouth!

AFRICAN SPIRITUALITY AND THE AFRICAN AMERICAN MALE/ FEMALE DYNAMIC: PART 2

A brother, via facebook, approached me some time ago wanting to converse. I thought it great! I, often, enjoy a lively conversation about the spirits. After, our initial greetings, the brother dropped so many of his titles on me that I got tired of reading them. He mentioned that there were very few Mami Wata priestesses out here; and, I agreed. So, to get the conversation started, I went about asking him who initiated him, in Africa, and to what temple was he affiliated. Again, he came off listing his various titles, out of Ghana, as though these were to mean something to me. It was not that I have a disrespect for titles...I do not! But, it's just that, in Africa, everyone has one... including me! So, again, I inquired as to his spiritual parent(s) and temple affiliation. However, according to him, he had been initiated into a spirit that, he said, wasn't Mami but controlled Mami. When I said that there was no such thing it all went downhill from there.

First, according to him, I did not respect his many titles; and, since I was a WOMAN, that perhaps he had to mention them yet again, so, that I might give the proper respect! Well, ya'll know that saying... you can take the sistah out the hood; but, you can't take the hood out of the sistah? I almost burned a hole, in my chair, trying to keep my composure. This was a broken and ignorant man!

His knowledge on African society was severely lacking! He did not understand enough, about African traditional spiritual systems, to realize that to be in a, particular, priesthood you must first be a part of that pantheon of spirits, as revealed by Ifa, and then endure initiation, into that pantheon, if instructed by them. He also did not understand that unless one is born to succeed someone in kingship, also revealed by Ifa, then for it to include an outsider, of no obvious kinship, was simply not going to happen. These kingships are passed down from generation to generation; and, a stranger coming out of the diaspora will not succeed a king, in Africa, unless of that ancestral family and proven to be the successor by authentic African divination. And, even so, the likelihood of a stranger, out of the diaspora, swooping in and sitting on a king's throne, thus, stepping over the heads of those already living there, and in the line of succession, are almost nil. They verify these things in Africa! Thus many of these so-called 'kingships', bought out of Ghana, are a farce to get American tourist dollars out of people's pockets. This brother's insistence that he had been put in charge of 19 temples, in Africa, with no obvious training, or kinship into these temples, was ludicrous! Oh, it could possibly be believed by a sister who could not see her way to Africa, for the moment; but, it certainly could not be palmed off on a sister who knew better! I had lain in and out of African temples for eight consecutive years, I have a home, there; and, I am married to an African chief priest. What was he thinking? So, that conversation went nowhere. After numerous texts of his attempts to convince me, through derogatory insults, I eventually went to his facebook page and blocked him from further communication with me.

Broken brothers who visit Africa and come back setting up shop as king this or king that have basically been taken. And it's only people who have spent consistent time on the continent who understand what has been done to them. One can certainly discover one's roots, through Ifa, while visiting Africa; but, full initiations and kingships into anything African takes months and often years, on end, if genuine.

This was not the first brother that has approached me disrespectfully. There have been a few others; but, like I have said these men were broken even before they left the continent. There ARE good men out there! Kind and gentle men with loving natures and willing to take care of you and yours. However, sisters, you must not put all your hopes in a man but, rather, in the spirits. For it is THEY that judge the hearts of men or women. And, If you continue to follow them and put your faith and confidence in them, then, they will give you the desires of your heart; and, that includes the right man.

AFRICAN POLYGAMY: A SPIRITUAL PERSPECTIVE

I would like to say, at the onset, that this essay is by no means an attempt to promote the concept of polygamy; but, it is an attempt to see it from not only an African but a spiritual perspective. While not a scholar, on the subject, I do speak from a unique perspective... an active participant married to a unique African priest and one who has a sister wife whose marriage was arranged by the African ancestors themselves as revealed by the great Ifa.

During a more Victorian era, in our society, sex was considered more for procreation than anything else. However, with the advent of the numerous sex revolutions in this country coupled with the age of feminism folks are having a jolly ole' good time. Promiscuity seems like a relative term now-a- days with some sistahs throwing it out of both 'drawer legs' as we termed it in my youth. When folks hear the term "polygamy" some men feel that they have died and gone to heaven, if they simply had the opportunity, with some women, on the other hand, crumpled up with the "stink face". Sistahs relate polygamy to "cheating on me" or better still "you must not love me!" And in both cases, it is about the "knockin" of de boots". Polygamy in our Eurocentric Christian minds is about a man getting all the sex he wants; and, especially for most women "you do not see me with any worth". Polygamy in America is related to the carnal. But, I would like you to indulge me for just a few moments and try to see it from another perspective...a spiritual one.

The African ancestor has absolutely no problem with polygamy. The concept is uniquely African with the Arabs and most traditional people as participants. The Muslims can have up to four wives and the African as many as he can support. The traditional African priest generally has more than one wife. Some come in his youth or when he's first starting out. She is usually the first wife. In some African tribes if a brother dies and his wife has children she may become the bride of another brother that the children and the surviving spouse is cared for. In this way this woman and her children are under the auspices of a responsible male who is to care for them. In some instances where there is a successful man or priest, in the village, a father will offer his daughter that this man will take care of her and whatever offspring. The key, in Africa, is that every woman is cared for and her children. Now this may seem crude to us in America; but, I assure you that all of the single head of household mothers, in America, seems just as crude to Africans as well. But for the polygamous African priest let me tell you what I have observed.

His wives have generally been chosen by the ancestors and divinities, themselves, or the man has chosen and sought their approval. In vodun there is a male/female duality. Prominent temples generally have a male and female counterpart of the vodun that runs that temple. If the female counterpart, sitting on the throne of that temple, is a family member, then, the priest generally has a wife or wives of the same pantheon of spirits as him. These women become an integral part of the priest's work. I have watched certain spirits in our temple that only come on the head of my sister wife. It is only the wives or close female family members that these priests can be fed by. Poison is a reality in Africa. While I am his counterpart, a Dattatreya, my sister wife, as well as my husband's sisters who are Mami Wata priestesses themselves, are important components for the mighty work that is done within our temple. In traditional Africa vodun is usually a family affair.

Now look folks, I am not saying that polygamous families are trouble free. I have heard of and witnessed some horror stories. But, I simply am attempting to give a glimpse of what polygamy could be for a traditional African if the man is honest, upright, following the directions of the spirits and treating the women fairly. When the spirits revealed that they had chosen a husband for me, believe me when I tell you that, I had no idea it was a priest. For I too am a woman with human frailties. But in hindsight this man has been a blessing in my life and the best gift that the spirits have ever given to me. When two people have their eyes on that which is divine and not on that which is carnal ALL things are possible.

WHEN A MAN LOVES A WOMAN

A man loving a woman has always been a beautiful concept to me. Today, sistahs are looking for 'Mr. Right', their fantasy of what the perfect man should be. In the old days, if a man worked hard and provided for his family, sistahs looked away at the small transgressions. I'm not saying that these brothers were perfect, by no means; but, men back then knew how to take their 'kept' women out of town. They didn't bring their indiscretions to your doorstep. And, if any of these floozies wanted to get stink, and inform the wife, they dropped them like a hot potato! These were hard working men! Blue color brothers working by the sweat of their brow. They took care of home and family, sent their children to college and built a life for themselves. These were the men of my generation. To me, this was LOVE! As I've said, they were not perfect; but, back then most children knew who their father was, most men believed in honest work; and, if your mother wanted you to go and hunt him down, for dinner, you could always find him! He may have been the brother walking home with a lunch pail or he may have been the neighborhood drunk; but, everybody knew whose father he was and where he fit in the neighborhood.

Today sistahs are looking for the brother who is 6'2", dreadlocked down, gorgeous looks with a streak of bad! Nine times out of ten a brother like this don't have a job, has a prison record and running from woman to woman looking for somebody to take care of him. He usually gets his way 'cause he can knock hard de boots! But sistahs, really, give that hard-working brother over there a chance. He may not look like Denzel, he may not make a lot of money; but, he believes in hard work and will flip burgers, if he has to, if it means feeding his family. He also may not be perfect; but, if you can love him in spite of his imperfections, girl, you've got something good! Mr. Right does not exist!

I learned my lesson, about men, while living in NYC. I was teaching in upstate NY. I had a very dear friend. She had two daughters by a brother that was a police officer; but, they were not married. When my friend decided to get 'religion' the sistahs of the church convinced her to give up her children's father for a dude sitting in the church. She did and died two years later from the aids virus. See the dude, sitting in church, was a former heroin addict and gave aids to his wife. We should have seen it coming. After they got married he stopped going to church, stole money from her and went back to heroin.

In traditional Africa when a man sleeps with a woman she becomes WIFE! The sex act, itself, makes the contract. One then goes to the families to work out the details. Paper doesn't make the marriage the commitment does. Of course, in our society, paper helps for legal reasons; but, as long as you brothers are willing to be responsible and take care of you and yours...I say give yourselves a hand!

WHEN THE SPIRITS DO NOT WANT WHAT WE WANT FOR OURSELVES

A young lady came for divination. And, as always, during the course of the divination session her ancestors appeared. The young woman was dating someone that her ancestors, and the divinities, were adamantly opposed to. For the young woman that was the whole reason she wanted the divination in the first place...to see if she could hold on to the young man. The spirits gave an emphatic no! As I explained the consultation to her, she pleaded that we intercede and do something...ANYTHING...to help pull this young man to her and keep him with her always. We refused!

Often when, we are approached, people arrive with baggage... dysfunctional relationships, desires that are not within their destiny, wishes to harm their neighbor due to incessant envy, revenge, wanting to rekindle relationships that flamed out years ago, desires to become rich, beyond anyone's wildest dreams, and all manner of things. But if, through divination, we determine that one's desires are against the desires of one's ancestors and/or spirits, we will refuse every time.

In traditional African vodun one's ancestors and the divinities are with us to help promote a more fulfilling and prosperous life. Our ancestors love and protect us. They intercede, with the divinities, when we have dark periods in our lives asking for their assistance in helping us. They desire the best for us; therefore, they will not agree to someone, in our lives, that will bring us misery, pain and/or shame! The divinities, as well, are here to protect us and help us in the completion of whatever spiritual missions we might have, on this earth; but, if there is someone, in our lives, making that a difficult task, the spirits will work to purge that person from us. And, if you refuse to obey, then, you will surely reap the consequences, because the heart, of that person, has already been examined, by the spirits, and found wanting. Whatever the spirits see, further down the road, about the incompatibility/ inappropriateness of this person, in your life, will certainly come to fruition. The voduns do not lie! And, in that we, at Temple Behumbeza, serve the spirits, we will refuse, to do anything contrary to what the spirits command. Our first commitment is to those who have ordained us into the priesthood... the ancestors and the divine spirits. It is they to whom we hear above all others.

I have seen many, destined for the priesthood, arrive in relationships where the spirits deem the spouse unsuitable. That person has wreaked havoc, in the person's life for years; yet, these people have stated their undying love. And, in refusing to give up such relationships, have chosen to no longer pursue the priesthood with us. They refuse to hear the voices of the spirits and obey. This is not good for the people involved. To continue in such relationships is to insinuate that one knows better than the spirits; but, it has always been proven that the spirits are correct. The problem; however, is that this realization often comes too late for the person(s) involved. They return with their lives in shambles and their spirits are annoyed with them or their ancestors are no longer willing to help them. They are often broke, from spending their money with those of the priesthood who have promised them what they desire, but haven't delivered, and their spiritual lives are so damaged that no amount of sacrifices can repair it! If we go to the spirits begging, on their behalf, the spirits are so annoyed we get admonished, by them, trying to help. Often, even if we can do something, they have no money left to even pay for the sacrificial animals needed to do the sacrifices. But, once the spirits are finished, with a person, they are finished! They are patient and long suffering; but, they do not tolerate constant disobedience and people who refuse to heed their warnings. As those who created the heavens and the earth...they can be most severe! So, in vodun, one always has choice, but, one must realize that there are always consequences to those choices.

The concept of 'faith' is known to be a Christian concept; but, I assure you that it is implicit in vodun. One must understand that the spirits love us and, because of that divine love, only want what's best for us and beneficial to the completion of our missions here on earth. This requires faith... the assurance of things hoped for, the conviction of things not seen. (Hebrews 11:1) And, one should know also that... without faith it is impossible to please him [the spirits], for whoever would draw near to God [MawuLissa, the spirits] must believe that he [they] exists and that he [they] rewards) those who seek him [them]. (Hebrews 11:6) The concept of faith is not an easy one and putting it into practice is even harder. But it is necessary in serving the spirits, believing in what they command of us and acting upon it!

This is yet ANOTHER reason why authentic African divination must be reinstated, to diaspora vodun. One must know what it is that the spirits want and require of us. Vodun is based on what the spirits want for us. Sometimes this can be incompatible with our own desires; yet, one must have the faith, in believing, that what they want for us is far better than anything we could have ever imagined for ourselves!

DOMESTIC ABUSE IS NOT JUST ABOUT PATRIARCHY

Whenever I want to visit my sister I take a particular route; and, in so doing, I pass a cemetery that always holds my attention for an instant. It isn't just that my mother, my brother, two uncles and a host of other relatives are buried there; but, my eyes always go to the three beautiful headstones, sitting perfectly side by side and the beautiful flowers and tender care that is lovingly paid to these three graves. The story of how they got there is sad, but, has become legendary for those of us living in the 'hood.

A brother was married to a sister coming from a very tight nit family. In any of the arguments, that ensued between the two, mama, the two sisters and anyone else, related to the woman, got involved. With these strong independent women, according to the man, meddling in his marriage he had taken all that he could take. In their last domestic dispute, he wound up in jail. He vowed that if he ever got out he was going to do damage. No one took him too serious however...he eventually got out. Slid by his former house... former because sister-love had found a new man. He shot and killed the wife, searched for the mother...she at work. After he visited the two sisters, shot and killed each one, then, shot himself. Now, it is mama who lovingly cares for the three graves sitting quietly side by side in the first row of the cemetery testifying to an awful result that can happen due to domestic discord.

I bring this up because domestic abuse is not just about patriarchy. Sure in more patriarchal societies one finds much more domestic abuse; but, as we unpack many of the reasons for domestic violence, envy, jealousy, feelings of inferiority, substance abuse, meddling relatives and a multitude of other factors, it is not all about patriarchy or even men.

A lesbian couple together as one. However, one, I suppose, wasn't so sure because when her lover came in early from work, one day found her in the bed 'knocking boots' with a dude. Sister-love goes to her car and comes back...shoots the lover and her newest squeeze. Goes to prison with 20 to life. She did 20 and is out and about, now, for the last 10 years. A second case more recent.

Two female lovers break up. Before it, however, they fought like cats and dogs. Jealousy, envy, strife, unresolved anger issues...there was a whole multitude of reasons as to why. With the last break-up, the one most in love wasn't having it. She waited for her former lover's new squeeze to come out of a nightclub one night. Saw her, approached her and a fight ensued. She stabbed the woman and the woman fell to the ground. To make sure she was dead, sister-love, jumped in her car and backed over the woman not once but twice. She's in prison, today, with a life sentence.

All I'm trying to say, here, is that DOMESTIC ABUSE is not all about patriarchy, men or cultures that are highly patriarchal. It can come from either partner/spouse or even in what some may term as non-traditional marriages/relationships, today, and stem from a multitude of reasons or triggers. To put it all on men, patriarchy, or use it as an excuse for feminist rhetoric could not only lead to undue male bashing but take our attention away from domestic violence that may happen in other domestic parings or with abusive caregivers of all types. So, let's be careful out there.

VODUN AND THE SPIRITUAL SHYSTERS FROM THE MOTHER-LAND

Earlier I posted a two-part essay entitled, "African Spirituality and the African American Male/Female Dynamic". The essays were prompted by the proliferation of sisters entangling themselves, in relationships, with so called "Afrocentric Priests"...brothers who have visited the motherland and return with bogus titles and using their 'perceived' spiritual superiority to seduce and mistreat women. This essay serves as a companion piece because the attempt to take advantage of women, by priests, happens not only in the diaspora; but, in the motherland as well. What makes the situation more dangerous, however, is that these men are not bogus by any means. The majority of these men happen to be the genuine article...which could cause a woman much heartache and havoc in her spiritual life. Before we began, however, I must be clear. I love Africa!

I respect the African ancestor and would give my very life to defend them and vodun. I believe that the African priest, in terms of knowledge and training, has no equal...they are the standard. But, just like in any other society, there are those that would, if given an opportunity, take advantage; and, in that I have gone to the motherland before many others, must warn against possible mistreatment toward vulnerable diasporan women who travel to the motherland alone or with no viable contacts.

Our economy has suffered greatly over the last few years; and, if America is suffering Africa is seeing economic devastation. Feeding oneself, as well as our loved ones, can be a daunting task on either continent. Since the early 1990s and "Remembering the Slave Project", by UNESCO on the west coast of Africa, those of African descent, and others, are visiting Africa, in earnest, and searching for reconnection to traditional African spirituality. But, women who travel, alone, are especially vulnerable to con games, mal treatment and outright deception. Some African Priests, with no qualms with the idea of multiple wives, may seek to make you one of theirs. The motivation is often to secure financial support from America. Many Africans, unknowingly, believe that the diaspora is a land of milk and honey. If they can, somehow, connect with a woman, born in the diaspora, they can visit, get possible citizenship and/or have a steady flow of cash coming to them in Africa.

Be careful, therefore, of picking up "boyfriends" in Africa. If one is busy spending their time laying on one's back, in Africa, then whatever spiritual quest one might have been on get's thrown out the window! And if a priest is more interested in getting into your panties than he is in performing your spiritual ceremonies, then, you are with the wrong priest!

As diasporans we are at a distinct disadvantage when we visit African priests. These Africans use Ifa. They can discover more about us than we even know about ourselves; and, they can withhold this information, from us, so as to use it to THEIR advantage. In addition, if they divine that you are prosperous, or may be in the future, they may employ spiritual techniques to bind you, to them, such as cut your hair and use it to control you. They may even put various powders or potions in your food to cast a love spell, or give you specific shrines/voduns, that they use to control you while you are back in the States. And, lastly, they can also go to various African Voduns to buy certain powers or favors to make you theirs. African priestesses can be part of this as well. These women can offer to initiate you but keep you dangling, on a string, for years extracting money but giving you nothing! In some instances, they may even take your money and initiate you into something but give you no voduns. With no voduns, you have NO POWER! African priests and priestesses, just like anyone else, should be checked out or possibly referred to you by others. Many are running to Africa to do their own thing. But running without the advice from someone that has gone, before you, or doing the proper research on what you should be looking for, before you go, is a fool's errand. To undo the trouble that authentic African vodun can do to you, if harmful, is costly and time consuming. In the meantime, your life is in shambles. A bogus diasporan priest can hurt your feelings, give you a wet bottom and bring you shame; but, an authentic African priest, who is dishonest and a shyster, can cost you your life or your very soul!

THE REGULATION OF AFRICAN PRIESTS LIVING IN AMERICA: SPOUSAL ABUSE

First, of all, let's be clear. There is no organization or spiritual authority that regulates African Priests in the United States. In Africa, yes, but not here. I bring this subject up because of a recent post, presented on a forum, about a African Babalawo who took hands to his American wife.

Sadly, domestic abuse is not new in the United States. It happens to many of us in one form or another...a spouse drawn to drink, so, he lashes out and beats his wife, a father who chastises his children, obsessively, or in cruel ways or a spouse who is verbally abusive, toward the other, because of unresolved issues in their past. This domestic 'cancer' can invade every cultural group and every class of people. So, why is it such a shock that it can happen to someone who serves in African traditional spiritual systems? It shouldn't be! These are people too!

When a person is born to a spiritual throne it does not automatically guarantee that the person will have spiritual integrity no more than it guarantees that a preacher will not 'whore' around in his congregation or a Catholic priest cannot be found guilty of pedophilia. While the odds certainly should be higher, that a man of the spirits, would not do such a thing...it so happens that man has choice to do what is right or wrong, at any given moment, whether he has a spiritual title or not. We are human so therefore fallible. One of the problems is this.

Sisters are so busy chasing the spiritual power of a man and his title that we are often looking through rose-colored glasses at what we are getting ourselves into. Growing up I have seen this same phenomenon in the churches. Sisters loved chasing the preacher if unmarried or his son if available. The perception is that marrying a spiritual title automatically gives us TITLE or respect in the community. Preachers wives are now called 'first ladies'. I often ask myself...first ladies of what? It is a beautiful thing, if in serving the spirits, a sister is blessed with the spirits choosing an appropriate mate for her. This is absolutely what we want; but, we must approach the spirits when choosing any mate, regardless, of where he hails from. And, in cross-cultural relationships, we must understand something of the person's culture before we commit! Let's be real folks...for an African, who may be looking for an American visa, marrying an

American is a win win situation. Oh, he is going to pay all of the bills, because, he understands his duty as a man. That is one of the up sides in marrying an African. African men are raised to understand their duties, as men; and, many of them do not even get married until they are sure they can support a wife. This is appealing to any woman. But, realize, ladies, that this man comes from a culture where everything in that house (where he pays the bills), wife, kids and all is considered his. So, when I hear sistahs saying..."He's in America now!" So, what? That is supposed to change him? The Queen of England stops being a queen because she comes to America? No, know what you are getting into before you go into it. Take off the rose-colored glasses and see what is before you! And, don't think that because I'm trying to explain the culture, to you, that I am on the man's side. Too many, falsely, think that! I'm on no one's side; but, I do know the culture. And, I do know that there are things, in marrying an African, that an American must adjust to or keep on steppin'. Polygamy is just one of them! Oh, well we say, he's in America now and can only have one wife here. Yeah, true; but, how many traditional wives he got in the motherland there huh? How many children on African soil? In traditional culture, these women are just as legitimate as you are; and, their children too! There is just so much I can speak of; but, let's get back to the main topic.

African priests are regulated by the spirits, themselves, because it is the spirits that ordained them. Through various, ordained, hierarchical spiritual groups, in Africa, we regulate ourselves. Examples would be the Supreme Chief of Vodun, in Benin, who hears and make decisions in disputes or the Chiefs of each pantheon, of spirits, when a complaint is logged against someone of the priesthood. These men carry spiritual authority to regulate or hear complaints against these men and women. And, if it is domestic, one goes to the family heads or priests to lodge a complaint and seek a solution. No one in America, serving in African or African-based spiritual systems have this type of authority as of yet. The diaspora priesthood simply is not on the same level as that in Africa due to training, experience and a whole lot of other variables. This includes me. The powers to regulate me comes straight out of Africa. As an ordained African priestess, I can be called before either of these groups if a complaint is logged.

So, my sistahs, if you get into a relationship with an African Priest; and, it goes downhill... plain and simple... either go to an African authority who can regulate him or his family members, if you have access, to address the issue and seek a solution...or divorce the man, he will lose his visa, be deported; and, let's call it a day. Go somewhere, to one of these capable social work agencies, and work through your abuse issues and continue on. Sitting around slandering each other in public is not going to get you anywhere. No one looks favorably upon a woman or man who airs their domestic disputes in public. 'Cause I'm gonna be honest with all y'all. If I was in that sistah's shoes... wouldn't be no talking...only person I want to talk to is the family member who got enough money, on hand, to get me outta jail for trying to kill that man! Sistah love don't be playin' that! Priestess or no priestess!

WOMEN'S ABUSE AND INNER STRENGTH/FAITH

I want to try and address the issue, of women's abuse from a more personal perspective in this essay. The reason being, I am a firm believer that our ability to make better and more informed decisions and/or choices, as women, could help us prevent some of these very bad situations that we find ourselves in. And, in order to do this, one must look for that inner strength within ourselves...that spirituality or faith needed... to lead more whole and productive lives. The tendency, for far too many of us, is to look without...to a man or to some 'other'...for our emotional or financial wellbeing; and, in so doing leave ourselves open and vulnerable to exploitation and abuse

I grew up in a segregated south. Most Black men, from my generation, worked long hard hours of backbreaking labor. These men were being oppressed every which way but loose by White

America. Black folks had their own neighborhoods; and, in them lived the richest to the poorest. Our fate, as Black folks, was, basically, 'we are all in this thing together!' Our neighborhoods were dotted with liquor houses, gambling spots and juke joints. It was nothing for a man to go home, tore up from the floor up drunk, and start taking it out on his wife. As kids, we would, all, sit out on the stoop, on the weekends...'cause brothers worked all through the week, and wait and listened to the fights until somebody broke it up or the police came. We didn't term it, back then, as domestic abuse as folks do today. It was letting off steam; and, the women could fight just as hard as their husbands. We would bust a gut, laughing, at many a man who came running down the street with his wife, right in behind him, swinging a caste iron skillet. By nightfall all was forgiven; and, on Monday morning one would see that same man walking, with his lunch pail full of last night's super, headed out to work for the man. This is not to excuse any of this; but, what I remember about these women was their faith in church and family. These sisters lived in an era where times were difficult; and, they made due. Their faith was the greatest part in that. These were some bible toting, praying, church going women! So where are we today...those in African spirituality?

We should be in that same place, with that inner faith, that dependence on the spirits and our faith in knowing, that, if we are obedient to their spiritual tenants we too are going to make it through, is exactly where we should be, as well as, advice from older sisters or those who have been there to help us.

My journey to the African priesthood has been all of my life. I was born to it; but, like most diasporans I discovered it as an adult. And, as most diasporans, I have taken many various routes in my quest to get there. But, in all of them, I was searching for the ancestors and a better way to serve God. I was a spiritual person but also human. At 27 years old, I decided it was time to marry. As I was clinging to Christianity, at that time, I married a man without knowing him, because, the Bible said I needed to marry him before sleeping with him. So, that is what I did. It was one of the worse decisions of my life. The man hit me, one day, in front of his friends. But before that the things started small...the verbal abuse, the threats, etc. He even put a gun, without bullets in it, up to my head one day. This man was dangerous; and, I sensed it! It escalated into the slap! But I sensed more could come. After that slap, I waited until boyfriend went to sleep, rummaged in the back of my car, pulled out the only thing I could find...a tire iron...and tried to wear that man out! When the neighbors called the police, and they got there, I was still swinging! The marriage lasted all but 3 months! Took me 2 years to do a proper divorce; but, I got out from under. I had spent a lifetime, on stoops, as a kid watching fights; and, I wasn't about to endure them in my own house! My mistake was that I simply did not take the time to know the man. I was too much in a hurry to be married, and have a man, that I didn't take the proper care. But I had faith in what was right and what I wanted for my life. I had self-respect; and, I was a hard worker. I did not need anyone outside of myself to make me whole. That inner strength and faith, actually, saved my life. This same man... the one I divorced...is in prison, this very day, serving a life sentence for stabbing a woman, to death, 69 times! Each day I wake I thank the spirits for life. For it is they that have stood at my back and in my front since birth; and, it is to them I owe my allegiance, now, that I have come to know them.

I am thankful that there are organizations, available, that can help when we encounter such situations. Domestic abuse is a family terror; but, if you set your sights on that which is divine, my sisters, the odds are extremely high that you will make it through whatever difficulties may befall you. There are good men out there, my sisters, good, spiritual and honorable men. So, set your sights on the spirits, for, they have the ability to examine the hearts of all of mankind. Trust in them; and, they will find the proper one for you! And to that I can testify!

CHEATING

It seems to be the topic on a lot of women's minds today! Everybody looking for that "Soul Mate" or "Mr. Right" as we call it. You'd think an old priestess like me wouldn't know about such things; but, I was young once! I understand how difficult it was out there with your hormones raging and 'dem brothers all sweet smelling and fine... Oh yeah, 'chil, I remember what is was to see a brother so fine you done lost your mind! Brother so sweet 'dat all he had to do was flash, those pearly whites, and your panties hit the flo' and you don't remember how they got there... uh huh, how 'bout them brothers who can kiss so good that you ready to jump on a doorknob! Brothers with muscles rippling down their bodies and dreadlocks flowing down their backs, making love so good, to ya, that your toes curl up and your voice jumps a few octaves higher as you screaming "SHAKA ZULU!" Yep, I done been there and know all about that! So, I understand a woman's perspective. It hurts so bad when a man you love starts cheating. It feels like you just wanna die! So that's when women get a bit desperate and resort to all kinds of foolishness! But over the years I've learned a few things

For, one, men are different from us. A lot of times they DO think with their 'third leg'; but, I do not think it is all their fault. See I think men are polygamous by nature! Men were built to procreate. Women connect sex to love, men are able to separate the two. I firmly believe that men can love a woman, yet, still have sex with another. Believe me ladies I would give anything for this not to be so; but, what I see is man's attempt to conform to the manmade concept of monogamy, because of Christianity, and failing miserably. Africans are basically polygamous. Jews were at some time as well. Muslims can have four wives. The Bible ushered in monogamy. Now look, don't get me wrong, I'm not here trying to promote polygamy. But I am attempting to help women understand the nature of man. If a man stays faithful to one woman that is wonderful; and, that woman is truly blessed! But sistahs, while I am not, by any means, condoning bad behavior, it isn't the end of the world if he doesn't. Get over it! Concentrate on yourselves, and/or your children, if you have any. Work on making yourself the best you can possibly be. Seek to know the spirits and let THEM direct your path; and, as I've said before, THEY will find that suitable one for you. But listen...NO MAN IS PERFECT...because neither are you! But if a man is such that you can love him IN SPITE of his faults.... chil' you might have something! Hey, all this coming from a woman married to an African! : lol:

ARE MEN TRULY POLYGAMOUS BY NATURE?

Yesterday, in my comments on 'CHEATING', I stated that in my observation, of men over the years, I have concluded that men are polygamous by nature. The topic, itself, seems to have a lot of controversy. Google is teaming with sites on the subject! look them up if you like!

But, as for me, many of you know that I am married. I am blessed that the spirits paired me with the African Priest...BEHUMBEZA. Ours is a spiritual marriage, and arranged by them, due to us BOTH being Dattatreya (called Den'su in Africa). I have learned to love him deeply. But, if I did not put the spirits first, in my life, and trust in them it would have been difficult, as an American, to accept such a marriage. I was/am honored that I was chosen for this great man; but, I am not his only wife. Sometimes what the spirits have for us is not all that we envision for ourselves; but, this humble man has been the greatest gift (besides knowing them personally) that the spirits have EVER given me! He is a man of honor, humility, wisdom and grace. It is his love of the spirits and example in integrity that puts me in awe of him. Much that I have learned, about the spirits, has been from him through his example. So, again, sistahs set your eyes on the divine. They know us better than we know ourselves.

SISTAH TALK

For a while, now, I've had a few things on my mind I just wanted to get off my chest...sistah talk... as you will. Stuff be on your mind you just wanna say that's plain and simple. You see, as I've hung out on the internet, you get sistahs (women in general) who wanna come on and get you to fix their love problems. Somebody talk they wanna get a spell worked to get some joker to come back to 'em or 'dey done met up with some 'scoundrel', calling himself a priest, who done treated 'em wrong. Folks get indignant when I refuse to help 'em and can't understand when I become annoyed!

Well, think about this thing for a moment. Here's a woman whose foot, from Dec. 28, 1998 until March 6, 2006, never left the continent, of Africa, to touch American soil. Who, while on a spiritual journey, immersed herself into a culture, language and people initially foreign to her. A woman who spent eight continuous years in and out of African temples who sacrificed, struggled, sometimes out food, money and friends. Often out of friends, I later found out, because I didn't have no money; yet, I hung in there. Three times full of fever, due to malaria, told to, "go home, eslave"!, by one and that I would never make it back to the States unless in a pine box by another. A grueling journey, one that I'm still haven't completed. Yet, somebody think I did all of this just so I can cast a spell to get some dude back for them? Naw, my sistahs, it ain't that kinda party!

First of all, if a man is just rolling up on you because he wanna get in your 'drawer legs' ain't nothing spiritual about him! A spiritual man is about spirits not 'pu tang'. As women, we owe it to ourselves to focus on the divine. We are held to a higher standard, by the spirits, because it is through WOMAN that all creation flows! Prove your loyalty and devotion to the spirits first. Put them above all else and they will give you the desires of your heart. It has NEVER been the intention of the spirits that we journey this earth alone. But immerse yourself in serving them and they, who search the hearts of man, will provide that soul mate for you when the time is right.

I gladly help those, in the context of marriage, if trouble is occurring. However, the sacrifices I have made are to help, my people, reconnect to their ancestry and understand the spirits that live within us so as to provide an inner healing and a more prosperous life. I didn't do it to help folks get laid or drag somebody back who's not wanting you no mo'...

VODUN AND ABORTION

This is a hard topic. Like most progressive women I believe in a woman's right to choose; however, the spiritual consequences of aborting a fetus is high! It is by no coincidence that EVERY organized religion is against it! It is by no coincidence that it causes emotional, psychological and/or physical pain; for, it is the very spirits, themselves, that detest it!

What happens is that the precious little spirits, living within these fetuses, are cast out, before their time, and made to roam aimlessly about attached to their mothers and often wreaking havoc in their mother's lives. Therefore, the consequences of an unplanned pregnancy, and a swift abortion, is much deeper than one can ever imagine! One can get rid of the pregnancy but not the spiritual consequences, attached to it, unless ceremonies are performed and this precious 'little one' and it's spirits appeased.

Women come into the temple thinking their issue is one thing; but, when Ifa is consulted, find out that these cast out 'little souls' are often at the root of their problems. We are then instructed to do various ceremonies of purification, sacrifice and any other duties that the spirit commands. If done these 'little ones' become like little spiritual angels, for the mother, and tend and looks out for her all of her remaining days. But, as in all other spirits she might have, whether ancestral or otherwise, this 'little one' must be fed and cared for.

So, sistahs, I am not here to point fingers. I am not telling you anything that I, myself, have not experienced. But remember that the first purpose of sex is procreation. We know that it feels good. But unless you are deliberately choosing to bring a life into this world please stop by your nearest pharmacy and stack up on some condoms!

ABORTION: ARE WE THINKING OF THE CONSEQUENCES TO US AS A PEOPLE?

I recently read an article that is most shocking! I believe in a woman's right to choose; however, this appears to be one of the real tangible consequences of our many sistahs that make that choice to abort! According to the article, on cnsnews.com (2/20/2014) by Michael Chapman, more black babies were aborted than those allowed to reach full term in New York City in 2012. Apparently, that year, 31,328 black babies were aborted with 24,758 black live births. Our Hispanic sistahs didn't fare much better with 22,917 abortions and their portion being 31% of New York City's abortions for that year. Together our sistahs, of color, made up over 73% of the total abortions, in the Big Apple, for that year. White women only 9,704 abortions and Asian and Pacific Islanders 4,493. What is this saying about us? It can't ALL be the economy...

VODUN/PREGNANCY/ABORTION AND THE RIGHTS OF THE FATHER

This essay has been inspired by a young man whose girlfriend had an abortion, in lieu, of his extreme protests. In today's society abortions are plentiful. In my last essay, on the subject, I cited an article that showed more African American children aborted, in NYC, than brought to full term. This is genocide! The voduns are adamantly against it; and, so are some of the fathers!

Women complain about it being THEIR bodies! This is true! But, it takes two to make a baby, not one! When children ARE brought to full term we vehemently pursue these men for child support; but, it is OUR bodies when we want to dispose of a life as though it is an inconvenience? If the two, who thought not to use protection, produced this child, then, why is it that, in so many cases, the father's wishes are of no importance? These are social issues, of the day, I know; but, in everything there is a spiritual consequence for our actions.

We know biologically speaking that it is the male's chromosome that determines the offspring's genetic sex. What if this would have been this man's first and only son that was aborted? In most instances, a firstborn inherits the father's spirits and spiritual thrones. My head spirit, Dattatreya, was inherited from my father. He too is Dattatreya. He was 17 years old at my birth, my mother 15; but, if mother had aborted I would not be writing these essays, on facebook, today. They struggled, it was hard; but, I'm here! According to Ifa, the voduns sought a way to bring me, to this earth, for a mission and they brought me through this ancestry...Agassou...and these two-young people. Oh, sure, it was a shotgun wedding...big deal! Today you don't have to get married it seems. I've heard the terms, 'baby daddy/mama' until I'm blue in the face! But, that is also what extended families are for... to help in such cases...because it really does take a whole village to raise a child. When I was growing up everybody, on our block, were kinfolk whether biological or not. So, what are we accomplishing with our cavalier attitudes towards pregnancy and abortion? An ancestor wants to be remembered; so, he takes the clay and molds the child and ask a divinity to give the child life... .but we destroy it?

Pardon me for being stuck on this issue; but, fathers have rights too! And, remember, that with whatever decisions we make in this world, spiritual consequences, whether good or bad, result in all of them. And, that's for everyone involved. Put a raincoat on it guys! Or, rather, take the advice my aunt Jinx gave me ladies, "Gal, you'd better get out 'dere and get ya some of 'dem birth con'stone pills if ya doin' sumptin' out dere!' Aunt Jinx never went to no school; but, I adored her just the same!

VODUN AND THE VAJAYJAY

This is a bit of a spin off from my post on 'Abortion' but more inclusive. This is about how we are to be as women. In other writings I have said, that as women, spiritually, we are held to a higher standard Why? Because it is from Woman that ALL CREATION FLOWS.

Man was designed different, from woman, for another purpose. I personally believe that he is polygamous by nature; but, that is a subject matter for debate. What I am NOT confused on or have any doubt about is that women were designed as sacred creatures!

In this 21st century feminist world, that we live in, it is very easy to equate our worth with our equality to man. But I remind you of a saying that I heard once: "Man is the head of woman but attached to that head is a neck; and, it is the neck that turns the head where it wishes to go!" Therein lies the power of woman, for we are the neck! What we must do, as women, is to understand this power, claim it; and, allow it to help us to become better people...better mothers, sisters, daughters and lovers. But how does this relate to the vajayjay? It's about purity, modesty and conducting ourselves in such a manner that we do not shame ourselves or our loved ones.

Many of you no doubt has heard about young 'virgin' women being taken into the temples of Africa. There are two times, in a woman's life (besides purification rituals), that she is considered pure...before sex and after menopause. When a woman is sexually active, and dealing with vodun, she cannot enter the temple or touch her voduns while on menses. And, after menses, she must purify herself before re-entering the temple. The menses, itself, is unclean in the eyes of the spirits. This is a child that did not materialize; and, this bloody bacteria laden 'sloth off' is unclean or impure. Men who are priest cannot accept cooked foods from their wives, during this time, or share the same bed with them. The wife cannot touch her husband until her menses has finished and she has dutifully purified her body. She becomes 'pure' once her menses has finished...beyond menopause. The spirits are very strict on this issue. If a woman is in the initiation chamber and the menses appears she is immediately taken out of the sacred chamber, the chamber purified, and she is put somewhere else until her menses finishes. In Africa, where initiations are months on end, this can be tricky. I was in and out of initiation chambers so much, in Africa, that the spirits put me in menopause early. I was told that my mission, in vodun, was more important than my having the ability to make babies...so they took it! I have become a spiritual mother for all! Another worthy note is that in the places of the kings, in Benin, only pure women...women who are past menopause can take care of the king's burial sites.

Frequency of sex is also an issue for the voduns. African priests are only given certain nights that they can be with their wives; and, then after he must purify himself before re-entering the temple. A man must also be pure when working with the voduns. This idea of celibacy, in Catholicism, is actually based in spiritual fact. Virgins, celibate men and women are prized, by the voduns, to do great spiritual work! In our temple, when we travel to do work for the spirits, it is demanded, by the spirits, that the most experienced and pure are taken. Those that are sexually active most give up sex several days before this work is to be done. Purification baths are taken and sacrifices are given. Strict rules of purification are observed, on an everyday basis, in the temple as well.

But getting back to the subject, one can see that folks spending a great deal of time on their backs or 'knocking boots' ain't getting NOTHING done spiritually! These jack legged scoundrels claiming spirituality, and the priesthood, when they are only trying to get in your 'draw leg' should be dismissed from any type of consideration! Sistahs who busy hollering, "I'm sexual!" while claiming they pursuing spirituality is simply fooling themselves! We, as women, must conduct ourselves in a proper manner regardless of what a man might want or think! Women who choose to use their vajaja, as a playground, will not accomplish anything spiritually! The only thing they might guarantee is an STD, unwanted pregnancy or bad reputation!

VODUN AND CROSS-CULTURAL RELATIONSHIPS

Growing up in the Southern United States one didn't see many 'interracial', or what I chose to term, 'cross cultural' relationships

In the southern states, bogged down with the legacy of slavery, Jim Crow and overt racial inequality, of all kinds, such relationships were prevalent but rare. There was even a period in our history where they were against the law. Many parents, on both sides of the equation, sought to persuade their sons and daughters to stick to their own kind. The young Emmett Louis Till (July 25, 1941 – August 28, 1955) was an African-American teenager who was murdered in Mississippi at the age of 14, while visiting his relatives, after reportedly flirting with a white woman. Today things are very different!

While racism is STILL here, there are growing numbers of offspring from cross cultural relationships and marriages. As these young people become of age, one of the dilemmas that they face, is to whom do they owe their loyalty in the case of ancestry? How do they reconcile their own individuality when coming from two distinct cultures and/or heritages? Our President, Barack Obama, is the offspring of a cross cultural relationship, as well as, the children of the Mayor of New York City...Bill de Blasio. How do these young men and women cope? And to whom do they favor in searching for ancestors?

As a social scientist, I believe that everything springs forth from a particular cultural context. Whether it is spirituality, or whatever else, one understands a thing, person, or phenomenon better when studying the culture that embraced said phenomenon, person or thing it seeks to understand. To understand the New Testament, for instance, one needs to understand what was going on, culturally, during the times the apostles wrote the letters to the churches. By understanding the cultural context, we may come to understand why the apostles felt compelled to write these letters and to what objective. And, if there are any lessons to be learned, how these may be applied to our present-day situations. The same would be for a young woman of European descent in choosing a young man of African American descent. When arguing, something that happens in all relationships, one would know, in understanding his culture, that calling him the "N" word might cause a bother to 'lose his cool!' Culturally speaking that would be a derogatory term couched in all types of racial injustice! But, the consequences of not understanding this would certainly not end well for either person! So, to whom we choose to love doesn't really make a difference, anymore, if it is love that truly brought us together. However, in understanding a bit more, about the person, than what sexual attraction would allow helps to, not only deepen the bond and promote mutual respect, but help the relationship stay together. So, what happens to those cross-cultural offspring in reference to ancestry and the spirits?

Well, just like anyone else we go to Ifa...the West African divination system. And just like anyone else Ifa will tell us your ancestry, spirits, call to the priesthood, if any, and mission while here on earth. But just like anyone else, regardless of race, creed or color that oldest ancestor is more likely to have been from Africa. Why? Because Africa is the birthplace of mankind. So, it isn't about what ancestry we are favoring...it is about WHAT IS! Once one find the oldest ancestor one pulls forward bringing in all of the others no matter where they come from or of what race! These ancestors know who belongs to them; and, when you call them forward, to feed and honor them, will all show up! The African priest will stand in the 'crossroads' (the place where the sacrifice is given) and call all of them forth from the north, south, east and west. Yes, folks, the concept of the Christian cross and sacrificial lamb came from African traditional spiritual systems. That is because the spirits are in every single organized spiritual system on the globe!

In conclusion, it doesn't matter what nationality, race or gender one might be. The spirits are no respecter of persons. We were all born of the spirits. However, in truly understanding something or someone one needs to realize, or be cognizant of, the cultural context in which a thing, person or phenomenon comes from. Our environment, history and experiences often color our world view.

VODUN AND THE GREATEST LOVE

One of the greatest loves that the world witnesses, by far, is the love between a parent and a child. Mothers will do just about anything to protect or provide for their young. Fathers have been known, in the presence of danger, to shield their young or loved ones with their very lives; willing to die, themselves, rather than their children. Some folks, those who are parents of those of bad repute, murderers, pedophiles, and the like, where only their mothers could possibly find compassion for them, will go to their graves claiming, "my child didn't do it!" Such is the deep love and affection between a child and a parent.

I remember my uncle Smitty, who served in World War II, jokingly delivering his favorite line to me, "I love pretty women and pretty horses!" as I would watch him leave medical journals all around the house in an attempt to encourage my cousin to attend medical school. This man whom, himself, had dreamed of being a doctor was a humble janitor but desired better for his son. So, when my cousin became a prominent surgeon, in Columbus Ohio, and landed himself in the "Who's Who of African American Men" my uncle began to carry a continuous beam upon his face. But even further, I remember the unspeakable pain that gripped me at the death of my beloved adopted daughter, Constance Hounnon, from sickle cell anemia at the age of 3 and half years old in Benin, West Africa. Her biological mother had died in childbirth. The granddaughter of the Supreme Chief of Vodun, himself, I thought my life had ended. It took me over 2 years before I could say her name without breaking down with the voduns complaining that I had turned my face from them in my unbearable sorrow. But, through it all, I crawled and clawed myself back up into an upright position, again, understanding that this precious one was someone I loved just as much in death as I did in life with our relationship becoming stronger with each passing day of my existence. So, multiply this type of deep affection by one million times and you would just begin to fathom just how much the spirits, that gave us life, truly love us.

While it is true that we come to this earth with a specific mission or destiny there is an undeniable relationship of love and affection that develops between us and the spirits that live within us. For even before we become aware of them they proceed to protect and guide us. While we are attributing our life's accomplishments to others they are quietly working for us. When we are seeing life's troubles our ancestors are interceding and pleading for us that the divine ones do something to make it better. They run away the bad influences and those that wish to harm or make our lives difficult. They work to bring us the good fortunes, the good business leads, the good relationships, the good karma, the good vibes and the good life. And when things are most dire or they choose for us to know them, personally, they put us on a journey to discover them. But many times we never know them. Many times, in fact most of the time, mankind is not even aware they are there. This is the work of the divine, the work of the spirits that live within us...the work of unimaginable love...the work of the Creator(s) and that which they have created... a relationship between a child and their parent(s). The thought of it often overwhelms me. I am so honored to be a spokesperson for them, so honored to serve and be of service to the divine. AMEN

AFRICAN SPIRITUALITY: MATURE FAITH/MATURE LOVE

So much of my time is spent encouraging the re-connection to ancestry, the discovering of who we are as a people, the beauty of the spirits and their unconditional love and acceptance regardless of race, creed, sexual orientation or gender that I forget that it isn't just the young out here. I forget that it isn't just the young Africans or the young African Americans or the young, of European descent, who wave the banner of equality and diversity; but, within these groupings are those like me...older, mature who have experienced a bit of the world. I was so greatly surprised, by this, during my birthday greetings when folks admitted being born in the late 1940s and 50s. I love it! I am so proud of my generation! So proud that we have taken to the internet, and too, are wishing to learn and experience. I don't feel so bad that I type with only one finger, because, some others might be doing it too! We are aging; but, we ARE the original 'baby boomers' (people born between 1946-1964) and the world has much to learn from us!

This is important, folks, because while there is STILL horrible racism and injustices in this country, during the Civil Rights Movement; and, even in more recent cases, we have not been out there protesting by ourselves. Standing beside us were, and have been, some decent and God-fearing folk of other races. When you are an oppressed people you become an expert on your enemy; but, as a minority in this country, know that we couldn't have done it alone! We are a fabulous people; but, with any group of people there are the good and bad. And, while there has certainly been some seriously bad white folk out there...there has been some good ones too...I'm only trying to be fair! We cannot use the broad brush, of racism, to paint an entire group of people.

From my perspective, African spirituality is about all of mankind because that great continent nursed the origins of man, therefore, we all should respect and look toward her for our oldest ancestor. But we do have ancestors originating from all over the globe, as well; so, we must be mindful of others. The 'baby boomers' have seen some things. Many of us, as I, were raised in the church; so, for us to go from church to African spirituality you best believe we have figured out, over the years, that church isn't working for us. So, our past experiences are directing us to further spiritual inquiries. This is a part of maturity. It is the years that we have lived that help move our feet, as well as, less youthful distractions that help us to focus on the spiritual. Many have already done the parent thing. The children may be grown and gone; and, 'Mr./Mrs. Right' has come and went or the two are growing more mature together or someone may even be widowed. But in any event these folk are stepping out on mature faith.

They may have tried many things; but, this...African Spirituality...or traditional spiritual systems, in general, is the rest of their lives. My sisters and brothers I acknowledge you and honor you this day.

And looka here...don't you young folks, out there, think 'cause we are older and more mature we, too, do not hope for love! WE do; but, it comes different. What I've learned is that when your mind is focused on the spiritual. When all you want is to please the spirits and live your life serving and being directed by them...BAM! That's when it happens! That's when the spirits blesses your life in what you were searching for, and seemed elusive to you, in your youth!

So, do not be discouraged those who may be walking alone at this moment. The spirits have a way of working it! Let me give you an example. In, about, 2005 I was in Lome, Togo. I was visiting a friend who herself had the head spirit of Dattatreya. In that she was originally from Ghana she was a Nana. In her family those who were heir to the throne of Nana had to have been born with the spirit Dattatreya, called Den'su, in Africa. The Nana is ALL about vodun, something some of our young diasporan men do not understand. On that day she had another visitor, a young man with a head spirit of one of the Tchamba, ancestral spirits, who arrived sometime after me. After various greetings and small talk, the young man's spirit came on his head. He had a message for me as translated by my friend. The message foretold of a husband that the ancestors and the divine spirits had chosen for me many years earlier. When I finally met this man, sometime later, I did not know him as the one. He knew but kept it to himself. All I cared about was having this man help me with my voduns. He was so gifted. My mind wasn't on any man...only vodun. But later, much later it was revealed. I was over 50 years old. And, it took me 3 months to agree... turned out to be the best gift that the voduns has ever given me.... Hounnon Behumbeza.

So, my more mature sisters and brothers keep your eyes trained on the ancestors and the spirits; and, they WILL bless you with the desires of your heart. It is not their intention that you should walk his earth alone. In vodun there is a male female duality. To every pirit there is a male/female counterpart and to every child, of the pirits, there is someone out there for you. And, it is a mature love. 'm here to TESTIFY! So, slide over young folks and take a lesson, :ause we've got this!

CHAPTER 9

RACISM AND AMERICAN INJUSTICE: AFRICAN VODUN'S RESPONSE

"Bigotry's birthplace is the sinister back room of the mind where plots and schemes are hatched for the persecution and oppression of other human beings."

- Bayard Rustin

PAN AFRICANISM AND THE PROMOTION OF HATE!

From what I understand, Pan Africanism is an ideology and movement that encourages the solidarity of Africans worldwide. It is based on the belief that unity is vital to economic, social, and political progress and aims to "unify and uplift" those of us who are of African descent.

The ideology asserts that the fate of all African peoples and countries are intertwined. They say that at its core Pan-Africanism is "a belief that African peoples, both on the continent and in the Diaspora, share not merely a common history, but a common destiny". This appears good within itself. But, what I am observing about this movement is that, in many instances, it is being used as a cloak for overt racism against those of non-African descent. And THAT is NOT the way of the divine spirits! As racism is deplorable against those of us who are of African descent. It is EQUALLY deplorable against our neighbors. We do not need to spread HATE to unify ourselves. Promoting Black businesses and Black achievements is wonderful; but, reverting to what has been so horribly done to us does not uplift our people but shames us to the core! We must understand that while Pan Africanism has great aims...it IS AN IDEOLOGY! It is manmade; and, if it is used to tread upon the rights of others it will be, whole hardheadedly, rejected by the ancestors and the spirits. A young lady spoke to me, once, of Pan Africanism in relation to a United States of Africa. Africans, themselves, are not interested in such. While we are busy getting our 'Africa' on is it fair to make assumptions about what is African without consulting it's residents? Is it fair to change your name, to an African name, when you haven't even taken the time to consult Ifa as to what tribe you actually came from? Taking your name from that tribe and its elders instead of a book on African names? Is it fair to scream you've taken on the Akan tradition just so you can claim a kingship that Ifa, nor the ancestors say, you were actually born or entitled to? And is it fair to use Pan Africanism as a forum or platform to spew out your hatred of white people because you simply don't like them? Let me be clear...racism, in ANY form, is not condoned by either the ancestors or the spirits. This is YOUR misuse of a good cause, YOUR racism toward others; therefore, on YOUR head! The ancestors and the spirits are not with you on this and never will be.

But, if we are out to promote the respect of the African people, respect for it's spiritual systems, respect for its priests and priestesses who were initiated according to the tenants of the divinities, help in the promotion of its economic prosperity, with our investments, and so on, then, we are on the right track. Using Pan Africanism, which is a great idea, to bring up and promote the old racist attitudes of who is Black and who is not, who's got melanin and who has not, assumptions about the divinities with no clue as to what they are talking about and other such foolishness is a waste! The divine spirits are no respecter of persons. They created ALL of mankind... black, white, yellow and all which lies in between. It has been our PRIVILEGE, of men and women of African descent, to be given the quest of priesthood, our PRIVILEGE of being the creators' FIRST creation who walked upon this earth. Do not disgrace them in this manner. Gird your loins, stand up tall and straight, be no respecter of persons, men and women of integrity and peace and show that we have deserved that PRIVILEGE. For we are better than this... Let the legacy of Nelson Mandela...a man of integrity a man of peace...not die in vain!

VODUN AND THOSE OF EUROPEAN DESCENT

On December 14, 2013, I posted an essay entitled "Pan Africanism and the promotion of Hate!". In it I addressed my concerns about those who would use the concept of Pan Africanism, as a cloak, to promote overt racism towards those of European descent. Discrimination, in any form, is not tolerated by the ancestors or the divinities. And yet, time and time again I have noticed, in these internet vodun forums, coming from without...that is from some (not all) persons of

European descent... a callousness in how they treat those of African descent; and, in some instances outright hostility. I observed it on Haitixchange, was prolific to Tribe; and, now I am observing it on facebook. It is as though there is some type of resentment in the fact that we are Black and they are not!

I want to be clear here! All persons are born of the spirits; and, all persons, regardless of race, creed or color has the right to serve the spirits if Ifa says that they are born to do so. However, the fact remains that those of African descent are the FIRST inheritors of these African Spiritual Systems! It is THEIR/OUR ANCESTORS that were brought here, against their will and in chains, to the diaspora. Our ancestors brought these spiritual systems, with them, in the diaspora and held on to them the best that they could! And, now, as many of European descent has sought to become a part of these systems, THEY, want to dictate to us what is and what isn't from our very own culture? That's ludicrous! African Americans, and others of African descent, carry their heritage in their BLOOD! It is an innate part of who we are! This is what the enslaver did not understand! Whether we were born to serve the spirits, or not, we were endued with 'mother wit' and innate abilities that allowed us to survive one of the most horrific events of mankind...chattel slavery! We suffered, fought and died to hang on to that which we brought from the motherland. They took away our names, our culture, our history and our dignity as we were sold on slave auction blocks; but, they were not able to take away that blood that linked us to the African continent and our ancestors. We are a peculiar people to most; but, we are also a surviving people! It is through us...one single Black Woman... that ALL creation flows! So, WHY the DISRESPECT, WHY the DISREGARD for who we are as a people...our right as priests and priestesses, as the FIRST BORNS, to these African traditional spiritual systems that are ours in the first place? This is not good! You've got no right to stand on our heads, make up your own rules, squelch our voices, make us laughing stocks to your foolish jokes when these spiritual systems were not yours in the first place! And do you think the African ancestors, YOUR ancestors, even if you are the farthest removed, approve of such behavior? Absolutely not! For WE of African descent have PAID our dues...in BLOOD, SWEAT and TEARS!

And, again, it is not ALL persons of European descent that act this way. I have met some very humble and loving people while on facebook. Some sweet people, of European descent, that I truly adore. They are humble and kind and have approached me with the utmost respect. Because for me, it is not about color but what is inside of the hearts of mankind that matter. But it wouldn't be fair to chastise, my own people, about their disrespect towards those of European descent and not say something about those, of European descent, who outright disrespect us! It isn't fair. In vodun we are to do what is right, correct and just regardless of who dislikes it! For it is the SPIRITS that I serve in obedience to their commands.

And in conclusion...Folks like to bring up their spiritual titles and credentials when they are wrong like it's gonna correct the wrongs that they do; but, it doesn't. My grandfather had a saying, "Right is Right, and Right Don't Wrong Nobody!" A priest/ priestess is not one that would lord their title over you... A priest or priestess is a SERVANT!

VODUN AND THOSE OF EUROPEAN DESCENT: A EUROPEAN'S RESPONSE

Earlier I posted, "Vodun and Those of European Descent." When the post was shared one gentleman (several actually; but, I chose this one), of European descent, responded. Because I am no longer a member of the thread, that he responded on, I could not address his concerns. I found it to be a very honest response and was intrigued by it. I beg that the gentleman forgives me for quoting him here; but I think the response should really be heard and would like to address it as best I can. I am very sorry that he did not feel that he could voice himself, on the original thread. I have quoted him below:

"The poster who shared this did ask in the original page this was posted on why "they" meaning "white people" I presume were so interested in "our" culture. I would just like to say that perhaps others like myself were not particularly interested in your culture. The call was in many ways inconvenient, frustrating and something I would have happily ignored as I have little or no connection to it, coming from the north of Europe and having very little contact with the diaspora. How easier it would have been to get into the runes or something! There was never any intention to steal or abuse anything of anybody's. I am still confused, lost and somewhat alienated with the whole thing and feel a stranger very much in a strange land. I genuinely don't know why I was called but I have tried to follow the path laid out in the proper way, finding a Tata in the tradition that suddenly engulfed my life, following his advice and now planning for my initiations in Brazil. But I just wanted to say that "white" folks often have no idea why they are suddenly here! I certainly feel as unwelcome sometimes as I feel welcome and not only wish, but have actively tried in the past, to no avail, to ignore the whole thing. For now, I just follow the advice of my Tata, keep my head down, work with my ancestors and try to keep learning."

The writer's response touched me deeply. For one it hurts me that anyone would have to enter the priesthood, confused, lost, alienated and feeling estranged. We are family...those who serves the voduns. The life of the priesthood is difficult enough without having to carry such burdens along with it! This simply breaks my heart! This, to me, is one of the fall outs when Ifa (authentic African divination) is not used in the diaspora. If this young man had been taken to Ifa he would know, specifically, what his spirits are, to what station, in vodun, he is (a priest, vodunsi, diviner etc.) and through the traditional process of vodun would understand his spiritual mission if he has one. He would not be alone; but, taken into the gentle hands of an attentive spiritual parent.

Personally, I do not understand why Europeans seek vodun in

Haiti or anywhere else but Africa. Their oldest ancestors are in Africa and the newest are in Europe. Why would someone who never stuck a toenail in Brazil or Haiti go someplace where they would not have vodun? The voduns coming from these regions are culturally specific to these regions. Many of their local spirits are connected to their local history which deal with persons who died and were deified, in some way, or spirits that belong to the indigenous populations of the area. It is the Africans that are the most experienced with the divinities themselves. It is the SOURCE of ALL of these African-based spiritual systems. The Brazilians, for instance, are begging for African priests to come there. Not that these regions do not serve the spirits; but, they are serving the spirits that are culturally specific the them not Europe! Some reach back to Africa but not enough. These universal divinities, that come from all over the world, will only reveal themselves to those that have the knowledge to perform their ceremonies. And only through authentic African divination can one find out who these spirits really are. And even then, if they feel the person cannot perform their ceremony, will not show themselves.

So, to our European responder, I hear your pain; and, I truly appreciate your honesty. You were tending to your own business and this calling showed up; but, did it really? Have you been to Ifa? I advise you to find a reputable diviner to know if you are not sure. Only the spirits, themselves, can tell us for sure. I know, without a shadow of a doubt, that the voduns that I know and serve would never leave you confused alone or unwelcomed.

VODUN AND THE CASE FOR INCLUSION

I think the White Supremacists and those African American Racists who hide under the banner of Pan Africanism are going to have to, eventually, give it up and acknowledge the scientific fact that mitochondrial DNA indicates that all living humans descended from one maternal source—christened Mitochondrial Eve—who lived in Africa between 100,000 and 200,000 years ago. Similarly, the Y chromosome shows that all men have a common ancestor, Y-chromosome Adam, who lived during the same time. This has not only been proven through DNA but, further proven by the latest in Anthropology as well. So where do we go from here?

I have continually explained that the African ancestor...the ancestor to all mankind...as well as the divinities are no respecter of persons. That ALL, regardless of race, color, creed or gender have the right to access their ancestry and their spirits through Ifa, the West African divination system (or other such ordained systems) as handed down, to us, by the divinities themselves. This is our birthright. However, there is another reason, that I would like to address, for inclusion, besides the spiritual or moral one; and, that is that it makes ECONOMIC sense for Africa!

As people of African descent, we constantly speak of the rape of Africa! We pollute the atmosphere with our cries of the continual exploitation of our beloved motherland...all of the gold taken out, it's diamonds smuggled out, its oil reserves owned by non-Africans, it's mineral resources exploited, lands taken, mummies of our kings and queens and knowledge stolen out of Egypt! And, most of all, the loss of its most precious human resources due to slavery! I ask you, are our ancestors not owed something for these things?

Now that it has been proven, to many, that those furthest removed from African ancestry also owe their very beings to this continent should they not help to put back in some of what they took out? Does their being further removed, than us, take away their responsibilities to serve their oldest ancestors with their financial resources just as we? I give an emphatic NO! Can we, people of color, who in most cases, around the world, are at the bottom of the economic scale, try to stabilize Africa's economic instability by ourselves? Again, I say NO! The African ancestor is YOUR ancestor just like mine Mr./ Ms. furthest removed; so, just like some of your closer ancestors who took out, of Africa, you've got to put something back in. Serving your

African ancestors help in that process!

Pan-Africanism, devoid of the racism, is a marvelous idea! The ideology encourages the solidarity of Africans worldwide. It is based on the belief that unity is vital to economic, social, and political progress and aims to unify and uplift people of African descent. It also asserts that the fate of all African peoples and countries are intertwined. At its core is the belief that African peoples, both on the continent and in the Diaspora, have a common history and destiny. But, I contend, that since we ALL have ancestry in Africa, that the common destiny is for ALL not merely for those of color! So, let each person, regardless of race, creed, color or gender serve their African ancestors and the divine ones if called. And in doing so it is to the benefit of each individual and a down payment to the economic prosperity of MOTHER AFRICA!

VODUN AND DYING TO SELF

In vodun, when one is initiated, one goes through a death and burial process. This means that one dies to the old and wakes up anew. But, in reality, it is a lifelong process. As one works with one's voduns they continually mold and refine you to be a better person; but, it takes a while. It really doesn't happen overnight; but, it's necessary. It is necessary if we want to be of service to mankind...ALL of mankind.

Like anyone else I too have baggage. You cannot be born seeing racism towards your people and not be affected! You can not witness marches and Ku Klux Klan rallies without being affected. When a cross was burned in your yard because of a fight between you and the white neighbor's child it remains in your memory. You cannot be escorted, by the National Guard, to school in the enforcement of integration, and not be affected. You cannot experience gasoline bombs thrown at you, by racists as a child, while trick or treating and not be affected. Neither can you attend undergraduate school, at a Historically Black College, and not be influenced in some way. Your command of African American History, Politics and the lives of your people must put its stamp upon you. Your desire and re-connection to your ancestry helps to define you. And your years laying in African temples are part of you. You know WHO you are and WHAT you are; but, in the face of all that.... In the face of coming so far you are thrown a curveball by the very ancestors that you serve and the divinities you adore!

For they say you do not live on this earth alone. You are an African; but, you were born a priestess to ALL of mankind! But I still resist...I still hang on to that which has helped shape most of my life. With tenacity, I hang on...it is mine...it is ours...we have suffered we are in pain...I sacrificed so much to get so far for my people...I hang on... this is for us and the spirits say, "Wait our child you must learn you must grow." I hear the voices and the complaints...Why is she giving this information to our enemies, why does she consider them at all? I struggle inside myself...called a racist by the envious, a turn coat by those I love and then life changes...

A spiritual child comes A woman he is fond of is of European descent. As any mother I plead, son stick to your own kind; so, it will be easier for you. You are headed to the priesthood get rid of the baggage. Like a petulant child he defies me. His spiritual father is wiser. He goes to Ifa to determine the woman's spiritual appropriateness for his son. He returns with resolve, for the young woman, of European descent, is of his very own ancestry. She is Lankpan! She is also Mami-Dan with the head spirit of Hanuman. And living inside of her are African spirits in abundance!

On that day the death, my death to the old ways of thinking, and habits became expanded a whole lot more!

VODUN'S SOUL TRAIN!

People get ready, there's a train a comin'. You don't need no baggage you just get on board! These are the beginning lyrics of one of the great songs from my youth. It was sung by the Impressions in

1965. And I woke up singing it this morning. I'm singing it because my heart and soul are glad! For several days I had been embroiled in defending that which comes from the divine on a forum! That the divine spirits are no respecter of persons that we must overcome that which is worldly... the political agendas, the name calling, the racial hatred, the suspicions of the 'other' so that we can see that which is good and pure. And for a while I became tired. I lost my bearings, for a moment, confused and bewildered at this proliferation of hate stemming from my own people. I was so busy trying to teach that which is Godly that I had forgotten, for a moment, that in this world there are those that promote the UNGODLY! And to those I was trying to convince...those that were saying such horrible things about their neighbors, that they were born with no souls, that they were wicked and born with spirits of chaos...it was they, themselves, the very ones spouting this nonsense who were actually the ones that was the chaos! They, themselves, were the ungodly, the spiritually bankrupt and thus deceiving themselves into a false morality. For they were describing the very conditions in which they, themselves, were in. And I came out from among them! For that which is pure cannot dwell, effectively, among that which is impure. And then the spirits, in their divine wisdom, spoke. Not through me; but, through a Godly young woman. In conversation she reminded me, "That which is carnal is carnal, that which is spirit is spirit. So, they can't hear you!" The voduns have a way of sending us assistance when we most need it! I am so very grateful to this wonderful woman! With her assistance, at being a divine vessel, Mami is back on her game!

So, people get ready! The ancestors and the divine spirits are waking up their children! Vodun's soul train is in the station; and, its picking up passengers from coast to coast. All you need is FAITH to hear the diesels humming. You don't need no ticket...you just thank the Lord!

GEORGE ZIMMERMAN AND THE POWER OF THE AFRICAN ANCESTOR

On the morning after the George Zimmerman verdict I posted the following on an internet vodun forum I was a member of:

A Suffering People... Sun, July 14, 2013 - 9:36 AM

As I wake up this morning my heart hurts... Twenty years ago I experienced the same hurt for similar circumstances. Two people had been murdered. A man named OJ Simpson walked free. I was one of those who believed in his guilt. I also firmly believed that one day the African American community would regret it. Last night was that day. A young AA boy came out of the store on his way home with a bag of skittles and a fruit drink and was shot down in cold blood. He was profiled. And no matter what they say it WAS because of race. And WHAT does it have to do with Vodun you say? I'll say it plain. If this family...the Martins knew their ancestors. If this family could call them by name. They would not have to worry. We wouldn't need a court...they wouldn't need a prosecutor...cause Zimmerman would no longer be here...this I guarantee.

Wedosi

I was angry and tired. Tired of suffering, in a racist country, and angry at a typical racist and biased verdict! And knowing the ANCESTORS, as I do, meaning ABSOLUTELY everything I said above!

We've had a lot of discussions on the ancestors...the need to re-connect, serve and feed them; but, many do not understand their power! They have UNTOLD power! The ancestors are where we begin, our lives, and the ancestors are where we hope to return. It is an ancestor who wants to be remembered that brings us here...he reaches down and molds the clay and asks a divinity to breathe life into us; and, then, when our life, on earth, is done that portion of the divine lifts out and that which was formed, by the ancestor, returns to it. The ancestor, throughout our existence, intercedes for us, with the divinities, pleading for our safety, protection and pardon. And when he sees his child is threatened, or harmed, will lash out upon our enemies with DEADLY force! The ancestors do not play and they take no hostages! These are African warriors who know battle! The divine ones are long suffering and their vengeance, upon our enemies, slow but sure. However, for the ancestors, to harm one of theirs is to quickly offend! And, if they have been identified, through Ifa, honored, fed and given the appropriate attention will pounce upon our enemies with both feet!

GEORGE ZIMMERMAN AGAIN?

Why don't they just lock this man up and throw away the key? Now he is being accused of abusing his wife? He walks around, with his chest stuck out, asking officers, when stopped for traffic violations, if they know who he is? He is claiming this notoriety on the back of killing an unarmed black teenager. Whenever there is a miscarriage of justice, somehow, we realize it very early on. This is one man that I am very tired of hearing about! We knew he was a creep; and, he proves this more and more each day. When Zimmerman won his case, because of a biased jury, I posted my sentiments on an internet vodun forum I was a member of.

One of the worst things one can do, in vodun, or any other spiritual system for that matter, is to take an innocent life! This man did; and, he will suffer all of the days of his life for it! That southern jury may have set him free; but, the ancestors and the spirits, of Trayvon Martin, will not! That too I guarantee!

A RAP SESSION WITH MAMI: FERGUSON, MISSOURI

I guess facebook is so well loved because people are really able to say pretty much whatever is on their minds. My focus is vodun and African spirituality; but, vodun has been given to us to help mankind. Therefore, I would be remiss if I didn't voice how I feel about th events in Ferguson, Missouri. Most know that I am a political junkie and grew up during the Civil Rights era in North Carolina. In the 1970s, we had to be escorted to school, by the National Guard, due to newly federally enforced integration and busing. I have seen race riots, the KKK (in their hoods) marching, with them on one side of the street with us on the other, as well as, experiencing a burned cross in our yard. As a child, I have had gasoline bombs thrown, at us, when we tricked or treated in the wrong neighborhoods. My undergrad years were spent at a historically black university; and, my family has participated in community activism throughout the years. Every young person, in our family, is not only encouraged to vote but taken to the polls with their parents. So, you know this thing is affecting me and affecting me hard. I weep for the many young black men, and others, that die in these city streets daily just like I wept for the many that were lynched during my youth. So somebody tell me, please, ... when will this all end?

When will this fear of the 'other' stop? While we all can hope I do not think that it ever will. Each generation, it seems, is seeing the old skeletons continue to rear up on a society that was based on the inequality of one owning another...slavery...and all the horrible injustices and social stigma that has been firmly embedded in our society. Great strides have been made in our country; but, a first Black President seems to have brought it all back to the forefront again for some. But this war on Black Men is deeper than one thinks.

The African warrior is a fierce foe. He has always been whether on the African battlefields or the American city streets. And that's who you are young black men. For there are some that view you as an angry warrior...a black warrior. When your anger rises to the fore what is seen in your eyes are the centuries upon centuries of an African warrior. And the one who perceives you as his enemy will rise up, in fear, no matter what. In areas like Ferguson, Missouri you have a large population of blacks being controlled by a small army of whites. This mimics the massa/slave mentality of the old south. And, sadly, in places like Ferguson, this mentality still exists. So, when the slaves rise up.... the massa fears for his life and attempts, at all costs, to suppress the savages....those savage and angry African warriors.

Agree or disagree; but, this is how I view Ferguson, Missouri. And, that city councilman, or mixed brother, who was interviewed and claimed all his people were happy in Ferguson...well we all know what that was about.

I think the spirits that most of America is no longer living as if they were still in the antebellum south; but, with what I am seeing, in Ferguson, is like a scab being torn off a freshly healing wound. Just my 2 cents. And may the spirits be with us during these trying times.

FERGUSON, MISSOURI IS BURNING! BUT, IT'S WITH A RIGHTEOUS ANGER...

Since the prosecutor of Ferguson, Missouri's speech, two nights ago, I have been too bewildered to write! I am ANGRY! And, like others, it is with a righteous anger...But hey! What can I say? We are tired! Tired of being tired. Black, White and others alike! Folks who believe in justice, folks who believe in what is fair and right! So, Ferguson is burning! And I ask you? How is it that young Black men must continue dying in American city streets?

We were set up; and, they know it! For two days, I have gone from MSNBC to CNN to local news to the internet. I don't even want to turn on Fox News just to see those Republican bigots who ran from the southern Democrats after the Civil Rights Movement just to hear them defend their friends who dawn their invisible KKK hoods, that, Black folks can plainly see. And repeatedly they are showing the video where young black men are attempting to turn over a police car in Ferguson and the fires. So, they look at this; and, in the privacy of their homes they say see? Told you those "N" was out of control! But what did they expect? Here you have a prosecutor that was on the side of the police instead of the side of the people. Here you had a white police officer so scared of a burly black teenager that he used his gun instead of any other type of self-defense or disabling technique. Why kill the kid? Why not simply try to disable or prevent a possible alteration in some way? Do they not learn self-defense techniques at the police academy? No, in the officer's psyche this was an out of control "N" and he must be put down. That's the real deal. The National Guard was called out before time because the prosecutor was not intending to get an indictment and knew folks would be angry. But we all sensed what was coming down; but, folks still tried to hold out hope!

So now here comes our local Black elected asking for calm. Even the President. I say the h**l with calm. Ya'll set up this mess up now deal with it! 89 arrested the first night and 12 fires. I'm not promoting violence; but, I certainly understand it! And, if I was 40 years younger, I'd be out there with them!

Look, there are spiritual ramifications with all of this! But I'm too angry to get to them at the moment in any real detail! Of course there is the fact that this young man died an unnatural death. That involves zogbe. This is the place where all go after an unnatural death occurs. The officer took a life; and, the system failed us miserably. These local Black representatives need to be out there preparing to fight this in the courts. I have so much more to say on this in reference to the spiritual perspective; but, for now I'm where everyone else is... fuming with a righteous anger.

RACE, SPIRITUALITY AND INJUSTICE

As human beings, we are much more than the color of our skins. On a much deeper level we are individuals with dreams, desires, aspirations, hopes and a need to make a difference or leave a legacy after our sojourn here on earth. And it is within each of us that we want the best for those loved ones that we anticipate having to leave behind...those to which we are directly responsible for, their very existence and to whom we have most influenced and they, in turn, us. In this sense we look out for our own and are tribal if you'll allow me to use that basic terminolog . We cling to that which is most familiar and share a common bond, heritage and culture. The 'other' is outside of ourselves. That which is 'other' is of a different tribe. But I invite you to now let me take you even deeper into the realm of the spirits. That to which is sacred, pure and most holy.

Born within us are many spirits. Some are ancestral, some lived before the forming of the earth itself; and, still others were inherited from family members or come from various other places. As each person is born with a personal destiny they have come with us to help fulfill that destiny whatever it is. And as such they can be from anywhere on earth or beyond. Since, many of these destinies are connected to the master plans of the divinities themselves, they seek ways to come down in whatever ancestral groupings or bodies they choose according to what is expedient for them and their divine plans. And, as a result, we may have a black woman born of a spirit that is Arab, in origin, and known as one of the Hindu Gods as I or, if of Haitian parentage, born with the head spirit of another Hindu God that just happens to blue in color...Lord Rama. This is the spirit of one of my spiritual children. As a result, you may have a male spirit inhabiting a female body or a white person with distinct African spirits living within them as we have often found. For in the world of the spirits they can be of any color or of any origin. However, since the origins of man is distinctly African, it would appear foolish, under these circumstances, to dislike anyone of Africa descent or begrudge someone white from seeking the African priesthood. Yet we still must deal with mankind's instinctive desire to cling to one's tribe and to be suspicious of the 'other'. For the flaw is that we are human; and, only a part of us is divine. And if we do not discover and or acknowledge that part which may be divine, and are governed by, it we may thus live according to our own morality and/or cultural mores. A morality that could very well participate in man's inhumanity to man. In the world of the spirits, color or race simply does not matter. Whether a particular spirit is for the good of man or the destruction of mankind is their primary concern. But in our human frailties it matters to us because it distinguishes to which tribe or clan we belong.

And as such we desire to right old wrongs and engage in our many human imperfections. So the spirits gave us the world's religions to attempt to help us; but, for the traditionalist they have given direct contact with them. And for whichever one chooses some mode of spiritual help is available. Some systems afford more help than others; but, what I am suggesting is that it is only the man or woman who lives on the level of the spiritual that can even began to overcome our perceived problems with the 'other'. Some of them are real and others may not be. But the one thing I do know is that racism, by whatever people or person, is definitely an instance of man's inhumanity to man causing much dissension, destruction and unnecessary death. The spirits do not like it! As a result, it is a malignant cancer invading the lives of many and should be rooted out! For those, bent on destruction, who chose not to live by the spiritual, that which is pure and holy, it can be a slippery slope to the promotion and/or the involvement with injustice on a grand scale bringing against them justified anger...a righteous anger! True spirituality, I feel, is the only way to counterbalance racism and the world's injustices of man's inhumanity to man.

I am not sure if anyone is going to be able to make heads or tails of what I am trying to say; but, I'm just going to say it and pray for the best.

EPILOGUE

Like it or not vodun and African based spiritual systems in the diaspora will see a change. Of the many that are returning to Africa for reconnection to ancestry and more intensive spiritual training this cannot help but affect those that serve the spirits or simply practice vodun for profit. Yet for those who staunchly oppose these changes you will remain powerless against them. In reference to the African ancestors it is their season. They are coming with untold power and the full backing of the divine ones. They are waking those born to them and preparing their way home. The price has already been paid with the blood, sweat and tears of their children who were stolen, bound in chains and taken into chattel slavery. It is time my brothers and sisters to reclaim our rightful place as God's original men and women to which all others were born and to lay claim to the keys that unlocks the heavens.

When this book was first published I was standing on the precipice of 60 years of age. It has been an additional two years. Yet, for me, my spiritual journey has just gotten into gear. I still consider myself an infant in the faith. There is so much more to discover, to learn, to understand and to know. For vodun consist of infinite mysteries many of which the world is neither cognoscente of or privy to. It is my hope and prayer that, if the voduns are willing and before my time on earth is done, that I may learn enough to help those searching to find their way back home to them.

For it is from the spiritual world that we came and it is to the spiritual world that we will return. Therefore, to know one's ancestors and the divine spirits that gave us life is to discover and to know one's true self. For we are not just physical bodies with the ability to walk who just happen to contain spirits, but, rather we are spirits who have physical bodies that just happen to be able to walk. Until we meet again...

Mami Wata Priestess.

CPSIA information can be obtained
at www.ICGtesting.com
Printed in the USA
FFHW010717121019
55476924-61278FF

9 780692 901618